THE TESTED
WOMAN PLOT

THE TESTED WOMAN PLOT

∞

Women's Choices, Men's Judgments, and the Shaping of Stories

Lois E. Bueler

Ohio State University Press
Columbus

Library of Congress Cataloging-in-Publication Data

Bueler, Lois E.
The tested woman plot : women's choices, men's
judgments, and the shaping of stories / Lois E. Bueler.
p. cm.
Includes bibliographical references and index.
ISBN 0-8142-0872-X
1. English literature—History and criticism.   2. Women in literature.
3. English literature—Stories, plots, etc.   4. Literature and folklore—
Great Britain.   5. Man-woman relationships in literature.   6. Choice
(Psychology) in literature.   7. Temptation in literature.   8. Judgment in
literature.   9. Trials in literature.   10. Narration (Rhetoric)   I. Title.
PR151.W6 B84   2001
820.9'352042—dc21
2001000547

Text and jacket design by Bookcomp, Inc.
Type set in 10 pt Janson Text by Bookcomp, Inc.

9 8 7 6 5 4 3 2 1

CONTENTS

∞

PART IV   NARRATING THE SELF

PREFACE

THIS BOOK IS A PROJECT FOR WHICH I HAVE NO MODEL. THOUGH there has been a certain amount of criticism on the characteristics of plot-specific literary subgenres (e.g., Renaissance revenge tragedy) and on theories of plot structure (e.g., structuralist readings patterned after folktale analysis), very little critical work is available on specific plots and even less on their connections and permutations across genres and historical periods. Yet storytellers and their audiences have a strong sense of how certain kinds of stories go. In this book I discuss a single old and influential plot structure, what authors and readers seem to know about it, and which features seem central to its tradition. Especially is this book an essay in how plot and genre interact. The two great storytelling genres of Western culture, drama and third-person prose fiction, put different emphases on similar story material and make different demands on their audiences. Watching a single plot move between genres is a superb way to study generic forces at work. Linked to the story of genre is the history of cultural attitudes and changes. Owing to its antiquity, the tested woman plot provides a showcase for studying relationships between cultural phenomena and literary form.

My professional debts for this very broad project go back many years. The support of the National Endowment for the Humanities to scholars at smaller institutions has been life-giving. In addition to the NEH fellowship year in 1981–82 that allowed me to start shaping my ideas about the tested woman plot in Renaissance drama, I have profited from three NEH summer seminars: in 1979 with rhetorician Thomas O. Sloane at the University of California at Berkeley, on "Humanist Rhetoric"; in 1989 with philosopher Amélie O. Rorty at Harvard University, on "Virtues and Their Vicissitudes"; and in 1997 with literary and cultural scholar Leopold Damrosch, again at Harvard, on "The Enlightenment Invention of the Modern Self." In addition to the stimulating presence of scholars within and beyond my field of English literature, these seminars brought me deeper familiarity with key periods, authors, and texts. My home institutions have also supported my work at crucial points. Winona State University gave me a summer grant for early work on the plays of John Ford, and California State University, Chico, allowed me both a sabbatical and a semester's leave, the first to write a book about *Clarissa* that stabilized my understanding of the plot, and the second to put together a draft of this book.

For permission to use portions of previously published arguments about the tested woman plot in chapters 2 and 5, I wish to thank the Associated University Presses (for material from *Clarissa's Plots* [University of Delaware Press, 1994]) and the editors of *Studies in English Literature, 1500–1900* (for material from "Role-Splitting and Reintegration: The Tested Woman Plot in Ford," *SEL* 20 [1980]: 325–44).

Many people have helped my thinking about the tested woman plot. My dissertation director at the University of Colorado at Boulder, Jack Crouch, taught me by his theater craft. Dropping in day after day one summer to watch him direct a production of *Cymbeline*, I became interested in accounting for the power of the play. A few months later, during my dissertation defense, as I thought aloud beyond my work on Jacobean drama to a dramatic plot I was just starting to discern, Kaye Howe of the comparative literature department asked the central long-range question: "What about the novel?" "I don't know," I answered—and was stuck with the need to find out. Many years later, Leopold Damrosch generously read a version of this book and helped me get a reading from the Ohio State University Press, whose director at the time, Barbara Hanrahan, responded to my submission with enthusiasm. The press's thoughtful and tireless reader Peter Rabinowitz provided sympathetic and merciless critiques that helped make this a briefer and clearer piece of work. And from the mid-1980s on, when he provoked my interest in Richardson, my colleague Victor Lams influenced my reading and thinking, welcomed my talk, and read any number of think pieces and drafts.

Above all I must thank my family, Bill, Katherine, and Edward, who have heard about the tested woman plot for such a long time. This book is for them.

ONE

The Plot as Story Machine

THIS BOOK IS AN EXAMINATION OF A SINGLE LITERARY STORY STRUC-
ture that I call the "tested woman plot." The tested woman plot is one of
the great story machines of all time. It has been with us in Western literature
since the prototypal versions of the Mediterranean world. It has adapted to
myth and to drama, to chronicle and to history, and to prose fiction from
Hellenistic romance to the novel of psychological development. The tested
woman plot structures interpolated tales in *The Golden Ass*, *The Satyricon*,
and *Don Quixote*, as well as one of the literarily most influential episodes
in Ariosto.[1] Arguably the single most brilliantly exploited plot in English
Renaissance drama, it structures tragedies, comedies, and romances from early
Tudor homiletic plays through the greatest works of Shakespeare, Webster,
Fletcher, Middleton, Ford, and Shirley. Boccaccio capped the *Decameron* with
an example of the plot in the story of Patient Griselda, which was picked up
by Chaucer and English ballad singers and chapbook vendors for the next
five hundred years. Milton used the plot in both *Paradise Lost* and *Comus*. It
appears in the operas of Handel, Mozart, and Puccini.[2] Samuel Richardson's
success with *Pamela* and *Clarissa* may have been what led Henry Fielding, his
parodist and rival, to try his hand at the plot. A hundred years later Nathaniel
Hawthorne wrote a tested woman novel, as did Elizabeth Gaskell and George
Eliot. Hardy's *Tess of the D'Urbervilles* gave the plot its most disturbing post-
Romantic expression.

Criticism of specific plot structures, as distinct from the plots of individual
works or the features of narrative in general, is hard to come by. A reason may
be that the plot is the feature of narrative most interesting to literarily naive
readers, from whom literary critics are often eager to distance themselves.
More fundamentally, though, the absence of critical attention may reflect the
complexity of mature plot structures. Not only are they intricately patterned
from an interlocking, richly motivated, and staggeringly large set of components, they are found in certain cultural habitats and do specific kinds of
ideological work. Thus a critic interested in a plot type must have not just an
insatiable appetite for stories but an interest in the study of cultures. A specific

plot is also a hard thing to pin down. Its components, which consist of character types (an unmarried young woman, say), character functions (defending the heroine, perhaps), and action motifs (being cast adrift in an open boat) are portable objects found in many different plots and used for many different purposes.[3] Many different plots have women in them; many different plots have tests (in fact, "testing" in the broad sense is the foundation of most story lines). So the tested woman plot is not just any story about a woman who undergoes some sort of testing. It has specific kinds of characters, a stable event structure, and a particular ideological relationship to its cultural habitat. Because it is widespread from the beginnings of Western literature through the nineteenth century, however, no study can deal with all its stories. In this book I concentrate on British literature and its related historical and generic concerns to achieve an encompassable presentation of plot characteristics and possibilities.

In part 1, "Frameworks," I describe the tested woman plot and discuss the seminal Mediterranean stories that coalesce to make the plot type. I also explain in schematic terms how the plot is structured and explore the nature of women and of men as characteristically presented by the plot.

Part 2, "Dramatizing Patriarchy: The Renaissance Experiment," concentrates on English Renaissance drama, the literary corpus in which the tested woman plot was most brilliantly practiced. Like practitioners of the dominant literary form of any period, Tudor and Stuart playwrights wrote about ideas distinctive to their genre and their time—the rise and fall of great men, the necessity and horror of revenge, the making of politic marriages between country bloodlines and city money, the near-sexual and near-mystical bonds of male friendship. Perhaps most compulsively, they wrote about female chastity, about women whose virtue, construed in (if not always limited to) sexual terms, represents the ethical concerns of their society—or even symbolizes the moral state of all mankind. Why should sophisticated writers systematically devote their attention to such a notion and introduce it in so many contexts? There are sociological explanations about the importance of female virginity to the marital transfer of property, political arguments about the relationship between gender and power in patriarchal cultures, theological commentary on Christianity's dualistic symbolism of Eve and the Virgin Mary, aesthetic theories about the connection between political upheaval and artistic sensationalism or about the connection between gendered motifs and genre. Yet such explanations skirt the most basic literary questions: What kinds of dramatic power do these dramas develop by means of their plot characteristics, and how is that power used? Part 2 fits thematic explorations into the description of plot dynamics to attempt a unified understanding of the plot in Renaissance culture.

Part 3, "Experimenting with Genre," explores the developing eighteenth-century understanding of the self and its relation to problems of genre. The tested woman plot did not die after the Renaissance, but it could no longer be taken for granted. Because of the plot's suitability to drama, its exploitation had reached an artistic peak in the early seventeenth century, so that later dramatists had difficulty using it freshly. But the plot's opportunities for psychological exploration made it attractive to prose fiction increasingly concerned with concepts of the individual self. It is no accident that in the eighteenth century the plot's most powerful expression occurs in Richardson's epistolary novels, a genre combining features of both drama and prose narrative. Nor is it an accident that many of Richardson's readers were confused by the plot's increasingly vexed social dynamics. The tested woman plot originated in societies composed along patriarchal lines that fracture and re-form themselves around the woman as defining subordinate. As such, the plot predicates a broad social consensus and a hierarchical stability within which local upheavals may be explored and contained. As inherited social structures weakened and literary attention shifted toward the representation of the lived experience of individuals rather than the portrayal of social types, the plot opened up opportunities for psychological and social commentary that blurred its traditional outlines.

The developmental psychology of moral awareness, the cognitive problems posed by the innocence of ignorance, the double bind created by the claims of the self against the demands of traditional codes of behavior—these are the interests of the novels I examine in part 4, "Narrating the Self." By the mid-nineteenth century the plot had been thinned to the formula of naive girl seduced by sophisticated cad. This thinning vitiated serious attention to the competitive male power relationships by which the plot is traditionally framed—and from which it takes much of its social importance and dramatic interest. Working against this reductionism, however, some of the most important nineteenth-century novelists—Austen, Scott, Hawthorne, Gaskell, Eliot, Hardy—revisited the tested woman plot to probe the collapse of male relationships under the pressures of the modern world and to exploit an increasingly complex understanding of the plot's psychological opportunities.

My argument in this book is influenced by historical, feminist, narratological, and rhetorical criticism. It is made possible by textual scholarship. Because this is a study devoted to readings of a range of texts in their cultural settings, I am indebted to the painstaking work of textual scholars and analytical and thematic critics of the middle of the century, among them editors of Renaissance drama. Readers of the literature of the past owe unspeakable debts to their work. I am also grateful to the critics and scholars who have recovered works for and about women, especially in the second half of the eighteenth century, and whose efforts have led to a revaluing of the epistolary novel, of women as letter writers, novelists, dramatists, and theorists, and of the relations between theories of sensibility and literary sentimentality. My closest theoretical affinities may be with structuralist thematics.[4] Because I am interested in the relation between literary content and literary form—the ways form makes content possible, detectable and intelligible—I believe with Ludomír Dolozel that "content in literature is structured and cannot be studied independently of its structuring."[5] I also believe that studies of structure need to be tied to texts. Theory about literary structure divorced from recourse to instantiating texts quickly becomes ungrounded and sterile. Just as there is no such thing as theory alone, but only theories *about*, there is no such thing as structure alone, but only structures *of.* Describing why the study of thematics and the study of structure are so necessarily linked, Thomas Pavel notes that themes are "topics a text is built to make us care about."[6] In this book I am after the ways structure is used to help us see and care.

My formulation of the tested woman plot has consisted of a movement back and forth between increasingly firm description of the plot's structure and scrutiny of the details of individual narratives. In his discussion of how a student of the taxonomy of folktale types proceeds, the dean of tale-type studies, Stith Thompson, describes the paradox of needing to be able to envision a structure before you can see it:

> The only way in which a tale-type can be formulated is to study the variants of the type. This process is somewhat circular because in order to tell what is the variant of a type, it is necessary to have some idea of the type. In practice this means that the investigator finds many tales containing so many striking resemblances that he places them in a single category. He then studies these resemblances and notes the common characteristics. Later he brings together as many variations of tales having these characteristics as possible, and eventually he is able to make a satisfactory statement as to the contents of the tale he is studying. His investigation implies a basic assumption, namely that the tale he is studying is an entity, that it has had a history with a beginning in time and place and has suffered certain changes in the course of its life.[7]

The same procedure is needed to see a plot type. Out of the wide and overlapping range of possible structures, the observer develops a sense of "best examples" that most clearly spell "tested woman plot." That such a category cannot have fixed boundaries, that on its fringes some elements of the prototype may be lost, does not prevent our making meaning of tale types and plot structures. Though boundaries are not set, though plots mix and overlap, certain key and abiding features characterize our "best examples" and type specimens.[8] In my case the initial research materials were dozens of English Renaissance plays, from which the tested woman plot gradually emerged as an identifiable and powerful structure exemplified by a few particularly notable examples.

But how can we be sure that what eventually becomes visible to the student of folktales or the critic of plays is apparent to the teller or author? In fact we can be sure that it is not, at least not in the same terms. Just as people living inside an ideology or a language typically do not see it and cannot describe it, for it is what they look through to the world around them, people using a literary structure are unlikely to see it, for it is the naturalized means by which they imitate the human types and actions of their world. Seeing from the outside is the work of the student of culture, the linguist, the critic. Thus the tested woman plot is my construct; by its means I see relationships and account for patterns and influences. It is I, not the Renaissance dramatist or the Roman historian, who talks of the typical double stages of test and trial, or the typical configuration of character functions.

Does this mean that I have made it all up? Not at all. Works built on a given plot structure share affinities, and it is by the cultural and literary clustering based on those affinities that the critic comes to see relationships. Sometimes the affinities are pointed from the inside, as when literary works openly claim connections with one another. Chaucer's Clerk connects Griselda to Job, Mackenzie's Roubignés connect Julia to Iphigenia, Richardson's Lovelace connects Clarissa to Lucretia, Rowe's Lothario is named after Cervantes' Lothario, Rousseau calls his work *La Nouvelle Héloïse*. Though these seem to be examples of character calling to character, because a character exists in a matrix of relationships and events, calling up the figure means calling up situation, social habitat, and plot shape, for a character exists as one node in a collection of nodes. Sometimes the affinities become evident from external phenomena, as by means of fads. English Renaissance drama, for a few decades the flourishing product of an explosively popular industry, imitated itself as relentlessly as does Hollywood, and tested woman plays proliferated by virtue of their success. Without being conscious of all the features I will describe, without using the descriptive designations I use, Tudor and Stuart drama reproduced the same essential structure over and over. My job in this book is to define that essence, deciding what elements the partial references pull with them.

The plot's importance to Renaissance drama has influenced how I work with it. Literary drama (as distinct from the stagings of ritual, say) borrows its stories from the broader narrative matrix of the culture, then defines or classicizes those stories by sharpening their outlines and committing them to a public staging. A play made from a mythic or historical account foregrounds structure, notably by imposing the points at which the story begins and ends and allotting the action motifs to specific characters who are further characterized by being inhabited by actors. The absence of a characterized narrating voice completes the process of four-dimensional sharpening, presenting the staged action in all its unmediated time and human physicality. Any story material subjected to that process carries in its text its decisions about emplotment and invites genealogy along its two axes, the tracings of origins and the tracings of family resemblance. I have accepted that invitation.

Though there has been little sustained critical attention to specific plot structures, there has been an explosion of critical interest in narrative, containing some potentially useful work on plot. Part of the difficulty of plot studies is that the term "plot," "how stories come to be ordered in significant ways," as Peter Brooks defines it,[9] is conceptually sweeping and open to widely differing applications. One way to think of plot is to conceive it broadly and extratextually, as describing the biological, ethical, or religious shape of human life. Ethicists see that Aristotle's *Nicomachean Ethics* presents a "life plot" involving the striving for excellence through the competing pressures of various life stages to the achievement of beatitude in the final stage of contemplation. Christians know that Christianity contains two versions of the life plot structure, one inside the other, so that the journey of the individual Christian believer toward salvation is a whole-life-focused concept nested within a communal movement of the whole of humankind from Creation and Fall toward Last Judgment. Life plots need not be either ancient or prescriptive; a modern version is Freud's "master plot," in which all human lives are narratives driven by libido amid the competing pressures and stages of family life. There are roughly two ways to deploy the notion of life plots in textual criticism. One explores the fact that many subgenres of narrative are frankly conceived in terms of life plots: all hagiography, whether religious or secular, performs this emplotting work on the lives of its subjects (witness the inevitable life trajectory of a Horatio Alger hero); much allegory has the specific purpose of generalizing the life plot, making it, for instance, any pilgrim's progress. The other kind of textual criticism seeks out evidence of some version of a life plot in texts not so openly didactic. These approaches tend to be to some degree psychological, though not necessarily psychoanalytic. Peter Brooks's *Reading for the Plot*, for example, bases its analysis of nineteenth- and twentieth-century novels in the desiring versus the remembering/retelling phases of the Freudian master plot. Allen Tilley generalizes from Brooks's "binding of energy" notion to a "plot snake" structure of highs and lows that informs not just literary narrative but also the life narratives of actual people. Some criticism employing a life-plot theme focuses on period and genre, as in Leopold Damrosch's study of the concept of Christian Providence in the shaping of seventeenth- and eighteenth-century fictional narratives. An even closer focus is present in my study of *Clarissa*, where I argue for the existence of a "prudence plot" intermingled with the other plots of the novel and serving as the means by which Richardson construes the life tasks of his heroine and conducts her death and Christian apotheosis.[10]

The other major way to study plot is to look schematically at its form and structure, whether comparatively from one work or genre to another or in terms of the internal organization of single works. Again there are technical ways to proceed. An example stemming from a combination of historical and formal techniques is Richard Levin's *The Multiple Plot in English Renaissance Drama*, which examines the frequency, structural characteristics, and thematics of double- and triple-plotted Renaissance plays, some elements of which carry forward as far as the novels of George Eliot. Though Levin studies structure, he is not a structuralist in the more theoretical sense. Structuralist treatments of plot find their progenitors in the work of the Swiss linguist Ferdinand de Saussure, the formalist criticism of the Prague school, and the taxonomic work of students of folklore. The single most influential product of the Prague formalist school, Vladimir Propp's groundbreaking *Morphology of the Folktale,* informs almost all subsequent studies of plot characteristics and components, including mine. Stith Thompson's motif- and tale-type studies are extended, systematic taxonomies of the structures of folktales and the movable components of which they are comprised. Other studies are more specifically linguistically modeled: Tzvetan Todorov's study of the *Decameron* constructs a plot and character "grammar" of some of the stories of Boccaccio's hundred-tale compendium; Thomas Pavel (1985) constructs a move-grammar for the analysis of Christopher Marlowe's plays and of *King Lear.* Structurally oriented critics have also produced intensive readings of single works. In *S/Z* Roland Barthes constructs an extraordinarily detailed exploration of Balzac's short story "Sarrasine" which he organizes, in terms recognizable for their affinities with both linguistic structuralism and Prague formalism, into five codes (empiric, hermeneutic, referential, connotative, and symbolic). But though Barthes acknowledges the organizing power of the empiric code or "code of action" on the readerly properties of the text, he never investigates that ordering power itself; all he admits is "that when subjected to a logico-temporal order, [sequences of acts] constitute the strongest armature of the readerly; that by their typically sequential nature, simultaneously syntagmatic and organized, they can form the favored raw material for a certain structural analysis of narrative."[11]

None of these studies, however stimulating, attends centrally to the way a single plot, however defined, is used across a broad range of periods and genres. Folktale studies suffer from being restricted to brief, simple, and stereotyped narratives; the same is true for script theories of students of cognition, which say accurate and interesting things about how customers interact with waiters or bank tellers without throwing much sustained light on even a very short story about waiters or bank tellers. On the other hand, studies like Pavel's or Todorov's develop considerable explanatory power without moving beyond particular writers in particular genres at particular moments. At the opposite extreme, my study of *Clarissa,* while it develops an extended commentary on three different plot types, applies them in detail only to a single (albeit immense) novel. We simply do not know in any depth how literary plots work across periods and genres. There is a partial exception: when read as companion volumes, Leo Weinstein's historical and thematic study, *The Metamorphoses of Don Juan,* and Jean Rousset's structuralist analysis, *Le Mythe de Don Juan,* provide a rich, detailed, and theoretically multifaceted understanding of the Don Juan plot from its proto-Enlightenment expression in the drama of Tirso de Molina through its Romantic transmogrification. But even these works attend only unsystematically to the plot's relation to generic possibilities and constraints.

I have, then, undertaken an ambitious task. Combining various approaches, I identify the defining characteristics of a complex literary plot and follow it through its range of historical and generic manifestations and permutations. In picking examples I have tried to maintain a balance between very well known works (*Othello*) and less well known ones (Chapman's *The Widow's Tears*), between highly influential stories (Boccaccio/Petrarch/Chaucer's Griselda) and those so occasional as to spawn no heirs (Middleton's *A Game at Chess*). I have largely restricted myself to the British literary tradition. Though the tested woman plot is a property of the European story pool, thanks to the unique flourishing of first English drama and then the English novel, the British tradition has the richest and most clearly demarcated plot history. Beyond the stage setting involved in establishing the originary strains of the plot, I have turned to Continental literature only for the most influential examples—Ariosto, say, or Cervantes—and then only briefly, with one exception. My more extended consideration of Rousseau's *Julie ou La Nouvelle Héloïse* is motivated by its date and its intimate connections with the British tradition. Until the mid-eighteenth century, English literature hardly influenced continental literary practices, though there was extensive seepage in the other direction. But beginning with the Richardson vogue, translating English authors into continental languages became a fad, and cross-fertilization back to English sentimental and Romantic authors a significant phenomenon. Finally, American literature enters my story near its end, with Hawthorne's *The Scarlet Letter*.

Lying behind these technical considerations is always the gripping matter of story. My first desire is to introduce readers to the formal and thematic properties connecting some of the great characters and stories in our literary tradition. I investigate how Job on his dunghill, Shakespeare's Marina and Richardson's Clarissa in their brothels, Austen's Fanny Price confronted by Sir Thomas Bertram in her garret retreat are literary cousins. I show why Nicholas Udall's *Ralph Roister Doister* has a heroine named Christian Custance, how readers thought Richardson's Pamela like Griselda, and why Rousseau's Julie is called the new Heloise. I allude to the great journeys undertaken by Scott's Jeanie Deans, Eliot's Hetty Sorel, Shakespeare's Imogen and Thaisa, the medieval saints Constance and Mary Magdalene. I revisit some of the great literary trial scenes: those of the Biblical Eve and Susanna; of Livy's Virginia; of Shakespeare's Cordelia and Hermione and Webster's Vittoria; of Hester Prynne. I call up great tempters: Abelard and St. Preux; Tarquin and Iago and Richard Crookback; De Flores; Lovelace; Satan. And great martyrs: Jephthah's daughter, Iphigenia, Lucretia, Cordelia, the Duchess of Malfi, Tess of the D'Urbervilles. I find confirmed in Austen's Fanny Price, as in Richardson's Clarissa, the centrality of the plot to the modern development of concepts of the self. And throughout I hope to help readers understand the tested woman plot as a deeply political construct.

That is a lot of work for a literary plot to do. I hope this study helps support readers' deepest intuitions, persistent since Aristotle, that the most complex, revealing, and satisfying literary phenomena are what characters do and how stories go.

PART I

Frameworks

TWO

The Tested Woman Plot

STRUCTURE

The essential structure of the tested woman plot involves three elements: a moral test, a double-stage plot action, and a specific configuration of character functions.

The moral test. The moral test is a thematic requirement of the tested woman plot. In the Judeo-Christian tradition, moral virtue means obedience to moral law. Not all moral systems are legal systems; that of classical Greece, with its emphasis on the pursuit of excellence and the achievement of ethical balance, is not. But in the Judeo-Christian tradition, heavily influenced by the legalistic bias of Roman culture, the moral test involves obedience to authority, and because moral law is taken to be divine in origin, obedience to moral law means obedience to God. Since authority is exercised through a chain of command, divine law being administered by human hands, the moral test is connected to hierarchical relations. Moreover, moral law is for the most part couched as prohibition. While doing justly, loving mercy, and walking humbly with God may be the ambition of the genuinely devout, avoiding evil is what constitutes virtue in ordinary eyes. Evil consists primarily of such specifically prohibited activities as murder, theft, perjury, blasphemy, and adultery. This legal bias is firmly structured into Judeo-Christian versions of the tested woman plot beginning with Eve and into Roman stories from the founding of the Republic. But moral tests can occur only where there are choices; in a system in which morality is based on authority, moral choices can occur only when authority is less than monolithic. The competing claims made possible by placing a character at the bottom of a hierarchical configuration in which authority figures represent moral authority provide the material for the moral test.

It is important to be precise about what I mean by a *moral* test. Many stories are "testing" stories, in that the qualities of the hero or heroine are displayed or "tested." But not all such stories involve significant moral choices. The adventurer trying to stay alive and ahead of his pursuers is not being morally tested. The white knight engaged in mortal combat with the black knight is not making moral choices either; he is defined as good and his opponent as evil; the white knight simply carries out his destiny. The true moral test involves options. The tested character is not always tormented by the need to choose, but the story must treat the character's action as the expression of a deliberate moral position.

Why is the story of moral choice focused on a woman? The answer involves a paradigmatic inevitability. In Western patriarchal tradition women are natural subordinates. As the object of the test a woman thus introduces with efficiency and flexibility the competing claims among authority figures on which a moral test is based. Since a woman's sex determines her hierarchical status in relation to men, and since her sexual nature is chiefly at the service of men, authority is typically directed at women's sexual behavior. Sexual obedience is therefore a woman's primary moral obligation. The female equivalent of men's honor controls a woman's sexuality and uses it in the service of, and only in the service of, her duly constituted male superiors.

As subordinates, women thus have their entire moral character focused on a form of behavior that is necessarily responsive to the initiatives of men. Unlike the male chastity requirement (roughly speaking, the prohibition against coveting one's neighbor's wife, where a man may be regarded as virtuous simply by refraining), female chastity consists of refusing to do in the face of male-initiated opportunity. As long as men are the sanctioned initiators of sexual activity and women generally lack the social opportunity to be sexual aggressors, the culture cannot regard the absence of forbidden sexual activity on the part of a woman as virtuous. Without the opportunity to be unchaste, a woman's chastity is merely potential; only a test that forces a choice can make it actual. And men create the opportunity: as the bawd Dipsas sneers in Ovid's *Amores*, "She is chaste whom no man hath solicited."[1] This argument is at the heart of the tradition that untested female chastity is no virtue at all.

So plots about women's virtue are plots about tested women. The test is the only way to demonstrate female chastity, which means, in any public sense, the only way to have it. In literary works the temptation of a married woman to commit adultery is a particularly attractive type of test because it offers the broadest threat to patriarchal possession, offending against both father and husband. Other forms of testing occur, however. A widow may have to adhere to her vow not to remarry, a daughter to obey her father's wishes to marry, an unmarried woman to retain her virginity, a woman to resist or respond to rape. Or a woman may have to balance one demand against another: illicit sex against a relative's life, or a father's demands against those of husband or betrothed. And though testing occasions are usually sexual, they need not be. In the Griselda story, the tests demand patience and acceptance in the face of marital coldness, threats, humiliation, rejection, and the loss and apparent death of children. Scattered among the sexual tests in the Constance story are occasions for endurance and Christian witness in the face of religious persecution or casting away. Even these nonsexual tests typically demand passive virtue—not murmuring, not complaining, not becoming angry against the originator of the test.

Whatever the occasion, the issue underlying the test is obedience to conflicted patriarchal authority, and the tested woman plot moves toward a resolution of conflicts and contradictions. But the reconciliation sought is not primarily between the woman and the men to whom she owes obedience, but among the males who have claimed her allegiance. For example, when a calumniated woman has been vindicated, though the triumph would seem to lie in that vindication, it is really the comprehension of the misled men, the expiation of their guilt, the reconciliation with their friends, or the unified front against their common enemies that is the victory. The calumniated woman may be welcomed back from grave or exile, received back into a marriage, allowed back into the good graces of a household, made the figurehead of a political or military campaign. But the health celebrated is that of the patriarchal establishment that has regained its properly constituted hold on itself and its world.

Test and trial. Because obedience involves both fact and appearance, the tested woman plot has an important structural peculiarity: when exhibited in full, it has two stages or actions. The first plot action, which involves the occasion for unchastity or disobedience and which I call the test, is the point at which the woman chooses or refuses an act of clear moral significance. This test is forward-looking: Will she or won't she? The second action, which I call the trial, looks backward: What actually happened? How should offended authority regard these events? Although I have called the whole structure the tested woman plot, then, I distinguish between the moment of choice, which is the testing action strictly speaking, and the examination of that choice by means of a more or less formal trial.

This double action—first choice, then judgment—is the most striking feature of the tested woman plot. Other plots can have double actions; for instance, revenge tragedy requires both offense and retribution. In a revenge plot these events are linked by causation in what Northrop Frye calls a "hence" structure[2] and are necessarily in the same mode: a murder calls up a retributive murder, the taking of a throne demands a political overthrow. The tested woman plot is distinctive because the two actions represent two different modes of considering the same phenomenon. The first action, the test or choice, involves fact or reality and hinges on the behavior of the tested woman herself. The second action, the trial or judgment, involves appearance and opinion and hinges on the behavior of others.

These two actions allow a great deal of variation. The test is the opportunity for the woman to make a decision—to render a passive virtue active or to act in a way that makes the pretense to virtue a mockery. Although the moment of choice is in theory a moment of temptation, the tested woman may feel no desire to be unchaste or disobedient; she need not feel tempted, though she does have to review and renew a commitment. But the test may very well tempt, leading the woman to a psychological struggle—a weighing of the appeals of competing claims or a capitulation to worldly pressures. In either case, her response to the test is between her and her conscience, which in the Judeo-Christian tradition means between her and God.

The trial is a demonstration aimed at and usually conducted by the authority figures to whom the woman owes obedience. Often the more interesting part of the story, it is the one that allows the greater variation. If the woman is unchaste or otherwise disobedient, the trial usually establishes that fact and metes out punishment, which may or may not cause the woman's repentance and reform. Even if the woman is chaste, the trial action of the plot nevertheless must occur. Most tested woman stories involve virtue upheld, if not always rewarded. The woman may be proclaimed virtuous. Or she may face an honestly mistaken accusation of unchastity based on misleading evidence, against which she must be defended. Or she may be slandered, calumniated by the lies of someone who wishes her downfall.

The different modalities of test and trial are in good part responsible for the dramatic vigor of the plot. Responses to both test and trial are variable and repeatable, allowing continuing plot complications and making the tested woman story a paradigm for the Christian life. Just as each day the Christian faces opportunities for disobedience to divine injunctions, the tested woman may repeatedly face occasions for unchastity and may even change her response.[3] Many stories use the mechanism of deathbed or gallows exhortation, repentance, and good death to give a fallen woman a chance to reverse her original decision. That the conclusions of test and trial need not at first correspond provides even more dramatic potential,[4] as does the fact that the men who initiate the test or conduct the trial may be motivated by sharply differing impulses. The slippery relationship between appearance and reality helps give the double action of the tested woman plot its abiding dramatic power.

This variety is contained within the constant structural parameters of test and trial. The action may enter and leave the test-trial sequence at a number of different points, so that some of the stereotyped episodes may precede or follow the story the literary work displays. But the earlier or later portions of the plot are always understood to have happened.[5] And the trial action always continues until the truth is demonstrated to the patriarchal figure the woman must obey. The woman need not be present for this demonstration—or even alive—for the trial concerns reputation, not what the woman is, but how she is perceived. The man in possession is the one who must learn and accept the truth about her.

Characters and character functions. The other structural requirement of the tested woman plot is the distribution of agency among male authority functions. Tested woman stories always involve competing men in competing power positions. Without the power and the competition there would be no test. Beneath the woman's behavior, which is the catalyst, lies the plot's central concern: the nature of male authority; how it is exercised, why, and by whom; and what happens to the hierarchical paradigm when authority figures compete. The paradigm is based on the analogous relationships of father to child, husband to wife, and master to servant that underpin both Greco-Roman and Hebraic domestic ideology and provide the pattern for the political organization of church and state, with their hierarchical pairings of priest and layman, magistrate and citizen, prince and subject. In Judeo-Christian theory and practice these pairs are understood to imitate—and thereby to receive their ultimate moral sanction—from the patriarchal relationship between God and man. But hierarchical relationships are always in question and in flux. Stability may be undermined in two ways: from below, by inferiors who challenge the rights or powers of their superiors; and laterally, by those sharing power and possession who infringe on one another's prerogatives. The tested woman plot involves both challenges. The first (the potential for female disobedience) is the pretext for the plot, but the second (the power struggle among the men) is its ultimate point.

In plot terms, male authority falls into consistent and stereotyped categories or functions—those of tempter, accuser, defender, and judge. "Function" does not mean the same thing as "person" or "character." The four plot functions may be divided among four characters, or they may be doubled up, so that one character exercises more than one function, even plays them all. The tempter, who offers the woman the occasion for disobedience, acts as the antagonist in the test action of the plot. As the importunate lover or would-be rapist, he may seek sexual or at least psychological possession of the woman. Or, since the test is the only means by which a woman can make her chastity active, he may offer the opportunity for disobedience in the hope that she will reject it.[6] His motives may be confused or hidden, even from himself. Offering the occasion for unchastity, he may be genuinely uncertain not only what response he can expect, but what response he desires. Though in stories with strong romance elements the tempter may be a casual stranger, the demands of dramatic and patriarchal concentration usually make him intimately related to the woman. He is the suitor, the husband's friend, the husband, the brother, the father; or the master, the marquis, the magistrate, the king.

Acting as the antagonist in the trial action of the plot, the accuser brings the fact or possibility of the woman's disobedience to the attention of those in authority over her. The accuser may be the tempter under a different guise; having succeeded in his seduction, he may flaunt his possession, or having been rebuffed he may accuse falsely from wounded vanity or the desire for revenge. He may be the injured party himself, the person in whom patriarchal ownership resides. He may be a third party, who either on behalf of the male possessor or out of spite against the woman brings a charge of disobedience against her. Though theoretically it would be possible for a fallen woman to bring an accusation against herself, out of remorse, I do not know of plots in which that happens, except for a few works in which the woman accuses herself falsely as a subterfuge. The absence of self-accusation confirms two of the plot's characteristics: the fixed nature of the woman, who, once fallen, remains so until exposed and worked on by men; and the primacy of male over female responses and states of mind.

The third character function is that of defender. Occasionally the defender appears in the test action, strengthening the woman against the blandishments of the tempter, but his presence there is superfluous, since the essential action takes place within the woman. The defender must, however, appear in the trial action, whose judicial and evidentiary nature requires that someone speak for the accused, often in her absence. He may be a helpful outsider, he may be the male in possession, or he may be the tempter or accuser converted. Whatever the case, the defender's function is forensic; his business is to speak the truth about the woman, not to prevent the test.

The judge renders the decision in the trial action, determining the truth so as to uphold or reestablish duly constituted authority. As final arbiter, the judge is typically the highest-ranking character in the story. Sometimes he is an outsider; at least as often he is not a disinterested party at all, but the authority figure to whom the woman owes obedience. He may also serve, or have served, as accuser, defender, or even tempter. Whoever plays the judge, it is the man in duly constituted possession of the woman—the husband, the father, their surrogate—who must understand and accept the truth about the woman. Judgment is rendered on his behalf, not hers.

These four functions may be combined or exchanged in any number of ways. The tempter of the testing action, who offers the occasion for corruption, may not appear in the trial stage at all. Or the tempter may turn up again either in his original function or in another, such as accuser.[7] This function-shifting is the source of much of the plot's interest.

But how can one say that a plot "requires" certain character functions? What does it mean that a plot has a "central concern" or "moves toward" a certain kind of resolution? Though plots, as distinct from authors, do not have intentionality, readers commonly ascribe directionality or trajectory to them, as in talking of the shape of the action of a play. This sense of shape arises from expectations about plot conventions, expectations that may run very deep. The work of structuralist students of plot is based on the hypothesis, by no means fully confirmed, that literary structures resemble linguistic structures in certain ways. The use of a segment of a language structure may "naturally" call up connected segments, and something like this seems to be at work in literary plots. Users of a language tend not to be conscious of, much less able to describe, structural relationships that they agree on in practice. Most native speakers of a language agree on what sounds right and what does not even when they have never encountered a specific variant and have no linguistic training. To provide a single example, a speaker using the English transitive verb *give* "naturally" supplies both a grammatical subject (the agent) and a grammatical object (the gift) ("Trudy gave flowers"). He also has the option of designating an indirect object, the recipient ("Trudy gave John flowers"). Agent/gift/recipient thus supply a structure around the verb *give;* in fact the verb *give* evokes a very simple plot structure, with characters, action, and trajectory. When a speaker uses a seeming variant that lacks a gift designation ("Trudy gives and expects nothing in return"), native speakers agree that the variant is well-formed, and both speaker and listener easily supply the ellipsis (Trudy gives something). If, however, a speaker were to designate the recipient but did not fill the gift slot ("Trudy gave John"), listeners would reject the sentence as ill-formed or would be confused about its meaning. To a degree, plot structures work like this. Users seem to agree on which features are expected and which unexpected, which allowable and which aberrational.

FIRST STORIES

Prohibition and Obligation: Eve and Susanna

The Book of Genesis begins with one of the most gripping stories of all time. In its framing narrative God creates a complete world, and in the center he sets a paradise that he populates with the pinnacle of his creation, the human being made "in his own image."[8]

Why does he do this?

In many ways this is an absurd question. It is anthropologically absurd, since all creation myths are back-formations designed to motivate the unexplainable facticity of present existence, bypassing an infinite causal regress. It is theologically absurd, for the god, to name him in anthropological terms, is by definition the one who *has* no motives, in any human sense. But in literary terms the question is not absurd. As a culturally shaped artifact the story has a motivated trajectory and a controlling structure. The question may have to be answered in terms internal to the story, but in this sphere it is rational.

So what does the story tell us about why the god has made the universe? Why, above all, has he made the human being? The next narrative move—the creation of a second human being—illuminates the motivation by repeating the creative act. Telling us that Eve is created to become Adam's helpmate, the account clarifies a more fundamental fact: she is created so Adam can become Adam. Without her, he lacks a distinctive essence; he is not even *he*, for the fact of sex is the fact of the difference of sex. Further, she is created out of his body so that he may simultaneously enjoy both identity with and primacy over her, for she makes possible the distinct, male, progenitive, dominant human figure Adam becomes. This repetition of the plot move in turn answers our "why?" about the creation of the human being made in the god's likeness, because it shows us that creation takes place so "the god" can become God, separate from and superior to his creation, and that Adam is created in God's likeness to satisfy God's need for the combination of identity with and superiority over his creature. Adam exists so that God can be known to be God, as Eve exists so that Adam can be known to be Adam.

As the story continues, more insight into its structure becomes possible. When God states the prohibition of the tree of knowledge, its motivation seems straightforward: If you eat you will die; that is, the tree is poisonous. But the serpent's argument to Eve raises contradictory possibilities: God's insistence on the fatal result is a lie; his motive for the prohibition is not to protect man; he fears rivals. The serpent's intervention, in fact, raises the concept of *power*, a concept understandable only in terms of more and less power. The god who created the universe and human beings must have held a monopoly on power, but the idea does not enter the story until the act of disobedience actualizes the rivalry for power that originates in the relations among the characters. The serpent's intrusion makes it possible to interpret God's divine *we*. Given the laconic nature of Genesis, it is justifiable to appeal to Judeo-Christian tradition, which describes the serpent as housing Satan. Tradition tells us that Satan is the Adversary, a functionary of the heavenly court, the shadowy authority structure motivating the contradictory behaviors of the divine being. By introducing the Adversary the story shows us that God's power, the power of intellection or consciousness that generates desire and makes creation necessary, has now been divided four ways.

The Genesis story is thus a sequence of creative acts designed to increase differentiation and hierarchical distinction. By creating the other, the creator expresses his desire to be known as distinct and superior. The initial prohibition of the tree of knowledge creates the idea of distinction—I know, says God, and you do not; therefore I am telling you. But the serpent's interrogation of the prohibition tests its grounds by raising the idea of *obligation*. If mere self-preservation is not at stake, what obliges the man to obey? The answer is the hierarchical fact of God's primacy. A prohibition derives its force from the authority of its promulgator, an authority validated by framing the Garden narrative in the narrative of the Creation. The creator commands his creatures, who are obliged to him for their creation.

Nevertheless the narrative has a seemingly unnecessary complication. The initial prohibition required only two participants, God and his creature, but we end with four. The test might have been directed by God: instead it is directed by the serpent. It might have targeted Adam: instead it targets Eve. The reason has to do with the sharing of power that occurred first with the creation of the man, then again with the creation of the woman. Moral tests occur only when moral authority is in disagreement—or appears to be so. The mere statement of prohibition turns out to have been no test because there was no consciousness of divided authority. Not until Adam has his Eve, as God his Adam, does the test become activated. By putting the test on Eve, by placing her at the bottom of a hierarchy in which not just God but Adam and the serpent exercise authority, the story plays one claim off against another, forcing decisions up and down the chain.

The Edenic story is not finished with the Fall. Genesis now gives us a forensic action in which God observes, interrogates, judges, and passes sentence on each of the participants. This trial phase makes the divine being more dramatic. No longer the remote figure whose impersonal act of creation authorized the test of obedience, he steps directly onto the human stage where, walking in the Garden in the cool of the day, he judges like a magistrate. Suddenly the text is full of dialogue. Through God's interrogation and sentence, we have entered human historical time and human physical space. There is a dramatic thrill to this exchange, as though the terrible loss were offset by the power of the encounter itself. The presence of God in the garden—impassioned, caught up in the lives and acts of his creatures—has sealed the pact implicit in the creative act. Creator and created, superior and subordinate, are acknowledged as inseparable, for each defines the other. The unmediated intimacy of God's judgmental presence confirms the relationship.

The multiplication of characters in the story of the Garden tells us something fundamental about the tested woman. In plot terms she is a structural convenience for exploring hierarchical relationships among authority figures. Eve is God's creature. But she is also Adam's creature and Adam's wife, subject to his marital authority. The serpent's approach is made in part as though for Adam's benefit, and Eve must weigh her obligation to Adam as well as to God. Further, the approach is made in terms insinuating that the serpent himself is a superior worthy to be obeyed. Not Good against Evil, but one good against another seeming good—that is the stuff of the moral test, and that is what Eve is subjected to. Making Eve rather than Adam the object of the test introduces the competing claims among authority figures that make a moral test possible. It gives dramatic form to the real issue: To what degree does man, having been created in the image of God, have the right to share in his authority?

My other Old Testament "first story" is the tale of Susanna and the Elders. Though it revisits many of the Edenic motifs—the enclosed garden, the naked wife, the sudden attack by the tempters, the judges walking in the garden, even the doubled tree—detached motifs do not constitute a plot. It is the structure that bespeaks plot identity. Like Eve's, Susanna's story is first a test. Lusted after by the lascivious Elders, she is propositioned in her garden under the threat of a false charge of adultery, its believability to be based on the collusion of the tempters turned accusers. Each will serve as the other's witness, while she will have none. Susanna is tempted, not to unchastity, but to capitulation to extortion: yield to us, or we will accuse you of adultery here in the garden with a young man, and you will suffer the fatal consequences of the act you have refused to commit. One evil against another seeming evil: these are the terms of Susanna's choice. Once she chooses to scream rather than submit and hide the deed, the trial sequence is underway. The Elders counter with accusatory cries of their own, a crowd assembles, the charge is made, and Susanna is judged and sentenced to death by stoning. On her way to execution, God moves the young Daniel to demand a reexamination of the evidence. Interrogating the Elders separately, he elicits contradictory claims about the species of tree under which the alleged adultery took place. Susanna is cleared, and the Elders are condemned.

The tale of Susanna insists on the centrality of the trial stage. The attempt on Susanna is the motivating event, but the subsequent examination—accusation, defense, and judgment—is the heart of the narrative. That fact brings out the biggest plot distinction between Susanna's story and Eve's: Eve fell, but Susanna does not. Susanna is innocent, and readers know it because we have been privy to the events of the test. Nevertheless, the trial is carried out. But on whose behalf? The trial is not to inform us or God. By refusing the Elders, Susanna has made her choice about where her ultimate allegiance lies: "It is better for me to fall into your hands, and not do it, than to sin in the sight of the Lord" (v. 23). God has all the evidence he needs. But we are no longer in Eden, where God is a character, interrogating and judging. The Susanna story is situated in human time and place, and all its forensic roles—accusation, defense, and judgment—must be carried out by human agency. Hence the addition of Daniel to the cast of characters, which occurs by God's prompting when the distinction between the functions of accusation and judgment have become corrupted. The presence of the defender is linked to the non-allegorical nature of Susanna's story. In a fallen world justice is possible only through the most vigorous examination of the evidence. Even at that, God must prompt the human spirit.

The other expansion in the cast of characters, the entertaining doubling of the tempter figure, is less necessary, but it underscores the plot's concern with hierarchical relationships. Though the frame of Susanna's tale establishes her beauty and piety, it spends most of its time on the community's patriarchs. The narrative introduces her husband Joachim, the man "of greatest distinction" in his community, records the rank of the Elders, who have been appointed magistrates for the year, and places them at Joachim's house, where the affairs of the community are adjudicated. Then it spends the bulk of the frame undermining the patriarchal unity it has established. The Elders come to Joachim's house not to do justice business but to ogle Joachim's wife. They hide their intentions from one another and, on the day when each decides to attempt her in the garden, they leave the house in opposite directions to throw each other off the track. Naturally they meet coming back and, deciding to make the best of each other's presence, concoct the charge-of-adultery threat. The vigor with which this charge is carried nearly to its hideous conclusion makes clear that the Elders lust after more than Susanna's body. Their action, bent on her destruction as a model of chastity, is really aimed at Joachim. The injunction they violate by coveting their neighbor's wife is one designed to protect possession, and its violation targets the husband. This conflict within the authority structure is stressed right through the resolution, for Daniel's means for reversing the judgment is to break the criminal collusion between the Elders, restoring Joachim's marital right in his wife.

Rallying the Patriarchy: Iphigenia, Virginia, and Lucretia

Hebraic versions of the tested woman plot introduce us to divinely sanctioned hierarchy and to the scrutiny of the test stage by means of its trial sequel. Greco-Roman tradition contributes stories that elaborate authority conflicts within the patriarchy. Euripides' *Iphigenia in Aulis* tells one of the originary stories of Greek literature. The Greek fleet, assembled under the leadership of Agamemnon to sail for Troy to avenge the abduction of his brother Menelaus's wife, Helen, lies becalmed in the bay at Aulis. Informed by the priest Calchas that Artemis will grant wind upon the sacrifice of Agamemnon's firstborn child, Agamemnon lures Iphigenia and her mother, Clytemnestra, to Aulis on the pretense of marrying his daughter to the young hero Achilles, then gives her to the sacrificial knife. The wind blows, the fleet sails, and with this death, the first of the Trojan War, passes into a new generation the self-destruction of the house of Atreus.

Euripides' posthumously produced play[9] infuses this episode of betrayal and sacrifice with the complexities of competing power. Iphigenia's heroic response to her impossible situation, the feature that most appealed to the Renaissance and most bothered Aristotle, is preceded by the agonized attempts of father, mother, daughter, and the abused Achilles to evade the consequences of Agamemnon's rash pledge. The pressure on the father is not moral, much less spiritual. Agamemnon's pledge was given in a spasm of military ambition and group solidarity at the urging of Calchas, Menelaus, and Odysseus, and he is faced with mutiny if he does not honor it. Not even Achilles can control his men; the Myrmidons are as avid for blood and action as the rest. Her entrapment brought home by Achilles' inability to mount a rescue, Iphigenia takes control in the only way she can and gives her life to her father and her country.

Iphigenia's heroic self-command momentarily focuses the play on her. But the play is about the internecine quarrels of the house of Atreus. At its heart is Clytemnestra's charge that Agamemnon is willing to sacrifice Iphigenia because he has privileged the interests of his brother over those of his wife and daughter. Yet Agamemnon's circumstantial entrapment is more heart-rending than Clytemnestra's accusation admits, and Euripides complicates it by making the relationship between father and daughter the most loving in the play, so that Iphigenia's horror at what her father has promised is especially deep, her concern for his fate especially poignant. Euripides is dramatizing the conflicted move from the culture of the individual hero to the culture of the nation-state. *Iphigenia in Aulis* has a public world—the mob with its demagogue priest, Calchas, and its demagogue warrior, Odysseus. Against this public, no man, however firm, fearsome, charismatic, or skillful, can do single combat.[10] Achilles' impotence proves this both to Iphigenia and to the audience. Not even Achilles . . . When she realizes that traditional heroics no longer work, Iphigenia takes command of her death. Her heroics are perforce in the interests of this controlling public.

There are differences between Euripides' proto-version of the tested woman plot and those of the Old Testament. Some are differences of Greek versus Hebrew. Euripides' play is less legalistic, its god more remote and ambiguous. There is no clear double stage of test followed by trial. The woman is a daughter, not a wife, though the issue of marital fidelity reeks in the background. But Iphigenia's test is still provoked by a patriarchal power structure in profound disarray, forcing her to make a decision about where her obligation lies. Her metamorphosis from passive victim to sacrificial hero is not designed to change her fate; it is intended to address that disarray. Knowing that she will die, Iphigenia must choose how, and her choice is contrived to bring warriors, chieftains, and priests together into a ferociously harmonic Greek force. "We" versus "they" will become, not brother against brother, or mother-right against father-right, or the leader against his troops, but Greece against Troy. Iphigenia's concern for Achilles is that the bond between him and his men not be further strained. Her last injunction to her mother seeks to heal the breach within the family: "Do not hate my father who is your husband" (1453–4; line numbers refer to the Greek text). Her final dance is designed to work its unifying will on the god herself: "With my own blood in sacrifice I will wash out the fated curse of God" (1480–4). It is this theme of sacrifice that will be especially influential in the tested woman plot.

By contrast, the Roman version of the sacrifice of a daughter by her father, the story of Appius and Virginia, emphasizes the post-sacrifice dynamic of male reintegration. Thanks to its extended treatment in Livy and Chaucer, the story of Virginia[11] was even better known during the English Renaissance than that of Iphigenia. Whereas in Euripides issues of causation, necessity, blame, the standards of heroism, and the status of the gods are vexed, Livy shows no ambiguity of narrative intention. He is openly didactic, shaping chronology and commentary to an argument about the development of the Roman polity. The corrupt decemvir Appius lusts after the young daughter of Virginius, a citizen absent from the city on military service. After unsuccessful attempts to seduce her, he contrives with his minion Claudius to seize her in the street on the trumped-up claim that she is Claudius's slave. Her betrothed, Icilius, and her uncle, Numitorius, send for Virginia's father while they maneuver to keep her out of Appius's clutches. Though Virginius arrives in time for the trial, Appius holds the legal power. When he declares in favor of Claudius's claim, Virginius stabs his daughter to death rather than allow her dishonor.

Livy's story of Virginia is the melodramatic set piece in his account of the central political event of the early republic—the making of the Roman law. Since Rome is a legalistic culture, clear test and trial stages are present. The test, which ends with Virginia's death, occurs in a forensic setting because the effort to develop a just legal system is the subject of this portion of Livy's Roman history. The trial stage shows how the manner of that death forces Rome to discuss and decide. Piece by piece power is stripped from the decemvirs, the tribunes and consuls are restored, and Appius is brought to trial, prosecuted by Virginius. The story raises a complex of issues about power relationships. The right of supposed slave ownership is set not just against father-right but also against Icilius's husband-right: "I am to marry this girl, and I mean to have a virgin for my bride" (233). With his political savvy and his status as former tribune, Icilius continually seems on the verge of dominating Livy's account—as do the abused plebs, the troops, the patricians, and the political factions, the other loci of power through whom Livy maneuvers his narrative.

Livy is aware of the narrative shape of his account, for he introduces Virginia in terms of her predecessor, Lucretia: "[The origin of the crime against Virginia] was lust, and in its consequences it was no less dreadful than the rape and suicide of Lucretia which led to the expulsion of the Tarquins. The *decemvirs*, in fact, met the same end as the kings and lost their power for the same reason" (231). Like Virginia's, Lucretia's story is exemplary less for its moral than for its political force. The attack on Lucretia's chastity, which represents the abuse of kingly power, features in Livy's account at the other master moment in pre-imperial Roman political history, the transition from monarchy to republic. Though Virginia's story was well known in the Renaissance, Lucretia's eclipsed it as the type of the heroically virtuous woman. The events of Lucretia's story were common currency: how her husband boasted in the camp of his wife's virtue, how the young husbands rode to check up on their wives' behavior and found Lucretia spinning among her women, how Sextus Tarquinius, the king's son, returned to rape her under threat, how Lucretia called husband and father to her to report the deed and commit suicide before their eyes, how the outraged family rallied Rome to overthrow the Tarquin kings and establish the republic.

Unlike Livy's Virginia, Livy's Lucretia has real dramatic presence because she makes her choice herself. Faced with a situation like Susanna's—Tarquin promises to leave her dead body beside that of a naked male slave if she does not submit—Lucretia must make a moral choice about her physical chastity and tactical choices about her trial. Tarquin cannot seduce her, nor can he move her by threatening simply to kill her. It is rather the prospect of posthumous dishonor that forces her to yield so that she herself may supply both the accusation against her and her most compelling defense. The knife that passes among the men after her death, unlike the knife Virginius displays, is the weapon she used on herself. Moreover, because Lucretia is wife as well as daughter, carrying in her body the patriarchal interests of two great Roman houses, when she proves the rape by killing herself before her husband and her father, she implicates them both.[12]

Though Lucretia's and Susanna's situations are similar, their decisions are different. Superficially the difference is Tarquin's willingness to kill to prevent

Lucretia's witness. The more profound difference involves the question of whose judgment matters. Susanna does not expect her denial to be believed, but to her the important judgment is God's. To Lucretia, what matters most is the judgment of husband and father, who must be given irrefutable evidence that publicly corroborates her chastity. Placing the two tales side by side dramatizes how the complexities available to the plot type are magnified when it is transferred to a Christian world inheriting both classical and Hebrew traditions.

What about the story of Penelope? Is the twenty-year siege of the wife who holds off 108 suitors a tested woman story? The answer, a qualified no, helps draw boundaries around the plot type. The Homeric material is not structured to do the work the plot typically does. The *Odyssey* gives us almost no sense of the Ithacans as a patriarchal unit. Though lip service is paid to the distinction between suitors who are Ithacans and those who come from farther away, and though the political assumptions of later times try to see the household of Odysseus as the hierarchal center of Ithacan life, it really is not. There is no Ithacan polity; there is only Odysseus's family on the one hand, and all those other people on the other. Within Odysseus's family, which includes his son, Telemachus, and his father, Laertes, unity is absolute—no patriarchal conflict, and therefore no test of loyalties. Beyond the family there may be faithful servants or temporary allies, but mostly there are natural enemies, whom one defeats if one can and tricks if one cannot. Disarray exists among the gods, where Poseidon is anti-Odysseus and Athena pro-Odysseus, but though that conflict affects humans, it is not their conflict. Penelope undergoes a grueling siege, but there is little evidence that she regards herself as morally tested or that she has obligations except to hold Odysseus's patrimony for Telemachus. The poem opens with the Telemachiad because the son's majority has nearly arrived; the suitors grow more urgent because Penelope's importance is waning.

Loss and Recovery: Hellenistic Romance

Protecting the patriarchy from external threat is a different story from the exacerbation and reconciliation of internal conflicts we find in the tested woman plot. Nevertheless, the peregrinations of Odysseus resemble in some ways a group of stories that do lend material to the plot. These are the ancient novels, or Hellenistic romances, that typically propel their characters about the Mediterranean world on (primarily) amorous adventures.[13] Mikhail Bakhtin argues of the Hellenistic romance that it is not travel per se but what travel allows and signifies that is so characteristic of the type. Bakhtin describes the salient feature of this romance style as "adventure-time" in an "alien world" (89), where events occur by chance and the paired motifs of meeting and parting, recognition and nonrecognition, and acquisition and loss saturate the stories. While travel allows for the crossing of time and space that gives these motifs narrative form, the alien world removes the characters from quotidian concerns. On the road, they carry with them only their essence—their youth, their desire, their honor. If this "chronotope" (as Bakhtin calls the configuration of novelistic time/space) marks the conditions of the Hellenistic romance, the test of the heroes' integrity makes its action. This testing does not change the characters, but demonstrates their capacity to remain unchanged. The Hellenistic romance is designed to end where it began, with the recovery of its "initial equilibrium": "The hammer of events shatters nothing and forges nothing—it merely tries the durability of an already finished product. And the product passes the test" (106–7).[14]

In *The True History of the Novel*, Margaret Anne Doody argues against Bakhtin's perception of the static quality of the ancient novel's presentation of character, demonstrating the way that, for instance, the story of Daphnis and Chloë tells of the entrance into adult desire and adult sexuality, or Apuleius's *Golden Ass* uses physical metamorphosis as a path through spiritual suffering to religious rebirth.[15] But she agrees with Bakhtin in finding an emphasis on characters' active response to adversity and to designs on their integrity. A distinctiveness of Hellenistic romances is the love- and adventure-equality of the woman; hence the customary titles of the tales, names of a pair of people, male and female, who undergo parallel adventures. The rigors the woman undergoes, the tests she endures, the fidelity and physical courage she evinces, are fully as common and powerful as the man's. Unlike stories in which the tested woman fails her test and is morally and emotionally transformed, unlike those in which "rejective" chastity (Doody's term) is overwhelmed by force, unlike those in which the woman maintains her spiritual integrity at the forfeit of her life and is absorbed into the patriarchal postmortem of the men who examine her case, the tested woman of Hellenistic romance resists and triumphs, over and over.

This emphasis on the preservation of personal integrity makes Hellenistic romances the precursors of the saints' and martyrs' stories of the following thousand years of Christian hagiography. The romances measure integrity largely in terms of chastity, though that need not mean virginity. In the earliest of the extant romances, Chariton's *Chaereus and Callirhoë*, the young lovers marry at the beginning of the story.[16] Almost immediately Chaereus is tricked into believing Callirhoë unfaithful and kicks her in the belly, causing a deathlike swoon; grave robbers find her alive and sell her into slavery. This opening tells us that the tale will require marital chastity. Callirhoë's next crisis complicates our sense of chastity's nature, for Dionysus, who buys her, falls passionately in love and woos her to marry him. Determined to remain faithful to Chaereus, Callirhoë is preparing to kill herself when she realizes she is pregnant. To avoid killing her husband's child, she marries Dionysus and passes the child off as his without ever wavering in her psychological fidelity to her first husband. The chastity requirement extends to the hero as well. In Achilles Tatius's novel *Clitophon and Leucippe*, Clitophon too must decide what virtue requires. He has

entered into a paper marriage with the young widow Melitte, who begs him for
a consummation he delays while he searches for his beloved Leucippe. Having
found Leucippe just when Melitte discovers that her brute of a husband still
lives, Clitophon makes love to her out of pity and gratitude—and does not fail
to enjoy it.

In Hellenistic romance the preservation of spiritual and bodily integrity is
worked out in a world lacking the overarching authority of Hebrew or Roman
law. The characters' bondage to fortune is most often figured by capture
and enslavement, in which the power of landowner, military commander, or
brigand is set against the individual will. The many judicial proceedings are
not moral examinations but threats of the same order as shipwrecks or pirates,
and they catapult the action forward rather than scrutinizing the past. The
trial may include a display of resistance, like Leucippe's ringing defiance of
her lustful master Thersander's threats, forecasting the defense of integrity to
be met in Cervantes' Marcela and Webster's Duchess: "I am defenceless, and
alone, and a woman; but one shield I have, and that is my free soul, which
cannot be subdued by the cutting of the lash, or the piercing of the sword, or
the burning of the fire. That is a possession I will never surrender; no, not I:
and burn as you will, you will find that there is no fire hot enough to consume
it!"[17] Leucippe is credible because she carries the scars of the equally lustful
and unsuccessful overseer's whip on her back.

As Hellenistic romance evolves into the romances of the Middle Ages, some
motifs continue, while others change. The earliest extant text of *Apollonius
of Tyre*, the source story for Shakespeare's *Pericles*, is a sixth-century Latin
redaction in which the unmistakable Hellenistic romance material has been
subjected to strong Roman-Christian influence.[18] Like Hellenistic romance,
the story has highborn lovers separated and adrift in alien worlds, a wife who,
presumed dead, lives to be reunited with her husband, chastity triumphant,
priestesses of Artemis (who has become Diana), and pirates, shipwrecks, evil
kings, and threats of torture. But there are also changes. The title is different—
not a pair of lovers, but a single male hero. The frame is different—the
story opens not with the principals but with the contrastive account of King
Antiochus's incest with his daughter. Apollonius is already on the road and
on the run when he meets the heroine, Lucina. Their daughter, Tharsia, is
an active character; she rouses the jealousy of the foster mother and faces the
most rigorous tests of chastity. Above all, the characters age, living toward
resolution through a generation's worth of time. The marriage at the end is
not that of hero and heroine but of their daughter.

These changes in action motifs shift the thematic emphasis. *Apollonius of
Tyre* has the beginnings of a teleology. Its purpose is not just to test what is
but to explain what must be,[19] and the explanation is couched in moral terms:
Tharsia's incorruptibility not only protects her but converts her attackers.
Though both Chariton and *Apollonius* use the theme of paternity, the shift
in moral tone is striking. In Chariton's tale Callirhoë bears Chaereus's son to

Dionysus, and when it is time to reunite the lovers, she excuses her marriage to Dionysus by explaining about the child. While Chaereus accepts her justification, he shows no interest in retrieving his son, whom she leaves with Dionysus as a consolation prize without disabusing him about its paternity. But in *Apollonius of Tyre* paternity matters. Antiochus's sexual monopoly of his daughter represents the worst aberration of paternal power. As for Apollonius's depressive illness, it stems from the emotional suffering of loss combined with aging, and suggests a new theme, that the man who cannot create family and establish paternity dies not just in body but in spirit. And if paternity matters, then time must matter; it must operate to change the characters, not just to recover them. *Pericles* teaches us that the most moving reunion of all may be that of parent and adult child, because it represents such change. Nevertheless, *Apollonius of Tyre* retains the essential adventure heroine. Lucina's desire creates the central love affair, and Tharsia the maiden protects herself from pirates, pimps, and propositions, using her art to profit her master and heal her father.

THE BOOK OF JOB

Because the tested woman plot is fundamentally about the patriarchal power structure that expresses itself in the character functions of tempter, accuser, defender, and judge, I can argue that the woman's presence in it is a paradigmatic inevitability based on her position as natural subordinate. The notion of a natural subordinate arises from a patriarchal mindset about the relationship between father and child that regards the male parent as primary progenitor and natural possessor of his offspring. In a patriarchy sons inherit their fathers' positions and become superiors themselves, but daughters never do, being given instead into the possession of other men. Women's lifelong subordination makes them "natural" objects of competition and subjects them to tests of obedience to men.

In myth, however, men are not yet the ultimate superiors, for the gods still walk the earth. As Western literature becomes increasingly postmythic and literal, it less easily mingles gods and humans in the same scene. A literature that wishes to examine the issue of authority without being frankly a theodicy must therefore sublimate downward, substituting human power for divine. But in literary forms in which God the ultimate creator and possessor can still be brought on stage, a story may subject a man, God's creature and natural subordinate, to a version of the moral choice and scrutiny found in the tested woman plot. Such a story must posit, represent, and reconcile a motivating conflict within the Godhead. That achieved, the tested woman plot is present in every feature but the femaleness of its central figure. We have the story of Job. Job's story has always been seen as an analogue of the tested woman plot, and it makes unequivocal the plot's focus on the relationship between superior and subordinate. Because God enters the story as a dramatic character, no woman is needed; a man may be tested directly because he can confront that authority directly.

That the Book of Job has traditionally been viewed as the analogue of the tested woman plot is evidenced by some of the plot's best known stories. Chaucer's Clerk's Tale refers the story of Griselda to that of Job. Richardson's Clarissa cobbles together from the text of Job the account of her own suffering and eventual redemption into clarity of mind. The imagery of Job permeates the final two acts of Webster's *The Duchess of Malfi*. In fact, tested woman stories are characterized by internal references to the archetypes of the tradition, from Richardson's Mr. B jeering dismissively about Lucretia as he paws Pamela, to Udall's Christian Custance, named for one exemplar, calling up others to her aid. One of the most important ways the tested woman plot expresses itself as a coherent plot type is through such cross-references.

The greatest test case in the Judeo-Christian tradition, the Book of Job schematically displays the two-stage structure and competing character functions of the tested woman plot. In the brief opening, Yahweh provokes the test by praising the most virtuous of his creatures. Satan the Adversary, the functionary of the heavenly court who acts as tempter, returns the challenge by arguing that untried virtue is no virtue at all: "Doth Job fear God for nought? / . . . But put forth thine hand now, and touch all that he hath, and he will curse thee to thy face" (1:8, 10). Having provoked and permitted the test, God absents himself while Satan puts Job to the question. Will Job retain his faith in God, or, given the overwhelming evidence of his rejection by the Creator, will he separate himself, curse God as his wife advises, and bring on death as his only possible relief?[20] At the end of chapter 2, the conclusion of the test stage, Job has made his choice. Though confusion and grief silence him temporarily, he does not curse. What follows is the examination of Job's case. Satan the tempter disappears from the story, his function concluded. The friends step forward to act as accuser and defender, arguing on the one hand that Job must have brought this misery on himself, on the other that, however undeserved his lot, he is obliged to accept the inscrutability of his suffering. In agony of spirit Job refuses both positions. He examines and confirms his sense of his own integrity, presents his own case, and while not questioning God's right to act as he wills, insists that only the Creator can weigh his life. Eventually God takes up his function as judge, accepting Job's account and handing down an award of multiple damages.

The structural exactness with which the Book of Job employs the tested woman plot is no accident, for the plot repeatedly refers to the story of Job to form itself. Yet the Book of Job does more than display the architecture of the plot; it gives us deep insight into the plot's psychology. In particular, Job helps make comprehensible the origin of the test, frequently the most difficult moment of the plot to rationalize. The story has as its starting point Job's virtue: "There was a man in the land of Uz, whose name was Job: and that man was perfect and upright, and one that feared God and eschewed evil" (1:1). Job's virtue and prosperity established, the tale recounts a heavenly debate in which God makes a boast, Satan issues a challenge, and God gives Satan permission to act. So the test begins.

In this exchange God does exactly what Posthumus does in *Cymbeline* and Collatine does in the story of Lucretia. He holds up for admiration the perfection of his servant Job, the human partner who, analogically, stands to him as wife to husband. Like Iachimo, Satan immediately challenges the boast, and he and God together set the terms of the test. The boast/challenge pattern is so bold and its significance so central to the tested woman plot as to demand examination. What provokes Satan to attempt to violate Job's perfection? What provokes God to test his servant? The clues are found in the terms of the wager and in traditional views of the participants. Satan's response is the easier to understand, for it is caused by envy. God's description—"there is none like him in the earth"—establishes Job as first among men. Although in the universal hierarchy he is God's inferior, within his own rank he is preeminent, patriarch of a great clan. Satan lacks such preeminence. One of the heavenly courtiers, he is distinguishable primarily for his busyness in going to and fro on the earth and in challenging God's estimate of his creature. Satan's power to harm Job is a power delegated and circumscribed by God.

The traditional Christian elaboration of Satan's character ascribes this envy to his nature as a fallen angel, the once brightest son of God now reduced to a perpetually discontented instrument of temptation and chastisement. So strong is this tradition that when Milton's Satan makes his first testing approach to Christ in *Paradise Regained*, by denying envy as his motive he confirms the tradition: "Envy they say excites me, thus to gain / Companions of my misery and woe" (1.397–8). Responding, Christ cites the experience of Job: "What but thy malice mov'd thee to misdeem / Of righteous *Job*, then cruelly to afflict him / With all inflictions" (1.424–6). Having his attention called to God's servant Job is a triple affront: Job's relative perfection reminds Satan of his own imperfection, God's total power over his servant reminds Satan of his own limited power, and Job's most favored status with God reminds Satan of his own alienation from God. Satan's response is to attempt to exercise power by reducing Job's status. Satan does not seek Job's death, for he is indifferent to Job's existence as such. It is Job's virtue that he wishes both to own and to eliminate, by making Job like himself. Here is the lure and the paradox of violation, which, by transforming its victim, at once possesses and destroys. Though the means may be goods, family, or flesh, in order for violation to occur Job must be brought to curse God of his own free will. Job must take evil into himself.

If Satan seeks to violate, God seeks to prove. God's situation is the opposite of Satan's, because by definition he is the one in possession. God knows that Job is a perfect and an upright man. Why should he seek to establish what he already knows; to have what he already possesses? The wager gives us a clue. Satan's challenge provokes God's pride of possession. He must demonstrate what he knows to those who doubt. The creature Job reaches the height of his perfection and value only if acknowledged. The acknowledgment of the perfection of God's creation propels the entire tale. Satan must acknowledge the perfection of God's servant Job, Job must acknowledge the mystery of God's creative power, Job's friends must acknowledge both Job's righteousness and the justice of God's dealings with him, all God's creatures must say of him the thing that is right (42:7, 8). Proving, then, means demonstrating.

But proving also means testing, for God is stung by Satan's challenge into admitting uncertainty. That Job is already "perfect," which is to say complete—that he has done all the things a man in his position should do—is not enough. He must also refuse to do evil. Satan's prediction is that Job, if sufficiently tormented, will cut himself off from God, as God has seemed to cut himself off from Job. Job's response to increasingly severe tests reinforces that uncertainty. Truly he has not feared God for nought, for he is first among his people in possessions, power, and prestige. The initial test completed and Job's family and possessions stripped from him, it is also true that he finds consolation in his reduction to his essential form: "Naked came I out of my mother's womb, and naked shall I return thither: the Lord gave, and the Lord hath taken away; blessed be the name of the Lord" (1:21). When the wager's boundaries are extended to Job's body, he still insists on his own integrity and justifies his own righteousness. Job does not curse God, as God would have known had he, in Jung's evocative phrase, consulted his own omniscience.[21] But Job does maintain his own case, he does stand on his own separateness, he does insist on a response.

For God, the provocation of Job's virtue is that it is both his and not his. God may dictate the situations under which that virtue will be tested, but Job must define its essence. To possess Job's virtue fully, God must find a way to ask for it. And Job must willingly give it. When Job ends his words at the end of chapter 31, stopping what has been a fruitless plea for dialogue, the test falls on Yahweh, who must make it possible for Job to express the bond between them.

God does this by an appeal to the ineffable majesty of his creation, that is, to the natural relationship between creator and created. But how he appeals matters as much as what he appeals to. After all, Elihu has spent six chapters taking the same position, that God's power is beyond man's comprehension. But Elihu has told Job. God, when he responds to Job out of the whirlwind, asks, commencing a dialogue: "Gird up now thy loins like a man; for I will demand of thee, and answer thou me" (38:3). When Job in his humility refuses to answer (40:4–5), God repeats his proposition: "Gird up thy loins now like a man: I will demand of thee, and declare thou unto me" (40:7). The extraordinary statements and questions he uses to describe his creation are not simply rhetorical. They demand interpretation. By their means Job must become aware of the full import of the nature and power of the Godhead. Once aware, he may formulate the relationship between

Creator and creature. This is what Job performs in his response. He humbles himself before God, acknowledging God's omniscience and omnipotence as he should. But the definition of God's power comes from Job. The servant defines the master.

Does including the Book of Job as a seminal version of the tested woman plot open the plot to stories about the testing of a man? Why should not Melville's *Billy Budd* fall within the plot? Why not Shelley's *Frankenstein*? As in the question about Penelope, my answer, a qualified no, helps delimit the plot type. Though in the broad sense testing is at the core of most literary representations of human experience, the tested woman plot requires more than a tormented individual at its heart; it requires a natural hierarchy, a moral choice, test and trial stages, and the authority functions of tempter, accuser, defender, and judge. *Frankenstein* does have the natural subordinate in the shape of the creature, and, even more crucially, the creator/father, the natural superior. Playing this fact for all it is worth, Shelley frames her tale in terms of relationships between parents and children and constructs the intellectual privation of the creature to mimic in certain ways the privations visited on women. But *Frankenstein* lacks two necessary features of the tested woman plot. It lacks a clear sense that the creature is morally tested, that he makes a conscious choice to violate a moral obligation he understands and accepts. More fundamentally, it lacks any conflict over the creature. Until late in the tale, only the victims and Frankenstein even know of the creature's existence, and no one competes for possession of him because this natural subordinate has no exchange value. Though Frankenstein himself is certainly conflicted about what he has done, Shelley's tale has neither the test/trial distinction nor the competition over the subordinate that marks the plot.

Melville's novella comes closer to the type. *Billy Budd* features an authority structure in conflict over an innocent whose behavior is examined in a judicial proceeding that results in his martyrdom. Within the sequence of temptation, accusation, defense, and judgment we even have (in Captain Vere) a character who adopts one trial function after another, serving as Budd's accuser and defender as well as his judge. Certainly we have hints, especially in Claggart, of a desire for sexual possession. What Melville's story lacks is any sense of Budd's caste status as natural subordinate and social possession. Though he is portrayed as psychologically and culturally "simple," incapable of guile, deceit, or even abstraction, any view of him as essential inferior is undercut at every turn, from his original presence on the *Rights of Man* to his noble physique and the pretty silk-lined basket in which he was found. The superiority of the ship's officers is only the superiority of force. The tale's point is the capriciousness of his entrapment—by the British navy, the personalities of the officers, his tongue-tied response to Claggart's accusation. Though one might claim that by focusing a kind of testing structure on a man Melville undermines the idea of natural hierarchy altogether, I would argue that the story really shows the participation of all males in a gender equality so taken for granted as to be invisible. The absence of women masks but does not negate men's fundamental bonding and power sharing.

Given the portable nature of its elements, the tested woman plot naturally pulls toward itself stories that lack the central female figure but do some of the plot's time-honored cultural work. By the nineteenth century, one should expect to find elements of the plot harnessed to an examination of the psychology of power in contexts other than the domestic and familial. Rather than attempting to extend the plot beyond its traditional focus, however, I have accepted its circumscription. Its stereotypical features give the plot its historical identity and ethical power, both of which depend on specific cultural attitudes about the place of women in relation to men. As those attitudes wane and fragment, the plot wanes and fragments as well. But at its height, it is responsible for some of our most compelling literature.

THREE

Frames of Mind

THE TESTED WOMAN PLOT IS A PLOT ABOUT WOMEN AND MEN BE-cause it is a plot about power and the social structures through which power is exercised; the caste relationship between women and men is an efficient and dramatically interesting venue for the exploration of power. The story of Job shows us that the sex of the plot's participants, not to mention the sexual behavior on which it came to focus, is a contingent rather than an inevitable feature. It is a contingency, nonetheless, that requires careful investigation. At issue are the assumptions about the essential differences between men and women by which a sex-based hierarchy can function.

The Western tradition about the nature of women is both persistent and peculiar. One of the most peculiar things about it is the large amount of material available. This results from the binary sex-differentiation system of Western culture, in which males are regarded as the universal or representative form of humanness, the type sex. The other sex—the variant or differentiated one—is the female. Since woman is seen as varying from the type, she tends to be described only in terms of the features that create the variation, a categorical asymmetry accounting for the different traditions and texts about the sexes. In the Middle Ages and the Renaissance, there is a mass of material about the nature of women, meaning the characteristics ascribed to women on the basis of their femaleness. By contrast, about the issue of the nature of men, with which the Renaissance at least was even more obsessed, there is very little that has to do with their maleness. Though the material assumes maleness, the standard topic "the nature of man" really deals with what it means to be human, not what it means to be male. There is very little that isolates the phenomenon of maleness from the phenomenon of humanness entire. The topic "the nature of woman," however, has to do with what it means to be female, often to the complete exclusion of features that are not overtly sex-linked.

This difference in the historical record accounts for the conduct of this chapter. In the first section, I will characterize the tradition about women only briefly, since it is well known, and will focus instead on the logical and rhetorical character of its conduct. In the second section, faced with the absence of a comparable tradition on the nature of men, I will deduce some of the expectations about male psychology and behavior that influence the conduct of tested woman stories.

THE NATURE OF WOMEN

The question of what manner of creatures women are and whether they are essentially good or evil endlessly exercised medieval and Renaissance writers and worked its way into the assumptions of ordinary men and women. A fixture of classical rhetorical exercises and of medieval disputation, it was revisited with fervor by fourteenth- and fifteenth-century French participants in the "querelle des femmes" and led to a spate of pamphleteering in Jacobean England. The topic hung in the air, in relatively unchanged form, for two thousand years.[1]

The debate was conducted on several grounds—theological and philosophical, historical, medical, political—and was permeated by two methodological biases: organization by reference to types, not individuals, and support by reference to authorities, not firsthand evidence. Until the seventeenth century, this method was the dominant approach to any intellectual topic, however subject to empirical examination. The failure of those debating the woman question to look closely at individual women is itself evidence not of antifeminism but of a general habit of thought. A further bias lies behind the label "debate." Descriptions of women clustered around extremes, one favorable, the other pejorative. Women were virtuous or vicious, strong or weak, capable or incapable of intellectual effort, able or unable to control their passions, elementally refined or mixed, ethereal or base, stable or changeable. This polarization followed the pro-contra character of classical rhetorical presentation, which permeated both Christian theology and medieval and Renaissance education. The tradition encouraged the virtuoso elaboration of extreme positions rather than the reconciliation of opposites, and the pervasive authoritative evidence used to describe women was already in a form representing these extremes.[2]

The woman question was most commonly argued by reference to historical or pseudohistorical biographies of women from biblical, classical, and medieval tradition. The biblical figures of Eve and Mary were the poles of Christian experience; they were the types of weakness or carnal seductiveness on the one hand and of strength or divine purity on the other. Other biblical women fell into place accordingly. Susanna, Esther, Judith, Elizabeth, and Jephthah's obedient daughter joined the side of female virtue. Jezebel, Delilah, Salome, and Noah's querulous wife represented female vice. Occasionally women— Mary Magdalene is a favorite example—were converted from one extreme to the other without violating the duality principle. The women of the classical and medieval traditions were treated similarly.[3] The most popular way to join the debate was to compile a set of exemplary biographies. Some supported

only one side—Chaucer's *Legend of Good Women*. Others included both sides—
Boccaccio's nearly contemporaneous *De claris mulieribus* (Concerning famous
women).[4] Many histories of women appeared in sources not exclusively about
women—Jacobus de Voragine's *Golden Legend*, the most famous compendium
of saints' lives, or the 1563 edition of the enormously influential *Mirror for
Magistrates* that for the first time included in its collection of famous lives the
story of a woman, Jane Shore.

Medieval and Renaissance habits of thought were not only intensely antilogistic, they were also intensely hierarchical. Descriptions of the nature
of man were descriptions of his place in the scheme of the created world
that has come to be called the Great Chain of Being.[5] In this scheme man,
though lower than the angels and God, was higher than the beasts and the
members of the vegetative and mineral kingdoms, increasingly simple in their
organization and limited in their attributes, that formed the lowest orders of
creation. Within the kingdoms that constituted the major links in the chain
were smaller, imitative hierarchies—the nine categories of angels, the orders
of animals, the social classes of men. Along with this doctrine of hierarchies
went its philosophical accompaniment, the doctrine of attributes. Categories
of creatures enjoyed categories of attributes. God was the essence of pure
actuality, angels of pure intellect, man the creature of reason, animals of sense,
plants of growth, stones of being. Each corporeal category contained the
attributes of the member below it. Man had being, growth, and sense, but his
distinguishing characteristic was reason. Reason came from an intermingling
of these corporeal attributes with that of intellect, making him like the angels
as well as like the beasts.

The essence of the debate about the nature of woman concerned her
position in this hierarchy, for she was both man and not man. The hierarchical
habit of thought forced this question of similarity and difference into the more
emotionally charged one of superiority and inferiority. To the degree that
woman was not man, her otherness supposed attributes that would give her a
hierarchical niche either above or below him, a necessity neatly adapted to pro-
contra disputation. Woman might be considered purer, less compounded of
base elements, more ethereal or angelic than man. Or she might be considered
baser, more exclusively compounded of mere being, growth, and sense, less fur-
nished with the human attribute of reason. Either position could be argued—
and was.[6] Whichever way woman was shunted, up or down the hierarchy, the
result was to simplify her. Man's place in the Great Chain of Being gave him
a unique position with access to both spiritual and physical realms, as Walter
Raleigh explained in *A History of the World*:

> And whereas God created three sorts of living natures, (to wit) angelical, rational,
> and brutal; giving to angels an intellectual, and to beasts a sensual nature, he
> vouchsafed unto man, both the intellectual of angels, the sensitive of beasts,
> and the proper rational belonging unto man; and there . . . 'Man is the bond and

chain *which tieth together both natures*': and because in the little frame of man's body
there is a representation of the universal, and (by allusion) a kind of participation
of all the parts thereof, therefore was man called *microcosmos*, or the little world.[7]

Shifting woman from this swing position denied her full microcosmic complexity, a complexity the realization, enjoyment, and exploitation of which
came to constitute Renaissance man's great compliment to himself.

Determining rank was no mere theoretical game. Concern about the hierarchal position of women resulted from concern about the moral influence of
their sexual and reproductive capacities on men. If women were refined and
ethereal creatures, their capacity for steadfast virtue was a beacon to guide
men's baser instincts. So viewed, woman was a meet spouse and mother for
God himself, or a way station on the Neoplatonic ladder to the contemplation
of pure love. If woman was a lesser man, instinct with the sensual attributes of
beasts but lacking sufficient reason to control those senses, her attractiveness
to men was an attraction toward corruption and her reproductive use at best
a deplorable necessity. So viewed, woman was Satan's favorite avenue to men.
One view constantly paid tribute to the other, as in Boccaccio's *Corbaccio*,
the mocking dream-vision in which the Lover, tutored by the venomous
Spirit of Husband Past, is converted by his stay in the Pig-Sty of Venus
from infatuation with the perfections of a woman to disgust at her viciousness.[8] Paradoxically, although the earthly woman's vices eventually swamp her
once imagined virtues, the dream takes place under the aegis of the Virgin
Mary, most glorious of women. Although Christian theology and practice
have never been monolithic, and the Reformation gave competing opinions
the formidable persuasiveness of political power, the theological tradition,
especially in its monastic forms, overwhelmingly viewed women as less rational
and more sensuous than men, and more likely to lead men to damnation than
salvation.

In this tradition about the nature of women, there exist two logical difficulties important to the tested woman plot. One was barely acknowledged
because of its political ramifications: if each rank has its attributes, does rank
create attributes or do attributes determine rank? For the great links in the
chain, the kingdoms and their species, attributes determine rank: minerals
are classified together because they lack all signs of life. Within the category
of man, however, the acknowledged fact was that attributes follow rank. A
person's social place was determined by birth; his character, expectations, and
obligations followed. The Aristotelian concept of dramatic decorum codified
this social ideal on the stage.[9] Women's place could be argued from either
causal position. The awkward caste relationship of women to men, unlike the
relationship between species or social classes, was a reminder that the issue
of cause and effect inherent in the hierarchical argument was unsolved and
unsolvable. This lack of resolution led to significant social tensions. What were
the rank and attributes of a woman who was also a prince? Elizabeth Tudor

spent her reign guarding her rank from contamination by her femaleness. Or—a quandary many more had to deal with—what was the authority of a parent who was also a female? How could the commandment to honor parents give the mother equal authority with the father when the relationship that made her parenthood possible was her subservient position as wife? This was the dilemma that Robert Filmer's *Patriarcha*, written as late as the 1640s, dared not even acknowledge.[10]

The other logical difficulty about the nature of women—that opposite opinions existed in the same scheme and the same minds at the same time— was acknowledged and exploited with enthusiasm. Whereas the paradox of the nature of men was that they were mixed creatures, glory, jest, and riddle at once, the paradox of women was that they might be one extreme or might be the other. Though this is logically absurd—women may be of either kind, but opinion should choose between them—the doctrine of the two natures of women was too convenient to abandon. Moreover, the observer could never be certain which woman he was dealing with. The ability to inspire this uncertainty, which Rosalie Colie reminds us is one of the great paradoxes of an age that reveled in paradox,[11] gives power to every female character who steps onto the Renaissance stage.

Cultural attitudes about women's behavior were bolstered by opinions about their essence, which in turn were underpinned by medical opinion.[12] Given their culturally dedicated reproductive role, women were regarded as displaying their nature primarily through their sexual behavior, manifesting virtue, or "honesty," by means of chastity, and vice, or "dishonesty," by means of unchastity. Tautologically, chastity meant virtuous sexual behavior, but what constituted virtuous sexual behavior was not always self-evident. The patristic Christian ideal for both sexes was the natural or original state of virginity.[13] Virginity as the natural state is made imaginatively easier to grasp in the case of women by the existence of the hymen, the outward and visible sign, as it were, of the inward and spiritual intactness that represents God's power manifest in human beings. Regarding virginity as a sign of purity and therefore a source of spiritual power was not exclusive to a few repressive church fathers. In discussing Hellenistic romance, to which subsequent versions of the tested woman plot owe important features, Northrop Frye emphasizes that the frequent virginity of the heroine is an expression of her fundamental essence: "What is symbolized as a virgin is actually a human conviction, however expressed, that there is something at the core of one's infinitely fragile being which is not only immortal but has discovered the secret of invulnerability" (*Secular Scripture*, 86). The notion of the innate integrity of the virgin state is widespread and potent.

But the sense of the invulnerability of chastity is as strong in the married Leucippe defying Thersander as it is in any Hellenistic virgin. Sexual virtue does not have to mean virginity; it may include the pleasures of marital sex. In reaction against monasticism in all its forms, Reformation doctrine fostered married chastity as a Christian ideal, eventually influencing attitudes about the nature of women. Committed to the sanctity, though not the sacramentalism, of marriage, Protestantism stressed the practical importance of women as partners and among the fringe sects admitted women to increasingly prominent roles in church and eventually secular government.[14] The immediate effect of emphasizing marital partnership was, paradoxically, to strengthen rather than weaken the patriarchal household.[15] Protestant praise for the married state was not motivated exclusively by the desire for a freer expression of sexuality, as comments like John Foxe's make clear. In his exposition "Of Matrimony," part of the preface to *Acts and Monuments* which contrasts the Protestant ideal of the ancient church with the corruptions of Rome, Foxe is at pains as much to attack the dispensation vending of Rome—made possible by its numbers of vow-bound would-be celibates, its harsh measures against clerical marriage, its required seasons of marital sexual abstinence, and the extension of its incest prohibitions—as he is to uphold the doctrine of St. Paul, who "vehemently . . . reproveth them that restrain marriage."[16] Nevertheless, however complex the motivations, moderate enjoyment of the marriage bed became a Protestant ideal.

Different as these competing ideas of chaste behavior seem, for women they were both expressions of a single obligation, that women's sexuality was the property of men. The unmarried woman was the property of her father or his patriarchal surrogate, her virginity an expression of her filial duty to her father. The marriage contract transferred sexual rights to her husband, so that her sexual performance became an expression of her obedience to her husband. Female sexual activity in marriage was not for women primarily a means of sexual release as it was for men,[17] but an expression of marital duty. If sexual satisfaction resulted, well and good, but the focus of female virtue was the obligation to male familial authority. This relationship of female chastity to male authority is what creates its appeal for the tested woman plot. Female chastity is dramatic because its demonstration requires complex male participation, not just on the part of the man who solicits or is solicited, but also on the part of the men to whom the woman already belongs.

THE NATURE OF MEN

There is no comparable tradition about the sex-determined nature of male people. As the sex representing the universal characteristics of humankind, men are as all-inclusive in their nature and as wide-ranging in their social roles as are human beings altogether. If this binary system imposes on women the burden of restrictedness, the burden imposed on men is that of representativeness and inclusiveness. Nevertheless, some key ideas about the fundamental psychological and social nature of men may be deduced from tested woman stories.

Hierarchy

If the nature of man is the nature of men, the way is open for a wide representation of male character types. Even the relative restrictedness of classical decorum allows much more range for men than for women, whose roles are reduced to the marital categories of maiden, wife, and widow. Nevertheless, where the plot focus is the relationship between men and women, the logic of hierarchy enforces a similar mindset among males. Whatever their relationship to the tested woman, whatever their degree of sympathy or hostility to her needs or the difficulties of her situation, the primary male characteristic is a shared position of dominance. Even a subordinate male (the master of the horse, the ensign) shares in the dominance of the male world and struggles to maintain or achieve power in that world. This shared dominance causes male competition, for the danger to the man in possession of the woman comes from other men. But male competition predicates fundamental cooperation as well: a shared set of assumptions about women and a desire for status and power in the terms understood by other men. Competition also predicates a certain degree of fluidity. There must be institutionalized opportunities for reconfigurations of power or possession. Such fluidity is provided by marriage. Because it is the point at which the father's right is exchanged for the husband's right, it is the moment both of maximum male cooperation and of maximum male competition. And however amicable the transfer from father to husband, two loci of authority over the woman now exist. The husband may have received legal rights, but a certain amount of moral and psychological authority still resides in the father.

The pressure put on individuals by this exchange opens to scrutiny the assumptions about male nature that underlie it. Consider the first act of *Othello*, which sketches from a multiplicity of individual perspectives the male subworlds of the Venetian state. Cooperation is the key. The explosive action of the first scenes is set against the expectation of male cooperation that has configured the brilliantly successful world of the play's opening. Brabantio the senator is representative of the commercial and civic success of Venice. Othello, representative of Venetian military success, is Brabantio's contemporary in age, his counterpart and equal in public service, and his guest. Roderigo represents the younger males of the upper class, engaging in the expected courtship behavior of his age cohort. Iago and Cassio are successful young officers in the military hierarchy, with its clearly enunciated obligations and its expectations of advancement. All owe allegiance to the state, whose duke can call upon their energies in defense against the infidel Turk. Part of the play's genius comes from setting it in the heyday of the most successful Renaissance example of civic life in all its aspects—international and domestic, commercial and military, intellectual and artistic.

But it is a certain level of contained male competitiveness that makes possible the vigorous health of the Venetian cooperative enterprise. The male competition in act 1 occurs between Venetians and non-Venetians, between generations, between soldiers and the civilian upper crust, between cultural mindsets. Within the military, competition occurs between the field officer Iago and the theoretician Cassio. Iago even claims sexual competition between himself and his chief, though he half takes it back. Competition especially occurs between father-right and husband-right.

All these competitions are contained by the institutions that have spawned them. The state has mechanisms for putting foreigners to use, the military for choosing and disciplining its officers, the family for selecting among suitors and negotiating loyalties. How precisely all parties understand the mechanisms is made clear by the containment of each of the conflicts, of which the deepest and most irrevocable would seem to be that between Othello and Brabantio. When the father asks his daughter where her obedience lies, her answer is definitive and indisputable, because it speaks to the patriarchal roots of his worldview:

> My noble father,
> I do perceive here a divided duty.
> To you I am bound for life and education;
> My life and education both do learn me
> How to respect you. You are the lord of duty;
> I am hitherto your daughter. But here's my husband,
> And so much duty as my mother show'd
> To you, preferring you before her father,
> So much I challenge that I may profess
> Due to the Moor my lord.
>   (1.3.182–91)

The duty the daughter owes to her father as her creator has been transferred to her husband according to the model on which that father's authority over her rests.

In a world in which male institutions contain male conflict, Desdemona enunciates the means by which containment is accomplished. Brabantio knows it: "God be with you. I have done" (1.3.192). When he ratifies the transfer of his daughter to his friend, his address is generous: "I here do give thee that with all my heart," he says, "Which, but thou hast already, with all my heart/I would keep from thee" (1.3.196–8). His hand has been forced and his heart broken, but his private grief cannot touch his public code of male cooperation, and his "bad blame" does not, as he promised it would not, "light on the man" (1.3.179–80), for Desdemona was indeed "half the wooer."

What has forced Brabantio's hand? How can what is construed as property be handed over without the possessor's consent? The answer, at bottom, is Christianity. Though Christianity is a patriarchal institution, its fundamental relationship between the individual and God represents a radical break with the patriarchal structures of the official Greco-Roman and Hebraic worlds. Not even the covenantal relationship between Hebrew and Yahweh, essentially a relationship between the Godhead and the chosen group, prepares us for the contract between the individual believer and God that is the basis of Christianity. As St. Paul does not tire of pointing out, that contract is open to Jew and gentile, male and female, free and slave. It is not a contract of nations, lineages, or households, but of individuals. Not for nothing are the ceremony of baptism, which makes the contract, and the ceremony of the Eucharist, which reiterates it, the only two ceremonies universally accepted as sacramental by all branches of Christianity. Christianity superimposes a divine patriarchal authority on human forms, rationalizing human authority by making it representative of God the father. Once a patriarchal society makes binding a Christian form of marriage, in which individual consent and individual contract between husband and wife mimic the individual contract between God and man, the father loses ultimate control over the transfer of his daughters to other men. Marriage takes priority over father-right, and the woman herself, as consenting Christian, must subscribe to the marriage contract. Desdemona has given herself to Othello without the consent of her father. This much is understood as possible, if shocking, within the Christian framework. More shocking is that she has done so without his knowledge, for the manner of her deed has activated male fears about her nature. Of which kind is this woman? And *how can we be certain*? The father harps on what he thought he knew of her. And now this. Look to her, Moor. She has deceived her father, and may thee.

Paternity

Behind the complicated psychology of hierarchy, which seeks mechanisms for self-correction to facilitate a cooperative division of power, Brabantio's agony exposes the psychology of paternity. Christian marriage based on individual consent threatens paternal control from two directions. The father's power to effect the exchange of women can be undermined either by the daughter's contracting a marriage against her father's wishes or by her refusal to enter into a match her father desires. A more fundamental threat than the marauding male, this female right of contract contaminates hierarchy, rupturing male hegemony and damaging the male psyche. To Brabantio it is lethal.

This threat, which stands at the heart of the Christian patriarchal system, only compounds the social fragility of paternity. Between mother and child the physical connection is unimpeachable, but (until the advent of DNA analysis and in vitro fertilization) a man has known a child to be his only if he is assured of the mother's unavailability to other men. In any situation other than total female sequestration (and there myth always allows visitation by the god), establishing paternity is based not just on female cooperation but on male belief in it. For a daughter to be her father's by right of paternity predicates his faith in her mother. For a daughter to disobey her father in the matter of marriage taints her reliability as a wife and, by a kind of back-formation, casts a pall over her own antecedents. Men's total psychological dependence rests not just on the bodies of women or even on their cooperation, but on faith in those they construe as naturally inferior and untrustworthy. The male paranoia displayed in *Othello* is not surprising.

Medieval and Renaissance tested woman stories make the strain of maintaining this faith a constant theme—as passing jokes, as underlying threads, as the center of some of their most powerful works of literature. Leontes is the type of the man who cracks, and who shows us in the eventual healing of his psyche how faith can become possible. The first act of *The Winter's Tale* opens on the problem of paternity as explosively as *Othello* does on the problem of hierarchy. The exposition moves even more swiftly because the characters required to set the problem are more restricted: husband, wife, child in utero—and one other man of a standing sufficient to have access to the woman. Since the husband has insisted upon this standing for nine months running, Polixenes' sexual access is under Hermione's control, not under Leontes'. With astonishing speed, Shakespeare has arrived at the heart of the problem: Leontes has no way to be sure the child in his wife's womb is his except by his faith in her. The entire play is a battle between the male fantasy of betrayal and the faith toward which Paulina urges the king in the final scene.

What might be the avenues to male faith? *The Winter's Tale* advances several. Logic, rationality, and the nature of evidence form one. As Camillo, Paulina, and Hermione point out, there is no evidence of Hermione's misconduct. But argument from the absence of evidence is never conclusive. So Leontes manufactures evidence of Hermione's unchastity, arguing endlessly from the suggestiveness of her social charm and the flight of her alleged accomplices.

Then there is the avenue of religious or oracular testimony. If an unimpeachable outside source proclaims Hermione's virtue, Leontes says, he will accept that authority. But when the oracle speaks, Leontes rejects it out of hand. When his blasphemous response is followed immediately by the news of his son's death, he staves off further punishment by publicly retracting his charges against wife and friend and by admitting his attempt to suborn Camillo into murder. When Hermione's death is announced, he responds with sorrow and the promise of perpetual penitence. But his increasingly anguished responses do not stem from faith, either. They are focused on his self-created misery. Having commenced in fear of Apollo's anger, they continue out of guilt.

What changes can sixteen years work? In act 5 Leontes is a man with a different understanding of his own power. Scene 1, which shows him for the first time in the give-and-take of actual conversation, also shows him capable of turning over the question of his posterity to women. When Paulina asks "Will you swear / Never to marry, but by my free leave?" he responds "Never, Paulina, so be blessed my spirit" (5.1.69–71). This act of faith in the integrity of women is what Paulina has been waiting for. Even before the discovery of Perdita, whom Leontes embraces as his, the stage is set for Hermione's recovery. The rest of the act shows the change that has made this capitulation possible, for Leontes is a man learning not just to give up control but to admit his need for love. We see his sexual need at the sight of Perdita; we hear of his whirling exuberance at regaining family and friends. In the presence of the statue he gives himself over to his longing for his wife, as, imagining her alive, he enters a fantasy that is the benign counterpart of his jealousy. How closely Leontes' fantasies are now related to his faith is demonstrated by Paulina's final use of the term "fancy." As the "transported" king stares at his wife's statue, Paulina threatens to draw the curtain to protect him from his overwrought condition: "No longer shall you gaze on't, lest your fancy / May think anon it moves" (5.3.60–1). Here fancy has become the accurate, healthy mental state, for the statue does move, it breathes, the veins verily bear blood. This fantasy is necessary to the faith that Leontes must awaken; his faith in turn brings the fantasy to life. Paternity itself is a fantasy, the necessary male fantasy of a patriarchal world.

The Obligating Force of Male Desire

The deep-seated necessity of the fantasy of faith and the insecurity to which it is connected explains the frequency and nature of male fantasies about women in Renaissance literature. Beyond jealousy of another man, this necessity helps account for many compulsions: the compulsive attention to the topic of female virtue, the compulsion to test a woman's fidelity, the agonized need for certainty in the face of recognition that only the failure of chastity can be subject to tangible proof. It may even help explain the most unaccountable fantasy of all, that male desire *of itself*, even if unsought and unreciprocated, obliges its object. A case study of this strange notion occurs in *Don Quixote*. Cervantes' global theme is the literary forms taken by the operation of fantasies, especially fantasies about women, upon the male mind. Part of the book's charm is that the most fantastic are not those that overcome Don Quixote himself.

The "fantasy of obligation" story occurs early in an episode about a beautiful young woman, Marcela, who takes to the life of a shepherdess to maintain her freedom from the attentions of men and the desire of her wealthy father to marry her off. The story tells of her male followers, especially the rich scholar Grisóstomo, who falls in love with her, pursues her over the hills and pastures, and dies of her disdain. The goatherd Pedro evenhandedly introduces the cast of characters. This is not peasant behavior but gentlefolk's behavior, and Pedro recounts it with a kind of bemused neutrality. There is nothing neutral about the passion of the dead Grisóstomo, however. The verses a bystander rescues from the flames, reads, and finds overwrought and inaccurate in their description of an apparently chaste and modest woman speak of what Grisóstomo's friend Ambrosio acknowledges as his "jealous imaginings, fears, and suspicions," which became for him "a seeming reality" (103).[18] The most remarkable phenomenon is the quality of the language applied to Marcela. In Ambrosio's eulogy, "He loved well and was hated, he adored and was disdained; he wooed a wild beast, importuned a piece of marble, ran after the wind, cried out to loneliness, waited upon ingratitude, and his reward was to be the spoils of death midway in his life's course—a life that was brought to an end by a shepherdess whom he sought to immortalize that she might live on in the memory of mankind" (98). When Marcela appears on the rock above them, Ambrosio's accusatory language becomes even more intemperate: "So, fierce basilisk of these mountains, have you perchance come to see if in your presence blood will flow from the wounds of this poor wretch whom you by your cruelty have deprived of life? Have you come to gloat over your inhuman exploits, or would you from that height look down like another pitiless Nero upon your Rome in flames and ashes? Or perhaps you would arrogantly tread under foot this poor corpse, as an ungrateful daughter did that of her father Tarquinius?" (103). Marcela is a monster, a murderer. Worse, she is a Tullia—the unnatural daughter driving over the corpse of her father, whose name Ambrosio confuses with that of the husband. But no matter. By this point we have the collapse of any objective description of Marcela's behavior in a diatribe against female depravity. Because she did not respond to his friend's unsolicited passion, she is evil in the way of all evil women. She is a violator of the patriarchal order.

Marcela's response is straightforward and rational. First she lays out the issue: "Heaven made me beautiful, you say, so beautiful that you are compelled to love me whether you will or no; and in return for the love that you show me, you would have it that I am obliged to love you in return" (104). Then she lays out the response she has made to Grisóstomo as to every man: that she seeks freedom and solitude, that she has encouraged no one, and that she politely disabused her pursuer of the possibility of hope.

"Ask yourselves, then, if it is reasonable to blame me for his woes! Let him who has been truly deceived complain; let him despair who has been cheated of his promised hopes; if I have enticed any, let him speak up; if I have accepted the attentions of any, let him boast of it; but let not him to whom I have promised nothing, whom I have neither enticed nor accepted, apply to me such terms as cruel and homicidal" (105). When she turns and vanishes into the woods, a lustful murmur momentarily risks sparking pursuit, but Don Quixote sees an occasion for succoring a damsel and, whether from his threats or from the need to finish the funeral, she is left to what he rightly calls her own "modesty and good intentions" (106).

Where can such a male frame of mind have come from? Let us grant that the language and the posturing are literary. The tropes and the clichés, the space devoted to Grisóstomo's verses, the emphasis on his profession as scholar and his recent return from Salamanca, the whole bent of Cervantes' novel say that this is bookish excess. But that does not make it either innocuous or empty of significance. For one thing, framing the lyric language in narrative embodies it disturbingly. A man is dead, a woman threatened, and the Ovidian world of rape and narcissistic implosion is not far away. Nor is it any less an expression of the male fantasizing underlying the tested woman plot. In this version male fantasy no longer admits of doubt or considers the possibility of female independence or separateness. It is foolish to require that the person you love love you in return; love cannot be forced. But that is not what Grisóstomo requires. He demands that Marcela not be allowed to be indifferent, neutral, separate, or solitary. She may *not* not notice him. That is the obligation Grisóstomo insists upon. If he cannot force her love, he at least will force her continuing refusal, which he characterizes as disdain.

The several tested woman stories I have used as example texts in this chapter are notable for their willingness to express the extreme logic of male fantasy and obsession. The logic itself, however, seems inherent in relations between men and women as constructed by the patriarchal tradition. Despite the attempts, sometimes frantic, to relegate women to metaphysical and emotional, as well as political, insignificance, the logic of hierarchy is inexorable: the servant defines the master. Of the two, it will therefore be the master who is obsessed with the relationship.

FOUR

Finding the Dramatic Form

ITS ORIGINS IN SCRIPTURE, ANCIENT HISTORY, AND POPULAR TALES meant that the tested woman plot's materials permeated the medieval world. It became influential in British literature not just by reason of its omnipresence, however, but because it developed into a form peculiarly suited to drama. The spectacular burgeoning of English drama was accompanied by a sophisticating of the plot into one of that drama's favored story types.

MEDIEVAL STORIES AND TUDOR HOMILETICS

Tudor and Stuart drama grew out of medieval religious drama, employing technical features of mystery, miracle, and morality plays in works that often retained little specifically Christian flavor. Scripture, postscriptural history, and allegory provided the characters; testing and witnessing were the necessary events.[1] Present from the beginning, the tested woman plot was used to dramatize the hierarchical relationships of the Judeo-Christian worldview. In the mysteries of the Corpus Christi cycles, tested woman plays burgeon from the sketchiest scriptural hints. The analogy between wifely obedience and the obedience of man to God is the dramatic point of the Wakefield Cycle's Noah play, for instance. As Noah resists God's command to build an ark, Noah's wife resists his command to enter it. Only after argument, a domestic punch-out, and the first drops of rain does the wife capitulate. This repetition of the action suggests potentially blasphemous possibilities. In the wife's stubbornness we see Noah's agonies of dislocation. In the physical brawl between the two we see the suppressed possibility of rebellion against the Lord's commands. In Noah's use of his authority over his wife we see a reflection of the Lord's ability to order the lives of his creatures.[2] The *Ludus Coventriae* or N. Towne cycle develops the plot from New Testament materials. Introductory episodes about Mary's childhood and betrothal climax in the Trial of Mary and Joseph, featuring a pregnant Mary, her earthly spouse, and two enthusiastically lewd Detractors in a full-blown slander story in which the woman is innocent,

46

whatever appearances may suggest. In the Woman Taken in Adultery episode, where the woman is plainly guilty, Christ is cast as both defender and judge, implicating Him in all the human actions of the plot. In the same way the Noah play forecasts a host of later works in which marital strife mirrors other hierarchical relationships, Christ's roles as defender and magistrate forecast the combined functions of secular authority figures.

As medieval dramatizations became more extended and realistic, stage representations of the divine gave way to human figures whose heroic witness did not run the risk of blasphemy.[3] Unlike plays based on scripture, the story of the "Christian hero" (who might be Hebrew, Roman, or medieval) borrowed materials from wherever it could find them and blended its influences as it pleased. Medieval saints' lives were already permeated by the motifs of secular romances. Thus the Digby *Mary Magdalene* (1475)[4] has its sea voyage, its return from the dead, its birth of a child to an abandoned mother, its recognitions and reunions. Conversely, secular narratives were the stuff of hagiography. In the Italian popular drama called *sacre representazione*, the witnessing of the heroes or (characteristically) heroines need not be specifically religious, but their defense involves the interventions of the Virgin Mary— hence their "sacredness." In Chaucer's Man of Law's Tale, Constance is God's instrument to convert first Saracens and then Saxons. In her chastity and patience she imitates the Virgin Mary, and at her trial for murder she is saved by God's striking down her accuser. Even a romance that does not involve explicit Christian witness may read like a saint's tale. Boccaccio's story of Griselda attracted Petrarch because of the familial piety and fortitude of its heroine, it was given a range of Christian applications by Chaucer's Clerk, it appeared among the *sacre representazione* despite the absence of divine intervention, and it was dramatized by John Phillip in 1559 as one of the wave of Tudor hybrid moralities that otherwise feature specifically religious heroines.

Because saints' lives are the great stories of Christian witness, they are especially amenable to adaptation by literal drama. The tales of the early Christian martyrs are formulaic. By proselytizing, practicing Christian rites, or refusing to sacrifice to the pagan gods, a convert attracts the legal attention of the Roman state and undergoes a prolonged martyrdom, rejoicing in the opportunity to display Christian faith. Making the saint a woman adds two elements: stress on her chastity as a token of Christian witness and competing allegiance to a patriarchal figure like the father or the husband. St. Cecilia, who has consecrated her virginity to Christ, is forced into marriage by her family. On her wedding night she refuses her groom's sexual advances, converts him and his brother to Christianity and the virgin life, inspires them to martyrdom for their newfound faith, is sentenced to death for refusing to renounce her God, and for three days survives a severed neck bone before dying heroically. Her triumphant story has the two stages of Test and Trial: required to conform to her filial duty, she remains true to her obligation as the bride of Christ, and her subsequent persecutions, carried out in a variety of forensic contexts, allow her to convert increasing numbers of her abusers. Since by the seventeenth century explicit religiosity had come to lack appeal for an increasingly secular stage, Dekker and Massinger's *Virgin Martyr* (1620), based on the similar story of St. Dorothea, seems atavistic. Its existence, however, shows how the female saint's tale, with its stalwart female witness and copious opportunities for male conflict, underlies the Renaissance tested woman play.

So also does the morality play,[5] from which dramatists borrowed devices for moving the plot into literal drama. The morality presents the Christian test in its starkest form, as the war between the impulses of good and evil for the human soul. Staging this psychomachia creates a dramatically sound (though theologically and psychologically absurd) separation between the tested person and his qualities—the forces that test him. What results is not the classical agon of two, protagonist and antagonist, but an agon of three, as in the most famous English morality play, *Everyman*, where Good Deeds and other virtues, competing against Covetousness and other vices, encourage Everyman toward a hopeful death. This triangle has two features important to the full development of tested woman drama. First, the central figure, though morally active, is dramatically reactive. Virtue and Vice contend; Mankind chooses. Second, both sets of abstractions competing over Mankind are of supernatural origin. All virtues, expressions of the divine in man, emanate from God; all vices, components of mankind's divinely instituted free will, are allowed by him; judgment is his. Theatrically the agon involves three parties, but theologically it involves only two. As Tudor theater moved from allegorical to literal drama, it humanized its figures of virtue and vice and created in the central character a specific person rather than a generalized representative of mankind. At the same time it lost the divine presence. But dramatists learned to capitalize on the difference between men's and women's positions to create the literal counterpart of the morality play's supreme authority. The rash of middle Tudor plays about tested women combines the Christian hero of the miracle play with the testing configurations of the morality to create a hybrid in which the central female figure is the focus of overt competition among male exemplars of authority, both virtuous and vicious.

Tudor playwrights' adaptations of the Griselda story show the morality structure at work.[6] In Chaucer's Clerk's Tale, all power and willfulness are concentrated in the husband, Walter, and all endurance in the wife, Griselda. For drama, the problem with Chaucer's Walter is that, like God in the story of Job—to whom Chaucer's clerk compares Griselda[7]—he combines all four authority functions. He is the tempter who seeks to induce Griselda's disobedience. He is the accuser who condemns her as unworthy to bear his children. Only after far too long a time does he come to her defense, acknowledging her steadfastness and judging her obedient and faithful. By creating vice figures and sympathetic retainers who clarify and rationalize the extremes of Walter's nature, Tudor playwrights stage the contradictions without losing the sense of unified authority. The plot possibilities that most appeal to later dramatists develop from this complex of male powers and impulses.

Integrating Classical Drama: *Ralph Roister Doister*

By the mid-sixteenth century another dramatic influence was developing in England as the recovery of classical texts and an increasingly rhetorical education put the study and performance of classical drama into the school and university curricula.[8] The Roman comedies of Plautus and Terence, with their simple plots and language and their lively stock characters, were attractive to schoolmasters, and formal features of Roman comedy entered English plays. One of the best known, Nicholas Udall's *Ralph Roister Doister* (1552),[9] is invariably described in terms of its classical borrowings: as one of the first "regular" English plays (with act and scene divisions and unities of time and place), as an adaptation of Roman comedy (the prologue refers to both Plautus and Terence), as introducing the figures of the parasite and the braggart soldier to the English stage.[10] It is true that Merrygreek's flattery of Roister Doister is patently indebted to Plautus's *Miles Gloriosus* and that Roister Doister's attack on Christian Custance's house borrows directly from Terence's *Eunuchus*. Though some scholars have looked briefly at its "native elements," most critics accept it as essentially Roman comedy Englished.[11] But a dose of the real Plautus and Terence shows how different *Roister Doister*'s social and ethical structure is. Character types are totally unlike. Udall's play has no slaves, no pimps and whores, neither husbands and wives nor fathers and sons. Instead it puts a respectable, independent, marriageable woman at the center not just of the story line but of the stage action. The sanctions against which the characters struggle or which they seek to impose are moral and social, not economic or legal. Characters seek to ease or shame each other into civil behavior. They do not threaten penury, crucifixion, or enslavement.

These differences accompany a radically different central agon, the testing of a woman's faith.[12] *Ralph Roister Doister*'s plot focuses on Christian Custance. As a widow, the only legal category that gave a Tudor woman control over her property or her marriage arrangements, she is an independent head of household whose wealth has attracted Roister Doister the perennial wife-hunter. Her household is as cheerful, obedient, and hardworking as can be maintained within the bounds of human nature and the requirements of comedy, and her response to Roister Doister's courtship is firmly dismissive. Knowing better than to take him seriously, she looks forward to a confrontation: "Let him come when he lust; I wish no better sport" (3.2.96).

Yet Roister Doister does prove a threat, and the reason for that threat shows how un-Roman the play is. Custance is betrothed to the merchant Gawyn

Goodluck. Though she cannot prevent Roister Doister's suit, she may not in good faith either entertain it or be perceived to do so. Her mood changes when Roister Doister's attentions may be misconstrued and her allegiance called into question. That moment is marked by the appearance of Goodluck's servant Sim Suresby, sent to tell Custance that Goodluck's ship is in and its master will shortly be home. The simultaneous arrival of Merrygreek and Roister Doister creates the possibility of misconstruction, for Roister Doister's presumptuous attentions to his "wife" and "sweet spouse," despite Custance's repeated rejections, cause Suresby to hurry away in suspicion. Knowing the danger she is in, Custance turns scornfully on the suitors, leading Roister Doister to the conviction that only force will do. When he threatens, she sends for her friend Tristram Trusty, beats Roister Doister and Merrygreek off stage, marshals her servants, and arms them for battle.

Since Custance unarmed can rout both men, her doughty battalion, armed with kitchen implements and an attack goose, should be proof against all comers. So what is old Tristram Trusty for? His halting arrival tells us he is of no military use. His sole purpose is to witness Custance's behavior, for the issue is reputation, the interpretation that the public, in the persons of Suresby, Trusty, and especially Goodluck, will put on Roister Doister's effrontery. When Custance rebukes Merrygreek for his part in the business, he pleads the jest of it and the fact that he knew she was betrothed. That is just the danger, says Custance: "I feared thereof to take dishonesty" (4.6.24). So Custance, Trusty, and Merrygreek conspire to turn this jest to their use. By driving Roister Doister off, Custance provides a public demonstration of her contempt to which Trusty can bear witness, while Merrygreek, pretending to fight for Roister Doister, gets in a few good licks against him. The rout is riotous and complete, and a grand time is had by all. Nor is the main point forgotten:

> CUSTANCE   Friend Tristram, I pray you be a witness with me.
> TRUSTY   Dame Custance, I shall depose for your honesty.
> (4.8.58–9)

But Goodluck must receive Suresby's report and be disturbed, meet Custance and hold her at arm's length, and be convinced by Trusty's reassurances before he is reconciled to her. That accomplished, Goodluck demonstrates his peace of mind and his pleasure at homecoming by inviting everyone to dinner, while Custance demonstrates her confidence in her reputation and her obedience to her betrothed by agreeing to let Roister Doister come too.

Udall's is a comic calumniated-woman version of the tested woman plot. The double actions of test and trial and the character functions of tempter (Roister Doister), accuser (Suresby), defender (Trusty), and judge (Goodluck, the affianced husband) are all present. That Custance's adventure is light-hearted does not obscure its moral nature or its literary and hagiographical antecedents. The test of her obedience takes place in a single day's secularized encapsulation of the Christian life. Her name echoes Chaucer's spelling of Constance, one of the great Christian heroines.[13] Steeling herself for her encounter with Goodluck in the prayerful soliloquy of 5.3, she compares herself to a series of tested women, including Susanna.[14] Like Susanna, Custance requires no assistance in rejecting her tempter. She needs help only in the trial, where that rejection cannot be heard over Roister Doister's cacophony.

To combine a serious didactic point with a comic tone, Udall's chief structural device is to overlap the play's two actions, continuing the comic test created by Roister Doister's suit as he gets the trial of Custance's reputation under way. Unlike the *Eunuchus*, Udall's play needs a real fight because Custance needs a public display of her rejection of her suitor. To provide that fight, the braggart must be forced to engage. This is Merrygreek's job, and he can do it because he has already changed sides—or rather, as Bernard Spivack suggests, because he has no side. Less Roman parasite than mellowed medieval Vice, Merrygreek is committed only to a rollicking raising of the comedic temperature. Once Custance confronts him with the serious turn the wooing has taken, he redeems himself by helping engineer Roister Doister's public defeat. The battle lets Merrygreek "play with both hands" in a comic version of the ambidexterity that is a key trait of the morality Vice.[15]

The other major difference from Roman drama lies in Custance and the kind of help she seeks. Custance has attracted Roister Doister's interest because she is a widow, whom Roister Doister sees only as prey. Udall takes care that we understand her differently. As Merrygreek points out, it is because she is so unsuitable a target that he has amused himself by fostering Roister Doister's harebrained delusions. Once Custance realizes the danger of calumniation, she moves swiftly to the offensive. Roister Doister's delusions operate in the context of a moral test of high Christian seriousness that no Terentian or Plautine model can provide. Udall gives classical shape, secular language, and a flavoring of Roman characters to a plot type that becomes one of the most characteristic of English Renaissance drama.

WITNESSING WOMEN AND COMPETING MEN— CHANGES IN EMPHASIS

Whereas most early Tudor tested woman plays continue the hagiographical and romance emphasis on female witness, later playwrights often shift the focus to the antagonisms and reconciliations of the male world. Stress moves from the triumph of the woman's virtue to men's compulsions and competitions. This difference is a matter not of story but of its handling. A play about female witness usually emphasizes the test; one about male competition, the trial.

Jephthah and His Daughter

The biblical account of Jephthah and his daughter (Judges 11:30–40) appealed to Tudor humanists, George Buchanan writing his Latin play about 1543, and John Christopherson his Greek version about 1544.[16] Both were influenced by Euripides' *Iphigenia in Aulis*. Though it is the heroine's similarity to Iphigenia that attracted Christopherson,[17] his dramatization tells Jephthah's whole story: his exile because of his brothers' jealousy, his return to defend the tribe of Gilead from the Ammonites, his vow to offer in thanks the first creature to greet him on his return home, his military victory, and the fulfillment of his vow by the sacrifice of his only child. In Francis Fobes's modern translation the play is economical, vigorous, and moving. Though he adds the character of the wife who cannot accept her husband's determination to carry out his vow, Christopherson takes no other liberties with the biblical account. Jephthah has opened his mouth unto the Lord, and the Lord has given him the victory; not for a line does he question the rightness of carrying out his vow. But the play is made powerful by the equally unquestioning obedience of the daughter who, mourning with poetic clarity the life she is giving up, steels her distraught father to cut off her head with his own hands. Each suffers in harmony with the other to create a double pattern of obligation fulfilled.

Their references to *Iphigenia in Aulis* help explain what drew sixteenth-century humanists to these stories of sacrifice. Part of the appeal of Euripides' play is owing to its early translation by Erasmus.[18] But why did Erasmus, perfecting his Greek in preparation for translating the New Testament, choose this Euripides? Or Christopherson, who hardly needed a Latin pony? Or Buchanan, who took the mother of his *Jephthes sive Votum* from the model of the embittered Clytemnestra? All of them, we may assume, were seized by Euripides' portrayal of a family struggling to reconcile religious, political, and personal demands only partly of their own making and finally beyond their control. It was a struggle, often centered on the moral status of vows, that mirrored the awful dilemmas of sixteenth-century readers. For Christopherson, Euripides' power lies in Iphigenia's apotheosis; like the Greek maiden, Christopherson's daughter turns victimization to heroic sacrifice. This ability of the politically powerless to bring chaos and horror to a standstill through an extraordinary act of will is spiritual and dramatic power as the Renaissance most valued it. Euripides and Christopherson also share the motif of the daughter given to death as a substitute for marriage. Agamemnon laments that his daughter will wed Hades rather than Achilles, Clytemnestra contrasts her expectations of marriage to the Greek hero with the agony of sacrifice, and Iphigenia takes fire and purpose in her groom's presence, emulates his martial courage, and goes to her death as to a kind of marriage, with Achilles beside her in battle dress. Christopherson's heroine laments her unwedded state, makes her two-month pilgrimage to bewail her virginity, and performs her act of filial piety as the culmination of a perverted marriage rite.

By contrast, George Buchanan hardly uses the marriage motif. His point of scrutiny is the vow. Opening his drama at the moment of Jephthah's expected return, foretelling events not just by the Angel's choral overview but by the mother's dream of the guard dog that first drove off the ravening wolves, then returned to tear the lamb from her arms and "mangle it with merciless teeth" (l. 102; p. 66),[19] he misses no opportunity to introduce arguments against the vow's fulfillment. The wife, Storge (her name means "the one who yearns"), is clearly inspired by Clytemnestra. Accusing her husband of inhuman hardness and of adherence to a wicked vow, she also accuses him of preempting her parental share in the child in whom she has an equal right. Buchanan's Priest, who has no counterpart either in Euripides (where Calchas engineers the deed) or in Judges, also argues against the sacrifice with all his rhetorical power. In four long speeches he maintains that Jephthah's vow, whatever its letter, violates the spirit of man's relationship with God and the wisdom of tradition and authority. Jephthah responds by excoriating the priestly caste for its loss of true piety and resting his case on the sincerity of his convictions. In this debate between the voice of institutionalized religion and the prompting of the individual conscience—the central debate of the century in which Buchanan wrote—scripture allows Buchanan no resolution. The father regards himself as bound, the daughter takes up her own death as an act of filial piety, but the play ends, not with Christopherson's communal exode, but with the mother's grief: "The braver the spirit with which my daughter bore her death, the sorer the anguish which gnaws my heart" (ll. 1449–50; p. 94).

For a modern audience, Christopherson's may be the more satisfying play, for it makes more dramatic sense of the Gileadites and their flawed hero Jephthah, and more eloquent use of the daughter's death. But Buchanan's play directs attention more insistently to the story's psychological and political potential. Buchanan does not have open to him the savage scrutiny of the male power struggle or the unsavory role of the gods that imbues Euripides' treatment. He can give the wife eloquence and dramatic prominence, but he cannot give her the male relatives or the bloody sequel that makes Clytemnestra's anger a genuine threat. By means of the Priest he comes close to an examination of the role of sacrifice among both Hebrews and Christians. But given his scriptural source, given his pedagogical purpose in writing for the pupils of the Collège de Guyenne in Bordeaux,[20] given Inquisitorial scrutiny of his work, even if he had wished to do so he could not situate that conflict within Jephthah himself, nor probe the connection between the occasion of the vow and the context of tribal and familial animosity. In the sixteenth century the Jephthah story was not available for full dramatic exploitation of its male conflict.[21]

Patient Griselda

Secular stories, however, may question the rationale and conduct of the test as well as celebrating female constancy. The story of Patient Griselda, which entered western literature as the capstone of Boccaccio's *Decameron*, inspired Petrarch to write a Latin version, and received its first English rendering as Chaucer's Clerk's Tale, was dramatized three times by Tudor playwrights. Ralph Radcliffe's version has been lost,[22] but John Phillip's *Patient and Meek Grissell* (1559) and Dekker, Chettle, and Haughton's *Patient Grissil* (1600) show us both the story's didactic attractions and its dramatic difficulties. As Boccaccio tells it, Griselda, daughter of the poor but pious Janicula, attracts the attention of Marquis Walter, who marries her for her obedience and humility. Determined to test his wife's virtue, Walter removes and pretends to kill first their young daughter and later their baby son. Then, feigning dissatisfaction with Griselda herself, he sends her destitute back to her father. Finally, pretending to remarry, he brings Griselda to take charge of the nuptial preparations, has her dress the young bride, and only at the last moment reveals that the girl is their daughter and her brother their son. Griselda, who has accepted all without complaint, he proclaims a miracle of domestic sanctity and takes back to his hearth and bed. The fact that the testing is repeated over the period of a generation and denies to its object a single striking demonstration of obedience complicates a dramatist's task. The nondramatic writer may revive the tension through overt homiletic commentary, but playwrights must create characters who maintain the appearance of conflict and allow variety from test to test.

Opening his play with Grissell and her parents, John Phillip helps rationalization by stressing the link between wifely obedience and filial obligation. The mother, not present in medieval originals, is dying, and her exhortations about caring for the father allow Grissell to express her filial obedience. The mother disappears, but the emphasis on filial piety continues: Grissell reflects on her duties as she brings her pitcher home from the well, her father, Janicle, advises the marquis how to raise the children of the marriage, Gautier and his courtiers descant on the spoiling effects of sparing the rod, and the young son and daughter, once reunited with their parents, stress their filial obedience. Reflecting the increasingly rigid atmosphere of Tudor patriarchal control,[23] the play's subtitle combines the submission of children with that of wives: *The Play of Patient and Meek Grissell* "Wherein is declared, the good example, of her patience towards her husband: and likewise, the due obedience of children, toward their Parents."

Phillip's secondary characters come primarily from the morality tradition. Virtue is represented by the courtiers Fidence, Reason, Sobriety, and Diligence and by Grissell's handmaidens Patience, Indigence, and Constancy. Rumor and Politic Persuasion represent vice. Politic Persuasion is the most vigorous of these personifications, not just because the morality Vice is a witty scene-grabber, but also because Phillip must motivate Walter's discontent with the most obedient of wives. By 1559 Phillip also had the means of literal drama available, allowing him to enliven his play with realistic characters. The moral problem with Griselda is her acceptance of her children's seeming deaths. Phillip helps the audience through this awkwardness with his earthily outspoken Nurse, who condemns Gautier's ungodly acts, defends her mistress's rights, and attempts to keep the children, showing the strain of dramatizing this extreme form of the tested woman plot by voicing the humane protest Grissell cannot allow herself.

By 1600 theatrical sophistication demands even more rationalization. Though the *Patient Grissil* of Dekker, Chettle, and Haughton portrays a marital saint, the authors add two contrapuntal subplots, the frankly farcical story of Sir Owen's tempestuous marriage to the shrewish Gwenthyn and a sketch of Marquess Gwalter's sister Julia's refusal to enter the bondage of marriage. Dekker's main plot[24] relieves the repeated and motiveless persecution by reducing the number of tests (Grissil's children are twins, removed in a single episode) and by collapsing the duration (in stage time the children's return and the mock wedding festivities immediately follow Grissil's rejection). As in Phillip's play, audience dislike is focused on a pair of vice figures, the courtiers Mario and Lepido, who rejoice at the persecution of Grissil and are banished at the ritual ending.

The authors also admit an incipient struggle among the play's authorities. In Phillip's play the objections of the Nurse are domestic only. As a mother-substitute she has emotional power but no moral authority. Dekker's version, though it has no nurse figure, adds to Grissil's family a rebellious brother, Laureo, and an outspoken servant, Babulo, whose objections are political. Laureo insists that Gwalter has overstepped himself in courting Grissil: "If equal thoughts durst both your states confer, / Hers is too low, and you too high for her" (1.2.262–3). When Babulo is told to kneel to the duke, his response is instantaneous: "I have not offended him, therefore I'll not duck and he were ten Dukes" (1.2.288). When Grissil's family is sent home to their penury, Laureo calls Gwalter a tyrant and, in conversation with Babulo, condemns this treatment. When the family returns to court for the second wedding, Laureo refuses to serve the marquess or wear his fine clothes, while Babulo keeps up his disrespectful commentary. Given the jovial tone, these dissonant characters hardly portend revolution, and they are to a degree discredited: Babulo is the allowed fool, while Laureo is the disgruntled scholar moping over the absence of worldly preferment. But the brother's objection to Gwalter's intrusion into the freedom his family's social and economic distance entitles them to underlies his disgust at his father's supine acceptance of Gwalter's behavior. Dekker's typical emphasis on the rights and virtues of the lower classes encourages him to foreground points of stress in the plot's authority structure.

The Calverley Murders

Phillip and Dekker are tied to a story too well known to allow more than modest variations, but events which have not yet found literary form allow greater freedom, as in two very different plays based on an incident involving the Calverley family of Yorkshire in 1605. In fewer than eight hundred lines *A Yorkshire Tragedy* (1605)[25] tells of a virtuous wife who endures her husband's outrageous treatment and brings him to Christian remorse and repentance. The desperate husband, a wastrel gripped by despair and self-loathing, verbally and physically abuses his wife, his children, and his servants. "Bleed, bleed rather than beg, beg" (4.105) are the words with which he kills his oldest son. He stabs his wife in the same spirit: "Now, begone; / There's whores enow and want would make thee one" (5.31–2). But though the anguish of a class-proud man brought low is the putative cause of his rage, the husband's abuse goes far beyond his frustrated desire to protect and control. Despite her loving submissiveness, his language becomes systematically harsher, as though her very patience is the provocation. Yet there is no evidence of the wife's disloyalty. She speaks gently to her husband, seeks to sell her dowry for his benefit, forgives him her abuse and the murder of their children, argues to the court for mercy on his behalf, and by her love brings him to a sense that the devil that possessed him has literally glided from his body. The anonymous play's power comes from its brevity, the vigor of its language, and its concentration on the wife's unflinching loyalty.

George Wilkins's *Miseries of Enforced Marriage* (1606), loosely based on the same historical event, is a far less satisfactory piece of work, but by the kind of incident it multiplies, it shows the shift in focus from female witness to male conflict that dramatists learned in order to make full-length plays of the tested woman plot. Wilkins's play attempts, though clumsily and inadequately, to supply a motive for persecution in the form of male competition. The play has three tested women. Clare exchanges binding betrothal vows with young Scarborow, who is then forced into marriage to another; hearing the news, Clare kills herself to free him. Katherine, the niece of Scarborow's guardian, Falconbridge, becomes the unwilling Scarborow's wife, bears his twin sons, and patiently endures his profligate career. Scarborow's sister marries the rake Ilford in an attempt to free her brother from Ilford's financial and psychological clutches. None of these women, however, receives Scarborow's—or Wilkins's—concentrated attention. Although betrothal and marriage form the contractual skeleton of the plot, it is Scarborow's struggles with men that matter. The betrothal is broken by Falconbridge's anger at his ward's show of independence, the marriage is forced by Falconbridge's absolute control of Scarborow's patrimony, and Scarborow's decline is prompted as much by his rage at this bondage as by his guilt over his bigamy and Clare's death. The happy ending comes, not from the husband's recognition of his wife's and sister's virtues, or from his appreciation of his betrothed's sacrifice, but from the guardian's deathbed repentance, which frees Scarborow from both penury and, it would seem, guilt. Wilkins lacks both a firm sense of the play's overall structure and a good ear for the counterpoint among its parts, but for all that, he tries to make the most of the male power struggle.

Virginia

Thanks to their historical spread, my final pair of dissimilar dramatizations shows most clearly the difference between a play focusing on female obedience and one stressing male competition. For Livy the story of Virginia was the key episode in the struggle of Roman citizens to assert their republican rights against the tyrannous decemviri. For Chaucer in The Physician's Tale and John Gower in the *Confessio Amantis*, however, the emphasis was on female virtue attacked and father right painfully upheld. *Apius and Virginia* (1564?), by R. B., is a hybrid morality that follows the medieval treatment by simplifying the story to the pathos of female witness. John Webster's *Appius and Virginia* (written perhaps with Thomas Heywood and perhaps around 1625) is a far more complex affair designed to make the most of the story's underlying patriarchal tensions.[26]

R. B. (probably Richard Bowers, who was master of the Children of the Royal Chapel from 1545 to 1561) manages his story in a mere seven scenes, two of which are extraneous clowning sequences. With its exhortations from a dying Mater, its songs by Virginia's family and the clowns, its personified virtues and its vice Haphazard, the play resembles Phillip's nearly contemporaneous Griselda play. It opens with a scene celebrating filial piety: The mother tutors Virginia in chaste and obedient behavior, and father and daughter vie in expressions of mutual love and obligation. When Apius follows Haphazard's suggestion and sends Claudius to claim the girl, Virginius is apprised by Rumor of the plot against them and informs his daughter of the hopelessness of their position. He longs for Virginia to kill him, but she asks for death herself and binds her eyes to overcome her flinching. Her father strikes off her head. Spurred by Comfort to prefer vengeance to self-slaughter, Virginius carries his dead daughter to the accusing Apius, who is himself condemned by Justice. Apius kills himself, Haphazard is hanged, Claudius is banished, and Fame, Doctrine, and Memory enter to inscribe Virginia's tomb.

The names of some of the characters aside, the play has nothing Roman about it and contains little specifically political. Though Apius and his creatures are brought down, the author cares almost exclusively about the covenantal bonding of the patriarchal family. That bonding is established in the opening scene, threatened by Apius's attempt, tested through the father's and daughter's suffering, and reconfirmed by the denouement and the epilogue. The play omits all historical matter extraneous to this focus and shortens almost out of existence the trial in the Forum, at which the father snatches a knife from a butcher's stall to kill his daughter before the eyes of all Rome. In R. B.'s version, as in Christopherson's *Jephthes*, the most compelling scene is a private session between father and daughter, replete with overtones of the Abraham and Isaac story, in which Virginia becomes a willing partner in the maintenance of her chastity and the family's honor.[27] The play is Virginia's, hers is the great demonstration of loving and heroic duty.

By contrast, Webster portrays the clashes between domestic and legal authority, military discipline and political authority, and father-right and husband-right. The result is a full-blown patriarchal power struggle, with Virginia its catalyst only. Appius's attempt is an expression of his assumption that with supreme political power comes the right to possess what he covets and crush what he opposes. He is ultimately wrong, but it is raw power, not just virtue, that brings him down. Virginius's fierce sense of familial and military honor can deprive Appius of the girl and quell a mutiny that would open the army to Appius's demagogic control, but it takes Icilius, the prospective groom, to dispose of Appius. Icilius first occupies the city, then carries in Virginia's corpse at the head of the Roman mob to force Virginius to judgment and Appius to suicide. The politics of the play are anything but simple-minded. The mutinous troops that Virginius renders servile by his scornful dismissal are nevertheless shockingly mistreated servants of the state. The heroic sacrifice of his child, for which he is promoted by the army, is, as Icilius accuses, an act of unnatural horror. Yet, though Icilius threatens Appius for his attentions to Virginia, by doing so he precipitates her misfortune. As Virginius reminds him, he would hardly have married her had she been raped. As for Appius, that vicious spoiler of helpless citizens can kill himself with stoic fortitude. Webster's is a story of revolutionary times in which the camp has lost the trust of the city, the potentially noble Appius has lost his moral balance, the soldier Virginius has been catapulted into a political struggle he does not understand and a generalship he does not know how to use, and Icilius has half-acquired a familial role but been cheated of its consummation.

Only Virginia's place seems certain. The trial scene, the clearest and most brilliant of the play, has the simplicity of Virginia's nature and situation at its center. She is the lamb; the audience longs for the wolf to be kept from her. The wolf is stymied, but only by the device of turning Virginia from prey to sacrifice. In the tradition of the tested woman, so closely allied are the roles of prey and sacrificial victim, so often interchangeable the woman's attackers and defenders, that Webster's characters and his play can almost accept and use Virginia's death as the necessary instrument for the restoration of social health. But Icilius still cannot bear to clasp Virginius's bloody hand. And Virginius reminds us how little the sacrifice has been Virginia's own. Unlike Lucretia, to whom he compares her, unlike Iphigenia or Jephthah's daughter or R. B.'s Virginia, Webster's Virginia is denied the chance to give away her life. Not even with her death can the witnessing woman speak above the tumultuous conflicts of competing men.

THE PATRIARCHAL ANALOGY

Webster's use of the Virginia story to portray conflicts among familial, legal, military, and political powers is made possible by the Renaissance commonplace of the patriarchal analogy. The mindset that makes a Stuart play not just a dramatization of Roman history but an expression of contemporary civil tensions has that analogy at its center. The intensification of patriarchal authoritarianism in English society between the Tudor consolidation and the Revolution is well documented in its broad outlines. Consciously developed by political and religious propaganda, sixteenth- and seventeenth-century authoritarianism had two features important for my reading. First, patriarchy became the dominant trope for the expression of all (necessarily hierarchical) relationships between individuals. Partly as a result, moreover, patriarchalism became for a short but crucial period a formal political theory for the justification of political sovereignty.[28] Although medieval society had been strongly hierarchical and male-dominated, its sources of authority were multiple and diffuse. Authority over land tenure was exercised through an intricate system of fiefdom and overlordship. Authority over religious beliefs and practice was exercised by the clerical confessor on the individual conscience and layers of church hierarchy on matters doctrinal and organizational. Authority over family property and household governance was exercised by senior kin and advising friends. Authority in political matters was exercised by coalitions of families and clans. Authority in the economic sphere was exercised by guilds and trading leagues representing discrete economic entities bound by common interests.

During the Renaissance, by contrast, authority became more focused and rigid in the key spheres of state, religion, and family. In the state the Tudor monarchy consolidated power in the hands of the sovereign and the court officers, who by the middle of Elizabeth's reign had become ministers owing their allegiance to the institution of monarchy itself. As fealty to an overlord was transformed into commitment to the nation, as the military and economic power of noble families was undermined, as London concentrated more capital and entrepreneurial talent, as Tudor and Stuart monarchs made their favor the channel to wealth and political advancement, as the court became the center of the state, political propaganda and reality increasingly emphasized the two poles of a simplified political hierarchy: the monarch and the subject. In drama, the effect is a sense that the king holds direct power over his people and assumes direct responsibility for their welfare, the responsibility that Shakespeare's anachronistically Tudor Henry V momentarily finds so burdensome. Hierarchical concentration of religious authority also occurred. In the Anglican church, where the sacramental and organizational hierarchy of the clergy maintained itself against more extreme Protestantism, ultimate authority was vested in the monarch. Among Protestants of all stripes, even those committed to episcopal or presbyterian church governance, longing for the spirit of the primitive church resulted in pressure to eliminate middlemen from the relationship between believers and their God. The Protestant ideology of the priesthood of all believers was not an ultimate leveling. Quite the contrary. Simplifying the theological hierarchy to its poles, God and the believing Christian, focused attention on power—the awesome power of God and the insignificance and obligation of man.

The parallel changes in familial authority were equally ideological. The erosion of feudal kinship control, the increasing calculation of wealth (especially marriage portions) in terms of money as well as land, the growth of legal means for manipulating inheritance, the elimination of religious orders as a career option for both sons and daughters, and the growth of vernacular literacy in upper- and middle-class males strengthened the perception of the family as the basic unit of social organization and increased the power of heads of household. Domestic relations came to be thought of in terms of the authority and obligation pertaining between father and child, husband and wife, and master and servant. Since father, husband, and master were the same man, the male head of household enjoyed multivalent authority. In civil terms the nature of "free subjects," whose relationship to the monarch lay at the heart of the English political struggle leading to the Revolution, was a concept bound to the unit of the household. "Free subjects" were those men who as fathers, husbands, and masters had free or rightful use of the human and material property that gave them a legal stake in the body politic.[29] The attendance of heads of household was required at church; their opinions were courted, monitored, and coerced. Heads of household paid taxes, held local offices, served on juries. When debate raged during the 1640s over extending the franchise, the issue except among the slimmest of democratic minorities was how far among heads of household to extend it. When the first serious estimate of English population was made by Gregory King in 1696, it estimated households.[30] Small wonder that the publication of conduct books designed to educate householders in the performance of their duties was a conspicuous feature of Elizabethan and Stuart printing.

Tudor and Stuart domestic, religious, and political relationships all showed a polarization of the hierarchy of authority into governor and governed. In the domestic sphere this meant father and child, husband and wife, master and servant; in the religious sphere, God and man; in the political sphere, king and subject. Correspondences between the powers and obligations of governors and the status and duties of the governed were obvious. Stimulated by the fact that father, husband, and master were the same man and that God was (inevitably) and the monarch (usually) male, the patriarchal analogy was automatic. As a father is to his child, so is God to his people, a king to his subjects, a master to his servants, a husband to his wife. Where other hierarchical relationships pertained, the analogy was as apt. As a father is to his child, so is a clergyman to his flock, a teacher to his pupils, the oldest brother to his juniors, any brother to his sister. The analogy is as old as Hebrew and Greco-Roman culture.[31] Dominant in Christian theology from the doctrinal defeat of Gnosticism,[32] it has its greatest figurative expression in the concept of Christ as the son of God and the Church as the Bride of Christ. Its importance in Tudor and Stuart thought stems not from novelty but from concentration and extension. Consideration of any one of these hierarchical dualities came to trigger automatic references to the others. A threat to any could be a threat to all.[33]

The increasingly vexed and explosive issue of the nature of political sovereignty was argued in terms of the patriarchal analogy. "I am the husband, and all the whole isle is my lawful wife," said James I in his first speech to Parliament in March 1604, arguing for the unity of Scotland and England as a single kingdom and the impossibility that he "as a Christian king under the Gospel should be a polygamist and husband to two wives." Following this reasoning, "What power the master hath over his servants for the ordering of his family," said Robert Sanderson, "no doubt the same at least, if not much more, hath the supreme magistrate over his subjects, for the peaceable ordering of the commonwealth: the magistrate being *pater patriae* as the master is *paterfamilias.*" Moreover, if God was a father and governor to his people, the king, as temporal father and governor of his people, was a kind of god. So maintained the humanist Justus Lipsius in his statement on political organization: "Neither do the sages of the world dissent from me, which he well witnessed that sayeth, a king is as it were, a god amongst men." The analogy could apply to anyone in authority. "Let all men hereby take heed how they complain in words against any magistrate," said a Privy Councillor in Star Chamber, "for they are gods." But the aptness of the analogy was a matter for debate. Sir Henry Shirley, for example, said in a moment of heat that he "cared not for any lord in England, except the Lord of Hosts."[34] If the virtuous father Janicula in Dekker, Chettle, and Haughton's *Patient Grissil* warned his rebellious son, "Great men are gods and they have power o'er us" (5.2.177–8), the ethical spokesman Diogenes in Lyly's *Campaspe* denied it: kings "are no gods" (2.2.128). Whether its implications were accepted or rejected, the analogy remained the starting point for political debate.

The inevitability of the patriarchal analogy explains its presence as the basis of seventeenth-century theories of political sovereignty and the organization of the state. The most famous expression of patriarchalism as a political theory occurs in Sir Robert Filmer's *Patriarcha*, written in the 1640s (though published only in 1680), which defended the absolute power of the sovereign through an appeal to the primal authority of Adam, and hence of all fathers, over their children and other dependents.[35] Neither the historical nor the moral argument, the latter taking its weight from the Fifth Commandment—"Honor thy father"—was seamless, as John Locke pointed out in his *First Treatise on Government*. But however extreme Filmer's statement,[36] its patriarchal impulse lay behind seventeenth-century political theory of every stripe. So long as theorists felt obliged to base arguments about political power on a discussion of its origins, so long as the Bible carried indisputable weight as the primary historical document, so long as the Decalogue was the essential statement of moral law, Filmer's recourse to the condition of Adam and the explicit command of God was rational and unexceptional.

Filmer's work was related both to a great body of patriarchalist writing and to the work of the contractualists now thought of as his ideological opponents.[37] Contractualists differed from patriarchalists, as patriarchalists from each other, not in denying the applicability of the patriarchal analogy to human relations, but in describing its nature. No one denied that children were subordinate to parents or that other authority figures acted like parents or in the place of parents. Where patriarchalists differed was over whether the relation of Adam to his heirs or of modern kings to the kings of the Old Testament was one of identity or merely one of likeness. Was Charles I an actual descendant in the direct patriarchal line of Noah? Filmer implied that he was. Other patriarchalists were content to maintain the likeness. Kings had the power of life and death over their subjects. Did that mean that fathers once had had, in fact still had, the power of life and death over their children? Filmer said yes. Other patriarchalists settled for the degrees of chastisement suitable to fatherlike figures.[38] Nor did contractualists desire to sidestep the patriarchal analogy. Their intention was to undermine the claim of inherent right and to bolster that of implied consent obtaining between inferiors and superiors, especially between the subject and the state. For Hobbes, the issue was whether the parent-child bond was based on the right of the parent or the need of the child. His conclusion, of a piece with his other conclusions about man's exchange of political subordination for political protection, is that the child's helplessness caused it to accept subordination in exchange for nurture.[39] Not even Locke, gleefully attacking Filmer for his omission of mothers from the commandment to honor parents, denied the subordination of wives to husbands or scorned to make the marital analogy one of the key examples of the social contract.[40] His concern was to establish that the hierarchical relationship between the two was a matter of mutual agreement to fulfill a specific social purpose desired by both parties as individuals. This fundamental distinction between genitive and contractual authority is an old one. Aristotle had noted that the parent-child relationship is analogous to regal government (government by genealogical birthright), while the husband-wife relationship is analogous to political government (government by explicit contract between the ruler and the *polis*), and Aquinas had provided the Christian gloss on Aristotle's distinction.[41] Nevertheless, correspondence among all social hierarchies was the shared assumption of both "patriarchalists" and "contractualists." All Tudor and Stuart political thinkers were in the broad sense patriarchalists.

The patriarchal analogy was useful to dramatists because it could express social ideas by dramatic means, that is, by conflicts between characters. Though much of the published controversy involving applications of patriarchalist ideas came during the 1640s and 1650s when England had a relatively free press, the underlying commonplaces, intact through 150 years of Tudor and Stuart rule, provided even under rigid censorship a politically safe way of exposing potentially explosive concerns about authority. The usefulness of the analogy is self-evident in frankly political plays. In Shakespeare's *Henry VI, Part 3*, the son who has killed his father and the father who has killed his son represent both political and domestic disorder. Shakespeare's second tetralogy again plays variations on the father-son relationship to enrich the theme of political and social authority and obligation. But playwrights also learned the advantages of using women as hierarchical subordinates, for however analogous marital and civil relationships might be, women were politically controllable, whereas, as the seventeenth century came increasingly to see, men of whatever rank might not be. The exception was the anomalous position of female heads of state, whose existence made John Knox queasy[42] and whose presence in plays in which their individuality and power were expressed could create unsettling vibrations. In the domestic sphere widows, women who belonged to no man, were likewise a focus of nervousness and speculation.

Moreover, there were dramatically interesting contradictions in the subordination patterns involving women. All children were subordinate to their parents by virtue of biological necessity, but whereas male children naturally attained a legal majority, female children did not. For them the ground of subordination shifted from age to sex, contradicting the argument of the need for education and maturation that justified subordination of the young. Equally interesting was the contradiction about parenthood. On the one hand, parental authority was the origin, or at least the essential type, of social authority. Mothers were indubitably parents of some sort; Hobbes saw that it was their care or neglect that caused the infant to live or die.[43] Biblical injunctions commanded children to honor both fathers *and* mothers. Yet the very act of marriage and parenthood that created the father's authority undermined the mother's, making her position in relation to the husband analogous to a child's or a servant's. Conduct books admitted that women necessarily wielded power in the home, serving as first officers to their husbands' function of command, but the stress on women's innate subordination and limitations created a paradox. As a parent the mother exercised authority over the children, yet as a wife (a position inseparable from, and the cause of, her motherhood), she was inferior to her husband.[44] Women were also good subjects for playwrights because in marriage parental authority was passed to the husband through a formal contract to which both husband and wife gave explicit individual consent. The marriage contract was the type of the social (even the theological) contract, thus inherently suggestive about social contracts of all sorts. The transfer of inherited paternal authority to contracted marital authority, and the possibility of competition between the two, provided endless dramatic occasions. While reflecting the realities of marriage they exposed broader issues about authority in a patriarchal society.

I by no means argue that Tudor and Stuart plays involving the testing of women were always deliberate political explorations or that either playwrights or audiences always realized the ramifications. Because so much about the hierarchical position of women was taken for granted, plays about women

could carry the most shattering implications with an abandon that full consciousness would have rendered impossible. Only in retrospect is it possible
to understand the popularity of plots about forced marriage or the need of a
husband to test his wife's fidelity or a king's or magistrate's attempt to violate
the chastity of another man's wife or daughter. The tensions of patriarchal
relationships in a changing world were felt and dramatized long before they
were fully identifiable with the upheaval that eventually retheorized society
on the basis of individual consent.

PART II

Dramatizing Patriarchy:
The Renaissance Experiment

FIVE

Male Role-Splitting
and Reintegration

Tʜᴇ ʀᴇɴᴀɪssᴀɴᴄᴇ ɪs ᴛʜᴇ ɢʀᴇᴀᴛ ᴀɢᴇ ᴏғ ᴛᴇsᴛᴇᴅ ᴡᴏᴍᴀɴ ᴅʀᴀᴍᴀ.
The plot occurs in morality drama like *Virtuous and Godly Susanna* and
Patient and Meek Grissell, domestic drama like *A Woman Killed with Kindness*
and bourgeois adventure plays like *The Fair Maid of the West*, Shakespeare's
romance *Cymbeline* and his "problem play" *Measure for Measure*, tragic mas-
terpieces like *Othello* and *The Duchess of Malfi* and *The Changeling*, prototypal
tragicomedy like *Philaster* and pastoral gems like *The Faithful Shepherdess*, love
and honor plays of the Caroline court, Milton's masque *Comus*. The theme
forms the subplot of plays not usually associated with "female drama"—history
(*Perkin Warbeck*), political satire (*A Game at Chess*), revenge tragedy (*The
Revenger's Tragedy*). It appears in passing (*Cambises*) and in miniature (*Richard
III*) in plays which exploit its familiarity as a moral litmus test. This currency
suggests that the plot is responding to ideological and dramaturgical needs.

The shift from a focus on female witness to an emphasis on male competition is part of the increasing vernacularization and secularization of literary forms, which makes homiletic purposes less inevitable and allegorical
treatments less attractive. It is also a response to conditions in the theaters:
compared with "five-men-and-a-boy" itinerant players or students performing
school theatricals, acting troupes under stable patronage based in the growing
number of London theaters were able to increase the size of their troupes,
systematize their apprenticeship systems, build their repertoires, commission
works, and develop dependable audiences. Such troupes sought scripts with
a range of challenging roles and complex, agonistic action, which the competing male functions of the tested woman plot could supply. The shift from
female witness to male competition also allows English drama to represent
the psychological complexities of an intensely patriarchal age, among them
the reciprocal relationship between male competition and male bonding; male
responses to the power and provocation of female virtue; the analogy among

67

religious, political, and familial patriarchies; and the psychological stresses on the dominant male inherent in such analogical equivalency. As a result, the dramatic expression of male states of mind reaches a literary high point in Stuart theater. Not until the mid-eighteenth century, when the tested woman plot begins to be put to the service of the novel's experiments in interiority, do we get comparable attention to the psychology of the tested woman.

PARADIGMATIC ROLE-SPLITTING AND REINTEGRATION: *THE LADY'S TRIAL*

In late Renaissance tested woman plays, the homosocial bond is at the heart of patriarchal concerns. Men unceasingly compete and collude, trying out different hegemonic configurations: exchanging familial and marital rights, challenging and protecting patriarchal power, valuing themselves by the acknowledgment of other men. The configurations are clearest in the elegant balance of high comedy, and we see them in perfected form in *The Lady's Trial* (published 1639), a play titled as though to emphasize its type status. In this best of his comedies John Ford choreographs male roles to emphasize his structural design, exhibiting the plot's power and efficiency at displaying male rivalry and reconciliation.

In the main plot of *The Lady's Trial*, the middle-aged Genoese nobleman Auria must leave his young bride, Spinella, in order to recoup his fortunes in battle against the Turks. Everything about the situation—the play's title, the age difference between husband and wife, the Italian setting with its stereotype of passion and revenge—leads the audience to expect the testing of the wife's marital fidelity. To heighten expectation, Auria's bosom friend Aurelio burdens the husband's departure with assurances of the folly of leaving a young wife unsupervised. Ford first complicates, then undermines, expectations. Spinella is indeed propositioned by the young rake Adurni; in the midst of rejecting him she is broken in upon by Aurelio, who accuses her of whoredom and her sister of bawdy connivance. When Auria returns, triumphant and enriched, Aurelio denounces Spinella, who has disappeared. Auria listens to Aurelio's accusations but refuses to credit them without proof, and in a three-sided conference with accuser and tempter is convinced of both the attempt and the rebuff. Spinella, discovered at her cousin's house, defends herself in public against her accuser Aurelio, is supported by the witness of sister and cousin, and with the public confession of Adurni is triumphantly vindicated. To show that there are no hard feelings, Auria presses Adurni on his sister-in-law and Aurelio regrets his hasty misconstructions.

This quintessential tested woman story[1] has two clear stages, the test, in which Spinella must respond to Adurni's advances (acts 1 and 2) overlapped by the trial, in which her behavior is scrutinized by her husband and his male friends (end of act 2 through act 5). Equally clear are the character functions of tempter, accuser, defender, and judge, which create the dynamic of male unity, rupture, and reintegration. Since this is comedy, the play reintegrates the tempter by converting him to defender, and schematically exhibits the men's fundamental identity. Auria, Aurelio, and Adurni are three functions of one patriarchal phenomenon. By threatening their unity, Ford gives us the pleasures of insight into their relationship and reassurance at their reconciliation.

Yet the threat must be real, and it comes from two directions. Because Adurni must make a real attempt on Spinella's virtue, Ford characterizes him by means of a subplot, where he is shedding a mistress he seduced from her serving-man husband.[2] It is quickly apparent, though, that Aurelio's accusations are the greater threat, as calumniation can be lethal, especially in Italy. But Ford also prepares for reconciliation by portraying Aurelio and Adurni less as vicious than as "humorous," as people whose normal inclinations have become socially obnoxious. So Aurelio's "rudeness," "slovenly presumption," and "officious curiosity" are repeatedly mentioned, and Adurni's sexual opportunism is expected. Faced with Spinella's emphatic rejection and Aurelio's untimely intervention, Adurni takes the initiative, with some humility, in clearing Spinella's name.

Ford pushes the plot toward the trial stage by overlapping the temptation scene with Aurelio's initial accusation so that Auria is faced immediately upon his return with Aurelio's report about his wife. But Ford's couple, whose union was not forced but "by consent" (5.2; 2449),[3] have both sense and spunk. Auria assumes that Spinella will honor her vows. Urged by Aurelio to take revenge, he responds "Revenge! for what? uncharitable friend, / On whom? Let's speak a little, pray, with reason" (3.3; 1424–6). Thus the husband takes up the function necessary to a happy issue for the calumniated wife. Having judged her innocent on the basis of his estimate of her character and Aurelio's evidence, he becomes her defender.

Yet the problem of her reputation and his honor remains. Auria's honor does demand revenge, not against Spinella but against Adurni, who has attempted his wife. Because Aurelio's accusation is public knowledge, for Auria to seek revenge against Adurni would lend that accusation credence. Thus when Auria becomes angry at Aurelio's charges, the anger is against Aurelio himself, who has both driven Auria's wife from him and foiled his revenge against the tempter:

> . . . I am certain, certain it had been
> Impossible, had you stood wisely silent,
> But my Spinella, trembling on her knee,
> Would have accused her breach of truth, have begged
> A speedy execution on her trespass.
> Then with a justice lawful as the magistrate's
> Might I have drawn my sword against Adurni

> Which now is sheathed and rusted in the scabbard,
> Good thanks to your cheap providence. Once more
> I make demand—my wife—you—sir.
>
> (3.3; 1509–18)[4]

Briefly Auria is swamped with passion and reduced to incoherence—but not from jealousy.

The solution is to heal the apparent breach between man and wife by healing the real one between the wife's defender and the men who have tempted and accused her. Now Ford begins to use his emphasis on the men's friendship. At the play's opening Aurelio had castigated Auria for not revealing his penury, they had characterized their relationship as holy and sacred, and Auria had made the other man his heir. The central duet of accusation and anger between the two began with the strongest expression of their closeness:

> We have exchanged
> Bosoms, Aurelio, from our years of childhood.
>
> . . . .
>
> So dearly witness with me my integrity,
> I laid thee up to heart, that from my love
> My wife was but distinguished in her sex.
>
> (3.3; 1466–7, 1474–6)

Following his explosive anger, whose chief pain lies in the violation of that closeness, the scene ends with Auria's restatement of their bond: "Auria and Aurelio / At odds oh it cannot be, must not, and shall not" (3.3; 1547–8).

If Ford had given us a friend motivated by the desire to possess and a husband motivated by the desire to defend possession, there might be regret, bitterness, and catastrophe, but there would be little need for psychological analysis of the male bond. Putting the tempter's function in the hands of a third man and using the friend as the defender of the husband's honor against the husband's will raises fresher possibilities. Many seem obvious to modern minds. Aurelio could be the mouthpiece for deep fears in the husband as well as in the culture. Despite Auria's avowal to the contrary, he too may distrust his wife's faith, or at least her wisdom. Aurelio's accusation against Spinella could be an indirect attack on his oldest friend, an old man's kind of envy. Or perhaps he wants Spinella faithless to set off his own loyalty, as she accuses. When Auria makes Aurelio his heir, he might be including Spinella among his possessions, so that Aurelio is in emotional as well as legal *loco conjugis*. Aurelio might have misread the depth of the friendship, so that he is being not just unwise but presumptuous. As for Adurni, his trespass may actually be desired, a gesture of admiration that any husband of Spinella would be disappointed to be without. And given Adurni's age—for Ford first raises then blocks another stock situation, that of virile youth seducing old man's young wife—the attempted seduction might be the expression of the younger man's desire to join the older and more powerful men's circle. This competition over the woman could be primarily a means to strengthen male bonds, as such bonds are strengthened by competition in games, in arms, and in civic life.

These issues simmer beneath the surface of the play because the play's trajectory toward reconciliation requires that they be admitted in order to be controlled. In schematic terms the dynamic of containment involves keeping character functions clear so they can be clearly reconciled. Obvious alter egos, their names echoing each other,[5] Auria and Aurelio represent the husband split in two and engaged in open ethical debate. While Aurelio, the man of passion, behaves according to the stereotype of the accusing husband, Auria, the man of reason, acts the part of champion. The next step is to bring the tempter into harmony with them. This move has been prepared for by Adurni's regret after being rebuffed by Spinella: "she is a goodness / Above temptation, more to be adored / Than sifted; I'm too blame sure" (3.3; 1361–3).[6] Resolving to sue for mercy, he arranges to visit Auria, agrees to Aurelio's presence at the interview, and both accuses himself of wrongdoing and praises Spinella for her firmness. His conciliatory bearing prevents either jealousy or revenge, for as Adurni himself points out, "I have robbed you / Of rigor, Auria, by my strict self-penance / For the presumption" (4.3; 2188–90). Auria can do nothing but admit that, especially for Italians, "the trick is new" (4.3; 2193). That admission made, Auria's musing is exclusively about how to manipulate the public rehabilitation of Spinella's reputation. While Aurelio continues to accuse and Adurni to placate, he paces and mumbles like a trial lawyer or theatrical director. Having concocted the solution, Auria requires the others' help—"Aurelio, friend, / Adurni, Lord, we three will sit in counsel / And piece a hearty league, or scuffle shrewdly" (4.3; 2222–4). Once Adurni joins the colloquy, tempter, accuser, and defender confront each other, come to an agreement, and cooperate to clear Spinella's name. The breach between Auria and Aurelio is healed. Adurni, though he has been refused Auria's marital place, becomes husband to Spinella's sister. The marriage, publicly representative of the men's reconciliation, "rectifies all crooks, vain surmises," in Auria's words (5.2; 2516) and "frees / Each circumstance of jealousy," in Aurelio's (5.2; 2525–6).

The solution scene shows Ford's skill at making the most of the triangular agon he has contrived. Controlled, vivid character choreography is typical of his work. Often it is stark or minimalist, strengthened by devices of with-holding. Here what he withholds is the woman. Spinella's fate is discussed in her absence; Auria, though returned from the wars, has yet to see her. Public calumny demands public resolution. When Spinella reappears she will come before her husband in a formal trial. The resolution Auria plans is not without danger. Spinella must have as fine a perception of male functions as does her husband. Already the balance between her independence and her sense of appropriate behavior has been established. She visited Adurni at his house, but spurned his advances. She rejected Aurelio's construction on her actions, but refused Adurni's offer to champion her. Unable to tolerate false accusation, she retreated to Malfato's house but would not hear of his love for her, accepting his shelter as her kinsman only. Her expectations of Auria's behavior were summed up in the speech with which she turned aside Adurni's attempted seduction, words her husband repeats as he prepares her public vindication: "Auria, Auria, / Fight not for name abroad, but come my husband, / Fight for thy wife at home" (2.4; 1056–8). In these encounters Spinella has had to resist not just the temptation to grant other men her husband's sexual place, but the greater temptation to grant them her husband's role as defender. That temptation is strongest in the last scene, when she finds her husband holding her to public trial and playing, to her confusion, judge rather than advocate. In this final test Spinella refuses any aid but that of her own witness:

> Though prove what judge you will, till I can purge
> Objections which require belief and conscience,
> I have no kindred, sister, husband, friend,
> Or pity for my plea.
>
> (5.2; 2389–92)

Struck by her words, Auria repeats them—"Said ye, Lady, / No kindred, sister, husband, friend" (5.2; 2395–6)—reassuring himself that none of his marital functions have been preempted.

In the final scene Auria is playing the judge's role for public consumption.[7] He enters the mock trial with the elements of tempter, accuser, and defender already reconciled. But under the guise of scrutinizing the woman, the scene maintains the appearance of male fragmentation until the husband publicly admits that his appropriate role is as her defender. This mock trial is a less grueling version of the finale of the Griselda story, in which playwrights locate Walter's competing functions in a proliferation of tool characters. The Lady's Trial completes the rationalization by transmuting fairy-tale concentration and ferocity into a realistic form. From the moment Auria enters the play, escorted on stage by Adurni and then joined by Aurelio, the three men stand as representations of a single class, interest, and mindset. Accustomed to being first among these equals, Auria's concern is to reestablish both power and honor with his peers. The lady's trial is his means to orchestrate and publicize male unity.

THE TRAUMA OF MALE FRAGMENTATION

In The Lady's Trial Ford blocks full-fledged male fragmentation, which threatens only momentarily when Auria, swamped with frustration by Aurelio's interference, tries to find the words to recover his wife from the situation created by his friends: "Once more I make demand . . . my wife . . . you . . . sir. . . ." In his tragedies Ford specializes in dramatizing this trauma. He does not need to invent his basic situations, since treachery between friends and conflict between brothers are as old as the tested woman plot itself. *Orlando Furioso* serves the Renaissance as a sourcebook of exaggerated situations of romance. Early in the poem Ariosto uses the woman's calumniation to focus psychological damage on brothers. The initiating treachery in the story of Ariodante and Ginevra is the accusation "proved" by the visit of a man to the window of a woman dressed in her mistress's clothing (the prime source for *Much Ado about Nothing*). The story has the histrionic virtues of the tested woman plot raised a power, which is why it made good opera material for Handel.[8] There are the Scottish princess Ginevra and her waiting woman Dalinda; the brothers Ariodante (Ginevra's admirer) and Lurcanio (a formidable swordsman); Polinesso, duke of Albany, lover of Dalinda but ambitious to marry the princess and full of rancor because she prefers Ariodante; and the father/king, whose trial of his daughter is required by Caledonian law. As the locals explain to Rinaldo, "By the cruel and pitiless law of Scotland any woman, whatever her condition, who engages in union with a man, and is not his wife, must be put to death if an accusation is laid against her. And she has no recourse against death unless a mighty warrior come and undertake her defence, maintaining that she be innocent and not deserving of death" (4:59–60).[9] John Harington's argument for canto 5, in the first English translation of 1591, winningly summarizes what ensues:

> Dalinda tells what sleights her Duke devised,
> To get with fair Genevra reputation;
> Lurcanio of his brother's fall advised,
> Accus'th her publicly of fornication.
> A knight unknown in armor black disguised,
> Comes and withstands Lurcanio's accusation,
> Until Rinaldo made all matters plain,
> By whom the unjust Duke was justly slain.[10]

The initial calumniation of Ginevra is brought by Polinesso, but the psychological conflict in Ariosto's account lies between Lurcanio, the accuser, and the "knight unknown in armor black disguised," who is Ariodante. Both brothers have ocular proof of Ginevra's infidelity, for both have seen a shrouded man, Polinesso himself, enter Ginevra's chamber window to the practiced welcome of Dalinda in her mistress's clothes. Lurcanio, outraged by Ginevra's treachery and the report of Ariodante's suicide, accuses her. But Ariodante has swum back out of the sea in which he planned to drown himself. Softened by the news that Ginevra mourns his loss, he turns his frustration on his brother: "Anger towards his brother now enflamed his heart no less fiercely than his earlier love for Guinevere: Lurcanio's action seemed to him all too merciless and cruel, for all that it proceeded from brotherly affection" (6:8). In taking up Ginevra's defense to prove his love, Ariodante also has a more chilling motive. "By the same act I shall wreak vengeance on my brother, who has set light to so great a fire: I shall make him smart when he discovers the final outcome of his cruel undertaking—he will imagine that he has avenged his brother when in fact he shall have slain him with his own hand" (6:11–2). When Rinaldo clatters into the arena on his steed Bayard, it is first to save the brothers from each other and themselves.

The brothers are victims of rage, represented by Furor in the equivalent episode in Spenser's *Faerie Queene*.[11] In Ariosto, Lurcanio's rage is directed— on his brother's behalf—against the betraying woman. Once Ariodante is relieved of the function of accusation, his rage blooms against the brother who stands in for his accusing self. The psychic split in the lover finds dramatic form in the struggle of brother accuser against brother defender, which is why Ariosto's version works for Handel. Spenser's allegorical version, though less stageworthy, helps us understand the psychology better, for Spenser portrays his betrayed lover, Phedon, as doing battle with himself. He is pursued, chained, and beaten by Furor, who in turn is continually provoked by his mother, the hag Occasion. The moral message of Spenser's version, which narrates Phedon's vengeance against the beloved in a single line ("With wrathfull hand I slew her innocent" [stanza 29]) and his poisoning of the false friend in two lines (stanza 30), is that the true enemy is intemperance. "Wrath, gelosy, griefe, love this squyre have laide thus low," diagnoses the preaching palmer (stanza 34), denouncing "monster" love, bred from filth, as the seedbed (stanza 35). But the source of Phedon's anguish seems less Claribella's love or loss than Philemon's perfidy, brought up with him "from tender dug of common nourse" (stanza 18). Claribella's calumny is an expression of the male agon of desire, rivalry, suspicion, and rage, provoked by conflict between brothers but played out in truest form in the single male heart.

MONOPOLY AND MADNESS

Such rage is not the monopoly of the highborn. Thomas Heywood, the fore-most English Renaissance playwright of bourgeois life, suggests its destructive possibilities in both *A Woman Killed with Kindness* (1603) and *The English Traveler* (published 1634). But such rage is characteristically situated within the family, where intimate relations and complex expectations produce the greatest concentration of pressures. Ford is the premier Renaissance portrayer of insanity—not the wronged maiden strewing flowers or the disguised gen-tleman inventing fantasies, but the real thing. Part of his interest is a matter of fashion: melancholy was the preferred mental disease of the age, and his *Lover's Melancholy* is a tragicomedy about healing a sufferer from depression with the aid of music. In his tragedies, however, Ford develops extreme mental states to the point of disintegration and death, and at his best he motivates them by extreme situations and concentrated configurations played out within the family. His stories can get away from him: *Love's Sacrifice*, for example, is a botched mess. Yet where complexity and concentration can promote power as well as muddle, as in *'Tis Pity She's a Whore*, Ford profoundly exposes the psyche. As for *The Broken Heart*, its structural elegance, economy, and balance result in a nearly perfect theatrical representation of the madness of male competition and possessiveness.

Possessiveness is the disease, but in *Love's Sacrifice* Ford seems to have lost structural control of the insight. Criticism founders over the mixed messages that readers, not just the men of the play, receive about Bianca. Are we to take her as the blameless wife of the first two acts, the chaste Platonic lover of the play's middle, or the "shameless, intolerable whore" she seems in her final confrontation with her husband?[12] As for male character functions, the play gives us Fernando, the Platonic lover/tempter, D'Avolos, the Iago-like accuser, and Caraffa, the husband who first condemns his wife and kills her, then, faced with Fernando's insistence on her physical chastity, changes his mind and wreaks a second vengeance on himself. But husband and lover seem like leading figures in two confusingly different plots. Caraffa is the protagonist of a tested woman play in which the chief pressure is toward the integration of the husband's functions, with the wife the means of that integration. Hence the clear presence of the *Othello* skeleton. Fernando, however, is the protagonist of a Platonic courtly love drama in which the pressure is toward union with the beloved in death, with the husband merely the obstacle to a living consummation. Hence the strong echoes of *Romeo and Juliet*. In theory the patterns might come off in tandem. In practice, unfortunately, parts of the play are so derivative, and many of its signals so misleading, that the competing plots get bafflingly muddled.[13]

Whatever the uncertainties of Bianca's situation, that of Annabella in *'Tis Pity She's a Whore* is unequivocal. She is hardly calumniated even in the exaggerated terms of *Love's Sacrifice* since, when tempted by her brother Giovanni, she confesses herself already in love with him. Yet the comparative unity of *'Tis Pity* comes less from her attachment than from the degree to which Soranzo and Giovanni, unlike Caraffa and Fernando, compete to fill the same functions. The final act of *'Tis Pity* succeeds by emphasizing the functional resemblance between brother/lover and husband.

By the final act Ford has created a standard revenge triangle. The husband, Soranzo, having discovered the identity of his wife's lover, plots revenge, presumably against them both. But the triangle is also perfectly reversed because, through his successful temptation of Annabella, Giovanni has already preempted Soranzo's role, sealing it with ceremonial vows (1.2.249–59),[14] a betrothal ring (2.6.36–42), and a child in utero. Then Annabella's letter shakes his faith in her faith, he again perceives Soranzo as a rival, and he concocts "baneful plots" (5.3.73), presumably against both Soranzo and Annabella.

By every possible means—precedence, mutuality of affections, vows—Ford
has strengthened the sense of Giovanni's husbandly function. Sibling incest,
while it is an additional perversion, is also an additional reinforcement of
Giovanni's claim; it doubles his illegitimate authority by allowing him to play
both surrogate husband and surrogate father, a monopoly whose tension Ford
increases by providing a real husband and leaving the real father alive. Given
the weight of Giovanni's and Soranzo's conflicting claims and their mutual
belief in Annabella's faithlessness, the question of act 5 is which avenger will
get to his revenge the sooner. Giovanni does, preempting Soranzo in murder
as he did in marriage. "Shall I be forestall'd?" (5.6.16) cries the husband as the
brother intrudes one last time.

The terrible economy of a reversible love/revenge triangle should satisfy the
most demanding dramatist. But though this description represents Soranzo's
truth, it does not account completely for Giovanni's. Soranzo's judgment of
Annabella, once made, never changes. Giovanni does change his mind, but
(unlike Caraffa) appears to entertain his opposing judgments simultaneously.
In their last encounter (5.5) Giovanni begins by accusing Annabella of faithlessness, doing briefly what Soranzo had done at length in the hair-pulling scene
(4.3). Then, like Soranzo, he softens and seems to forgive. Soranzo's softening
had been a ruse, but Giovanni's change of tone suggests the judgment and
defense of the calumniated and vindicated wife, for his accusation of faithlessness is followed by his description of Annabella's purity: "Go thou, white in
thy soul, to fill a throne / Of innocence and sanctity in Heaven" (5.5.64–5). He
rests in the sense of their mutual and abiding love, their "fast-knit affections"
(5.5.69). The scene passes from judgment to advocacy as Giovanni defends
his sister by begging her forgiveness, killing her, saving her from Soranzo. Yet
although the orgasmic exhilaration of the deathblow increases our sense of
Giovanni's compulsion for total possession of his sister, his language defines
that compulsion strangely. To Annabella's question "What means this?" his
answer seems astonishing:

> To save thy fame, and kill thee in a kiss.
> Thus die, and die by me, and by my hand!
> Revenge is mine; honor doth love command.
>   (5.5.84–6)

As Auria says, "Revenge! For what? On whom?" If Annabella is "white in her
soul" and "fast-knit" to her lover, why revenge against her? How can her death
at Giovanni's hand save her fame and his honor?

To attempt an answer, we must remember the source of Giovanni's frustration. However completely he may assume marital functions, he cannot legally
be Annabella's husband. His only legitimate relationship to her is brother.
Given that relationship and the fact of her whoredom (by this point her
violation of her marriage vows), the honor of her family as well as of her

husband demands her death. This may be the sense in which to read Giovanni's "Revenge is mine; honor doth love command." His subsequent vauntings are corroborative. He has "prevented" Soranzo's "reaching plots" (5.5.100) by performing the murder himself, an act of "vengeance" that makes him "a most glorious executioner" (5.6.34). When a horrified Florio asks him "art thyself?" he answers as son:

> Yes, father; and that times to come may know
> How as my fate I honor'd my revenge,
> List, father, to your ears I will yield up
> How much I have deserv'd to be your son.
>
> (5.6.36–9)

In the demonstration that follows, Giovanni proves his kinship with Florio by proving Annabella's sin and death (5.6.57–60). The heart on his dagger, he assures his father, is hers.

On Giovanni's lips, however, claims of honor and vengeance are accompanied always by claims of love. After he kills his sister, he prepares to play a "last and greater part" (5.5.106), turning to Soranzo for another type of vengeance. Here he might merely be playing the lover who avenges the alienation of his mistress's affections, the husband in all but name who kills his wife's lover. But remembering the reconciliation between him and Annabella that preceded her death, remembering his evident acceptance that Soranzo meant nothing to her, we must read Soranzo's death in fuller terms. Giovanni has already killed the faithless wife, forestalling Soranzo. By so doing he has once again preempted the husband's role, has acted as Soranzo. When he turns now to kill the real Soranzo, it is as if against his sister's murderer. "Soranzo, see this heart, which was thy wife's; / Thus I exchange it royally for thine / And thus and thus! Now brave revenge is mine" (5.6.73–5). The second death mimics the first with gestures and language reminiscent of the killing of Annabella. It is the only intimate exchange in a scene of public display.

All that remains is for Giovanni, now united as closely as may be with his double, the legal husband, to work against himself that husband's final vengeance. Here he is forestalled by Soranzo's servant, who acts as his master's posthumous tool. When the Cardinal urges a plea for divine mercy, Giovanni professes himself complete: "Mercy? Why, I have found it in this justice" (5.6.103). Justice? The justice of his own death. Mercy? The consummation of having played out every marital function toward his sister. Giovanni has tempted her, wooed her, won her to sin and to marriage, killed her, and avenged her on his double and on himself. He is as complete as it is possible to be this side of death.

This is madness. But the forms taken by Giovanni's obsession are motivated at every step by the forms of authority available to the men whose places he takes, which is why, until the end, he does not sound mad. Loving Annabella, wooing her, contracting himself to her, impregnating her, accusing her of infidelity, doing her to death—as in his debates with the Friar he always has available a language that mimics the legitimate. The corruption lies in the fact that all agency is his. Only in the last scene, with his increasingly bizarre efforts to replay all the roles in the absence of his sister and the presence of their real possessors, do we receive the full impression of his frenzy. Though Annabella is equally obsessed, her sequestration—except for the marriage to Soranzo (4.1) Ford never gives her a public scene—allows her so few options that her fixation somehow seems more comprehensible. Nevertheless, the incest that monopolizes the woman in her father's house rather than transferring her to a husband creates the play's claustrophobic madness.[15]

In *The Broken Heart* the madness is less sensational but more widespread and devastating. The play is set in Sparta, not Parma; in a court, not a private household; among three interlocking families whose loves and hatreds are carried to their laconic conclusions in a choreography as austere as the other play's was frenetic. Here Ford turns the character-function configuration of *'Tis Pity* inside out: instead of centering all functions in a single man, he groups around the central woman three intensely competing males. The tested woman is Penthea, a calumniated wife tormented by her sense of unwilled impurity. Originally betrothed to Orgilus, whom she loves, she was forced by her brother Ithocles into marriage with Bassanes. Despite her chaste behavior, Bassanes is consumed by jealousy. As the play opens, the tempter is Orgilus, the accuser Bassanes, and the defender Ithocles, who takes charge of Penthea to protect her from her husband. But the male competition, already perverse, is exacerbated by further perversions of each man's role.

Orgilus has been nearly as wronged as Penthea, for he has contractual precedence. By legal and emotional right he should be her husband. Ithocles, who by the death of her father and the irrationality of her husband plays the role of defender, is the original tempter, for he forced his sister's marriage with Bassanes against both her contract and her love. Bassanes is cured of his jealousy when he loses his wife to her brother's protection, but he remains useless to her. Instead of taking on her defense, he retreats into an unresponsive stoicism. Penthea is trapped in a situation that is a reverse of Annabella's. Though her spirit belongs to Orgilus, as she confirms in a kneeling reiteration of their vows (2.3.61–7), in body she belongs to Bassanes:

ORGILUS	Penthea is the wife to Orgilus,
	And ever shall be.
PENTHEA	Never shall nor will.
ORGILUS	How!
PENTHEA	Hear me; in a word I'll tell thee why.
	The virgin-dowry which my birth bestowed
	Is ravished by another; my true love
	Abhors to think that Orgilus deserved

ORGILUS

PENTHEA

> No better favours than a second bed.
>   I must not take this reason.
>   To confirm it,
> Should I outlive my bondage, let me meet
> Another worse than this, and less desired,
> If, of all men alive, thou shouldst but touch
> My lip or hand again.
>
>   (2.3.96–107)

The vehemence with which she drives Orgilus from her is her response to his dangerous presence, the more dangerous because her heart is utterly his. The phenomenon behind the vehemence is irreversible: the "enforced divorce" (2.3.56–7) between her body and her heart has severed her from her self. Her slow madness and slower starvation are the physical expression of that divorce.

The multiplication of functions includes two husbands, and even, by accusation, two lovers, for Bassanes charges Ithocles with incest. Incest is not one of Ithocles' sins. The sin he did commit against his sister, however, contaminates his ability to protect her, heal her husband, ease Orgilus's anger, or consummate his courtship of the king's daughter Calantha. Penthea should have found in Ithocles another father:

> By yea and nay, an oath not to be broken,
> If you had joined our hands once in the temple,—
> 'Twas since my father died, for had he lived
> He would have done't,—I must have called you father.
>
>   (4.2.140–3)[16]

There could be no more succinct account of the crucial transfer from father to husband gone wrong. Ithocles' inheritance should have been his father's wishes. The promises of the father having been overridden by the son's ambitious folly (2.2.43–53), the younger generation is hopelessly contaminated. Penthea starves. Orgilus stabs Ithocles to death beside her body, then opens his veins in obedience to the sentence of Calantha, the new queen. Calantha performs her own marriage to the "shadow of [her] contracted lord" Ithocles (5.3.62–3) before dying of a broken heart. Figures of exchange haunt the play from the first blighted troth to Calantha's last dance. Each seeks the integration possible only to moral and emotional balance, and yet each goes awry, thrown off center by the ambient pressures. "Remember," says Penthea to Orgilus in her final scene, "When last we gathered roses in the garden, / I found my wits; but truly you lost yours" (4.2.19–21). Gains are also losses—Penthea has found her moral wits but lost her sanity, while the witlessness Orgilus shakes off by interpreting her admonitions as a spur to his revenge kills him, her brother, and the queen.

SIX

The Provocation of Virtue
and the Burden of Faith

V IRTUE HAS AN INNATE POWER OF ATTRACTION. IN A CULTURE THAT
views sinfulness as the normal human condition and virtue as the refusal to
sin, the virtuous person must be powerful beyond ordinary human capacities.
Part of the drama of such a person's portrayal thus lies in the admiration
and envy of others. Making the virtuous character a woman—socially inferior
and morally suspect—only heightens the drama. The tested woman plot gives
the playwright two psychologically rich ways to exploit the presence of the
virtuous woman. He may emphasize her power to define herself and maintain
her integrity in the face of extraordinary pressure. Or he may emphasize
the provocative effect of her virtue on men: their compulsion to force its
demonstration to enhance their possession or violate it to assuage their sense
of inferiority. Either emphasis gives female virtue psychological and dramatic
power because it exposes male insecurity and triggers male response.

THE POWER OF INTEGRITY

Morality plays like the Tudor hybrids favor a focus on the power of female
integrity and witness in which sacrificial wives and daughters embrace their
enforced martyrdom. The repeated abuses the heroines undergo not only
demonstrate the wickedness of the perpetrators; in dramatic terms they actually create the woman's extraordinary virtue. *A Yorkshire Tragedy*, for example,
achieves literary form because the horrors committed by the husband initiate
and shape the wife's obedient and loving response, which finally brings him to
recognition and repentance. Her virtue is crafted from the repetition, variety,
and severity of her tests. In the final scene she is carried out in an invalid's chair
to receive her husband's confession because the attack that put her there was
the culmination of his wickedness. Like Iphigenia or Jephthah's daughter she
seizes the occasion, making from her endurance of tribulation the stuff of her

power. Though more psychologically complex, the same effect occurs with the Duchess of Malfi, whose anguish and dignity bring even her tormenters—first Bosola, then Ferdinand—to awed devotion. The manner of her martyrdom makes not just her character but the play.

The power does not come unassisted. The duchess's meditative dialogue with Bosola (4.1) is replete with the probing and consolatory language of Deuteronomy and Job, and her religious confidence at the moment of her garroting is set off by her waiting-woman Cariola's frantic sense of spiritual unreadiness. Lucretia and Virginia draw their strength from their familial piety and the power of the *manes*. Susanna puts her integrity in the hands of the Lord, and Constance calls on the example of Susanna. Spiritual succor may verge on the magical: Milton's *Comus* (1634) has its moly, and in Fletcher's *Faithful Shepherdess* (1608) chastity can repel fire.

Comedy allows literal weapons as well, like Christian Custance's kitchen implements and goose. In male disguise Heywood's Bess (*Fair Maid of the West Part I* [1610]) threatens Roughman into submission with her sword, and Middleton and Dekker's Moll (*The Roaring Girl* [1608]) wounds her molester in a fully staged duel. Although adopted to afford protection, male disguise actually allows the playwright to multiply the threats to the woman's person and will. Shakespeare's Imogen/Fidele runs the risks of exhaustion, starvation, a hostile reception by mountain men, premature burial, the seeming discovery of her husband's headless corpse, an encounter with the Roman army, and a pitched battle, not to mention the revelation of her sex by the pursuing Cloten bent on rape. To repeated demonstrations of her moral courage and endurance Shakespeare adds physical tests to enhance her dramatic centrality and power.

Male disguise may also allow the woman to intrigue her way into a position of power so that she can direct the reformation of the men who mistreat her. In Heywood's *Wise Woman of Hogsden* (1604), Second Luce pursues her jilter Young Chartley and by means of a disguise inveigles him into first marrying and at last acknowledging her. A like freedom to travel, talk, and manipulate is granted by male disguise to Mistress Lowwater in Middleton's *No Wit, No Help like a Woman's* (1613), who uses her freedom to win back her fortune, shake off the attentions of a lecher, and help her brother to a suitable marriage. In these comedies male disguise adds variety and sometimes the trappings of male power to the tested woman's expression of her virtue. It gives her a wider stage and a richer set of circumstances in which to play. Disguise does not make a woman less womanly. Instead it allows her to maintain her womanly integrity.

All these means to power—endurance, magical or divine intervention, male disguise, martial prowess—spring from the woman's sense of self. She defines her own virtue in order to act on it, and her power comes from that definition. Middleton and Dekker's Moll, after demonstrating by force of arms her contempt for a man "that thinks every woman thy fond flexible whore" (3.1.71), confirms her control over both mind and body: "My spirit shall be mistress of this house, / As long as I have time in't" (*The Roaring Girl*, 3.1.139–

40). In Fletcher's *Faithful Shepherdess*, Clorin marvels at the strength of her female purity, which has overcome the Satyr and turned his lust to Ariel-like service (1.1;103–5; 127–9). Although such virtue corresponds to the patriarchal ideal of chastity, the women who possess it hold it in their own right. Their virtue lies first in how they define themselves.

THE LURE OF VIOLATION

A different kind of power is created by male definitions of female virtue. The men who value the woman and own or seek to own her typically present her through catalogues of stereotyped qualities: Posthumus's boast that Imogen is "more fair, virtuous, wise, chaste, constant, qualified and less attemptable" than other women (*Cymbeline*, 1.4.59–61) is commonplace in its extravagance. Here the woman's power clearly is created by the act of valuing. The rarer and more admirable the woman, the more she attracts the desire and the pursuit of men. This kind of power lies not primarily in the woman's essence or actions, but in the possessiveness of the men who value her. The stereotypes in which she is described establish her worth by reiterating those qualities that men have agreed to value.

With the virtuous woman's power to evoke or enforce admiration, even reverence, comes her power to provoke. The most cloying plays are tempered by their awareness that extraordinary virtue is hard not only to encounter with indifference, but even to tolerate. Such virtue, while eliciting admiration, also provokes the urge to boast, to prove, and to violate. These extreme reactions shift the plot's focus to male assumptions about their patriarchal roles and the ways they define themselves through possession, or attempted possession, of the woman.

These diverse reactions occur in the Book of Job, where God's boast triggers Satan's urge to violate and God's alarmed need to prove. The urge to violate, the reaction of the outsider, is the more understandable and at first glance the more sensational. The language in which the protagonist of John Fletcher's *Valentinian* (1614) ponders an attack on the virtuous Lucina is remarkable only for its bluntness, not for its novelty: "she is such a pleasure, being good, / That though I were a god, she would fire my blood" (1.3.249–50). Her rape cannot affect his compulsion because it cannot reach her intransigent chastity:

> Were it to do again (therefore be wiser)
> By all this holy light, I should attempt it:
> Ye are so excellent, and made to ravish,
> (There were no pleasure in ye else)—.
> (3.1.101–4)

Though atypically comical in its absence of postcoital misgivings, the voice of Valentinian strikes a note common in tested woman stories. The "lust-breathed

Tarquin" of Shakespeare's poem, hurrying to Collatium to attempt Lucrece, is lured by virtue: "Haply that name of 'chaste' unhap'ly set / This bateless edge on his keen appetite" (*The Rape of Lucrece*, ll. 3, 8–9). Heywood's *Rape of Lucrece* (1609) gives Tarquin the same motive. In *The Revenger's Tragedy* (1606),[1] the younger son's rape of Lord Antonio's wife, "That general honest woman" whose "name has spread such a fair wing / Over all Italy" (1.2.46; 56–7), owes its inspiration to her marital virtue. The more virtuous the Lady of Middleton's *The Second Maiden's Tragedy* (1611),[2] the more hotly the Tyrant pursues first her, then her corpse. The Black Knight of Middleton's *A Game at Chess* (1624) lusts after "the rape of devotion" (2.1.21); as the Fat Bishop explains to the White Queen, "The Black Knight's blood burns for thy prostitution / And nothing but the spring of thy chaste virtue / Can cool his inflammation" (4.4.64–6). The iconography of the assault on Susanna tells it all: the bath whose privacy and cool purity represent Susanna's chastity is the occasion that inflames the Elders.

The most eloquent examination of the provocation of virtue is Angelo's soliloquy in *Measure for Measure* (2.2.167–91). It is doubly illuminating because Angelo, like the Elders, is a magistrate turned tempter. As he examines the paradox of power, every turn works toward the issue of provocation. What preoccupies Angelo, beyond the recognition of his hitherto unadmitted capacity to sin, is the paradox of the power of Isabella's virtue. Because desire is in him but not in her, her virtue is passive; only his lust is active. But he struggles with the contradictions inherent in his words even as his speech exploits them. Isabella is the "tempter," yet Angelo knows she does not tempt. Her modesty "betrays" him, yet she performs nothing; it is he who would pitch his evils in the sanctuary of her virtue. She "subdues" him, yet she has not fought. His own desire "goads" him on, but its force seems to come from her. The very word "virtue," to which he returns repeatedly, seems to carry not just its narrower sense of chastity or even goodness, but also its deeper meaning of capacity and strength, the power beside which the "double vigor" of the strumpet is nothing. Save for a brief moment Angelo is too clearheaded to excuse himself by blaming Isabella. Instead his speech grapples with the phenomenon of a person whose power lies in her integrity.

As Angelo's speech is the type examination of the power of virtue to provoke violation, his situation is typical of the man who violates. As lieutenant he has been given the authority to search out evildoing, punish infractions, and test virtue (3.1.160–5). But Angelo is the law-enforcer only, not the law-giver. His power is circumscribed by his commission and rank. He is also a man emotionally deficient, for his preciseness translates into wifelessness, lovelessness, friendlessness. He has no confidant, no relative, not even a servant—a telling lack in a Renaissance play for a person of his rank. The roles of the overseeing duke and his increasingly tarnished deputy are especially reminiscent of God and Lucifer in this use of the solitary deputy as the testing and chastising tool. Angelo's response to his sudden if limited power is to attempt to expand it. His attack on Isabella is made by means of his magisterial role. He never attempts to seduce her as a man, only to force her as a judge. Angelo's situation as the eternal second-in-command cankered with the personality and longings of the dispossessed is typical of characters whose response to virtue is the urge to violate. Shakespeare works many variations on this type. Sextus Tarquinius is not merely the issue of the "hated family of the [usurping] Tarquins" but is also envious of the rich patrician happiness of Collatine. The ravishers of Titus Andronicus's daughter Lavinia are the younger sons of Tamora, the captured queen of the Goths. As mere stepsons of the emperor Saturninus, they have power only for mischief and rapine. And Iago, who carries out his violation of Desdemona through the agency of his commanding officer Othello, is the most notorious also-ran in the canon.

Because the woman's chastity represents broader marital and familial power, the violator's ultimate target is the male possessor. Dramatists tend to emphasize this fact schematically. In *Richard III* Shakespeare makes Anne the wife rather than the betrothed of the dead Prince Edward and stages her encounter with Gloucester over the coffin of her murdered father-in-law in order to direct upon her family the full brunt of her violation. What Tamora's bestial sons term their love for Lavinia turns out to be a taste for the murder of a rival and the violation of his wife's marital purity. In *The Revenger's Tragedy* Castiza's corruption is the ambition of Lussurioso, the duke's eldest son who spends the bulk of the play waiting for his father to die. The rape of Antonio's virtuous wife in the same play is the work of the duke's youngest stepson, a youth who rampages as viciously through the ducal halls as do most stepsons in Renaissance plays. In Middleton's *Hengist King of Kent* (1618), Horsus, who engineers the rape of a virtuous wife by her disguised husband, is the lieutenant first of Hengist and then of Vortiger, doomed by his infatuation with a slut always to serve other men and eventually to share his mistress with his king. Even violators who occupy supreme positions of authority are insecure or circumscribed in their power. In Garter's play Susanna's accusers are old men frustrated by their longing and incapable flesh. Milton's Comus governs only the "drear wood" (l. 37) in which he holds court, is subject to the thwarting intervention of the Attendant Spirit, and seems hardly equal to the Lady's father, that "noble peer of mickle trust and power" (l. 31) who has in charge "all this tract that fronts the falling sun" (l. 29). The necrophiliac Tyrant of *The Second Maiden's Tragedy* is a usurper who falls at the hand of the rightful prince.

In Renaissance plays rape is both the act and the sign of a political loser, but the oldest sources of the tested woman plot may not subscribe to this dynamic. In classical myths rape comes close to being the defining act of the god—a personality-neutral expression of power. The impartial savagery of family feuds and tribal disputes recounted in the Mediterranean story pool makes rape seem just another atrocity; Hellenistic romance, for instance, does not necessarily moralize it in political terms. But Renaissance drama unquestionably does. The genre's capacity to exploit the political resonance of male/female relationships helps account for its cultural vigor.

THE BURDEN OF FAITH

The man who seeks by violation to assuage the envy and longing of his dispossession gives straightforward expression to a common human weakness. More complex is the case of the man in possession who, knowing the virtue with which he is blessed, nevertheless puts his blessedness to the test. This response is so unexpected and intricate that it creates a distinctive plot subtype. In it the hierarchical superior comes to understand that he is defined by his subordinate and that his virtues are the virtues of his subordinate. When a husband describes his honor as residing in his wife, the aspect of himself that he values most is granted by a person other than himself. The patriarchal analogy, moreover, makes the superior believe that superiority in one hierarchical relationship corresponds to and helps create superiority in all. By losing his belief in Desdemona's virtue, for example, Othello loses his sense of himself as a soldier. A man's realization of his dependence on a woman's virtue is especially unsettling when her virtue can be demonstrated only under threat, and then only negatively. The necessity of faith becomes a burden; the loss of faith creates an unassuageable hunger for proof.

In such stories the sexual test begins stereotypically. A husband comes to entertain a gnawing uncertainty about his wife's virtue despite the lack of evidence of her infidelity. He either decides to woo her in disguise or convinces his most trusted friend to perform the test. If he chooses the second course, his friend initially resists but eventually agrees on the grounds of friendship and in the hope of easing the husband's anxiety. The wife refuses the wooer's blandishments, and at this point the story bifurcates. In one version the husband, unable to believe that his wife has resisted, insists that the test continue until she yields; in another version he accuses her and the friend of sexual misconduct. Given the possibilities for mistaken opinion, accusation, blackmail, self-recrimination, repentance, and forgiveness, either response may lead to a comic or a tragic conclusion. Whatever the conclusion, the motive is the husband's loss of faith, which is impossible to restore by evidence because the virtue involved in not doing is not susceptible of definitive proof.

This story is as old as the Greek myth of Cephalus and Procris, rendered most memorably for the English Renaissance in Arthur Golding's translation of Ovid's *Metamorphoses*. Disguised by the power of the goddess Aurora, Cephalus performs his own test and overcomes his wife's resistance. What aberration of the human heart causes such behavior? Ovid's Cephalus is never sure, though he recounts how the insinuation of Aurora coupled with the opportunity provided his wife by his absence grew into a full-blown mental debate about her fidelity:

I gan to dread bad measures lest my wife had made some scape.
Her youthful years begarnished with beauty, grace and shape,
In manner made me to believe the deed already done.
Again her manners did forbid mistrusting over soon.
But I had been away: but even the same from whom I came
A shrewd example gave how lightly wives do run in blame:
But we poor lovers are afraid of all things.

(7.920–8)

The very clumsiness of the fourteeners, with their rhymed closures that conclude nothing, their individualized reasons that turn out to be clichés, the recursively antilogistic "again . . . but . . . but . . . but," which jerks the argument from one side to the other, expresses the muddle between faith and doubt. Arriving home in disguise, Cephalus finds Procris chastely mourning his absence. When he tempts her with gifts and "great assaults" (7.950) she repeatedly turns him aside, urging her marital fidelity. Though he knows that to continue is folly, "I could not be content: / But still to purchase to myself more woe I further went" (7.953–4). Finally he wears her down.

This version, in which the husband acts the tempter, so that in seducing his wife he leaves her both chaste and unchaste and himself both unhorned and cuckolded, has rich psychological potential, but, like the Griselda story, it so concentrates male functions as to be complex to dramatize. The version preferred by Stuart playwrights uses the friend as tempter, relieving the concentration on the central couple and enriching the plot with the theme of friendship under stress. The most influential sources are again nondramatic: Robert Greene's novella *Philomela, or the Lady Fitzwater's Nightingale* (1592), in which the virtuous wife is calumniated, and Cervantes' interpolated tale, "El curioso impertinente," in *Don Quixote*, in which the wife succumbs. Unlike Ovid, Greene and Cervantes exploit a spacious literary form that allows them to debate psychology and ethics at length. The crux, as with Job, is what it means to possess the virtue of another person, a person who is both one's own and not one's own.

Cervantes' Anselmo provides the classic rationale for the test: "I let thee to understand, friend Lothario, that the desire which vexeth me is a longing to know whether my wife Camilla be as good and perfect as I do account her, and I cannot wholly rest satisfied of this truth, but by making trial of her, in such sort as it may give manifest argument of the degree of her goodness, as the fire doth show the value of gold" (326–7). As Anselmo begs his friend to subvert them, ironically he elaborates his wife's virtues: "I will give thee opportunity enough to perform the same, without omitting anything that may further thee in the solicitation of an honest, noble, wary, retired, and passionless woman" (327). Lothario's counterargument stresses not just the danger of the test but also its pointlessness. Not only will any change be a change for the worse; the very fact of desiring the test poisons the pleasure of possession: "Tell me,

Anselmo, if Heaven or thy fortunes had made thee lord and lawful possessor of a most precious diamond, of whose goodness and quality all the lapidaries that had viewed the same would rest satisfied . . . would it be just that thou shouldst take an humour to set that diamond between an anvil and a hammer, and try there by very force of blows whether it be so hard and so fine as they say?" (331).

Cervantes' classic debate between doubting husband and reluctant friend exhibits not just the type psychological issues but the type metaphors. These metaphors are supremely telling. If "proving" in the sense of metallurgical assay is the point of the wife's testing, then Anselmo's recourse to the gold metaphor is to be expected. If she passes the assay, the refiner's fire will prove Camilla as pure, hence as valuable, as he takes her to be. But common as the gold metaphor is, it has its drawbacks. By the seventeenth century it is too closely associated with coinage, with the mercantile, with the public medium of exchange, to be fully expressive of Camilla's virtue or Anselmo's possessiveness. And the hoarder of gold is always tainted with the farcical. Thus Lotharic shifts metaphors: the jewel, especially the diamond, expresses female value and male possessiveness in more socially accurate terms. Though it has nothing inherently female about it, none of the organic attributes that make the rose, say, a "natural" female symbol, the jewel is the most important metaphor for female virtue in Renaissance tested woman stories because of its combination of innate and socially constructed attributes. The jewel's hardness, brilliance, and richness of color promise enduring worth; its small size concentrates great riches; its rareness marks its possessor as singularly fortunate; its desirability makes its possessor wary of theft and its giver surpassingly generous. Not the kind of wealth, like food, that is necessary to sustain life, nor yet like gold the primary medium of commercial exchange, jewels are the prime example of wealth owned for pride of possession. They are to keep; they become heirlooms, are handed down over generations, are often individually identifiable. And they are uniquely adapted to both concealment and display, the forms of which the owner may control to his fancy. A jewel may be left in its original state or it may be polished and cut; it may be unmounted or mounted; it may be hidden away, set into furnishings or utensils, or worn on the body. Wearing a jewel, bestowing a jewel, secreting a jewel—these are symbolic actions in which the jewel as a possession becomes a sign of the owner's relations with other people, and the value that others put on it as a symbol of not just monetary but social wealth creates the desire to show it off or perhaps to hide it.

As a flagrant expression of possession, the jewel metaphor signals the shift of emphasis from the power of virtue as defined by the woman herself to the value assigned her by her possessor and ascribed to by other men, to whom she is "like your diamond, a temptation in every man's eye, yet not yielding to any light impression herself" (*The Atheist's Tragedy*, 1.2.168–9). By its means her power is expressed through the attention and passion she arouses in men.

Even her chastity is a curiously depersonalized symbol for a kind of wealth, often her only wealth, that she both guards and flaunts. Yet when chastity is gone the jewel image remains potent, for a woman's virtue can be construed as whatever power she has to attract a man's possessive longing. "What value is this jewel?" asks Bracciano of Vittoria (*The White Devil*, 1.2.214). The answer is whatever Bracciano will pay, which turns out to be his lust for her lust. At the heart of the metaphor is social complicity. The jewel and the woman are valuable to the possessor as they are valued by others.

Thus the richest version of the story involves the friend. Both Greene and Cervantes begin by stressing the depth, durability, and vigor of the friendship. The husband chooses the friend to test the wife because the friend can be trusted to be secretive and restrained, as well as to enhance the husband's pride of possession by his admiration. But this version of the test puts an even more extraordinary stress on the friendship than on the marriage, so that the breaking of the male bond precedes and causes the breaking of the marriage bond. Cervantes' Lotario eventually finds himself loving Camilla in earnest, and the very fervor of his passion wins her. Greene's Lutesio does not woo in earnest, nor does he win Philomela, but Philippo thinks he does. Philippo's mistrust of his friend brings on accusation, perjury, and the adultery trial.

Ovid, Greene, and Cervantes show the major permutations of the sexual test by the man in possession. When the test goes on the stage, as it did at least a half dozen times between 1605 and 1632, playwrights exploit contrasting or complementary subplots, dramatize the confrontations between husband and wife, and emphasize the men's conflicts. Robert Davenport's *The City Nightcap* (1624), whose main plot is taken from Greene's novella, makes instant, self-mocking capital of its familiarity. The play opens

> *Enter Lorenzo and Philippo*
>
> LORENZO   Thou shalt try her yet once more.
> PHILIPPO   Fie, fie.
> LORENZO   Thou shalt do't.
>   If thou be'st my friend, thou'lt do't.
> PHILIPPO   Try your fair wife?
>   You know 'tis an old point, and wondrous frequent
>   In most of our Italian comedies.
> LORENZO   What do I care for that? Let him seek new ones
>   Cannot make old ones better; and this new point,
>   Young sir, may produce new smooth passages,
>   Transcending those precedent. Pray, will ye do't?
>
>   (1.1; 1–11)[3]

The first scene has all the necessaries in abbreviated form: the husband's ambition to gain glory by improving his possession, his long friendship with a confirmed bachelor, the trial already underway, the wife's initial steadfastness. Chiefly, however, it dramatizes the degree to which the woman's virtue is the provocation. After the friend offers the usual encomium, borrowing heavily from Greene so that the old-fashioned antilogisms and euphuistic comparisons strengthen the impression of revisiting commonplaces, he concludes "And therefore, good my friend, forbear to try / The gold has passed the fire" (1.1; 46–7). But Lorenzo knows what Abstemia's seeming virtue means: "she that is lip-holy, / Is many times heart-hollow" (1.1; 59–60).

Dramatic economy and a well-known plot also allow Davenport to rewrite Greene's ending. For the husband's death in an agony of reconciliation he substitutes a test of the wife's willingness to exchange her chastity for her husband's life. In doing so he manages to suggest that Lorenzo would prefer the certainty of knowing his wife unfaithful to the burden of maintaining his faith. The parallel subplot of the complaisant Lodovico and his wife Dorothea, who is lip-holy to the point of suspicion and completely heart-hollow in the proof, openly explores the possibility. This husband's motto against cuckoldry, *Crede quod habes, & habes* (Believe that you have, and you have), "holds it impossible for any to be a cuckold can believe himself none" (1.2; 320–1), but it is equally applicable once his wife's confession has confirmed her unchastity. Lodovico finds as great a peace in the certainty of his wife's infidelity as he did in the conviction of her chastity, because fornication is an active, sure, and therefore reassuring deed. It is Lorenzo, brought to humility and repentance by his admission that Philippo and Abstemia have not sinned, who retains an uncertainty so great it nearly outlives the play. When Antonio promises him and his wife their freedom from execution for a supposed murder in exchange for Abstemia's sexual favors, the husband finds in his wife's rejection of such dishonor the very proof of her unchastity. To her question "Could you live, / And know your self a cuckold?" Antonio's interjection comes close to exposing Lorenzo's soul: "What a question's that? / Many men cannot live without the knowledge" (5.4; 2356–9). Lorenzo seems close to affirming Antonio's ironic diagnosis: his compulsion is to know—which can only mean to know loss.

Using the friend as tempter allows a plethora of highly wrought psychological states, as, for example, in the subplot of *The Second Maiden's Tragedy*, which comes from "El curioso impertinente" but reworks the end to allow a communal slaughter rather than the lonely deaths of Cervantes' principals. The play's interest lies in such moments of heightened psychological anguish as when the neglected wife, watching from their bedroom window, sees her husband, consumed by doubt, pacing in the moonlight (1.2.98–107). The bitter tone is in part a function of the absence of Cervantes' pitying, moralizing narrator. In the play the moralizing burden is carried by the friend Votarius, who finds the husband's destructive curiosity, his own growing passion for the wife, and his postcoital shame a source of ironic melancholy: "All's gone; there's nothing but the prodigal left. / I have played away my soul at one short game / Where e'en the winner loses" (2.2.1–3). The irony of the friend's position is greatest in the plot twist that brings about the bloody calamity, for Votarius, who has become the husband's surrogate in bed, also becomes his counterpart in causeless jealousy. In the face of his friend's assurances, Anselmus is content to think his wife chaste, but Votarius, seeing the waiting-woman's lover Bellarius skulking about the house and fearing this man's access to the wife, insinuates to Anselmus that she is wavering and drives her to the ploy of staging a mock demonstration of her virtue. As Anselmus eavesdrops on what he takes for a genuine test, his wife, pretending to drive the unwelcome Votarius from her chamber, pricks Votarius with a sword poisoned without her knowledge by Bellarius and kills the man she has come to love. Votarius dies thinking her false to *him*, Anselmus springs from his hiding place to stab the waiting-woman who by her accusation against his wife helped kill his friend, Bellarius attacks Anselmus for killing the waiting-woman, and the wife dies by running on both their swords at once.

Two of the three principals are now dead, but the author has not yet milked the husband's loss of faith for its maximum effect. Wounded by Bellarius, who has called the wife "an honourable whore" (5.1.124), Anselmus refuses to believe the charge, dying with her praise on his lips. When Anselmus's brother enters, and the dying Bellarius rouses himself to describe the events that led to the carnage, however, his account brings Anselmus out of his death swoon to curse his wife's corpse with his (this time truly) dying breath. In emphasis and tone this conclusion is as different from Cervantes' as may be. There the husband dies writing a clear-sighted confession of his own folly at bringing to temptation and ruin the two people he loved most. Here the participants have seen nothing clearly. Votarius dies believing his mistress false, the wife believing her passion reciprocated, Anselmus believing himself victimized. The end first of friendship, then of marriage, then of life itself all stem from his initial act, as Bellarius's succinct summary reminds: "That lord, your brother, made his friend Votarius / To tempt his lady" (5.1.153–4).

The latitude in combining individual elements makes a wide spectrum of tonal effects possible. Nathan Field's *Amends for Ladies* (1611), which combines four examples of tested and triumphant virtue in a seamless romp, builds its main plot from elements of both the Greene and the Cervantes types. The wife is attempted in earnest, stands firm, is calumniated, and finally wins over both friend and spouse. Despite the fact that he has three plots and four examples of female virtue to juggle, or perhaps precisely because of the analogic economies of simultaneous actions, Field manages a sharp critique of male motives and states of mind, including the male rivalry that passes for friendship. The friendship theme can take the plot over, as in Beaumont and Fletcher's *The Coxcomb* (1609), a lighthearted inversion of the "Curioso impertinente" situation in which the husband woos his wife for his friend. Fed up with her husband's follies, Maria eventually invites the friend to her bed, thus fulfilling her wifely obligations: by proving unchaste she has obeyed her husband's will, neatly retaining her virtue by losing it. The unwitting husband ends the play regretting that he has failed to prove himself the paragon of friends.

Given the exposure of male conflict and the dissection of male unworthiness that the plot entails, it is not surprising that the woman occasionally rewrites the denouement, surreptitiously and ambiguously like Maria, or overtly and frankly like James Shirley's Julietta (*Hyde Park* [1632]). The woman Frank Trier tests is his "mistress," to whom he has professed his affections and who considers him her "servant," but to whom he is not formally bound. Nevertheless Trier is sufficiently conscious of his proprietary claim to put his friend, the rake Bonvile, to attempt her, without, however, telling Bonvile of their relationship and in fact introducing her as a "lady of pleasure" (2.3). But Julietta knows she is being tested and insists on the test's continuing until Lord Bonvile has made his proposition and she her refusal. Once the test is completed, she has the grounds for condemning Trier's impertinence, bringing him to understand that he has lost what he already had:

TRIER	Know, lady, I have tried you.
JULIETTA	You have, it seems!
TRIER	And I have found thee right
	And perfect gold, nor will I change thee for
	A crown imperial.
JULIETTA	And I have tried you,
	And found you dross; nor do I love my heart
	So ill, to change it with you.
TRIER	How's this?

(5.2)

The operative point to Julietta's dismissal is her characterization of Trier's motive: "out of fancy," a wanton refusal of faith, he has played a selfish and destructive game. Her response has been not to refuse the time-honored plot but to win it on her own terms by rewriting its reconciliation phase. First she wins the test by refusing Bonvile and the trial by converting Bonvile and using him to convince Trier. Then she turns the plot back on Trier himself, making explicit the fact that the man who engineers the test is the one chiefly tested by it. Having made this point, she quits the game. Henceforth, she says, "I will value myself" (5.2). Julietta knows that the provocation of women's virtue stems from the valuations, boasts, and wagers of men, and she refuses to play. Because this is comedy, the date is late, the audience is upper-class, and Julietta is unmarried, she gives us a sprightly preview of Restoration comedy, where negotiating the sexual contract is the central game.

How the woman values herself is at the root of the test, just as what the men come to learn about themselves is at the root of the trial. Because action on her own behalf is most available to an unattached woman, especially a widow, while exposure of male motives occurs most starkly when the husband performs his own test, George Chapman's *The Widow's Tears* (1605) achieves maximum concentration by having the husband carry out his own test on his apparently widowed wife. The play has two variations on the "widow's bond" story, the wooing of a widow who has vowed to remain faithful to the memory of her dead husband. In the plot dominating the first two acts, the brash Tharsalio courts the rich widow Eudora until she yields to both sex and marriage. A second plot, involving Tharsalio's brother Lysander and his wife Cynthia, takes over the play from act 3. Based on the Widow of Ephesus story (best known from Petronius's *Satyricon)*, it tells of a widow who entombs herself with her husband's body until seduced by a sentry guarding some crucified thieves. Chapman has used a number of details from Petronius: Cynthia's hair-tearing and face-scratching grief over her dead husband; her five days' immurement in the tomb in the company of her maid; the seductive visit of the sentry with his food, wine, and sexual nourishment; the theft of a corpse from the cross in his absence; and the widow's willingness to save him from execution for negligence by substituting her husband's body.

Despite such details, the substance of Chapman's story is radically different. Petronius tells of a woman whose widowhood has left her free to please herself extravagantly through both her mourning and her new attachment, emphasizing "the incongruity of human intention and human deed" that Cyrus Hoy sees as the essence of comedy.[4] But Chapman tells the story of a wife tested by her husband to their mutual discomfiture. Stimulated to doubt his wife by his brother's insinuations and Cynthia's scorn of Eudora's capitulation, Lysander feigns his own death at the hands of highwaymen, wagering with Tharsalio that Cynthia will not keep her vow to remain faithful to his memory. When she and her maid accompany the coffin into the tomb to mourn, fast, and die, Lysander, unbeknownst to his brother, assumes the disguise of a corpse-guarding soldier, offers the women food, and at last makes love to his revived and compliant wife.

The play's climax, one of the most sophisticated and intricately designed sequences in Stuart drama,[5] creates a series of ironic recognitions. Visiting the tomb, Tharsalio finds Cynthia in the arms of the soldier, considers his bet won, and goes off to punish the soldier by removing a crucified corpse. The disguised Lysander, unable to leave the tomb because of a search party, explains his danger, and Cynthia volunteers her husband's corpse despite the sentry's claim that it was he who killed her husband. When Lysander does leave the tomb for a tool to open the coffin, has ripped off his disguise, and is inveighing against the faithlessness of women, Tharsalio enters singing the praises of the grief-stricken Cynthia. Lysander asks if there has not been a soldier succoring her; upon his departure Tharsalio realizes that his brother must have been the sentry and warns Cynthia, leaving her to make the best of it. While Tharsalio is replacing the crucified body, Lysander returns to take up his disguise, promising himself that if Cynthia opens the coffin he will kill her.

Cynthia carries the action as far as a scuffle over the crowbar before turning on Lysander as a

CYNTHIA	transform'd monster;
	Who to assure himself of what he knew,
	Hath lost the shape of man.
LYSANDER	Ha? Cross-capers?
CYNTHIA	Poor soldier's case; do not we know you sir?
	But I have given thee what thou cam'st to seek . . . .
	Farewell; I leave thee there my husband's corpse,
	Make much of that.
	. . . .
LYSANDER	What have I done?
	O let me lie and grieve, and speak no more.

(5.5.78–82, 85–7)

The scene is not over, for the characters assemble for a judicial process under an asinine governor that collapses with the discovery that there has been no murder and that the thief's body is back on the cross. Eudora and Tharsalio patch up a peace between Cynthia and Lysander, and the one remaining question, at what point the wife recognized her husband, is never asked, for the governor is too befuddled to put it and Lysander has lost both inclination and authority. Tharsalio's closing speech addresses one message to him, quite another to the witting wife and audience: "So; brother, let your lips compound the strife, / And think you have the only constant wife" (5.5.291–2).

Though it invites cynicism, the play's denouement is protective. Under the witting eye of the audience, both Cynthia and Lysander end up better than they deserve, learning their lessons without the misery of revelation. Lysander learns the folly of testing his wife without discovering that she was false. Cynthia learns to know her own weakness without having her reputation destroyed or her chastity physically impaired. At the play's end the self-righteous cant of the opening acts is gone. Whatever else this pair may know, their silence tells us that to their chagrin they know themselves.

Though the play satirizes the pretensions of lip-holy women, the denouement also takes us back to admire the economy with which it explores the provocation of virtue and exposes the figure of the tester. The provocation proceeds in waves, acting first on Eudora and Tharsalio, then on Cynthia, and finally on Lysander. Stimulated not only by Eudora's wealth but by her vaunted intention to remain a chaste widow, Tharsalio successfully woos her first to his bed, then to the altar. No disease here, only gusty laughter at the desires of the flesh and the opportunities of an independent woman to please herself. Provoked by Eudora's capitulation, Cynthia's expressions of contempt and of confidence in her own superior self-control expose the self-serving competition behind the veneer of virtue. If there is disease here, it is relatively benign; Cynthia is silly and tiresome, not destructive. But Lysander's response to Cynthia's vauntings must harm them all. By pretending his own death and turning Cynthia into a putative widow, Lysander criminally changes her status and thus her legal and moral obligations. By then taking on the role of seducer, he stages their mutual dishonor. Though Cynthia's scathing attack on her husband is self-protective, it is also accurate. His attempt to improve possession, to assure himself of what he already knows, makes a monster.

SEVEN

Living in the King's Two Bodies

IN THE OPENING SCENE OF WILLIAM DAVENANT'S *FAIR FAVORITE* (1638), the young king, who has just been welcomed home from a triumphant military campaign and should find himself at the pitch of contentment, turns introspectively savage about the "monstrous state" of kingship. Why "monstrous"? "What am I else, that still beneath / Two bodies groan, the natural and the politic, / By force compounded of most different things?" (1.1).[1] The king is in a romantic predicament. Recently married to one woman for reasons of state, he loves another. His politic body must be satisfied with a woman he disdains, while his natural body longs for a woman who refuses to become his whore. The trope in which he describes his quandary seems all too fleshly, but its medieval and Renaissance use is broad, including legal concepts about social organization. The same metaphor is still active in the terms "corporate" and "corporation." In his study of the political theology of the metaphor, Ernst H. Kantorowicz traces a strand in one of the great paradigm shifts of the early modern period, the growth of an impersonal state out of social organizations based on personal relationships. The concept held that the king was both "a mortal being, and yet immortal with regard to his Dignity and his Body politic."[2] The trope of the king's two bodies became a centerpiece of the Renaissance ideology of kingship, predicating both the private, mortal, erring, natural body and the public, immortal, infallible, politic body. As a legal formulation, the concept attempted to distinguish the continuing obligations and prerogatives of the state from the literal lifespan of its sovereign. As a political formulation, it attempted to account for the obvious incompatibility between the wisdom, virtue, and power claimed for the king as sovereign and the fallibility and weakness evident in his private person.[3] To divine right theorists, the concept enriched the analogy of king to God by giving the king a Christlike duality of nature.[4] To dramatists in totalitarian times, the metaphor allowed some scope for portraying kings realistically and even the opportunity to explore competing political ideas.

The political and legal invention of the king's two bodies was designed to unify his roles, increase his power, and enhance political continuity. In the mouth of the human being who lived its ambiguities, it just as often expressed division. In *Basilikon Doron* James I used the trope to describe the burdens as well as the glories of kingly office.[5] Among kings in plays it underlies Richard of Bordeaux's fluctuation between his role as the Lord's anointed and his understanding of himself as mere "subjected" man (*Richard II*, 3.2.176).[6] It causes Harry of Monmouth's restless passage through the camp the night before St. Crispin's Day and his almost despairing contention that, "his ceremonies laid by, in his nakedness [the king] appears but a man" (*Henry V*, 4.1.104–5). "They told me I was everything," says Lear; " 'Tis a lie" (4.6.104). We expect the trope in these political plays and in propaganda like *Basilikon Doron*. It is less expected in *The Fair Favorite*, so predictable a romantic tragicomedy that Davenant could have entitled it *Love and Honor* had he not used up that title on another play. Yet the concept of the king's two bodies is at home in the tested woman plot, which has the tools to dismember the sovereign's functions.

WHAT MUST THE KING DO?

The Fair Favorite is about governing the kingdom by governing the king, and there are no easy villains to deflect the burdens of choice. The king loved Eumena, but considerations of state led to her being locked away and declared dead while a politic marriage with a neighboring princess was promoted. The wedding once performed, Eumena was revealed to be alive. Refusing to consummate his marriage, the king longs for Eumena, who honors him, pities him, and refuses him either body or vow. The queen also loves him and pities her unwilling rival, who in turn feels only sorrow and respect for the queen. The situation is exacerbated by the accusation of Eumena's brother Oramont that his sister cannot have become court favorite in exchange for nothing, and by the defense of Oramont's friend Amadore, who credits Eumena's chastity and wins her love. Through all and to all the queen responds with such dignity and selflessness that the king comes to honor and love her. He agrees to consummate his own marriage and forward that of Eumena, bringing peace to Oramont through the alliance of honorable friend with honest sister.

Circumstances have demanded that the king learn to find his natural satisfaction in his political marriage or bring catastrophe upon the kingdom. Finally faced with the choice between his marriage and the divorce urged on him by sycophantic counselors, he decides in favor of politic virtues and against the body natural: "How accursed would subjects be, were we / Not born with far more virtue than we are taught? / I'll make my function loved, and rather die, / Than owe my life to such a remedy" (5.1). He does not mean to be self-denying or ascetic, but to reeducate himself. "I'll make my function loved" means "I will learn to love my function as king," thus unifying political and sexual roles. The alternative would be tragedy.

The Fair Favorite follows fifty years' refinement of English drama's analogical shorthand. The question, What must the king do now? is the one Richard II both asks and plays at answering in his descent from the walls of Flint Castle. By the time of Caroline drama the question is increasingly asked in plays whose conflict seems primarily sexual. Modern readers tend to view these plays as less concerned with kingship and governance than are the war-and-alliance plots of Shakespeare's chronicle plays. The increasing popularity of plays with familial and sexual themes, and the virtual disappearance of chronicle plays, has been interpreted as a symptom of Jacobean aesthetic decadence, but I see it as part of the protective ideological shorthand of the times. Chronicle plays were artistically old-fashioned in Stuart England partly because they were dangerous. Plays about sexual politics were superficially safer because women were not yet in a position to openly threaten a patriarchal society. But something else is also at work in this change of dramatic fashion. In an age of increasing royal absolutism challenged by revolutionary notions about individual worth, the seventeenth century had a sense that the essence of government lay not in dynastic struggle but in the relationship between sovereign and individual subject. In a patriarchalist social argument, the hierarchical relationship between individual and individual is fundamental in all analogical realms—civil, religious, and familial. When the Stuart playwrights Middleton and Ford return to the dynastic conflicts of the English crown, they stress the tension between the functions of a king and the analogical functions of a man in a patriarchal culture.

Comparing the king's conduct in love with his conduct in affairs of state was hardly new to English drama. Henry V woos an acquiescent Katherine of France to demonstrate a prowess as politically significant as his leadership at Agincourt. But Katherine is destined for Henry. When the tested woman plot is used, it introduces the king's courtship of a woman in some way unavailable. In such a plot his courtship comes to stand for any exercise of royal power in which the king's will to possess clashes directly with the claims of other men. Here the king performs as a man not just in his sexual relationship to a woman but also in his attempt to take the patriarchal place of another.

The rivalry is already displayed in John Lyly's *Campaspe* (1584). As Peter Saccio argues, *Campaspe* is about "being Alexander," learning to distinguish the role of king from the other roles he has experienced or is tempted by.[7] Alexander makes some of these distinctions with ease and grace, acknowledging his war captive Timoclea's valor and virtue, the philosopher Diogenes' metaphysical and ethical mastery, the painter Apelles' technical superiority and tutelage. But his sexual role is more complex, and distinguishing it from other acts of kingship is more difficult. When Alexander first announces his love for Campaspe, his friend Hephestion raises two questions: Is the soft sentiment of romantic love appropriate for a military commander? Is love for this woman, a lowborn captive, appropriate for a king? If Lyly had been interested only in considering love's effects on kings, these questions would have been enough to make his play. But ethically the plot thickens when it becomes clear that Campaspe is unwilling to be Alexander's concubine. Her status may be lower than Timoclea's, but she has every bit as much virtue. And politically the plot thickens when Campaspe and Apelles fall in love. Now we have the tested woman plot, for to gain Campaspe Alexander would have to force her, thus violating the rights of the man to whom she has committed herself.

Apelles, in the process of falling in love, highlights the competition: "But, alas, she is the paramour to a prince: Alexander, the monarch of the earth, hath both her body and affection. For what is it that kings cannot obtain by prayers, threats and promises?" (3.5.31–3). Even when assured of Campaspe's love, Apelles knows the magnitude of his audacity: "Now, Apelles, gather thy wits together. . . . It is no small matter to be rival with Alexander" (4.5.1, 4). Yet Apelles is not put off by this rivalry. In his artistic sphere he commands powers that the king will never have; as the favored suitor of Campaspe he commands a position not even a king can honorably take from him.

Campaspe's sense of the threat is stronger. She knows what it means for a lowborn woman to catch the king's eye. Yet despite his declaration to Hephestion that as a king he loves with a greater fervor than ordinary men and "therefore must obtain" (2.2.113), Alexander's sense of the obligations of kingship eventually subdues his sexual longing. His self-control is possible because he has a proxy for sexual possession. By conquest Campaspe's person, if not her will, is already his, so he can overcome his sexual desire by playing the surrogate father, giving her to Apelles rather than keeping her for himself. Lyly directs our attention to the shift in the possessive act. In admonishing his rival, the king sounds like a fond parent overtaken by the young folks' ardor: "Methinks I might have been made privy to your affection; though my counsel had not been necessary, yet my countenance might have been thought requisite. But Apelles forsooth loveth under hand, yea and under Alexander's nose, and—but I say no more" (5.4.108–12). Having mastered his jealousy and brought the lovers together, he makes the match. He knows what he has accomplished—"How now, Hephestion, is Alexander able to resist love as he list?" So does his friend: "The conquering of Thebes was not so honourable as the subduing of these thoughts" (5.4.164–7). Like Davenant's king, Alexander's way out of his predicament is to learn to love his function as king. He is in a position to give because he already possesses, and he chooses social health, that is, comedy.

Making the king the tempter in the tested woman plot forces a comparison of his patriarchal prerogatives with the prerogatives of other males. When the woman is single, the king's power opens the role of parental or marital surrogate. But when a king sues to a married woman, he cannot sublimate his sexual desire by adopting another patriarchal role. If the woman yields, plot interest shifts to the wronged husband, but if she holds firm, the play throws the burden of moral choice on the tempter/king. We see the difference in two similarly titled Elizabethan chronicle plays. *Edward IV Parts 1 and*

2, probably by Thomas Heywood and probably written in 1599, has as its central action the capitulation of Matthew Shore's wife Jane to Edward's sexual importunities, an historical event popularized by inclusion in later editions of *The Mirror for Magistrates*. Because the king succeeds with Jane, the play places the burden of moral response on the husband. Though part 1 shows Edward acting the charming tyrant over the affections of his people—Hob the Tanner, the military officers of whom Matthew Shore is one, Jane herself—part 2 concentrates on the domestic agonies of the Shores, to which Edward's death and the rise of Richard III is subordinated.

In the anonymous *Edward III* (1590), because the wife holds firm, the focus is on Edward's testing and education. It is customary to see this play as broken-backed, for acts 1 and 2 portray Edward's attempted seduction of the wife of one of his peers, while acts 3 through 5 portray the wars in France and the blooding of the Black Prince. But the play is not about first love, then war. It is about obligation, what the king (and others) must do, and the sexual action economically lays out the issues of hierarchy, loyalty, and oath that the war sections expand on.[8]

Edward's attempt on his hostess the countess of Salisbury is made by means of moral blackmail. When she responds to his moping by swearing to relieve his melancholy, he calls in her promise: "Didst thou not swear to give me what I would?" (2.1; 578). But she cannot be divided: "That love you beg of me I cannot give, / For Sara owes that duty to her Lord" (2.1; 588–9). Since marriage has transferred the sexuality that was once her father's property to her husband, she speaks fact when she tells the king that what he seeks is not hers to give. So the king tries the same ploy on her father; having sworn, even to the loss of his honor, to assuage the king's unspecified malaise, Warwick is asked to woo his daughter for his king. Warwick passes the king's words and his own urgings on to his daughter. But he stresses that although it is his duty to persuade, it is not her honesty to consent. By refusing to address her as either child or wife, he avoids violating his obligations as father and as husband's friend. The countess rejects the proposition, loathing the unnaturalness of being besieged by her natural defender, and her father rejoices in her steadfastness.

By raising the question of the oath, the play has set individual integrity against political power. The obligation of the oath is grounded in the relations between the bound pairs—God and Christian, husband and wife, father and child, king and subject. Using an oath to break an oath means enforcing the primacy of one relationship over another. The king seeks to reconfigure the analogical web into a single hierarchy in which royal power always takes precedence. In act 4 the play returns to the same point, but with a different king in a different setting. Salisbury has been given a safe-conduct by the French prince Charles, but during his passage through the French army he is brought before Charles's father, King John, who orders him hanged. The prince argues that the safe-conduct must be honored because it represents his good faith. King John counters by appealing to an absolute and linear hierarchy that would set his power above all other relationships. Moreover, he tries to foist on his son the Tarquinian argument put to a woman faced with rape—if you are forced, you are not responsible. Fortunately for both right and the English, Charles's insistence on his own faith in the face of the French king's absolutism saves Salisbury's life, just as the countess of Salisbury's insistence in the face of her king's absolutism saved Salisbury's marital honor.

FINDING THE FATHER

The king who overcomes his longing for an inappropriate woman by asserting the primacy of the political body over the natural body does so by a functional sublimation. Nevertheless, in playing the priest, the judge, the father, or the brother, he reminds himself that the analogy between kings and other patriarchal figures does not constitute literal fact. Though he may exercise some of the powers of those analogical roles, there are others he may not perform. The lesson is most dramatic in its sexual form because the relationship between husband and wife includes an act the king as man is physically capable of performing but as non-husband is morally and legally forbidden. The blocking of the king's sexual will and its expression in other patriarchal acts delimits the kingly role. The king learns what he is by having to confront in his body what he may not do.

Yet a man may legitimately occupy more than one patriarchal role at once, for unlike the biological fact of fatherhood or brotherhood the roles of husband, king, priest, and magistrate are social analogues only. A man may be both father or brother and king, which gives him a double set of responsibilities and powers sometimes difficult to distinguish. In a hereditary system of kingship based on the male line, where kingship is dependent on fatherhood, it is possible to take the conflation for granted. But biological and social roles are not the same, though they are lived in the same body. How can they be uncoupled? What happens to the king, and the kingdom, if they are?

King Lear explores a version in which the king unkings himself as the first move in a tested woman plot that scrutinizes the relationship of daughters to a mere father. But since Lear has been king, the uncoupling cannot be definitive. There are other versions of this ambiguity, such as the story of a claimant or an impostor. In Beaumont and Fletcher's *King and No King* (1611), Arbaces turns out not to be the hereditary king, though he has occupied the throne since birth. To protect Arbaces' interests while maneuvering his supposed sister Panthea to her rightful place on the throne, Gobrius, the lord protector, engineers a seemingly incestuous passion between them. Once Arbaces has been driven by frustration toward murder, rape, and suicide, Gobrius reveals that Arbaces is no king, that Panthea is the queen, and that the two are not related. In an ecstasy of relief Arbaces gives up his throne to Panthea and begs for her hand, which she gives with equal relief and delight.

Here is a play that deepens the psychological and political issues behind the question of what the king must do by linking them to the heredity of the natural body.

At *A King and No King*'s center is a tested woman story that uses supposed incest to make sexual interest inappropriate. Fictional incest has a particular dramatic use: unlike the prohibition against adultery, which only death or sexual sublimation can resolve, Arbaces' and Panthea's obstacle can be removed by revelation and recognition. Fictional incest has a genre-linked use, to make comedy.[9] But it is also useful because by doubling roles it increases dramatic tension. Usually the king gets himself out of the position of seducer of an unmarried woman by playing the father or the brother in a giving away that eases his sexual frustration. In this play, however, playing the brother is no relief; it is the block, not the release.

Beaumont and Fletcher set up the giving away action even before the full development of the seduction action to capitalize on the dramatic fact that giving away is as impossible as consummation. The play opens on Arbaces, victorious in Armenia after an extended war that has kept him away from Iberia and his sister since they were children. Determined to be as generous in peace as he was triumphant in war, he hauls the captive king of Armenia home in silken bonds to be his sister's husband. The presentation sequence of act 3, scene 1, whose purpose should be to introduce Tigranes to Panthea and foster their mutual love, becomes, however, the occasion on which the king meets his sister and is overwhelmed by sexual desire. So at the moment when Arbaces first struggles against the horrors of incest, he also reacts in jealous fury to Tigranes' developing interest in Panthea.

In the magnificently orchestrated presentation scene, the conflict between the roles of brother and husband is dramatized in dialogue, stage movement, and event sequence. Arbaces first disclaims Panthea's kinship to him, then when Tigranes moves to court her, Arbaces claims her back. The scene ends with the king pleading to her for forgiveness:

> You did kneel to me
> Whilst I stood stubborn and regardless by
> And, like a god incensed, gave no ear
> To all your prayers. Behold, I kneel to you.
> (3.1.281–4)

Though they intend to pledge only their familial devotion, when Arbaces seals his brotherly love with a kiss, he follows it with another, and yet another. Again he comes to his senses, orders Panthea locked up to protect her from him, and ends the scene exhausted and desperate, begging the gods not to punish him with the "unmanly" sin of incest (3.1.334).

This scene shows the king ricocheting between godlike arrogance and the utter debility brought about by loss of control over any of his patriarchal functions. Yet his moral agony is framed and caused by the greater conflict between parent and child. In Armenia his trauma sprang from his mother's attempts to have him assassinated. The presentation scene started with Arane kneeling to her son to request forgiveness for her pursuit of his life. The unnaturalness of her assault prepares for the unnatural sentiment of incest. But Arane's penance before her son is no more health-giving than Arbaces' before his sister. Though Arbaces has tried to be a father to his kingdom, his gestures to his enemy, his courtiers, his people, his family continually misfire. It is the family itself that is built on lies, for the mother is not mother nor the sister sister, and the unnatural acts that torment Arbaces stem from natural causes. The real father is Gobrius, the lord protector, who married Arane at the old king's death, managed Iberia in Arbaces' absence, kept Arane from succeeding in her murderous schemes, encouraged Arbaces' and Panthea's attachment, and discouraged the prospect of the princess's marriage to Tigranes. Hints assure us of Gobrius's involvement, and Arbaces' bluff confidant Mardonius assures both the king and us of Gobrius's virtue. When Arbaces can do no more against his lust and, bent on rape and suicide, aims his sword first at the old man who has goaded him into his unnatural plight, Gobrius knows the scheme is ripe. Admitting he tantalized the absent king with descriptions of Panthea's "witching" beauty, he administers the first check to the king's frenzy: "Sir, you shall know your sins before you do 'em. / If you kill me— . . . Know / You kill your father" (5.4.116–8).

Gobrius is indeed Arbaces' father, but he has not whored Arbaces' mother. The story finally comes out. The former king had been old and incapable of giving Arane the child she longed for. Desperate for the position and dynastic assurance that a child would bring her, she pretended to be pregnant. When Gobrius and his first wife produced a son, Arane persuaded Gobrius to give her the baby with the promise that the child would be raised as the king's heir, and Arbaces became the crown prince. When the old king died six years later, however, he left his wife truly pregnant with Panthea. Arane has endeavored to maneuver her daughter onto the throne, while Gobrius, though desirous that the princess should enjoy her own, has tried just as earnestly to protect his son's interests. His scheme has been to encourage Arbaces' sexual interest in Panthea to the point that, when revelation becomes inevitable, the hotheaded king will gladly embrace the loss of his throne in exchange for the wife of his choice. But Arbaces must welcome the change in his status or the kingdom will explode in civil war. Cautiously Gobrius creeps up on the truth until Arbaces finally understands "the happiest news / That e'er was heard. . . . Panthea is the queen, / And I am plain Arbaces" (5.4.265–6; 269–70). The ensuing explosion is one of pure joy. Tigranes has returned penitent to his betrothed, Gobrius and Arane have brought their contrary interests to common fruition, and Arbaces and Panthea will marry. Arbaces ends the play jubilant: "Come everyone / That takes delight in goodness; help to sing / Loud thanks for me, that I am prov'd no king" (5.4.351–3).

The underlying failures and triumphs of the action in *A King and No King* are the failures and triumphs of paternity. Even before the play began, the old king's impotence and his last generative spasm shaped events. Gobrius's renunciation of *his* paternity complicated the royal inheritance. Now Gobrius's attempt to reconcile his paternity with that of the old king makes the play. The attempt to reconcile familial with political hierarchies is seen over and over in physical expressions of superiority and subordination like the gesture that announces Arbaces' true paternity. Having proclaimed himself "plain Arbaces," he asks his courtiers to put on their hats:

MARDONIUS	We will, but you are not found
	So mean a man but that you may be cover'd
	As well as we, may you not?
ARBACES	Oh, not here;
	You may but not I, for here is my father
	In presence.
MARDONIUS	Where?
ARBACES	Why, there.

(5.4.282–6)

Being "in the presence" no longer means being in the presence of the king, but of the father.

This "here/where?/there" sequence echoes the presentation scene, when Arbaces refused to identify his sister. His pleased humility shows us a man at peace with himself and his functions. Knowing who he is, he knows at last what he is and how he must behave. The revelation that he has a father to whom he owes life and honor and a wife only through whom he will again be king makes him a whole man. Mardonius sardonically remarks on the gain— "Indeed, 'twere well for you / If you might be a little less obey'd" (5.4.265–6). The deftness of the play's dramaturgy is demonstrated in the way Gobrius's scheme arises from Arbaces' psychological makeup. The first two acts take pains to establish how greatly his winner-take-all victory over Tigranes in single combat has reenforced his headstrong sense of himself as lord of the earth. Were it not for his wit, honesty, valor, and generosity, he would be insufferable, as Mardonius tells him to his face (1.1.338–78). Yet his lack of temperance hampers his ability to govern himself or others. To unking such a man is a hazardous undertaking requiring Gobrius's utmost ingenuity. The lord protector—dramatist and impresario—uses a tested woman as his bait, basing his entire hope for this political coup on his gamble that Panthea, by holding firm against Arbaces' pleas and threats, will bring the king to his lure.

The play is Renaissance drama new style, its ideological explorations carried on not in set speeches but in its dramaturgy. These characters do not debate the nature of kingship. Instead they live the slippery, tension-filled lives of a court at the mercy of a mercurial king. Yet in its entirety the plot makes a strongly ideological point. Arbaces' royal role, which gives scope to his great natural gifts, is an accident of birth and nonbirth. All his roles are gifts, or accidents, of which parenthood may be the greatest accident of all. Because this is no chronicle play—Iberia at war with Armenia situates us in romance—its exposé of the arrogance and accidents of kingship can capitalize on a convoluted plot that takes politically alarming turns. The convolutions are entertaining, but Gobrius's control of the plot is a plot indeed, meant to center Arbaces so firmly in the desires of the body natural that the pleasures of power pale in comparison. If his natural desire were sexual only, the play would have nothing like the power it does. But Arbaces' desire for parents is as potent, and if he loses a mother whose unmotherly behavior has haunted his life, he gains a father. We must understand what Arbaces understands: gaining Gobrius as his father equals losing his throne. Thanks to the father's wisdom and skill, it is an exchange in which the son finds joy.

ACTING THE KING

Unlike *A King and No King*, which uses the tested woman plot to exacerbate the king's contradictions almost beyond reprieve without expending energy on a consideration of marriage, in Ford's *Perkin Warbeck* (1634), the marital role is at the heart of the play. A powerful throwback to the Elizabethan chronicle play about Henry VII's consolidation of Tudor rule, *Perkin Warbeck* is not about who ought to be England's monarch, despite occasional attempts to read it so.[10] Ford's portrayal of the impostor who, with the blessing of Margaret of Burgundy, sister of two Yorkist kings, presented himself to Europe as heir to the English throne does not debate Perkin's genealogy. The verdict of history, embodied in the capacities of the play's Henry Tudor and 150 years of English history free of dynastic upheavals, makes Ford's framework. His focus is not on who England's king should be but on what it means to act like a king.

Ford shows his purpose in his dedicatory letter to William Cavendish, earl of Newcastle, where the inevitable praise for a patron is couched in far from inevitable terms. "Eminent titles," Ford writes, "may indeed inform who their owners are, not often what." By definition Newcastle has eminence of title. Against this fact Ford balances his patron's "known ability in examining" and "knowledge in determining, the monuments of time." By praising in Newcastle the coupling of the *what* with the *who* of eminence, Ford points toward the ideally balanced figure in whom the dignity of the position is complemented by the capacities of the man. The *what* of eminence is his theme.

The play portrays Perkin Warbeck as a cultivated figure of unflaggingly regal comportment,[11] a presentation contrary to Tudor historians' partisan descriptions of the man, the reports of Henry VII's court in the play's opening scenes, and presumably the expectations of a Renaissance audience about the character of an impostor.[12] Though Warbeck's followers are tradesmen and small-time politicians, their leader is a gentleman whose "brave aspect" and "goodl[y] carriage" (2.1.116) win him the respect and pity of noble folk. The chief manifestation of his alleged royalty is language. "He must be more than subject, who can utter / The language of a king, and such is thine" (2.1.103–4), says the Scottish King James IV, embracing Warbeck's person and cause. "If we tried to imagine for ourselves how an unfortunate young prince with such a history might sound," remarks Jonas Barish, "we could hardly improve on what Ford has provided" (160). Even King Henry, meeting the captured Warbeck, praises him as "an ornament of nature, fine and polish'd / A handsome youth indeed" (5.2.38–9).

The play is replete with reminders of the histrionic element in what we see or read. The dedicatory letter draws the distinction between history "discours'd" by historians, and actors themselves discoursing; the prologue reminds that *Perkin Warbeck* is "history couch'd in a play"; Henry remarks that the captured Warbeck is always a player—"'tis his part; / 'A does but act" (5.2.68–9). When the ladies of James's court comment from the upper stage on Warbeck's presentation below (2.1), when Warbeck's followers plan and perform a celebratory masque of "scotch antics" and "wild Irish" whose burlesque crudities mirror their condition (2.3 and 3.2), and when Warbeck's placement in the stocks gives him a martyr's stage from which to perform (5.3), the staging emphasizes the play's theatricality.

For almost every comment on Warbeck's royal language and manner there is an admonitory counterpoint. Crawford marvels at Warbeck's reception in the Scottish court created by the "argument of fine imposture" (2.3.2). Daliell marvels at Warbeck's confidence with women: " 'A courts the ladies / As if his strength of language chain'd attention / By power of prerogative" (2.3.6–8). To James's presentation of Warbeck as "Plantagenet undoubted," Huntley responds aside: "Ho, brave youth, / But no Plantagenet by'r Lady yet, / By red rose or by white" (2.3.73–6). Henry the master king undercuts in the same way: "I behold, 'tis true, / An ornament of nature . . . ," he admits, "but not admire him" (5.2.37, 39). This counterpoint does not necessarily represent truth either, but it does increase our histrionic sensitivity. What does speaking the language of a king mean? An actor does just that, as these actors personating Warbeck and James and Henry are doing. If an actor can personate a king, what relation is there between the manner and the fact of royalty?

The play never directly pronounces on Warbeck's claims, omitting the confession of imposture that preceded the historical Warbeck's death. But when James asks for proof of his royal antecedents (2.1.81–4), Warbeck produces none. What he does produce is a fine speech explaining why he will not provide evidence, and the king succumbs to its language. In the struggle against Henry, Warbeck is outmaneuvered at every turn by the de facto king, a failure that must diminish his royal claims. Faced with crisis after crisis, he never manages to *do* anything. His customary note is patience in adversity, acceptance under fire, dignity in defeat. Yet though Warbeck the political and military leader is routed by Henry, Warbeck the player king is not. Ford maintains to the last our sense of Warbeck's kingliness. How does Ford maintain this image in the face of increasingly hollow claims and disastrous consequences? Through language. But language must be *about* something, and as Warbeck's political and military pretensions fade, their place is taken by an increasing emphasis on his analogous role as husband. The play's architecture establishes the importance of Warbeck's marriage to James's cousin Katherine, for the king gives her to Warbeck as the token of his political support, a gesture that raises the pretender to the high point of his fortunes in the face of her father's vociferous objections.

But is Katherine herself forced? She speaks for herself in the matter only twice. At Warbeck's presentation at court, she responds to the king's summons in characteristically obliging fashion: "The duke / Must then be entertain'd, the king obey'd. / It is our duty" (2.1.122–4). When, with James's approbation, Warbeck asks for her hand, she accepts in the same tone: "Where my obedience is, my lord, a duty, / Love owes true service" (2.3.84–5). Duty, obedience, and service—these are Katherine's character. Their expression is her function in the play.

James's action brings an odd twist to the role of kingly suitor. In playing the surrogate father, he has not only used his patriarchal position to override the actual father's, but has also used the marriage to certify Warbeck's royalty. If Warbeck is a suitable husband for Katherine, he must be a legitimate claimant to the English throne. James makes this point himself: "The Welsh Harry henceforth, / Shall therefore know, and tremble to acknowledge, / That not the painted idol of his policy / Shall fright the lawful owner from a kingdom" (2.3.62–5). But before long James withdraws his support for Warbeck's political claims. Then the question becomes what position the marriage confers in its own right.

Ford has managed a subtle double use of the tested woman, for his variation on the king's courtship of an inappropriate woman sets up the testing of the faithful wife. Once married, Katherine never deviates from her wifely loyalty to Warbeck. In her first extended speech after her marriage, she responds to Warbeck's celebration of his marital and political hopes with a pledge of her constancy (3.2.163–7). When next we see her, James is saving his political neck by reneging on his promises, stripping Warbeck of all his support and gifts— except the lady. Again Katherine declares her marital loyalty: "I am your wife; / No human power can or shall divorce / My faith from duty" (4.3.101–3). Landed on the coast of Cornwall in an effort to recoup his fortune, Warbeck turns to his wife for the loyalty he has come to expect and receives it in full measure (4.5.11–4). Never does Katherine express her opinion of Warbeck's dynastic legitimacy; Warbeck is her lord because he is her husband. That claim becomes more insistent as his fortunes wane. When his military hopes have collapsed and he has fled, Katherine, though free to return to Scotland, submits patiently to a genteel captivity at Henry's hands. At the play's end, with

Warbeck displayed in the stocks before the horror of his execution, she seeks him out to pay homage—not to her king, but to her husband. The English lords find her devotion to a publicly proclaimed traitor scandalous, but when Oxford tries to separate the two he is rebuked in ringing terms:

> OXFORD   Remember, lady, who you are; come from
> That impudent imposter.
> KATHERINE   You abuse us;
> For when the holy churchman join'd our hands,
> Our vows were real then; the ceremony
> Was not in apparition, but in act.—
> Be what these people term thee, I am certain
> Thou art my husband. No divorce in heaven
> Has been sued out between us; 'tis injustice
> For any earthly power to divide us.
>
> (5.3.111–9)

Thus Katherine earns the accolades that place her in the pantheon of triumphantly devoted women. "Great miracle of constancy!" her husband calls her (5.3.89), and her father, even while recalling his distaste for her marriage, rejoices in her conduct as a wife: "I glory in thy constancy / And must not say I wish that I had miss'd / Some partage in these trials of a patience" (5.3.163–5).

Warbeck's marital claims stand in striking contrast to his political ones. The marriage has the de jure legitimacy of a legal contract, and Katherine's loyalty gives it a de facto legitimacy as well. Warbeck's sovereignty is increasingly by analogy as, less and less the potential king of England, he is more and more the king of Katherine. Warbeck makes this metaphoric transfer between roles in his initial address to Katherine:

> An union this way
> Settles possession in a monarchy
> Establish'd rightly, as is my inheritance.
> Acknowledge me but sovereign of this kingdom,
> Your heart, fair princess, and the hand of providence
> Shall crown you queen of me and my best fortunes.
>
> (2.3.78–83)

Katherine's farewell before the Scottish campaign uses the same language: "You must be king of me, and my poor heart / Is all I can call mine" (3.2.68–9). The final parting at the stocks marks Warbeck's apotheosis as husband and therefore a type of king: "Even when I fell, I stood enthron'd a monarch / Of one chaste wife's troth, pure and uncorrupted" (5.3.126–7). The play's glorification of Katherine's constancy,[13] which enriches her "poor heart" to the status of a precious kingdom, is largely responsible for enhancing her lord's status. Accompanied by more than a whiff of Christological language in Warbeck's preparation for martyrdom,[14] the marital analogy to kingship allows Warbeck to claim a kind of victory over the man he would displace: "Harry Richmond, / A woman's faith has robb'd thy fame of triumph!" (5.3.101–2).

Being husband is Warbeck's most substantial and enduring means of playing the king. Katherine's response is crucial because the role of husband, like that of king, is absolutely dependent on its hierarchical subordinate. A king must have both a demonstrable legal claim and his people's support. So must a husband. There must be both a ceremony "not in apparition, but in act" and the allegiance of the woman over whom the husband claims sovereignty. Those obtained, the husband is a kind of king indeed. And the wife, like a kingdom's citizens, holds her patriarchal superior hostage to her loyalty.

EIGHT

Acts of Persuasion: "The Subtlest Forms of Violence"

THE TESTED WOMAN PLOT IS SATURATED WITH OCCASIONS FOR PER-
suasion. The temptation of the test stage involves persuading the woman
to disobey and the tempter to cease and desist. The examination of the trial
stage involves persuading the accuser of the woman's disobedience and the
defender of her rectitude. These two in turn seek to influence the judge. How
to explore and understand the operations of what we call persuasion? "What
does it mean to persuade?" asks Paul Ricoeur. "What distinguishes persuasion
from flattery, from seduction, from threat—that is to say, from the subtlest
forms of violence?"[1] We might expect that the classical art of rhetoric, which
presents itself as the art of verbal persuasion, would have the analytical tools
to understand acts of persuasion in literary works. But rhetorical analysis has
no systematic way to examine the internal processes by which people come to
be persuaded or the formal capacities of various literary genres to present acts
of persuasion. Here we must feel our way.

Drama presents literary forms of persuasion at their most complex. Who is
the target of persuasion in the persuasive situation of a play? For that matter,
who is the speaker? The dramatist speaks not in his own voice but in the
voice of a character. In different ways he works with at least three targets of
persuasion—the character for whom he has shaped the speech, the character
or characters the speaker addresses, and the audience. The tested woman plot's
focus on the relationship between the deed and its perception offers unusual
opportunities for manipulating the dramatist's several targets. The supreme
example in English drama may be the intricately crafted effect of Iago's
conversation with Cassio about Bianca for the benefit of the eavesdropping
Othello, where Cassio's stock reaction to Iago's stock description of a whore
fulfills Othello's expectations about Desdemona and the theater audience's
expectations about all women—or, it may be, men. Even when one character
addresses another directly—I call such an addressee the primary audience—
acts of persuasion vary greatly from one setting to another.

Three of Thomas Middleton's plays written in the early 1620s[2] explore the spectrum of primary persuasive possibilities. Middleton is typical of Jacobean dramatists in his thematic interests but extraordinary in his dramatistic and psychological sophistication. *Women Beware Women*, the most standard treatment, focuses on its characters' seduction of one another through sexual, social, and material power rhetorically applied. *A Game at Chess* only pretends to be concerned with the persuasion of its characters; a political allegory, it uses the tested woman plot in a drama of fixed types that frankly manipulates its theater audience's xenophobic prejudices. *The Changeling* attempts something rare in Renaissance drama, an exploration of the operations of self-persuasion and self-education. In it Middleton constructs a detailed examination of the relationship between the ethical language of a character and the character's actions. The power of this explanation makes *The Changeling* Middleton's most interesting play for modern readers. It also shows the limits of drama's ability to explore internal states.

Persuading the Enforced

The persuasive powers of the characters of *Women Beware Women* are turned on each other until the logic of their rhetoric runs its bloody course to the classic blood-drenched banquet/masque finale. Moreover, the tested woman theme is multiplied into a trio of plots focused on the conventional configuration of wife, maid, and widow. Bianca, the young wife of the merchant's factor Leantio, is seduced by the Duke of Florence. The maid, Isabella, is decoyed into the arms of her uncle Hippolyto, with marriage to a simpleton as a cover-up. Having pandered both Bianca and Isabella, Hippolyto's widowed sister Livia succumbs to her passion for the bourgeois cuckold Leantio. Distinctive for the economy with which the three plots are intertwined, the play brilliantly varies the persuasive properties of its seductions. Though directed at characters primed by lust and self-interest, each seduction is tailored to its target's situation and embodies the rhetorical properties that most readily bind tempted to tempter.

The attack on Bianca is swiftly elegant, a combination of entrapment, bribery, and enforcement of a victim who becomes a willing participant in adultery. Having eloped from her patrician Venetian home to a clerk's apartment in Florence and the supervision of her unimaginative mother-in-law, the sixteen-year-old Bianca begins the play superficially contented with her new marriage and modest surroundings. But her eyes have met those of the duke as he passed beneath her balcony and, lured to her neighbor Livia's house under the pretense of a companionable supper, she finds herself confronted by a mature man of absolute authority and total rhetorical control. Though brief, the confrontation includes the range of nuances through which power can be brought to bear. In response to her pleas in defense of her virtue, the duke both warns Bianca and masterfully, caressingly woos her (2.2.359–68). In exchange for her marital honor, he offers her wealth, social position, and the security of intimate alliance with him: "Come, play the wise wench, and provide for ever: / Let storms come when they list, they find thee sheltered" (2.2.383–4). For all her youth and conventional statements, Bianca understands precisely what the duke is, what he threatens, and what he offers. She understands the language and the appeal of power, which is why they work on her. Moreover, the duke's language offers a compelling combination of force and tenderness. Nearly every phrase combines hard practicality with an invitation to ardor: though he has no pity, he affects a passionate pleading; he can both command and take infinite pleasure; she should play the wise wench and accept his shelter. "Should any doubt arise, let nothing trouble thee. / Put trust in our love for the managing / Of all thy heart's peace" (2.2.385–7) is his summation of his executive capacity to enforce, excite, and protect.

Isabella's entrapment is more indirect but every bit as well tailored, for it too rhetorically elaborates the interests that link tempted to tempter. Groomed by her greedy father for marriage to the cretinous ward of a family friend, Isabella finds her only pleasure in her innocent friendship with her paternal uncle Hippolyto. When she recoils from his declaration of incestuous passion, her aunt Livia undertakes to pander for him by means of the "pitying" fable that Isabella is the result of her mother's adultery. Though her real motive is her brother's comfort, Livia pretends to be freeing Isabella from her father's authority. Livia's language is as far from the vigorous directness of the duke's approach to Bianca as could be imagined. Chatty and suggestive, it is designed to let the virginal but emotionally longing Isabella contrive for herself a family past and a marital future that will open her to Hippolyto's advances. But the subtext of temptation, tailored to the niece's psychological needs, underlies the aunt's chatter. In her main seduction speech (2.1.152–74), Livia professes pity and piety, makes the application to Isabella's marriage, retreats to suggestive aphorism, reminds of the need for social cosmetic, advises discretion, and subtly introduces the name of uncle solely, it would seem, to require from Isabella a vow of secrecy. Motivated by the one tolerable prospect of her life, Isabella readily draws the desired conclusions: "Troth, I begin / To be so well, methinks, within this hour— / For all this match able to kill one's heart— / Nothing can pull me down now" (2.1.208–11). Isabella, we see, has seduced herself.

The third seduction is the crassest and, by virtue of its reversal of sexual roles, the most amusing. During the banquet of act 3—at which the duke displays his new mistress, her husband is palmed off with a preferment, Isabella must dance and sing for the ward, and the mother-in-law stuffs herself with sweetmeats—Livia meets Leantio and sets out to buy herself a lover. At first Leantio, still longing for Bianca and miserable in his public shame, can hardly hear her. Only when he has convinced himself that his only recourse lies in hating where he once loved is he ready for her approach. Livia's appeal is frank; she offers clothes, servants, racehorses,

LIVIA	or any various pleasure
	Exercised youth delights in: but to me
	Only, sir, wear your heart of constant stuff.
	Do but you love enough, I'll give enough.
LEANTIO	Troth then, I'll love enough and take enough.
LIVIA	Then we are both pleased enough.

(3.2.373–8)

This meeting of minds made possible by the meeting of worldly desires forms the persuasive pattern of the play. It is no accident that each of the three very different seductions ends in expressions of specious sufficiency and contentment. Nor is it an accident that each of the targets has been subjected to a frank exercise of power. The duke's threat to Bianca is the most overt, as his power is the greatest; "I can command: / Think upon that." Isabella too is enforced, for the lie that enables her to embrace her uncle merely softens the inescapable horror of a marriage that makes the liaison her only hopeful prospect. As for Leantio, who lacks masculine power in a male world, in his shame and depression he sells himself to a woman who herself has no prospects that are not vicious. Middleton emphasizes that none of these objects of seduction is a free agent, none powerful enough to take part in the equal exchanges of courtesy the duke claims to seek in love. All are trapped before they are approached by their tempters, and the persuasion to which they are subjected takes force from an appeal to the victims' circumstances. "Given who you are and what I am offering," these speeches argue, "better yourself." Abetted by force, by lies, by bribes, language merely provides the excuse for acquiescence.

In what sense are Bianca, Isabella, and Leantio persuaded by their tempters? In all cases the persuasive speeches have two functions: to spell out the situation in which the targets find themselves and to offer a way out. Hierarchical in-equalities and situational force have already been applied before the persuader speaks: Leantio's wife has been stolen, Isabella's marriage is inevitable, Bianca will be raped. The rhetorical emphasis is on the situational manipulation and explanatory skill of the tempter, not on the victim's state of mind. When we do go inside the victim, as in the case of Isabella reflecting on the marriage "able to kill one's heart," her decision is already made. Like most Renaissance drama, *Women Beware Women* does not show characters being persuaded in the emotional sense. Their previous understanding has already made vice attractive.

MANIPULATING THE IGNORANT

In *A Game at Chess* the tested woman develops no understanding, nor does she need any. The play is political propaganda in the form of a dramatized chess game satirizing the Roman Catholic Church, a contemporary Spanish diplomat, and the Spanish monarchy. The Black House patently represents Spain and the White House England. The fistula-ridden Black Knight carried in the very litter used by the former Spanish ambassador, Count Gondomar, was instantly identifiable to the play's first audience. Enjoying an unheard-of run of nine days during August 1624 after the much-hoped-for failure of Prince Charles and the duke of Buckingham to conclude a Spanish marriage, the play attracted a riotously appreciative audience of all classes, occupations and religious persuasions.[3] Among the plot elements comprising the chess game, the most systematic is the attempt of the Black Bishop's Pawn, a Jesuit of surpassing deviousness, to seduce the White Queen's Pawn, a young woman of surpassing naïveté. That the tested woman plot occupies so large a place in so political a play is a demonstration of its adaptability to persuasive situations. Its allegorical interpretation is easy. The innocence of the White Queen's Pawn is to be viewed as wholly admirable, and her defense of her chastity as a display of virtue pure. The casuistry and trickery through which she is attacked are to be seen as the foulest corruption, and the seducer and his bawd as masters of the rhetoric of depravity. The ultimate persuasive target is the theater audience, a congregation of the converted. All elaborations of the testing plot are devices for subjecting the White House to the maximum threat from the Black House for the titillation of partisan Londoners.

Middleton keeps the persuasive focus on the theater audience by making his tested woman incapable of genuine knowledge; because she learns nothing, the audience may continue to view her as an icon of innocence rather than being caught up in the adventure of her moral maturation. The play nevertheless ironically explores the relationship between the language of virtue and the actuality of genuine moral understanding. The White Queen's Pawn's sexual ignorance not only constitutes the greatest weakness in the defenses of the White House, it also complicates the process of her temptation. Though she is too inexperienced to recognize the subtleties of masterful seduction, educating her risks triggering her shamefastness. The Black House must teach her a double language that allows her to mouth the cant of virtue while understanding and performing the acts of vice.

The attempts at tutelage are subject to hilarious contretemps. In the first, the Black Queen's Pawn is a rhetorical softener, portraying the would-be seducer as a charitable confessor who cherishes "All his young tractable sweet obedient daughters / E'en in his bosom, in his own dear bosom" (1.1.39–40). From this bawd's disquisition the White Queen's Pawn extracts only the commonplaces that firmness, obedience, and penitence are good and that earnest tears, a comely presentation, and a reverend habit denote righteousness. Attempting her directly, the Black Bishop's Pawn is unable even to lead her into a conversation about lust. Falling back on handing her a printed homily on obedience, which she duly repeats—"And here again it is the daughter's duty / To obey her confessor's command in all things / Without exception or expostulation" (2.1.1–3)—he realizes to his frustration that she has not seized his full meaning: "She's farther off from understanding now / The language of my intent than at first meeting" (2.1.43–4). Yet she longs to have her obedience tested, for she knows the abstract terms of female virtue. So her confessor tests his "daughter" by commanding her to kiss him and accuses her when she balks: "At first disobedient, in so little too! / How shall I trust you with a greater then, / Which was your own request?" (2.1.52–4). For the rest of the scene the White Queen's Pawn stands on her modesty like a nervous animal: "If this be virtue's path, 't is a most strange one, / I never came this way before" (74–5). No casuistry will move her, even to a genuine comprehension of vice, and her seducer must resort to threats and physical force, though the rape is interrupted.

Middleton is engaged in a sophisticated critique of virtue founded on ignorance. Though in a sense the White Queen's Pawn has refused to be seduced, she has hardly been tempted by what she cannot understand. Further, the interruption of the rape by the Black Queen's Pawn was no genuine defense but the first step in a far more dangerous attack. This time the game is the Black Queen's Pawn's own, her object revenge for her seduction by the Jesuit five years before. Its first move again lays out, in Middleton's dramatic shorthand, the White Queen's Pawn's untainted conventionality and the Black Queen's Pawn's aphoristic exploitation of her victim's desire to do what good girls do. When the bawd hints that she foiled the rape in expectation of her victim's marriage, the White Queen's Pawn reiterates her vow to live single. But the White Queen's Pawn does not understand the relation between an individual's word, her will, and her actions. Her vow of single life is a talisman to keep fortune at bay rather than a sacramental expression of her intentions. Because she searches for reality in the projection of her conventional expectations, that is the reality the Black Queen's Pawn shows her. She is set facing a magic mirror, her future husband is evoked with music and her name, and the Jesuit, disguised as a richly dressed gentleman, steps into the mirror's path behind her. She sees his image and is caught, "and which is strange, by her most wronger," as the bawd puts it (3.3.71). Unable to detect the priest beneath the disguise, the White Queen's Pawn meets him face to face, agrees to a contract of marriage, and prepares to welcome him to her bed because it is her duty. Only the fact that the Black Queen's Pawn substitutes herself saves the White Queen's Pawn from complete sexual entrapment.

The play spells out the source of the White Queen's Pawn's inability to defend herself. When she first asks to see "the man," the bawd requires that she observe "the right use as I was taught it, / Neither looking back or questioning the spectre" (3.1.343–4). This formula refers to the physical arrangement necessary for the mirror trick. But the lines also refer to the operation of prudence or wisdom, whose places are memory, which takes account of the past, understanding, which examines the present, and foresight, which projects the future.[4] By her instructions the Black Queen's Pawn undercuts the operations of memory (not looking back) and understanding (not questioning the spectre) so as to prevent her victim from controlling the future. Yet the White Queen's Pawn is saved from her lack of prudence to remain the symbol of the audience's faith in its own partisan virtue. The bed trick revealed, the White Queen's Pawn ends her part of the play where she began: "I'll never know man farther than by name" (5.2.199).

Middleton's sweetest satiric twist on the defense moves of the tested woman plot is to save virtue by a vicious application of the conventional bed trick. Though he demonstrates the threat that determined casuistry holds for unreflective innocence, though vice fails only because its troops turn on each other, the applications are indirect. In the meantime the White House sweeps the board and the game is in the bag, to the delight of its politically engaged audience.

SELF-DECEPTION AND SELF-RECOGNITION

However comic, partisan, and satirically pointed *A Game at Chess*, in the person of the White Queen's Pawn Middleton is making a searching moral argument, one that concerned thinkers of his own age more than most. We know it under Milton's term: is cloistered virtue really virtue at all? Must not virtue know in order truly to choose, and to choose truly? Middleton's contribution is to push the conventional plotline and character type far enough to challenge their too frequent assumption that shrinking from vice is sufficient virtue for an adult life. This is the issue Thomas Wright, the author of the psychologico-rhetorical treatise *The Passions of the Mind in General* (1604), discusses in distinguishing between virtue itself and the propensity for virtue: The "shame of vice is a good commencement of virtue, because it proceedeth from a judgment disliking of evil, which is an apt beginning of good. Wherefore Aristotle calleth shamefastness a virtue, not for that it is a true virtue indeed (for it most often reigneth in children, who are not capable subjects of moral virtues) but because it is the seed of virtue, or a spur to virtue, or a bridle from vice; or a way, preparation or disposition unto an honest virtuous life" (lix).

The degree to which shamefastness is only a proto-virtue is underlined by its connection to children and to women, perpetual minors under the law: "shamefastness in women restraineth them from many shameful offences" (18). To grow into mature virtue, shamefastness requires active exploration of the relation between the negative strictures of shallow morality and the opportunities and actions of active and worldly people. Eventually novelistic literature will find the means to make that exploration self-generated and internal, but on the Jacobean stage it can come about only through minds meeting in dialogue.

The persuasive sequences of *A Game at Chess*, like those of *Women Beware Women*, are one-sided, and in neither case is internal change the primary goal. In *The Changeling*, by contrast, Middleton's attention is on self-education and self-understanding, and his rhetorical and dramatistic skill with grippingly naturalistic dialogue makes the play a masterpiece of psychological exploration. He takes the tested woman plot as his means because it is about the shift from ignorance to knowledge, and this time he shows us, in the dialogue itself, a woman coming to understand the import of her actions.

The Changeling has a tragic main plot, with a comic subplot by William Rowley.[5] Though thematically parallel, the subplot has only a tenuous situational relationship to the main one. In it the young wife of the director of a mental hospital, another Isabella, is subjected to the jealous strictures of her aged husband, the obscene attentions of his assistant, and the sexual advances of two gentlemen (one disguised as a madman, the other as an idiot) who enter the hospital to seduce her. Surrounded by examples of folly and derangement, she schools herself to a wary comprehension and rejection of lust, and so educates the men who plague her. Yet though Isabella undergoes a moral education, it is expressed primarily in the before-and-after psychological statements typical of Renaissance testing sequences.

The main plot, by contrast, takes us through the painful steps of its protagonist's moral education. Newly betrothed to Alonzo de Piracquo, Beatrice Joanna becomes enamored of the more attractive Alsemero, hires the detested servant De Flores to kill Piracquo, must yield her virginity to De Flores in payment, and enters marriage with Alsemero burdened by her increasing need for the man whom once she regarded as a loathed and dispensable tool. Whereas in the subplot tragic results are averted by Isabella's moral descriptions before the event, for Beatrice Joanna vicious deeds come first, made possible by the distance between her language and the specific acts to which it refers. Our sense of her naïveté is sharpened by the savagery of the deeds, the specificity with which Middleton explores her psyche, and the brilliance of the scene in which her education commences. Beatrice Joanna is convinced of her own righteousness and cleverness, the result of an abstractly homiletic education superimposed on native cunning, and she easily manipulates her father and her social surroundings. Only her detestation of De Flores, the gentleman with the disease-ravaged face who serves her father and burns with lust for her, unsettles her complacency. When she turns to him to clear the way for a more exciting marriage, we seem to have the conventional type of the woman who can mouth the cant of virtue while understanding and performing acts of vice. But Middleton's intention is more original. Picking up the Ciceronian distinction between the questions proper to logic and those proper to rhetoric, he is interested in showing how the mind superficially at home in the generalities of infinite questions is brought through the vehicle of rhetoric to the comprehension of specific applications. In the central seduction scene, Beatrice Joanna begins to *understand* what she has already been able, all too easily, to do.

In this scene the change in Beatrice Joanna results from self-persuasion and self-education. Middleton eschews the set before-and-after speeches typical of Renaissance tested woman plays—exemplified by Anne Frankford's refusal/capitulation diptych in *A Woman Killed with Kindness*—that give the effect of a wholesale, mechanical substitution of the tempter's will for that of his target. Middleton's attention is on process. Moreover, though De Flores's persistence is the catalyst for her comprehension, Middleton does not present Beatrice Joanna's intellectual deepening as a matter of contamination by her tempter's mindset or language. De Flores hardly uses any moral abstractions; his is a vocabulary of agency and causation. It is Beatrice Joanna whose vocabulary employs moral terms—wickedness, honor, vice, sin, modesty, shame—and only by a laborious internal reordering does she come to understand them as applicable to her deeds and thus to herself.

The scene opens with Beatrice Joanna congratulating herself on her skill. Piracquo's demise has been arranged. De Flores has merely to be paid off and sent packing, thus ridding her "of two inveterate loathings / At one time: Piracquo and his dog-face" (2.2.146–7). As for the favored suitor, Alsemero, he is being given a tour of the paternal house and grounds:

> So, here's one step
> Into my father's favor; time will fix him.
> I have got him now the liberty of the house;
> So wisdom by degrees works out her freedom.
> And if that eye be darken'd that offends me
> (I wait but that eclipse), this gentleman
> Shall soon shine glorious in my father's liking
> Through the refulgent virtue of my love.
>
> (3.4.10–7)

To Beatrice Joanna this is wisdom. The formal places of memory, understanding, and foresight have all been brought to bear, and wished-for consequences are predicted and provided for. Contemplating the painstaking trajectory of her intrigue provides satisfaction in itself.

But there has been a slight misunderstanding, for De Flores expects Beatrice Joanna herself to be his reward. The shortest of exchanges establishes that the fiancé is dead:

BEATRICE	De Flores
DE FLORES	Lady.
BEATRICE	Thy looks promise cheerfully.
DE FLORES	All things are answerable: time, circumstance, Your wishes, and my service.
BEATRICE	Is it done then?
DE FLORES	Piracquo is no more.

(3.4.21–4)

This laconic exchange is a rhetorical miniature that sets the issue of the rest of the scene. Systematically it visits the formal places of demonstration, clicking off the deed, the time, the circumstances, the purpose, the agency. Yet the stative neutrality of the final line leaves one thing unspecified—the actor. De Flores unquestionably performed the murder, but as tool, not as instigator. It is her "wishes" as well as his "service"—the classical "wherefore" combined with the "by what help"—that together constitute the doer of the deed. The remainder of the scene must bring that actuality home to Beatrice Joanna, and more than anywhere else in English Renaissance drama this moral work is accomplished step-by-step through the sinuous path of the dialogue.

De Flores starts off on the wrong track because he cannot believe that a woman so violent by proxy can be so unwitting of the moral import of her complicity. Confused by Beatrice Joanna's seeming unwillingness to give him what he has come for, he emphasizes the distinction between them, the difference between his service and her instigation. Angered by her gift of the ring from the dead man's severed finger, still more by his "salary" of three thousand florins, he finds himself trapped again in the role of hired hand:

> DE FLORES Do you place me in the rank of verminous fellows
> To destroy things for wages? Offer gold?
> The life blood of man! Is anything
> Valued too precious for my recompense?
> BEATRICE I understand thee not.
>
> (3.4.65–9)

Indeed she does not. But this distinction between them is not what De Flores longs for. In his urgency he speaks more plainly, tries to kiss her, begins a subtle thread of threatening. The intimate patterning of the language of the sequence, as each speaker catches up the words and warnings of the other, builds unity—though not yet understanding—between them. Refusing Beatrice Joanna's command to flee, De Flores tries to keep her with him psychologically as well as physically. There follows an exchange remarkable for the intricacy of its psychological and rhetorical moves, in which the characters pick up each other's wording and syntax both to combat and to incorporate each other's meaning.[6]

Once Beatrice Joanna has at last heard distinctly what payment must consist of, she reacts to what she hears rather than to what she has done, offended by the language of unchastity and the presumption of forcing consequences upon her:

> BEATRICE Why, 'tis impossible thou canst be so wicked
> Or shelter such a cunning cruelty,
> To make his death the murderer of my honor.
> Thy language is so bold and vicious
> I cannot see which way I can forgive it
> With any modesty.
> DE FLORES   Push, you forget yourself;

	A woman dipp'd in blood, and talk of modesty!
BEATRICE	Oh, misery of sin! Would I had been bound
	Perpetually unto my living hate
	In that Piracquo than to hear these words.

(3.4.121–30)

Beatrice Joanna's use of the word *sin* for her own actions suggests a sudden increase in moral self-consciousness. De Flores has made something apparent to her, in part by his refusal of her misuse of language. She is the one who makes the connection, however: this, *this*, is sin. Nevertheless she still struggles to keep De Flores and his message at a hygienic remove: "Think but upon the distance that creation / Set 'twixt thy blood and mine, and keep thee there" (3.4.131–2). Overriding her attempt to hold language between them, De Flores must force her to acknowledge their unity in the act of murder that makes inevitable their unity in the act of sex:

> Look but into your conscience, read me there;
> 'Tis a true book; you'll find me there your equal.
> Push, fly not to your birth, but settle you
> In what the act has made you; y'are no more now.
> You must forget your parentage to me;
> Y'are the deed's creature; by that name
> You lost your first condition, and I challenge you,
> As peace and innocency has turn'd you out,
> And made you one with me.

(3.4.133–41)

"Y'are the deed's creature": This declaration of the existential act that has united her forever to De Flores blocks Beatrice Joanna's further appeals to innocence or social distance. Yet this unity must be made palpable, physical, for still she tries to hold wealth, euphemistic language, and the talisman of her virginity between herself and him. Responding to his threat to reveal all, she offers De Flores her wealth: "Let me go poor unto my bed with honor, / And I am rich in all things" (3.4.158–9), to which his refusal is absolute: "The wealth of all Valencia shall not buy / My pleasure from me" (3.4.160–1). At last Beatrice Joanna understands that she is contaminated to the core:

> Vengeance begins;
> Murder, I see, is followed by more sins.
> Was my creation in the womb so curs'd,
> It must engender with a viper first?

(3.4.163–6)

The utter weariness of her capitulation and the hideous image with which she concludes it silence her at last. In that silence, "one of pleasure's best receipts" (3.4.168), De Flores takes his satisfaction.

This extraordinary scene exhibits harmonizing but contrastive motions, the directness of the dialogue and the circumlocutory progress of Beatrice Joanna's moral understanding. In the contrast between what the mouth can say and what the heart has truly learned, Middleton has delineated the difference between the enforcement usually called "persuasion" and the true persuasion that comes from deep comprehension of the self as a moral agent. In the enforcement sequence De Flores swiftly blackmails Beatrice Joanna, and she capitulates once her attempts to break his will prove futile. Concurrently a slower, more tentative process is going on. Unprepared for the depth of her obtuseness, De Flores must grope his way toward verbal expression of their identity. Trapped but uncertain how, Beatrice Joanna begins to explore her own moral condition only when she gives up hope of escape. The process is barely begun in this scene. Although she ends it convinced of her contamination, she still has not properly ascribed the cause. The remainder of the play is driven by her terror that Alsemero will discover her loss of virginity and her continued liaison with De Flores, who has become a "wondrous necessary man" (5.1.91). A manipulated virginity test, a bed trick, another murder follow as she attempts to save appearances. At her end, stabbed by De Flores who will kill them both rather than lose her, she publicly acknowledges her own corruption, warning her distraught father away from her defilement. Her final words at last bring her language into harmony with the facts: "Forgive me, Alsemero, all forgive; / 'Tis time to die, when 'tis a shame to live" (5.3.179–80).

Beatrice Joanna is interesting partly because, like real people, her habits lag as far behind her dawning comprehension as her glibness precedes it. Her mental process is different from the psychological experiences undergone by a fully blooded character like Macbeth, who understands the moral import of his murders as soon as he conceives them, however far from prepared he may be for how they will take him imaginatively. From Shakespeare's first scene we intuit Macbeth's political ambition and his experience in weighing the methods by which he forwards it. Although Lady Macbeth's persuasion is a form of sexual extortion, it does nothing to strengthen his desire or educate his psyche. His deeds are fully his; he conceives them with malice aforethought and owns them before he commits them. By contrast, in focusing acts of persuasion on a character virginal of mind and emotion as well as body, Middleton is able to give us some sense of how the process of moral discovery, decision, and maturation works.

Self-Persuasion and Soliloquy

For all his skill with language and gesture, for all his willingness to carry the process throughout the entire play, Middleton is up against the dramatic constraints of limited stage time and the necessity for nearly constant dialogue between characters. If the real work of persuasion must be self-persuasion, which goes on in the individual psyche over an extended period and results in a new worldview as well as a new set of habits and behaviors, drama is ill-suited to the work. Moreover, to earn the name of persuasion the phenomenon must consist of more than mere mental and emotional change, because it must be conscious. Persuasion moves toward the point at which the individual says "I am persuaded that . . ."; what follows must have deliberated origins. Analysis of circumstances, marshaling of arguments about evidence, and subtle overcoming of resistance are all involved in the rhetoric of external persuasion, and internal persuasion is no less subject to these techniques. The dramatic tool for the presentation of self-persuasion is the soliloquy. But drama tolerates soliloquy only in short bursts; even the most soliloquy-heavy play in the Renaissance dramatic corpus, *Hamlet*, has only a handful of such passages, and those are short by comparison with the dialogue in which they are embedded. Full literary expression of self-persuasion requires more expansive genres.

Nevertheless the term "soliloquy" is helpful in considering self-persuasion. Partly this is because it arises from the classical antilogistic tradition. At its literary origins the soliloquy—both the term and the internal debate—is the invention of St. Augustine, who coins the word for a kind of Neoplatonic dialogue he wrote in 386–87, that momentous winter between his conversion and his baptism. In this work, he tells us elsewhere, "I asked myself questions and I replied to myself, as if we were two, reason and I, whereas I was of course just one. As a result I called the work *Soliloquies*."[7] For my argument the significance of the coinage, as of the work, lies in its relation to the pro-contra procedures of classical rhetoric. In format the work maintains the sense of verbal combat of its Platonic forebears. The powerful difference lies in the relationship between the interlocutors "Reason" and "Augustine," who are the same person talking to himself. This identity makes possible not only the continuing sidetracks and messy explorations of the work, but also its single most illuminating moment, which occurs midway through Soliloquy 2, when "Augustine" realizes that he has been boxed into an untenable position by "Reason": "I don't know what to say, and I'm ashamed of myself." Reason replies, "It's ridiculous to be ashamed. Think of the very reason we have chosen this type of conversation. I want them to be called 'Soliloquies' because we are talking with ourselves alone." And Reason goes on to critique the pro-contra method as a means of genuine persuasion:

> There is no better way of seeking the truth than the question and answer method. It is, however, hard to find anyone who would not be ashamed to be beaten in an argument. The almost inevitable result is that a babble of dissent caused by wilful obstinacy will destroy a topic which up to this has been carefully canvassed in the discussion. People are cut to the quick, and even if they generally conceal their feelings, on occasion, too, they show them openly. It was for that reason

that the most peaceful and most profitable procedure was for me to question and
answer myself, and so with God's help to search for what is true. So if you have
committed yourself too quickly anywhere there is no reason for you to be afraid
of retreating and setting yourself free: there's no way out here otherwise. (*Sol.* 2,
¶s 13–14, p. 89)

In this self-reflective mode, where the "you" and the "I" are one "we," acts of
self-investigation and self-persuasion can truly be carried forward.

The soliloquy as Augustine invented it is not usable in literal drama, though
it renders the tensions of the self-questioning mind in dramatic form. For the
tested woman plot the most important trend in post-Renaissance literature
is the eighteenth-century experimentation that learns to combine dramatic
immediacy, the intimacy of the self-revealing mind, and the capaciousness of
narrative into a text of extended self-examination. The breakthrough comes
in Samuel Richardson's experiments with first-person epistolary narration
written not retrospectively but in the heat of thought and action, "to the
moment" as he called it, and his story of the moral testing of a servant girl
exploits internal conversation and debate. Like many a literary lover, Pamela
addresses and exhorts her heart: "O my exulting heart! how it throbs in my
bosom, as if it would reproach me for so lately upbraiding it for giving way
to the love of so dear a gentleman!—But, take care thou art not too credulous
neither, O fond believer! . . . And I charge thee to keep better guard than
thou hast lately done, and lead me not to follow too implicitly thy flattering
and desirable Impulses." Yet the flight toward allegorization is cut short, as
is Augustine's spasm of shame at being bested by himself, by reclaiming the
psychological reality at the core of the textual device: "Thus foolishly dialogu'd
I with my heart; and yet all the time this heart is Pamela."[8] The novel of interior
exploration that exploits the psychological resources of self-conversation has
been invented; it is the literary form in which from this point on readers will
expect to study the acts and arts of persuasion.

PART III

Experimenting with Genre

NINE

Dramatizing and Narrating

THE STORY OF THE TESTED WOMAN PLOT IN ENGLISH LITERATURE
between the English Revolution and the end of the Napoleonic era is the
story of genre. If in the early seventeenth century the great storytelling medium
was drama, by the early nineteenth century it was the novel of third-person
narration. The developments in the novelistic form during the long eighteenth
century are manifestations of the culture-wide waning of rhetorical literature
and the development of expressive literary texts.[1] They include changes in
subject matter—expressions of interiority, women's experience, middle- and
lower-class experience. They experiment with narrative form and voice—
first-person confession, epistolary exchange, the narrative of indirect speech.
Nevertheless, play-going and play-reading continued to flourish, and drama
interpenetrated the novel. The dramatic narrative of Samuel Richardson's
epistolary works was designed to achieve the effects of both forms. The leading
English dramatist and theatrical manager of the 1730s,[2] Henry Fielding, was
a great novelist of the 1740s. By the end of the century professional writers
like Elizabeth Inchbald routinely wrote both plays and novels. When in 1779
the young novelist Fanny Burney, still reveling in the success of *Evelina*,
met the young playwright Richard Sheridan, recently made famous by his
success with *The School for Scandal*, he urged her to try her hand at a play, and
the diary entry in which she describes the encounter falls into a "playbook"
scene,[3] a form *Clarissa*'s Lovelace delights in using in his letters. The plots of
drama became the plots of novels, and conversations about plays were carried
on in novels. Richardson's Pamela does a critique of Richard Steele's *Tender
Husband* as though her readers knew the play; Lovelace and Belford have the
same expectations about Nicholas Rowe's *Fair Penitent*. In *Mansfield Park* Jane
Austen's characters rehearse August von Kotzebue's *Das Kind der Liebe* under
Inchbald's title of *Lovers' Vows*, and Austen counts on her readers' knowledge.

How the tested woman plot works in eighteenth-century drama is thus part
of the story of its use in prose fiction, for which readership exploded. Though
many Britons were not even minimally literate, vernacular literacy became
the ideal for adults of most classes, and the expectation for men and women in

managerial positions—domestic, military, artisan, or mercantile—as well as for all Christians in the dissenting tradition. The effort to write the literature of private lives contributed to a social theory of domestic patriarchy, an aesthetic theory of sentiment, and a physically grounded psychology describing the relation between sense experience and emotional response. This social and literary shift changed the emphases and uses of the tested woman plot. The shift in genre especially changed the plot's relation to time—both story time, the amount and sequencing of story that may be introduced into a literary form, and text time, the length of the text and its availability for exploration of its characters' lives.

THE CONFRONTATION WITH DRAMATIC THEORY: DRYDEN AND RYMER

The closing of the London theaters in 1642 caused a loss of theatrical continuity for playwrights, acting troupes, and audiences. By the time the theaters were reopened in 1660, dramatic style had changed. The new style was marked by changes in diction and rhetorical preferences, the influence of French literary criticism, increasingly elaborate stage sets and machinery, and the presence of women actors. One important dramatist's career connected the two periods. William Davenant, whose first play dates from 1627, in 1660 received one of the two patents granted for theatrical companies. Davenant became a major source of such understanding and appreciation as the Restoration felt for its theatrical tradition.[4] Moreover, much of the repertory of Restoration and eighteenth-century theater was Jacobean and Caroline, and this repertory provided endless opportunities for emulation as well as updating. Nicholas Rowe's *The Fair Penitent*, for example, was an unacknowledged revision of Massinger and Field's *The Fatal Dowry*.[5] John Dryden's *All for Love* was a return to the characters and catastrophe of Shakespeare's *Antony and Cleopatra*. Despite such indebtedness, however, English drama of the last forty years of the seventeenth century seems more different from that of its first forty than can be accounted for by the loss of eighteen playing seasons.

The theatrical interregnum was caused by the political one. The closing of the theaters followed Charles I's loss of London and Parliament in 1642, and the drama that returned with the Restoration was the drama of the victors, of court and gentry. From the 1580s through the 1630s, London theaters had entertained a large percentage of the population, and even during the Caroline years, with their expensive private theaters, there were still writers and a repertory for the merchant, artisan, and laboring audiences of the public theaters. But the patents granted in 1660 limited the number of acting companies to two, and admission prices were high to pay for the costly sets. Though the theaters admitted anyone who paid, during the reign of Charles II they were principally the playground of a coterie of court-connected gentlemen-intellectuals whose tastes governed the responses of their audiences. Only after several decades, a quicker and less bloody revolution, radical reorganization among the acting companies, and a fin-de-siècle aesthetic shift did London again have anything as varied or as stable as the prerevolutionary theater industry.

In the meantime arose the first surge of modern literary theory. Classical poetics had combined rhetoric, philosophy and psychology, but without being prescriptive or imposing itself on popular literature. Though some Renaissance writers were interested in what is now called literary criticism, the concern of Philip Sidney, its prime English practitioner, was to inculcate a moral attitude, not to dictate technique. English theater before the Civil War was primarily a business, built on a largely native, untheorized tradition. As Thomas Rymer, that sharpest-toothed of Restoration critics, put it, "till of late years England was as free from critics as it is from wolves, that a harmless well-meaning book might pass without any danger."[6] But with early Restoration drama the case was sharply altered. A small number of gentlemen wrote the plays, they had them performed for each other, they competed in a milieu in which intellectual weapons had political and social consequences, many of them had spent years on the Continent—and theory mattered. More precisely, French neoclassical literary theory as it was being prescribed by French aestheticians and expressed in the drama of the admitted greats— Corneille, Racine, Molière—mattered. So Englishmen turned their eyes across the Channel as they attempted to resuscitate the most glorious of their native art forms.

One of the influences of theory was sharper distinctions of genre than had held in Tudor and Stuart drama. The pre-1642 English dramatist felt free to mix genres and language forms. Parody, satire, clowning, and horseplay, often in prose, abound even in late tragedy, while high seriousness and elevated verse are found in comedy. Arguments about dramatic unities, classical models, or poetic license were not unknown but they resulted in options, not dogma.[7] Restoration drama, by contrast, operated under layers of theoretical doctrine. The distinction between comedy and tragedy was shored up wherever possible, in part by language. Comedy required prose and tragedy verse, meaning that serious scenes in comedy lacked a secure legitimacy or style.[8] The dramatist's obligation to mete out just deserts, for which Rymer coined the term "poetical justice,"[9] further confused the grounds for distinctions between tragedy and comedy. The most notorious stricture on dramatic practice was the neoclassical principle of the unities of action, place, and time, which were draconian in theory, though stretched in practice.[10] All elements of the play were to be knitted into a single plot by the interaction of characters and events, which meant the disappearance of the thematically related but socially distinct multiple plots of Renaissance plays. The stage, being only one place, must represent only one place, which meant bringing all the characters to it rather than taking it to them. As for time, elapsed stage time should correspond to plot time: "the time equal to that of the presentation," as *The Way of the World* has it. Where the focus is manners, as in Congreve, this stricture is rational and workable. In the drama of political dilemma and debate, much less the drama of moral change, however, such a constraint proved unworkable even for purists, who had to allow twenty-four hours or even two days with their connecting night. In neoclassical tragedy, nights are frantically busy.

Issues of genre, plot, time, and the representation of persons can be debated on a continuum between maximum inclusion and maximum exclusion. The neoclassical impulse limits the range of characters. The limitation may be expressed in class and genre terms, as when tragedy is considered the province only of characters of high degree. The limitation may also be expressed in terms of unities, with the play's characters restricted to those who would naturally meet at the single time and place in which the play is set. Thomas Sprat understood what the English tradition had been when in 1665 he replied to a French criticism of the mixture of persons, humors, conditions, and actions on the English stage in terms of the master metaphor of Renaissance drama, the trope of *theatrum mundi*: "Nor is it sufficient to object against this, that it is undecent to thrust in men of mean condition, amongst the actions of princes. For why should that misbecome the stage, which is always found to be acted on the true theater of the world?"[11] Neoclassicism, demanding separation of castes and classes, rejected this argument.

Neoclassical theory was in pursuit of coherence, which is complicated in drama by the presence of story. Yet story could not be ignored; as Aristotle understood, plot is the first concern of the dramatic poet. When Dryden looked back at his revered but faulty predecessors, in good part what he faulted them for was offenses against the coherence of the story. Agreeing in his 1672 "Defense of the Epilogue to *The Conquest of Granada*, Part 2" that "their wit is great" and "their expressions noble," he goes on:

> But the times were ignorant in which they lived. . . . Witness the lameness of their plots, many of which . . . were made up of some ridiculous incoherent story which in one play many times took up the business of an age. I suppose I need not name *Pericles, Prince of Tyre*, nor the historical plays of Shakespeare, besides many of the rest, as the *Winter's Tale, Love's Labour's Lost, Measure for Measure*, which were either grounded on impossibilities or at least so meanly written that the comedy neither caused your mirth nor the serious part your concernment.[12]

"The lameness of their plots": under this head Dryden must include Antigonus eaten by a bear on the shores of Bohemia. But he is concerned about more than the obvious impossibilities of *The Winter's Tale*. Restoration criticism continually returns to questions of plot: what kind of and how much story a drama should try to tell. Among the competing positions in Dryden's "Essay of Dramatic Poesy" (1668) are different answers to specific versions of that question: whether the French desire for unity and regularity has impoverished their plots to the point of inanition; whether English pleasure in variety of action and effect has stuffed theirs to the point of absurdity; how close to the climax of a story the dramatist should open the action; what is the most effective balance between description and enactment. Dryden understands that the handling of time is key. The romance materials of *Pericles* or *The Winter's Tale*, like the materials of chronicle, tell the story of an age, a generation, which of itself gives grounds for his charge of incoherence.

It is no accident that three of the four plays Dryden names are tested woman plays. The tested woman plot needs time, which means that its Renaissance exemplars especially offend neoclassical theorists and its Restoration exemplars cause its practitioners time-related problems. Other characteristics of the plot also come up against neoclassical strictures. Because it exploits the analogy between domestic and public patriarchal relations, it compulsively mingles contradictory social roles in a single character. The resulting paradox, a potent engine of Renaissance art and thought, seems like a disease to neoclassical criticism. Under the banner of decorum, neoclassical theory seeks to restrict characters to single human roles or conditions; all-too-human mixtures of social obligations and character traits are suspect for the very paradoxes they embody. Under the banner of generic purity, theory seeks a related narrowness of social setting, so that the mixture of worlds in which characters might express the tensions of their mixed functions is refined out of existence.[13] The neoclassical stress on the maintenance of sharp distinctions between comedy and tragedy also works against the generic indeterminacy and unpredictability of the tested woman plot, in which the same test responded to in the same way may produce different results depending on how the woman's choice is interpreted.

The problem of interpretation raises the question of Rymer's "poetical justice," the doctrine of just deserts. If the good must triumph in act 5, much of what the tested woman plot can offer at its most powerful is vitiated. Learning and accepting the truth is the goal toward which the plot moves, and such learning is consonant with tragedy. But though this is a truth that Shakespeare's *King Lear* knows, it is one Nahum Tate's neoclassical *King Lear* cannot stomach. In neoclassical theory the tragedy of the loss of the good— of the daughter who practices and tells the truth yet cannot be saved within time—has become impossible. Neoclassical theory has problems with comic versions of the tested woman plot as well. When comedy must be restricted to satire on the social manners of fixed types played out in the few hours of a single action, the tested woman plot, which demands that virtue matter and have real-life consequences, is unavailable. If Charles Lamb is right that the glory of Restoration comedy of manners is its seamless amorality—its unbreachable assurance that these creatures *have* no hearts to break or virtues to assail[14]—then the tested woman plot cannot operate in it. Comedy will have to crack the facade of manners before it can use the plot.

The question of what kind of action and what conception of humankind a tested woman play is imitating is evident in Rymer's critique of *A King and No King*. When in *The Tragedies of the Last Age* (1677) he attacked his predecessors for their violations of neoclassical rationality, he was doing several things at once. Rymer attacked plays Dryden had mentioned by name in his "Essay of Dramatic Poesy," and he adopted Dryden's technique of extended analysis of individual works.[15] The three plays from the Fletcher canon[16] that Rymer addresses are mentioned favorably in terms of their plotting by Dryden's disputants. Lisideius commends *Rollo*'s unity of plot (38) and *A King and No King*'s excellent fifth-act unraveling (42); Neander praises the well-guided tour through the plot labyrinth of *The Maid's Tragedy* (49). Rymer disputes each of these judgments. There is much to sympathize with in his critiques, especially his jibes at the improbabilities of *The Maid's Tragedy*. What bothers him most about *A King and No King*, however, is the complexity and inelegance of Arbaces' character: his clowning and swagger, his familiarity with his officers and attendants, his abuse of his mother and his "brutish insolence" to his sister which "as she is lawful sovereign, nothing could be invented more opposite to all honesty, honor, and decorum" (46). Arbaces should have the "instincts" of a son toward his father Gobrius, and Panthea should have the noble and lofty instincts of the queen she really is—even though neither knows the true state of biological affairs.

What Rymer refuses to engage with is the kind of imitation this tragicomedy is attempting.[17] The trope of *theatrum mundi* lies behind *A King and No King*, and Gobrius, the father and Lord Protector, is the dramatist and theatrical director of its plot. The play's structure makes the exploration of Arbaces' neurosis-inducing multiplicity of roles its point, the fifth-act unraveling that Lisideius admires and Rymer condemns revealing the family's past and Gobrius's rationale. But the family's past is not the plot of the play, though Rymer thinks it is (41):

<blockquote>
The Plot Is This

The queen of Iberia, Arane, had feigned herself with child and made use of Gobrius's son to carry out the cheat. She afterwards proves truly with child, which came to be Panthea, durst not discover the first cheat, so that Arbaces (Gobrius's son) became actually King, [//] is made really so by marrying Panthea.

The Rest is All Episode
</blockquote>

The plot of the *play* actually happens where I have put the virgules, and the love interest at its center provides the tested woman focus which allows Arbaces' roles to be dramatically expressed as functions at war within the single male figure.

Neoclassical pressure on plot structure is even more apparent in its concern with unity of time. In theory, how much lived time characters have from beginning to end of the play directly affects how much story can be dramatized. Thence the neoclassical trait of beginning close to the catastrophe so as to fit the action into the available time. But the closer to the catastrophe the play opens, the more background must be filled in by means of choral commentary or explanatory monologues. How this fact translates on stage depends on the story the dramatist is telling. Late Renaissance drama tends to represent the woman's choice as more or less instantaneous, and to extend the second, or truth-finding, stage, especially when the woman is virtuous but besieged. Because Truth is the Daughter of Time, Renaissance plays seek to increase the illusion of time passing to emphasize the forces at work on the lives and psyches of their characters. After Claudio's repudiation of Hero in *Much Ado about Nothing*, during the indeterminate period of her sequestration we are meant to feel the passage of time. Though Dogberry's testimony and the literal fact-finding do not actually require it, Claudio's public mourning, the intensity of Beatrice and Benedick's courtship, and Beatrice's demand for vengeance all give that illusion. In *Cymbeline* a variety of ceremonial actions— journey, funeral, vision, battle—spread over indeterminate but extended time and space to give Providence (which includes Jupiter, a Roman general, and Posthumus's conscience) time to work. The chorus who opens act 4 of *The Winter's Tale* is Time itself, helping time pass and promising to bring forth Truth in the flesh:

> let Time's news
> Be known when 'tis brought forth. A shepherd's daughter,
> And what to her adheres, which follows after,
> Is th' argument of Time"
>
> (4.1.26–9)[18]

When Rymer attacks the time scheme in *Othello*,[19] he is literally correct about its inconsistencies, but wrong in damning it for them. One of the points of the play, after all, is that Iago is in mortal combat with Time for the control of Truth. "Thou knowest we work by wit and not by wisdom," he tells Roderigo, "and wit depends on dilatory time" (2.3.366–7), which must be harried and manipulated. Wisdom by contrast depends on time in its full and natural extension, in which cooperate past (memory), present (understanding), and future (foresight). By truncating time, neoclassical strictures short-circuit the wisdom of tested woman plays.

ROWE'S SHE-TRAGEDY

Nicholas Rowe's drama shows us neoclassical theory at work on the tested woman plot. The author of eight plays performed between 1700 and 1715, the editor of Shakespeare, and the coiner of the term "she-tragedy," Rowe practiced a neoclassically regular drama that nevertheless sought to capitalize on the English dramatic tradition as well as the new century's growing affinity for pathos. Rowe's three tested woman plays all change their sources in ways that show Rowe wrestling with contradictions of maintaining theoretical purity while capitalizing on the plot's power.

Ulysses (1706), the play Samuel Johnson objected to for its rewriting of the story—"this is not Homer"[20]—traps Rowe between the famous original and his theoretical constraints. Rowe turns the story of Odysseus's return into a tested woman plot, particularizing the suitor Eurymachus into an effective threat, developing the suitor Antinous as an Ithacan competitor for local power, making Ulysses-in-disguise a pander/tester, dividing Penelope's loyalties between husband and son, and giving the role of defender to the son as well as the husband. *Ulysses* exhibits the central problem of neoclassical tragedy: the shorter the time and the smaller the variety of characters allowed, the more the playwright must multiply events to maintain tension and the illusion of action. Because he is bound to unity of time and place, Rowe cannot portray Telemachus's maturation, Ulysses' adventures, or the long siege of Penelope. Yet decorum prevents his filling the final twenty-four hours with the suitors' riotous behavior and Odysseus's bloody revenge. As for his Telemachus and Semanthe subplot, invented to fill in the gaps, it creates a problem in the denouement. Rowe must end the Ulysses-Penelope action with the original's martial and marital success, so the superfluous subplot peters out.

Rowe's refusal to use a Renaissance-style mixture of character types or an extended time scheme shows in *Jane Shore* as well. Here we can compare a Restoration play with both a Renaissance play and nondramatic forms. The variety of motifs accounts for the tale's popularity. These include its class-consciousness (the wronged husband is an artisan/merchant and his wronger is the king), and a spin on dynastic upheavals (Edward IV seduces citizens' wives, but Jane's persecutor Richard Crookback murders little princes). These features mattered in 1713, as the Whig consolidation filled theaters with audiences grateful for the acknowledgment that a merchant could have honor, and as the problem of Queen Anne's succession kept the public eye on the prospect of dynastic upheaval.[21]

Rowe probably worked up his play in part from Heywood's *Edward IV, Part 2*, which seems to be the source of his device of the wronged husband returned in disguise.[22] Heywood's double play is outrageously irregular in both of the kinds Dryden describes as lame-plotted. It is formally broken-backed between the two plays and broken-backed again in part 2 as a chorus returns us to England. There are scenes representing simultaneous action, there is a split-stage scene, there are multiple locations of the wildest variety. As for the time represented, it can be computed by the king's marriage to Elizabeth Grey at the beginning of part 1 and the age of their ill-fated sons at the end of part 2. Rowe must work differently. His *Jane Shore* begins three days before Jane's death, a decision that controls everything. Jane's seducer is dead—if Rowe wished to dramatize the test stage, he could not use Edward. Jane's error and her subsequent purgative years are assumed to have passed, but the audience does not experience them. Thus Rowe has virtually eliminated attention to

Edward's sexual misconduct, including the historical fact that the king used his position to seduce a subject and publicly dishonor a man to whom he owed a public debt. By situating the action during the period when Richard is Protector but not yet king, Rowe avoids examining royal behavior while capitalizing on allusions to the villain of Restoration political ideology, that other Protector, Cromwell.[23] The new seducer Hastings, a vehicle for the time-honored re-temptation of the reformed woman, is powerful—but he is not Jane's sovereign. Whereas Heywood's play dramatizes the rise and fall of Jane's fortunes, Rowe begins with Jane's fortunes already destroyed, so that she is a victim only.

Rowe's version of the story of Jane Shore also has a narrowed social range. Heywood conceives the patriarchy in national terms and gives important roles to a wide range of commoners, so that his king may play the father, husband, lover, captain, magistrate to his entire people. In Rowe's version servants lose their names, personalities, and dramatic functions. Mistress Blague, the citizen, becomes Alicia, a lord's mistress. Heywood's citizen soldier Shore/Flood becomes the Frenchified, gentrified Dumont. Dumont, it is true, is no lord. The best scene in the play, effective because physically vigorous and psychologically satisfying, is his defense of Jane against rape in which he duels with and disarms Hastings:

HASTINGS   Confusion! baffled by a base-born hind!
DUMONT   Now, haughty sir, where is our difference now?
            Your life is in my hand, and did not honor,
            The gentleness of blood, and inborn virtue
            (How e'er unworthy I may seem to you)
            Plead in my bosom, I should take the forfeit.
            But wear your sword again; and know, a lord
            Opposed against a man is but a man.
                                        (2.1.273–80)

This scene knows the appeal of talking class differences and rivalries, but it does not, as Heywood's play had, enact them.

Thanks to theoretical constraints, Rowe refused the opportunity to dramatize the story of erring king, dynastic conflict, and wronged husband in a fully developed tested woman play. That he understood some of its potential is suggested by the Heywood he does use: the Shore-in-disguise device moves the play toward a concentration of the accusation/defense/judgment complex in the single person of the wronged husband. That Rowe also knew the appeal of the erring wife is wittily spelled out in the epilogue, where he first uses the designation "she-tragedy."[24] What is missing in *Jane Shore* is any way to dramatize the past sufficiently to ground the characters' passions in lived events. Male interests are not unified around the figure of Jane, are not fundamentally in competition with each other over her behavior and its interpretation. In eliminating not just the marital past of the principals but the sweep of historical time and the hierarchical relation of sovereign and subjects, Rowe has eliminated both the literal and the analogical families that give depth to the plot.

The Fair Penitent (1703), Rowe's even more popularly successful[25] tested woman play, though it too rewrites a Renaissance original into a more "regular" drama, displays more female error and male intimacy and competition because it is more fully domestic. Relieved of the politically delicate problem of erring king and mistreated subjects, The Fair Penitent focuses on Calista and the men of her family. In his prologue Rowe proclaims the potential of domestic tragedy to strengthen his audience's powers of empathy. Arguing that "We ne'er can pity what we ne'er can share," Rowe rejects the stories of kings and empires for "a humbler theme": "No princes here lost royalty bemoan, / But you shall meet with sorrows like your own" (ll. 11, 12, 18–9). Further, he is resolved not to be so "nice" as to disguise moral blemishes, "But show you men and women as they are" (l. 28).

Because of its domestic setting, this is the tested woman tragedy in which Rowe uses the plot to best advantage. Nevertheless, it too is hampered by theory. Whereas his source, Massinger and Field's Fatal Dowry (1619), emphasizes the excruciating moral and emotional choices forced on the father and the husband by the woman's adultery, Rowe emphasizes Calista's anguish over her premarital affair with Lothario. Rowe's play is less a tragedy of familial rupture and more one of the destruction of the individual spirit. Nevertheless, familial relationships hold the male figures tightly in Calista's orbit, for not just her husband, Altamont, but also her father, Sciolto, and her husband's bosom friend and brother-in-law, Horatio, share the family's stake in her honor. As for Lothario, though he cooled to Calista the morning after he had her virginity, now that she has married his hereditary enemy Altamont he is back to his illicit wooing. The test of the woman constitutes the main suspense, and Altamont's overhearing it sets up the family-destroying catastrophe.

Rowe has not lost the essential familial situation. What he underplays, in comparison with his source, are the social forms and political and economic origins of male bonding. Unlike the Heywood plays he used for Jane Shore, in The Fatal Dowry he found a tightly focused forensic drama displaying in single-plotted concentration the complete architecture of the tested woman plot. The opening of Massinger and Field's tragedy builds the male unity that the woman's error will disrupt. The filial piety and patriarchal bonding of the first two acts is the business of the whole play. Because the woman's sexual sin is not a premarital lapse but adultery, the play speeds and clarifies the judgment process—not just by father and husband but by the woman on herself. Beaumelle's position as a pawn between male factions is stark, her treatment so unsentimental as to seem almost unemotional.

To a degree The Fatal Dowry's structure results from Massinger's preference for having characters "perform a dramatic action and then discuss it,"[26] the pattern fundamental to the tested woman plot. By contrast Rowe achieves his she-focus by dropping the court scene and male bonding sequences of the first two acts of his source and opening his play on the wedding day. This cropping creates unity of time. But neoclassical unity of time is an expression of a literary attitude toward the relationship between emotion and the social structures and events out of which emotion arises. What makes a play dramatic is the heightened expression itself, its grandest version the French neoclassical *tirade*, and the unities are the means to increase the concentration of such moments by reducing exposition of the social interactions that give them life. Because Calista's moral choice has taken place before the play opens, because Horatio's accusation about her involvement with Lothario is essentially accurate, because the husband is bound to find it out and the father bound to be offended, because the play's softened emotional tone will forbid the execution of the woman by her family, choices are reduced to their minimum. What is extended is the expression of the desires and sufferings of the entrapped characters.

Hence Rowe's histrionic devices. He retains the dramatic services of the tested woman for as long as possible. Though Calista's seduction took place before the play and is known to the us from act 1, to Horatio from act 2, to Altamont from the accusation scene of act 3, and to the father from the death of Lothario in act 4, Calista stabs herself fewer than a hundred lines from the end of act 5. Likewise with Sciolto: the father's first expressions of joy in the union of Altamont and his daughter come early in act 1; his sorrowing farewell to that daughter, followed by the news of his death, triggers her suicide and the play's end. Most important, Rowe vastly extends the theatrical presence of the tempter. Though Lothario reveals early in act 1 that he seduced Calista, though his quarrel with Horatio occurs in act 2, though much of act 3 is given over to Horatio's accusation against Calista to her husband, it is not until act 4 that Lothario is killed—and his body remains on stage for another 150 lines. Then there is the liberal use of the feint. Characters repeat actions of high drama or threaten deeds they are prevented from performing so they may threaten them again. Altamont swoons in act 4 under the stress of Calista's betrayal and Horatio's contempt, then swoons again at the end of act 5 in response to Calista's and Sciolto's deaths. Even more histrionically, after the fight between lover and husband in act 4 Calista offers to kill herself and is stopped by Altamont, then Sciolto offers to kill her and is stopped by Altamont; in act 5 Calista again offers to kill herself and is stopped by Sciolto, then when she finally does stab herself Altamont offers to kill *himself* and is prevented by Horatio.

Because Rowe retains the classic virtues of the tested woman plot—focus on family structure, balance among character functions, and a combination of social and individual emotional concerns—the concentration he imposes on *The Fair Penitent* gives it the power of a carefully refined symmetry. His exquisitely orchestrated roles must have been the delight of the actors who played them. Yet the play works not because of the focus on female suffering, but in spite of it; it is the overall familial situation that gives Calista's quandary its power and the story its energy. The play, however, has problems conveying real tragic conviction because of the weak links between the nature of the events and their emotional flavor. By the time it finally happens, Calista's death seems supererogatory; it is merely that the ending has been signaled so often as to have become obligatory. "Poetical justice" demands death for female unchastity, no doubt, but the play is not primarily interested in the workings of that justice. There are no court scenes because Rowe's is not forensic drama in any sense. Its gestures toward justice grow out of its emotion. Calista feels she must die because she has disappointed her father and her husband and is grief-stricken over Lothario's death. But Altamont does not believe in the necessity of any of this, with the bare exception of the lethal duel with Lothario (duels immediately taking on their own passions and justifications), which is why his reaction is avoidance, fainting. The sense of a world in which honor would demand this behavior is nearly lost. Theory even prevents Rowe from staging the pomp of public scenes whose practices and expectations might give the characters' actions social force.

TAKING TIME IN *PARADISE LOST*

To the degree that his tested woman plays lack conviction about the plot features that drama is best able to represent, Rowe's example shows how close the early eighteenth century is to the turn from dramatic to novelistic renderings. His struggle also reminds us, however, that in its earliest expressions the tested woman plot achieves its power through its concentration. How brief are the deeds on which originary tested woman stories hinge: a single word or even a refusal to speak that word; an act of eating; a giving of the body to sex or to death. Cordelia's word stands for a lifetime of love and duty; Desdemona's flight from her father's house is the deed of a lifetime. Of the changes accompanying the plot into novel form, none is more potentially complicating of this synecdochal clarity than the textual spaciousness and variety of narrative means that make possible a developmental portrayal of the self.

An examination of the post-Restoration tension between text time and story time must turn at last to the time-capaciousness of *Paradise Lost*, the most influential experiment in the tested woman plot's nondramatic telling. What the English-speaking tradition now knows of the Fall it knows through Milton.[27] The revolt and battle in heaven, the creation of hell, the association of the serpent with Satan, the love and the misery of Adam and Eve—not one of these is in Genesis, yet all live for us in our Miltonic inheritance. The construction of Milton's moral cosmos on the skeletal design of the Genesis story is the most expansive exploration of the possibilities of the tested woman plot in literature.

The text is also thickened by the fact that *Paradise Lost* is an experiment with genre. Combining dramatic tension with epic sweep, Milton writes a novelistic epic coupling some of the most powerful resources of both narration and direct discourse, a combination that frees it into the richness of psychological as well as historical and cosmic time. His early outlines show that Milton first envisioned then turned away from drama as his genre. One lure of epic was its prestige as the pinnacle of literary genres. Apart from its status compared to drama, however, epic has advantages of scale. Its subject matter conventions allow extended and flexibly presented chronology, a variety of locales, and an expansive cast of characters human and divine. Its textual conventions allow both dialogue and narrative, as well as great length. Yet Milton's epic gives the impression of a residual craving for the possibilities of dramatic form. In addition to the blank verse associated with the vigor of Renaissance dramatic poetry, *Paradise Lost* makes prominent use of direct speech—soliloquy, quasi-monologue, and dialogue. A large portion of the poem is narrated by the two angels, Raphael the heavenly historian and Michael the prophetic mouthpiece. By this epic technique, Milton gives Adam and Eve access to the larger story in which their personal history is embedded, so that they become witting participants rather than mere playthings of the gods. Narration by characters distances the author from the burden of superhuman access to divine actions and intentions. But conversation is also one of the themes of the poem, for Milton explicitly valorizes conversation as a human good in ways that are not typically epic: Eve's withdrawal during Raphael's account of celestial motion so as to have the pleasure of Adam's retelling and Adam's delight in Raphael's company and conversation that he unabashedly seeks to extend (book 8); the bitterness of Adam's and Eve's "mutual accusation," which constitutes a breakdown in conversability and results in "words constrained" (9:1187, 1066). One of the losses Adam mourns most after the fall is the loss of unmediated conversation with God and his angels (9:1–4, 1080–2; 10:119–21; 11:315–33). The most memorable valorization is Eve's response to Adam: "With thee conversing, I forget all time" (4:639).

The notion of a novelistic epic can be clarified by some of Mikhail Bakhtin's distinctions. *Paradise Lost* incorporates all three "constitutive features" that Bakhtin regards as distinguishing epic from the novel: "(1) a national epic past—in Goethe and Schiller's terminology the 'absolute past'—serves as the subject for the epic; (2) national tradition (not personal experience and the free thought that grows out of it) serves as the source of the epic; (3) an absolute epic distance separates the epic world from contemporary reality, that is, from the time in which the singer (the author and his audience) lives."[28] These features appear in the historical material of the Old Testament, the high heroic literature of the unreachable past of a people at its peak times. In the military and political history of the Book of Judges or the journey of the children of Israel out of Egypt to the Promised Land, Bakhtin's epic formulation holds absolutely. Some characteristics of the story material of

Paradise Lost, however, exist outside of Bakhtin's formulation, especially the poem's treatment of time. Although much of the Old Testament tells the epic story of the Hebrews, in the Garden Adam and Eve have not yet entered that time, nor are they yet Hebrews. They exist outside of nationhood, as progenitors of all mankind, and only with the expulsion from the Garden will they fall into time, the "absolute past" of the Hebrew nation. Moreover, the story's religious significance, including the effect of Christian typology, gives its human characters a transcendence uncharacteristic of epic. The Garden is less the peak time of humanity's past than the womb state in which it practices its becoming. Milton's version is concerned with the human psyche in the process of its development into full personhood, a journey not only not separated from author and readers by "an absolute epic distance" but meant to mirror the journey undertaken by us all.

The resources of conversation are Milton's chief means of combining the advantages of epic and drama. Conversation allows him to present a developmental psychological narration that creates selves and forwards their tasks of self-presentation, self-persuasion, and self-examination. None of these self-stories is in Genesis. The shifting of blame aside ("the woman gave to me"; "the serpent tempted me"), in the original story neither human has anything personal to say. By contrast, Milton capitalizes on the chronological and sequential flexibility of epic to present the complexity of human lives in the making. Lacking the technique of *style indirect libre*, which in any event would sit oddly with the rhetorical character of epic verse, he has no graceful way to use the narrator's voice for extended character self-presentation. So he seizes the opportunity epic provides for telling self-stories. Drama has very little place for such stories. Though other characters may tell a character's story, though a character may lament her condition or allude to her history, dramatic soliloquy and dialogue do not primarily narrate the histories of selves. When they narrate at all, it is to recount events too physical and often too large in scale to be staged. Milton employs epic form for the most intimate imaginable account—the coming to knowledge of the adult child, fully formed in all but experience. When Adam detains Raphael in book 8, he tells the only story he has, his own beginnings. This is the conventional epic *topos*—the beginnings of the people—but personalized, psychologized.

The telling is not easy: "For man to tell how human life began / Is hard; for who himself beginning knew?" (8:250–1). At first consciousness Adam has little urge or capacity for introspection. He knows the external world— seeing, describing, naming it (Milton must perforce assume language as part of his innate adult equipment)—but he has no way to know himself. It is God's visit that begins the interaction from which self-knowledge arises. God's conversation stimulates wonder, gratitude, curiosity. God's presence as interlocutor creates Adam's ability to distinguish himself from others. Not until the creation of Eve, God's great "amendment" (8:491), however, does Adam experience passion—the sweet "commotion strange" (8:530) of desire for bonding with the other who is like his own self. Raphael the Angel is always censorious of this passion, always seeking to temper and neutralize it. Readers by contrast understand that Adam's commitment to his other self will be mankind's making and the model for its salvation.

Self-stories now seem a defining characteristic of what it means to be human. The multiple layering of psychological narration, with its self-presentation, self-persuasion, and self-examination, is the necessary feature of well-rounded novelistic characters. In part this explains most readers' initial attraction toward Satan. In books 1 through 3, Satan's boldness and heightened rhetoric make him appear the preeminent practitioner of psychological self-exploration. But what Satan does with self—and what he can do—is limited by his fixed nature and his solitariness. Given the *in medias res* opening of the poem, we never directly meet other than a Lucifer damned, whose nature is beyond change: this is what damned means. The more he exposes himself, the clearer becomes the static nature of his character, which is why there is no dramatic point in his having a friend or confidant. How much this solitariness is a literary phenomenon as well as a moral fact is evident only when we reach book 4, where we first meet Adam and Eve engaged in the practice of forming their selves, deepening their personalities through repeated interaction with each other and with their divine visitors. With each encounter, the two emerge as more complex beings. Satan cannot grow in this way. He is the classic epic figure less because he is larger than life than because he is static. With their human opportunities to create themselves, it is Adam and Eve who are novelistic.

Though in the mythic event sequence Adam's self-formation comes first, textually his self-presentation has been preceded by Eve's story in book 4. As we read Adam on himself our strongest point of curiosity is how his account of coming to consciousness will differ from hers. Adam's account is far longer, more connected to the external world, more filled with expressions of wonder and longing, whereas Eve's account had been intensive, more self-reflective and self-protective, and already framed within Adam's world. These differences respond to Milton's models of the ideal male and female, and they are designed to be hierarchical as well as complementary. The characteristic to which I wish to call attention, however, is the impression of Eve's inwardness and completeness. This is the quality that moves and commands Adam most, and it is repeatedly invoked in the descriptions before the Fall.[29] At their evensong Adam addresses her as "Daughter of God and man, accomplished Eve" (4:660) and the sense of "accomplished" as "completed," "perfected," is prepared by the bold Christological allusion: by genealogy this woman is the female equivalent of the Son of God and man. When later, in conversation with Raphael, Adam repeatedly tries to explain his response to Eve, it is in terms of her "allness": "what seemed fair in all the world" seemed "in her summed up, in her contained" (8:472–3). He knows that, created second, she has less dominion over the other creatures than he; and as a good Aristotelian, he also knows that she is imperfect, contributing less than he to the process of generation. But that is not how she seems:

> when I approach
> Her loveliness, so absolute she seems
> And in herself complete, so well to know
> Her own, that what she wills to do or say,
> Seems wisest, virtuousest, discreetest, best.
> (8:546–50)

No wonder Raphael must deliver a lecture on masculine self-esteem and the dangers of uxoriousness. The distinction between male activity and female passivity may seem merely a time-encrusted paternalistic construct, but the result is a very specific explanation for the presence of the tested woman. From Adam's point of view, Eve is the image of integratedness and thus of integrity. She is perfected, which means both that she seems to have less need of him than he of her and also that for him she is essentially unknowable. This is the point of the test: to confront the paradox of perfection, to find out what is otherwise unknowable. One of Adam's charges against himself after the Fall is presuming upon the impression of her completedness: "perhaps / I also erred in overmuch admiring / What seemed in thee so perfect, that I thought / No evil durst attempt thee" (9:1177–80). From whatever moral perspective her otherness is construed, we see here the male making of the female mystique.

Yet from the reader's perspective Eve's nature seems more tentative and provisional than Adam perceives. In the account she gives of her awakening, her movement is inward, while Adam's was outward. As though born with the genetic memory imparted by her biological parent, she already knows enough of self to concern herself with her own nature and origins: "much wond'ring where / And what I was, whence thither brought, and how" (4:451–2). After brief wandering, she lies on a bank, looks into a still lake, and is captivated by her image. The allusion is to Narcissus, but the use Milton makes of the motif of self-absorption is different from Ovid's because it goes on to include both self-examination and comparison with the not-self, the man to whom she is introduced by God and from whom she initially turns away. With this episode begins the presentation of Eve as the poem's premier adventurer in individuation. Adam has been created such that from his beginning he can distinguish himself from both God and beast. The various ceremonies of his initiation into humanhood—his conversation with God, his journey through Eden into Paradise, his viewing of the Garden, naming of the animals, pleading for a mate—all swiftly create a separated sense of self. His voyeurism during Eve's making gives him both image and metaphor of his relationship to her. Eve knows none of this. Like the rest of us, she is born into a world already peopled. It is her adventures of self-differentiation and self-definition that are most humanlike.

The waves of self-exploration gain power by the manipulation of textual time and space to suggest the expansiveness of the symbolically compressed moment in the Garden. Foreshadowing the human condition of endless choice, Eve actually undergoes two tests, first the seducing dream of book 5, presided over by the angelic simulacrum who fades at the point of "high exaltation" (5:90), then the real-time temptation in book 9, presided over by the human-seeming serpent. Her emotional and intellectual adventures in the course of these temptation sequences are vivid and varied. As when awake, in her dream she is the longing focus of all eyes, including the eyes of the heavens themselves (5:44–7). (The vanity of "longing to be seen / Though by the Devil himself" of which Adam accuses her [10:877–8] is a temptation prepared by repeated references to the male gaze of Adam, Raphael, and the narrator.) Stirred by the prospect of superior knowledge, she reacts, not like Adam the attentive student, but like a philosopher, with a series of thought experiments. On the one hand she wrestles with the temptation to leave Adam ignorant and enjoy her superiority over him ("for inferior, who is free?" [9:825]); on the other hand she invents jealousy, recognizing that if she should indeed "die," whatever the term means, he might receive another Eve. Later, as the two cease to accuse each other and acknowledge the misery of their mutual fall, it is she who explores the options of sexual abstinence and of suicide.

After the serpent's dance prologue, the temptation sequences of book 9, first Eve's then Adam's, are nearly entirely dialogue. One would expect them to be highly dramatistic, yet they seem different from dramatic dialogue in their pacing, in the dynamic between the interlocutors, in the detail with which the speakers weigh the pros and cons of disobedience. The difference has much to do with the nature of the disobedient act under discussion and with the tempter's relation to that act. To exploit most sensationally the presence of the woman as natural subordinate, stories built on the tested woman plot usually use sexual obedience as the crux. Milton's story does not. Though Adam and then Eve's disobedience is sense-based, has sexual ramifications, and uses sexual metaphors like Adam's description of Eve as "deflower'd" after her act (9:901), it is not a sexual act. The distinction shapes the level of intellectual and moral explicitness with which the temptation debate can be carried out. In a sexual temptation the tempter's task (absent the services of a bawd) is itself sexual, and the temptation sequence takes on a secret, euphemistic quality in keeping with the private and mutual nature of the act. Sexual temptation is always postlapsarian. Shame and guilt, which demand privacy, have already been invented, so that the sexual tempter usually includes the promise of secrecy. Eve has naive hopes of keeping her deed secret, but that is the only feature of her temptation similar to a sexual one. Satan's whole pretense is that he has preceded Eve in the forbidden deed. Far from seducing her to a mutual act of secret intercourse, he encourages her to follow him on an adventure from which she may profit as he has done. He presents himself as a disinterested but generous benefactor, something the sexual tempter is rarely in a position to do.

Moreover, the act he urges is symbolic only. The fruit is not poisonous in the usual sense, it is not even corrupting, only enlightening—unless corruption arises from knowledge. Eve is right in arguing after the Fall that there was nothing in her experience to enable her to crack the serpent's argument. The sole objection to eating the fruit is that it has been forbidden by the One who has the right to forbid.

This distinction in the nature of the act being urged allows Milton's characters to linger informatively over their decision-making. As the experienced tempter (first the serpent, then Eve) seeks a disciple and a companion in the act, the tempted one (first Eve, then Adam) ponders advantages and disadvantages, exploring what it means to become persuaded, to make another's position one's own. Adam's decision is immediate and nearly instinctual: "with thee / Certain my resolution is to die" (9:906–7), he states in the interior monologue that follows Eve's exuberant invitation to eat. This response carries out the declaration of that morning: "Where danger or dishonor lurks" the husband guards his wife, "or with her the worst endures" (9:267–9). More, it expresses his inability to return to solitariness: "How can I live without thee, how forgo / Thy sweet converse and love so dearly joined, / To live again in these wild woods forlorn?" (9:908–10). It is the "link of nature" (9:914), the "bond of nature" (9:956), that holds him. The maternal imagery of this longing is its strongest feature. Adam is not persuaded to the deed, but to Eve herself, which means to his past and the emotions of the past. Though he goes on to explain his decision and the alternating distress and hopefulness with which he regards the future, he never really debates his course of action. Taking her into himself through the act of self-persuasion is a return and a homecoming.

Eve's self-persuasion is more complex, though not more moving, because though she also is led into temptation, it is toward the new state the serpent offers, not toward any version of the past nor, directly, toward the serpent himself. Central to the serpent's persuasiveness is demonstration by analogy: since he who was a beast is now humanlike, she who is human must by eating become like a god. Eating the fruit is a displaced sexual act because it involves taking Satan's argument into herself, but Eve does not see this. To her Satan's presence is contingent and his argument fortuitous. The act of eating seems a positive good, which no forbidden sexual act, however convincingly excused or hotly desired, could seem. Eating the fruit will even reestablish the distinction that ought to lie between her and the serpent. Because the tempter plays an indirect, mediated, and seemingly disinterested role, eating the fruit is not personally intimate or disloyal in the way sexual disobedience must be.

What Eve's version of the deed does have is a powerful component of self-shaping. This self-shaping bears a double burden of hierarchical subordination because of her double parentage. Though she is God's creature, as Galatea is Pygmalion's, shaped and molded and breathed into life, she is also Adam's creature, as a child is her mother's, born from his body and treasured, guided, and clung to like a child. Little surprise then that Eve's temptation mimics the child's striving toward adulthood, as Adam's epithet of address ("advent'rous Eve" [9:921]) acknowledges. The serpent rehearses most of the points of her self-argument. His favored form is the rhetorical question, designed not just to give the impression of involving her in reasoned inquiry, but to preordain her response. One of the subtlest of the serpent's points, because so responsive to Eve's adolescent striving toward self-created independence, is about generational precedence: "The gods are first, and that advantage use / On our belief, that all from them proceeds" (9:718–9). For Eve, it is not the gods only but her earthly parent/spouse against whom she must grow. Like any child making its way to adulthood, she must work against that precedence, against the forbidding of the child to be as wise and experienced as the father (9:759). This is the self-shaping of rebellion and breaking free. Book 10 involves the opposite movement, Eve's voluntary return to a sense of unity with Adam. Yet because her ultimate expression of her need for him also includes her full acceptance of her responsibility for their fate, it continues the action of self-individuation: "both have sinn'd, but thou / Against God only, I against God and thee" (10:930–1). When she proposes to return to the place of judgment and importune God to sentence "Mee mee only just object of his ire" (10:936), she has made herself fully responsible and therefore fully human.

This distinguishing and freeing of individual selves from the generalized plot line of the Creation story is made convincing and gripping by its distribution throughout the text. In the absence of the natural progression of human birth, growth, and education, Milton creates in his poetic structure an equivalent spaciousness and flexibility that allows him to visit and revisit his human pair, repeatedly exploring their psychological states and moral awareness, educating them through tutelage and experience, developing the opportunities for conversation that create as well as express personality. In good part the sheer length of the text gives the illusion of elapsed time so necessary to this constructing, but Milton's theological and poetical purpose makes this construction necessary. For him the point of the plot is neither disobedience nor divine judgment, but the human opportunities created by the plot's natural stress points: the requirement of choice, the freedom to err, and the necessity of living with consequences. Because this is the story of the Garden told from outside the Garden, the trial portion of the plot is no longer merely backward-looking and purgative but also forward-looking and propitiatory. Adam and Eve's fall leads forward to their lives, a move that is profoundly novelistic.

TEN

Pamela as Epistolary Drama

FOR ALL ITS PASSION FOR THE THEATER, THE EIGHTEENTH CENTURY did not find its own form for serious drama. Neither pseudoclassical nor Renaissance structures rang true: the history of heroic drama, the revivals of classical forms, the few attempts at bourgeois drama, the she-tragedy that represented the period's take on its Jacobean predecessors, all are the history of a theater seeking a convincing contemporary form and repeatedly failing. The tested woman plot hung on as the stuff of sentimental drama, but it failed to achieve anything as powerful as the best Renaissance plays. The problem was partly social. The more drama sentimentalized the plot's relationship between the woman's act and the patriarchy's judgment of the act, the more blurred the plot's purposes became. But when the drama attempted to retain the social distinctions and sanctions (cults of honor, family feuds, rituals of bride exchange, female sequestration) out of which various versions of the plot had arisen, it no longer reflected its world's social beliefs and practices.

The theater, moreover, hardly acknowledged the biggest literary change of the period, the development of the modern concept of literature. At the Restoration what is now called literature was heir to the humanist rhetorical tradition of antilogistic argumentation last represented by Donne and Milton[1] and the humanist poetic tradition of imitation of classical forms last epitomized by Jonson. This world thought in terms not of "literature" but of the practices of grammar, rhetoric, and logic; the making of discourse as public argument; and the socially hierarchical mimetic genres of classical poetics. A hundred years later European culture had a new way of regarding texts. The concept of literature developed along with the concept of the expressive text. Instead of applying the topics and practicing the authoritative forms of the culture at large, the expressive text "consecrates the writer,"[2] claiming to express individual experience, sanctify individual sensibility, and glorify the private voice. This development legitimized and empowered the writer and fictive narrator, the first-person fictive character, the writer of the expressive essay. But its popularity created a technical impasse for drama, which buffers the writer's voice through the medium of characters and avoids assigning a dominating voice to any single character who might speak for the writer at a second level of expressivity.

THE IMPULSE FOR *PAMELA*

Samuel Richardson's radical epistolary experiment, *Pamela*, charts the move of the tested woman plot into expressive narrative fiction. Published to unheard-of public interest in 1740, *Pamela* seems designed to counter the incompatibilities between the tested woman plot and the constraints of eighteenth-century drama. Richardson's non-theatrical use of the plot was not the result of an active choice. It is true that he distrusted the theater business. He objected to the sneers of upper-class drama at bourgeois morals, was repelled by the behavior of many theater people, and welcomed the repressive licensing of the theaters in 1737. But he was not anti-drama or even anti-theater. As a printer he published hoards of plays and read some of them. His closest literary friend and adviser was the playwright and dramatic theorist Aaron Hill. He became the friend of the great actor and impresario David Garrick. Some of his wittiest writing occurs in *Clarissa*'s "playbook scenes," stage-managed by his superbly theatrical character Lovelace. *Pamela*'s critique of the disparity between the high seriousness of Ambrose Phillips's Andromache play, *The Distressed Mother*, and its salacious epilogue is Richardson's plea for theater to take seriously the moral power of theatrical illusion.[3] But it would not have occurred to him to write a play. A successful printer and occasional editor and author of didactic texts, he began the servant girl's letters that mushroomed into a novel while at work on a commissioned volume of model letters for the business and personal use of the lower classes. His intentions in both the *Familiar Letters* and the novel were ethical, and he considered himself firmly in the conduct tradition. But the novel he wrote was, in his words, a "dramatic narrative," and the psychological and social issues that engrossed him confronted the features of the tested woman plot that caused the drama the most discomfort.

One of these features is character decorum. In *Pamela*, Richardson was interested in the portrayal of behavior in relation to social class. The decorum of character, though rigidly established in dramatic theory, received little attention in other literature because no other literature mixed classes and their daily concerns, which is one reason *Pamela* attracted so much attention.[4] These class issues, the motivating force of his first novel as he initially wrote it, would be replaced in *Clarissa* by other concerns. But in *Pamela* Richardson was determined to write from his servant-girl heroine's point of view. Whether servants have honor; what might be the patriarchal rights of Goodman Andrews as against those of Squire B; how one should view, describe, and respond to the abuses of the gentry toward their inferiors; what the obligations of inferiors to their superiors are, and where those obligations must be overridden by the duty of self-respect—these were matters of compelling personal concern to

Richardson, the master of apprentices and employer of skilled workmen, the public-minded citizen, the husband, the father of daughters, the child of the urban working poor. These matters are central in the novel. The drama of the eighteenth century, with the exception of a few plays of which George Lillo's *London Merchant* and *Fatal Curiosity* are the best known, had found no way to break the stranglehold of character decorum and its tie to genre, no way to write the serious story of people from "low life." In *Pamela* Richardson set out to do it.

Richardson also set out to render women's voices. From childhood he had entered imaginatively into the psychological and ethical world of women,[5] and in his social life he had cultivated learned, accomplished, and sensitive women friends. The theater had already expanded histrionic opportunities for women—as actors, playwrights, characters—and drama had perfected two kinds of female voices: the aria of anguish and the innuendoed repartee of the comedy of manners. The increasingly popular novel form was linked to the growth of female vernacular literacy, the woman leisure reader, and opportunities for women writers. Earlier writers of fiction, notably Defoe, had featured female-adventurer protagonists. But Richardson was determined to give Pamela her own voice, both individualized as Defoe's female protagonists' voices never are, and personally questioning and expressive in ways drama has no room for. His choice of epistolary technique and a character impassioned about the act of writing stems not just from his experience as a writer of the homiletic letter form, but from his respect for women's voices and his fascination with the writer writing.

Richardson's fictive technique works against concentration of time. Both his epistolary form and his first-person point of view take time for psychological pressures to build and psychological reactions to be explored. His commentary over the next twenty years about issues connected with "writing to the moment" establishes his interest in the relation between dramatized time and lived time and his desire to express fully and with extension his characters' emotions in moments of crisis and choice. *Pamela* is initiated by the resistance of a lower-class virgin to a rake's sexual and economic enforcement. The "time" encompassed by this action is the fraught transfer of the woman from father to husband. But as Richardson worked with his character and her circumstances, as he was forced into a sequel to counteract unauthorized continuations, as he later embarked on a greater novelistic experiment, he became increasingly interested in the ethical and psychological shape of whole lives.

Yet because epistolary, *Pamela* is also a kind of drama. Less fully epistolary than *Clarissa* with its large cast of characters writing in all directions in fully individualized voices, its sense of dialogue is limited. Nevertheless, the buffering of the author by the voice of the letter writer enabled Richardson to publish the work as the letters of an actual serving maid. Because that voice was so distinctive and gripping, Richardson's work supplied a new answer to the question of what constitutes dramatic and emotional impact. As the eighteenth century theorized about and experimented with emotional identification, the results could be sentimental. "We ne'er can pity what we ne'er can share," argues Rowe, and the evocation of easy anxiety, sorrow, or admiration on behalf of abused characters is one of the traits the age increasingly valued and Richardson's work accommodates. But *Pamela* also promotes a different understanding of identification—lived time in the character's mind, circumstances, and language. This kind of imaginative participation in a character's life need not be sentimental. It may be strenuous rather than easy, unsettling rather than gratifying, anger-inducing rather than tear-jerking, provocative of analysis and reflection as well as emotion.

With this kind of identification, *Pamela* brings us to a crux at the heart of the new concept of literature. What is the authority of personal experience? The experience of an ordinary, anonymous, uneducated, unimportant person? In the strictly theological and moral sphere, the question had been answered by Pauline Christianity: in Christ there is neither Jew nor Gentile, male nor female, slave nor free. Protestantism had committed ultimate authority to the individual believer. But the practices of socially significant and morally serious literature had until recently answered the question differently, and it is with these practices that Richardson breaks. Before Pamela's experience slips into the exemplum category developed in the sequel and revised into the original, there is a potent sense of the authority of the socially modest individual's examined life. Part of the novel's affirmation of such a life is owing to its adherence to a time- and authority-honored plot. But part of that affirmation arises from Richardson's "writing to the moment." Unlike previous epistolary fiction, which reports past events reflected in some kind of tranquility, Richardson's letter writers report the near-present. Pamela is frequently interrupted in her writing; later letters may unsay what earlier ones promised or reported; Pamela often uses the letter form to debate her course of action with herself and her image of her correspondents, and to come to a decision before our eyes. This sense of actuality, however naive, flustered, and uncertain, is of itself authoritative for the reader.

The authority the technique develops depends on time: contact time between the character and the reader, which must be more extended than the stage can accommodate; time over a significant stretch of the character's life that cannot be encompassed in a drama constrained by the unities. What seems to be operating in this kind of identification is the reader's own character formation. The reader needs to participate in enough of the character's life to develop something like the same experience bank, especially the same memory of events and the same grounds for decision-making. Particularly useful for such fiction is a focus on the naive protagonist faced for the first time with momentous life decisions that require the greatest agonizing and debate. The reader can join in these decisions as the character herself builds her rich or deep memory bank. Because such fiction seeks wholeness—the whole mind in the widest variety of states, the whole experience in all its emotional ramifications, the whole life in its entire extension—the more wholes the fictive representation develops, the stronger the reader's ability to participate.

MR. B's TOTALITARIAN ENTERPRISE

To achieve this identification between reader and narrating character, Richardson adopts a version of the plot, exemplified by the story of Griselda, that maximally deprives his tested woman of outside help. In a study of the tale structures of the *Decameron*, in which the Griselda story first appeared, Tzvetan Todorov sees exchange as the common thematic denominator of the entire work. Generally, he says, exchange has the two-way action the term itself leads us to expect: X gives to Y and Y gives to X—a dowry for a wife, a gift for an act of kindness, an insult for an insult. Trickery or falsification of the facts of the exchange—some kind of one-upmanship—is the norm in the *Decameron;* Todorov sees the "message" of the work as breaking the old system "in the name of the audacious personal initiative."[6] Nevertheless, the form of the relationship is reciprocal. But Todorov also notes another form of exchange that does not seem reciprocal. A story opens with a stock sequence: X enjoys Y's wife while Y is away. Clearly there is a sexual exchange between the lover and the woman. But the woman's status as wife means that another, one-way, exchange is at work as well. "One must note that in such cases the exchange is not undertaken with the object of the action but with a third person, the one in legal possession, who may even be completely absent from the story; thus if a man has sex with a married woman, the exchange takes place with the husband."[7] Unreciprocated exchanges especially occur in situations of hierarchical inequality, where the superior simply takes (life, body, goods), or the inferior out-and-out steals (goods, body, life).

Most of the struggles of Renaissance tested woman plays occur between hierarchically more or less equal males. Even where the king infringes on the marital property of his vassal or subject, the play dramatizes the reciprocal rights and obligations of both patriarchal figures. That is, after all, the whole point of the infringement. Yet a few powerful stories so undermine, distance, or eliminate the power of the possessing male that the woman comes to stand alone, bereft of patriarchal support. The male possessor never completely disappears. The Duchess of Malfi's husband and steward of the horse may be helpless to protect her from her brothers, but in psychological terms he is neither negligible nor contemptible and it is her marriage to him that has enraged them. But the broader the social gulf, the more faintly his figure can be sketched, as in Boccaccio's Griselda story, which is why I have introduced Todorov's distinction here. Though Elizabethan dramatists scrambled Griselda's family back into the equation to restore the typical patriarchal balance of the plot, Boccaccio's tale presents a ruler who so monopolizes power as to be able to take, have, order, control at will. When Walter turns his attention to Griselda, he occupies *every* position of power. His graciousness to her father is condescension, not reciprocity. The father becomes negligible except as a formal place-holder in the morality structure. The full weight of Walter's transactions bears directly on the woman. This is Richardson's model for *Pamela*.

I need to fill in something of the form and the publication history of the novel to help explain how Richardson uses his model. *Pamela I* here refers to the novel Richardson first published in 1740. It takes the characters through the wedding and the response of Mr. B's circle to his bride. Richardson revised *Pamela I* repeatedly until his death, making his heroine "progressively more grammatical and less colloquial," as his biographers say.[8] Though the history of Richardson's revisions is important for the study of his developing intentions, I am using the first edition because of the information it gives about Richardson's first responses to his literary and cultural influences. When Richardson published *Pamela I* after extremely rapid composition, he had no immediate impulse to continue, though the latter part of the work introduces some themes that are not carried to fruition. But in 1742 unauthorized sequels drove him to publish the continuation I call *Pamela II*. This work also was printed in two volumes with two title pages, and it supplies the story of the Bs' married life and Pamela's homilies on ethics and the education of children.[9] Though *Pamela II* had a respectable readership, it was hardly the sensation its predecessor had been.

Pamela I opens in a totalitarian world. Compared to the oligarchical systems of tested woman drama, with their balanced male power loci, its concentration of power is striking. For the entire first half, not a single character equals B in either status or power. Everyone is his dependent in some respect. Most are servants; even the genteel Mrs. Jervis and Mr. Longman owe their economic positions to him. Offstage equals are mentioned—Lord and Lady Davers, the Darnfords—but they do not appear. The closest thing to a social equal is Mr. Williams, the young clergyman who, though he also is Mr. B's dependent, attempts to protect, liberate, and even marry Pamela, a degree of rivalry that enrages B into having him jailed on trumped-up charges of debt. Not only does B occupy all positions of authority in the world of the novel; he also deliberately combines and confuses them. He is the son of Pamela's revered late mistress and mentor, a kind of surrogate big brother. He is a rich, prominent, and well-educated public man. He is her employer, the master of the estate on which she lives, and the local magistrate, her source of just dealing and legal recourse. He first demands as by right, then attempts to buy, her sexual services. The patriarchal system fosters this concentration, and Richardson portrays from the inside the closed, arbitrary world it creates. The effect is both gripping and horrific.

I use the word "totalitarian" in the modern sense. Consideration of how the "government of B" exercises power over the unwilling yields a catalogue of modern totalitarian techniques. B subverts civic life and forbids assembly (pitting servants against each other and refusing to allowing the household to see Pamela off). He corrupts the morals of individual underlings (John), organizes private enforcers (Jewkes and company), spreads disinformation (to the Lincolnshire tenant family), directly lies (the letter to Goodman Andrews), feints (pretending to be planning to marry), threatens economic sanctions (firing Mrs. Jervis), manipulates and misuses the legal system (Mr. Williams), violates the privacy of the public post (Mr. Brett). He also steals and spies (Pamela's letters), bribes (gifts of clothes and money; the written proposal of concubinage), accuses the victim (every encounter with Pamela), and even makes his victim disappear for long enough to terrify her parents. If B's position is that of governor—and he is so presented—these forms of behavior make any kind of healthy society impossible, fostering distrust between members of the group and focusing every eye in cringing or self-seeking fascination on the center of power.

But the most totalitarian feature is his manipulation of language, the rhetoric of his own benevolence and victimization. B has a splendid line in syntactically fluent and semantically slippery self-justification. His favorite epithet for Pamela is "saucy," with "ungrateful" a close second. Both point to her subservience and obligation. His favorite argumentative ploy is to totalize hierarchy and obligation. Because as master he is owed respect and obedience, Pamela is obliged to respect him by obeying his demand for sex. His favorite response to the least resistance or rebuke is to accuse others of mistreating him—he will not be spoken to, plotted against, resisted in this way. His favorite form of psychological bullying is to put Pamela "on trial" for the offense of refusing his sexual advances. Pamela's frequent tears during their encounters are not just tears of terror at his physical familiarities but tears of frustration at his abuse of language, as her bedtime prattle to Mrs. Jewkes, freed from the tension of his presence, makes plain. Describing in the most straightforward terms she can how her parents' and mistress's lessons to live virtuously have been replaced by her master's demand "Be not virtuous, Pamela," and listing with scorn the gewgaws with which he would buy her body, she continues laying out his latest offer:

> Well, forsooth, but then I was to have I know not how many pounds a year for my life; and my poor father (there was the jest of it) was to be the manager for the abandon'd prostitute his daughter: And then (there was the jest again) my kind, forgiving, virtuous master, would pardon me all my misdeeds!
>
> Yes, thank him for nothing, truly. And what, pray, are all these violent misdeeds?—Why, they are for daring to adhere to the good lessons that were taught me; and not learning a new one, that would have reversed all my former: For not being contented when I was run away with, in order to ruin me; but contriving, if my poor wits had been able, to get out of my danger, and preserve myself honest. (174)

Here Pamela is translating, verbally taking her experience back from B's disguising, inverting, controlling language into a bald description of fact. This is one of her ways to stay balanced and sane.

Such emotionally powerful translation is made possible by Richardson's choice of protagonist, of epistolary method, and of concentration on the temptation/choice stage of the tested woman plot. It also raises a fascinating possibility that Richardson investigates more intensively in his next novel. Could Pamela's account be as partial, twisted, sophistical, propagandistic as B's seems to Pamela to be? After all, our perspectives are limited to what Pamela tells us. Pamela's terms for her present state ("honest") and her threatened future ("ruined"), terms about which B "fleers" and "jeers," are themselves self-interested. Yet we get help from the other characters' reactions and the fact that B has to keep hiding his enterprise. We get the help of his stated intentions—"I will have her!" coupled with his "Indeed I cannot marry." We have our knowledge of the world in which these characters live: what his "keeping" would mean for her life; the fact that her code words describe a disaster from which her parents would go to their deaths in shame, and a Mr. Williams would never think of offering marriage. In fact Richardson hardly lets us question Pamela's account. We are convinced, finally, less by any particular example of B's perfidy than by the fullness of her story. The minuteness of detail and the elaboration of her states of mind carry the conviction that, whatever B's intentions, his power and the terror and toadying it creates are evil.

In the most interesting portion of *Pamela I*, the end of the first volume and beginning of the second, the tone between Pamela and Mr. B starts to change. Like us, B becomes Pamela's reader.[10] First he overhears her, for he was present at Pamela's prattle to Mrs. Jewkes after all, disguised as the drunken Nan sleeping it off in a chair with her apron over her head. Then he gets access to increasingly large chunks of her papers and comes to imagine the events of the past weeks from Pamela's perspective. His surprise at her astuteness and seriousness of purpose suggests that he may never before have imagined another person's life—certainly not a lower-class person's or a woman's. Several scenes show him practicing this new angle of vision as he listens to her differently, engages in real conversation with her, tries almost literally to see her in a new light. In the scene where he interrupts her and Mrs. Jewkes at their meal to demand that she carve a chicken and eat a wing of it, then paces thoughtfully before marching out again, he seems to be trying to visualize her as mistress of his table—what she would look like as Mrs. B. This shift in Mr. B's perspective is of enormous importance to literary practice. One of the great contributions of the new expressive literature of the eighteenth century, elaborated in novels of the next 150 years, is its initiation of millions of readers into the lives and imaginations of other people, people unlike themselves, ordinary people. Richardson's readers repeatedly singled out this participatory effect as the most remarkable feature of his rendering of Pamela's life.

But something else also causes the change in tone. As B's kindnesses and the easing of her terror give her space for contemplation, Pamela realizes that she has come to love her captor. She has recognized her preoccupation with him, her attention to his every move, her attempt to read his tactics and intentions. She has admitted that she cannot hate him, expressed her gratitude at his escape from drowning. Now she notices—and admits—something more: "O my dear Father and Mother! now I know you will indeed be concern'd for me!—For now I am for myself!—And now I begin to be afraid, I know too well the reason, why all his hard trials of me, and my black apprehensions, would not let me hate him" (185). Not that Pamela is unarmed against the bad cop/good cop effect: having overheard B's declaration to Mrs. Jewkes that, since freezing will not move her, he will try what melting can do, she repeatedly warns herself not to be seduced by kindness. But a deeper psychological effect of totalitarian terror is also at work. In studies of hostage-taking this is known as the Stockholm syndrome, in which hostages emerge bonded, pleading for their captors. Total dependence does that: total dependence on an absolute power that can both punish and reward. For B can reward—and convinced of both Pamela's rectitude and her love, and acknowledging his need for her, he designs a marriage where once he designed seduction and concubinage.

The second volume of *Pamela I*—even given the tensions of the wedding day or the fight with Lady Davers—is as joyful as the first was anxious. Mr. B finds that he enjoys organizing generosity and marital felicity even more than he enjoyed organizing seduction, and Pamela's education—sexual, social, linguistic—fascinates him unendingly. As for Pamela, her preoccupation with him only increases as her gratitude burgeons. From a modern point of view, the world of the second volume is still totalitarian, though now the subject is willing. Mr. B's monopoly of patriarchal functions is to be expected in a patriarchal world, but his intrusiveness into every feature of Pamela's life is nearly as smothering as his intrigues. We realize that B's qualms about the difficulties of marriage to a servant girl have been overridden by his recognition of its advantages. If he has told Pamela how difficult it is for him to marry *her*, he has said even more often how difficult it is for him to marry at all. He has shied away from marriage within his own class. No woman of family, education, and fortune has been attractive to him (184). Like the Marquis Walter, in such a marriage he would have to negotiate power with his wife and her family, whereas with Pamela all advantages, including that of a legitimate heir, and all power, including that of condescending benevolently to her parents, remain his. This is the reward (if reward it is) of the man who marries an apprentice into his social sphere.[11]

As *Pamela I* comes to an end, Richardson is developing ever more insistently the theme of the imperious male will. It has always been a characteristic of Mr. B, but there is nothing like marriage to institutionalize it. At least that is the effect of B's lordly injunctions on marital obedience, the forty-eight "Rules I am to observe from this awful Lecture" (369). Enough to tax even Pamela's excellent memory, they evoke her bemused, understated assessment to her parents: "Yet, after all, you'll see I have not the easiest Task in the World" (372). They are provoked by her daring to approach him in his anger at his sister's interference, and they could be summarized as "Thou shalt not talk back." With them we have returned to the Griselda story.

EDUCATING MR. B

Perhaps because Richardson launched himself into his story of virtue tested and triumphant without any certainty of its novelistic shape,[12] his new way of writing assumed the profile of an old tale. That Richardson's work has a fairytale flavor is not new.[13] *Pamela* and the Griselda story share folkloric motifs with rags-to-riches tales like Cinderella or King Cophetua and the beggar maid, the most important motif being that the beggar maids marry their princes. Readers have always found that feature attracting: "Who does not, *Pamela*, thy suff'rings feel? / Who has not wept at beauteous *Grissel's* wheel?"[14] But whereas Cinderella stories are about how the woman's marriage up is achieved, the Griselda story is not. Though the poor girl/rich husband motif helped turn *Pamela* into the first novelistic bestseller, it does not control the structure of either *Pamela* or the Griselda story, nor is upward social mobility its primary moral. As Chaucer's Clerk's Tale points out, in its deep structure the Griselda story resembles the story of Job;[15] it is about the testing of the subordinate and the education of the superior.

Pamela's version of the tested woman plot is like the Griselda story in specific structural ways. It has only two characters who really matter. Mrs. Jervis and Mrs. Jewkes, Mr. Williams and Goodman Andrews, Lady Davers and Mr. H are walk-ons, mere conveniences or diversions. Though often memorable, they do not control the plot, and any number of characters could serve their turn. *Pamela* is the story of a monumental struggle between Pamela and Mr. B, just as the Griselda tale is about Griselda and Walter. *Pamela* also resembles the Griselda story in B's monopoly of authority functions. These are exercised in a series of waves, bringing us to the third similarity, the repetition of the test/trial pattern. Repeatedly Pamela, like Griselda, is offered an opportunity to err, after which her behavior is scrutinized. This pattern of testing and examination is one of the novel's distinctive features; the sequel shows that it could be made to continue for as long as Pamela lives, since like Griselda's, Pamela's tale is a type of the Christian life.

The Griselda event sequence also controls the event sequence of *Pamela*. Recognizing it, however, requires reading both parts of the novel as a whole. Richardson was galvanized to resume writing by the pressure of unauthorized sequels, especially John Kelly's. Critics have tended to see Richardson's sequel as nothing more than a flogging of reiterative exempla. Yet throughout the correspondence on the composition of *Pamela II*, Richardson insists on his

intentions regarding his characters and his "plan," though what those intentions were is never detailed. His letters do tell us that he thought of the two
parts of the work as of a piece, and that his story was not just about the courtship
of a virtuous woman, but about her life. In a letter to his brother-in-law the
printer James Leake, in August 1741, he said that if a continuation were to be
done "I was resolved to do it myself, rather than my Plan should be <basely>
Ravished out of my Hands, and, probably my Characters depreciated and
debased, by those who knew nothing of the Story, nor the Delicacy required
in the Continuation of the Piece." If Kelly's work did go forward, the printer
"should have it publish'd under some other Title, and not infringe upon my
Plan or Characters" (Carroll, 43). A few days later he was delicately rejecting
his friend Dr. Cheyne's recommendations for a series of "Characters" of the
good woman as unsuitable to "either my Design, or the Story."[16] A letter
to Stephen Duck, probably from October 1741, briefly lays out a "general
Sketch of my Design (How it will be executed, is another thing)" (53), the
sketch referring to such episodes as Pamela's charity to the poor, the debate
about mothers nursing their own children, Mr. H's intrigue with her maid, and
the "Distress" arising from a masquerade. Another letter to Cheyne, probably
from January 1742, reminds that "the four Volumes were to be consider'd as
one Work" (54).

    In comparing *Pamela* with Griselda, I wish to comply with Richardson's
intention and consider the two parts as one work, looking first at the event
sequence. *Pamela I* is about Pamela's change of station. The initial event,
Mr. B's decision to marry his mother's waiting-maid, is enormously protracted.
Whereas Chaucer simply states Walter's determination to marry a peasant
in order to ensure total power over his wife, Richardson elaborates all the
conflicts attendant on such a decision. Once B comes to entertain marriage,
events focus on the making of the marriage contract. To assure himself of
Pamela's total obedience and commitment, Mr. B scrutinizes her virtue by
reading her letters, satisfies himself that she has had no amorous interest in
Mr. Williams, and wins her father's consent and admiration. In turn Pamela
accepts B's complete authority over her heart and her person, like Walter's
over Griselda. Married life itself, the climax of *Pamela I*, tests Pamela's ability
to adopt her new status and carry out her wifely duties with humility, grace,
and dignity.

    At this point the Griselda story is just getting going. It continues with
the removal of the children and the threat of replacement by the highborn
woman, which have analogues in *Pamela II*. Given the realistic surface of the
novel, it will not do for B to pretend to slaughter babies, so the removal-of-
the-child motif takes more plausible forms. B forbids Pamela to nurse her
child, a prohibition causing her such moral conflict that for the only time in
her marriage she appeals to her father, who counsels submission. When she
becomes convinced that B will cast her off in favor of the Dowager Countess
of C——, she agonizes over the likelihood that he will take the child from

her. Richardson even manages to incorporate the older daughter motif while allowing Pamela a firstborn son (a triumph denied Griselda, whose story needs an older girl for the bride trick). B's bastard daughter, Miss Goodwin, whom Pamela has longed to mother from the moment they meet, is eventually allowed to join the family. The protracted affair of the dowager countess, the heart of *Pamela II*, threatens Pamela with being cast off in favor of a highborn replacement. It includes an episode in which Pamela must graciously entertain the countess and her sister, an encounter for which she dresses with deliberate simplicity in the equivalent of Griselda's smock ("only a white damask gown" [*Pamela II*, 4:161]), though her motives include jealousy and a little cattiness. The one major event Richardson does not complete in this part of the sequence, except through the agony of anticipation, is the return to her father's house; he had already used an incomplete version in *Pamela I*. The novel's main plot ends when B accepts his wife's virtue and moral outlook and the family is reconstituted. After the concern with the moral education of these particular people, the tailpiece consists of an extended discussion of education in general.

There is no way of knowing whether or to what degree Richardson was conscious of the Griselda analogy. But he knew the Griselda story and had ample access to both literary and popular versions.[17] One way to corroborate the importance of the analogy is to see how the most significant of the unauthorized sequels, Kelly's *Pamela's Conduct in High Life*, undermines the Griselda skeleton. Kelly's first major plot move is to eliminate Pamela's lowborn status. Her parents turn out to be poor but genealogically impeccable members of the Kentish gentry, so that all class tension and all rationale for the scrutiny of Pamela's obedience, humility, and grace immediately vanish. Mr. B is left with no reason for uneasiness about his wife's conduct. In fact, Mr. B is left with no plot function at all. Most of Kelly's continuation is devoted to finding excuses for interpolated tales and to sketching the "characters" of the Bs' circle of acquaintances. When, midway through his second volume, he remembers the possibilities of the test, he makes it a sexual one and directs it at Pamela in three variations of increasing severity. First she receives the attentions of the odious Lord D——, next she is carried off from a masquerade and nearly raped by a man disguised as her husband, and finally she is pursued all over Europe by Lord P——, a libertine abetted by a nymphomaniacal and ultimately murderous sister who has seduced Mr. B. In all three attempts the emphasis is on external proof that Pamela has resisted and remains uncontaminated. For instance, it takes the rapist's word rather than his wife's to convince Mr. B that his wife escaped violation. Mr. B's own sexual misconduct is used primarily as leverage against Pamela; he himself learns nothing except that wives are safer than whores.

The sexual testing of the wife is not part of Richardson's plan. The verses Pamela finds under the cushion in church are not a sexual test but a test of her ability to defuse B's jealousy. The major events of *Pamela II* do not imitate the more theatrically stereotyped variations of the tested woman plot present in Kelly's sequel. But Richardson still had to rationalize the events in ways acceptable in a realistic work. Some require little displacement. B's fear of the yoke of matrimony, his refusal to marry his family's candidates, his observation and evaluation of Pamela from afar, his use of fearsome underlings to carry out his more distasteful orders, his insistence on absolute obedience and warnings against provoking his disfavor, the public scrutiny of Pamela's exemplary domestic economy, the poverty and piety of Goodman Andrews and his harmonious colloquy with B over the marriage, Pamela's role as peacemaker among her husband's friends and family—all these are the stuff of the Griselda story. Richardson conveys them with vivid particularity.

Of these relatively easily managed similarities, the role of clothing is striking. Griselda's changes of status are invariably marked by changes of dress. Once the marital agreement is reached at her father's hut, she is stripped of her rags and beautifully arrayed. Returning to her father, she strips herself to her smock and walks home bareheaded and barefooted. When she goes back to the palace the story repeatedly refers to her poor clothing, about which she is "not the least put out." After Walter again welcomes her as his wife, she is again clothed in fine robes. The changes from homespun to cloth of gold are sexual as well as class-related. Peasant clothing signifies Griselda's condition first as maid and then as "widow," while princely clothing represents her condition as wife. The completeness with which she understands this patriarchal transaction is indicated by the way she manages her marital rejection. When she is sent back to her father's house, she arranges a precisely calibrated reversion of her sexual status to be announced in the language of clothing:

> "My lord, you know how you had me stripped of my miserable rags in my father's house, and graciously dressed me in splendid clothes. It is plain I brought you nothing except my faithfulness, my nakedness, and my virginity; and here I return to you your clothes, and also my wedding-ring, for evermore. . . . *Naked I came out of my father's house, and naked I must return.* I will gladly submit to all your wishes; but hope you do not intend I should walk naked out of your palace. . . . My own dear lord, remember that I was your wife, though unworthy; and so, in recompense for the maidenhead that I brought to you but do not take back with me, vouchsafe to grant me in return a smock such as I used to wear, with which to hide the womb of her who was once your wife." (My emphasis.)[18]

Echoing the Book of Job, this speech confirms for Chaucer's distressed readers the integrity of his tested woman. We recognize that at each of her tests she has chosen freely, with full understanding of what she does. In reply Walter grants the smock in which she stands.

Although the tone is different, clothing has the same function in Richardson.[19] From the opening of *Pamela I*, in which Pamela is given some of her late mistress's clothes by Mr. B but feels herself too humble to wear them, to the climax of *Pamela II*, the encounter with the countess—in which Pamela's simple white gown expresses her prospective loss of status as well as her uprightness of heart—changes in her clothes match her sexual and social moves. Carey McIntosh enumerates the ways clothing serves as an "illuminating leitmotif" in *Pamela I* and points out that its "peculiar aptness . . . is a consequence of intrinsic and functional relationships between clothing and, on the one hand, sex, on the other, social position" (89, 93). That "intrinsic and functional relationship" is especially true for women like Pamela and Griselda, whose social positions are dependent exclusively on their sexual roles. But though Richardson gets comic mileage from the sexual opportunities that clothing affords, appropriateness is the main point. Like Griselda's, part of Pamela's test involves responding to status-signifying changes of dress with humility and grace. When she divides her clothing into three bundles in preparation for returning to her father's house and proposes to take away with her only what she has made or truly earned, she is imitating the scrupulousness with which Griselda takes a smock in exchange for a maidenhead and returns to her father's cottage with her debts cleared.

For the tested woman, the thematic point of the repetitive cycles of test, examination, and praise is to convey the sense of an entire life—and to set the issue of female chastity within that larger framework. Despite Griselda's unquestioning patience, the old tale is not cheaply reductive. It does not imagine that virginity is itself virtue, or that once married is always happy. The same holds with *Pamela*, which insists that chastity is merely one part of a wider obligation. Hence the importance of the whole of *Pamela*, including the ongoing tests of married life.[20] The choices the married Pamela must make help illuminate the moral quandary of the tested woman. Pamela has no problem comporting herself with those over whom she is made mistress. Once the hierarchy is clear and she knows her place, she is radiantly capable and comfortable. It is when one obligation is set against another—when authority is in conflict—that she is tested. How to prevent rape when the rapist is the master, how to respond to courtship when the wooer is too elevated to be an appropriate husband, how to behave as the contracted equal of those to whom she is not the born equal, how to perform her maternal duty when it conflicts with marital duty, how to perform her marital duty to a husband who breaks the marital contract: these are her tests. The first is easiest, for the obligation of obedience to her father—to maintain her virginity until marriage—takes moral precedence over obedience to her master. But later tests are harder, for when conflicting demands issue from the same authority, how can Pamela know where virtue lies?

Nevertheless, the business of plot is to get some change made, some journey accomplished. Repeatedly showing that Pamela is virtuous is not enough; before the end of *Pamela I*, it is clear that she will find a graceful means to fulfill her every obligation. But the reader, like Lady Davers, is anything but sure of Mr. B. As in the story of Griselda, Pamela's tests set up episodes of examination and discussion of the woman's response designed to work a transformation in the male authority figure: to reconcile Walter's contradictory impulses, to educate Mr. B. *Pamela I* tests Pamela until Mr. B is brought to reject seduction as not merely impossible but undesirable, then to rejoice in marriage as the source of health and contentment. But because he continues tyrannical and untrusting, in *Pamela II* Pamela is tested until the spoiled heir is definitively transformed into a thoughtful master, the rake into a family man, the arrogant exponent of upper-class totalitarianism into an admirer of middle-class virtues—including independent decision-making by his wife.

Mr. B's education is accomplished by two means. One is the ongoing examination of past experience. The first volume of *Pamela II* is primarily a retrospective on events up to and through the riotous honeymoon eruption of Lady Davers. As she and Pamela cement their friendship as sisters-in-law, they discuss and eventually reach a common interpretation of B's behavior— and B gets to read it. When Pamela finds the wooing verses in church, she leads the party of family and friends in a discussion of the mentality that would spoil the virtue it claims to admire, a critique of the provocation of virtue that sends B back to his own past. Such continuous reviewing and commenting gives Richardson a lot of emotional mileage from a limited number of events, links him firmly to Protestant techniques of self-examination, and starts the modern novel on the road to the psychological exploration of private experience.

The other means of educating B is through forensic procedures. There are trials, in the broad sense, throughout the novel. The metaphor of legal judgment recurs repeatedly, and repeatedly Mr. B subjects Pamela's virtues to examination and judgment. These trials are not always law-related. Whether she can carve a chicken need not be demonstrated forensically. But the more serious retrospective examinations often are actual trials. Noting the pervasiveness in *Pamela I* of the legal metaphor of the trial, Albert Lyles ascribes it to Richardson's having made Mr. B a justice of the peace (103). I think the causation works the other way. Since the prime authority figure in the tested woman plot acts the magistrate and stands in judgment over the woman, it is convenient to make Mr. B a justice of the peace. Lyles notes several key legal episodes from *Pamela I*, especially the deposition/trial after Mr. B's return to Lincolnshire. In this episode Mr. B serves as prosecutor, accusing Pamela of tempting Mr. Williams and disobeying her master, and as judge, handing down a sentence of rape. But the test/trial alternation and its underlying legal metaphor extend through both parts of the novel.

B's infatuation with the countess, the great crisis of *Pamela II*, leads to Richardson's most openly forensic confrontation and shows most clearly the way the woman's trial is the means to the man's reintegration. Pamela has been unable to hide her distress at her husband's response to the attentions of the nun at the masquerade, at Mr. Turner's accusations, at Lady Davers's gossip, and at B's trip to Tunbridge with the countess. Rather than act the shrew, she has withdrawn to the solace of the nursery and her writing, with the result that B accuses her of becoming cold and inattentive. Upon his return from Tunbridge she puts herself on trial, her ultimate purpose, by provoking the question of *her* fate, "to be an humble means of saving the man I love and honour, from errors that might be fatal to his soul" (*Pamela II*, 4:183). Arranging the chairs in her closet into a bar behind which she stands to judgment, she requires that her husband take up his judicial functions: "And now, my dearest Mr. B. you must begin first: . . . you must be my accuser, as well as my judge" (184–5). The trial proceeds, the evidence is aired, and Pamela begs that when she is sent home to her parents she be allowed to take the child. Suddenly it is B who finds himself on trial, as he later acknowledges, referring to "*your*, or rather *my* trial" (200). Once his ignominious behavior and his wife's loving virtue have been displayed, B pulls back from taking the fatal step, proclaims Pamela's wisdom in all spheres of human endeavor, and henceforth lives faithful and virtuous himself.

What has happened to Mr. B? Reading *Pamela* in the light of the Griselda story has given some structural help. But just as in terms of personality the sprightly, openly self-satisfied Pamela is no Griselda, the mercurial, openly complacent Mr. B is no Walter. His impulses can be summed up as the desire to continue to have his own way. His demands are not only not openly cruel and unusual, they are too obviously the result of his upbringing, his sex, and his class. Nevertheless, Walter's case clarifies Mr. B's. Walter has all the habits of authority but lacks the habit of faith. Having demanded obedience and received a pledge, he cannot reciprocate, for the reciprocal of a promise is faith, a kind of grace. Walter lacks that grace. He cannot believe without proof, and he cannot prove without the test and the scrutiny that follows. Only after repeated tests does he come to believe truly in Griselda's virtue, at which point the tests stop. Walter says that Griselda's response to the final test convinces him, but there is no reason why one act of virtue should carry more conviction than another. We must conclude that Walter receives the gift of faith. As Chaucer tells us, his heart changes: "Now when Walter saw her patience, . . . the obdurate marquis felt his heart take pity on her wifely steadfastness."[21] An integration takes place in Walter. At last he sees clearly and judges truly. Ceasing to trouble himself, he can live henceforth with a steadiness and virtue corresponding to that of his wife.

Mr. B too begins with all the habits of authority but without the habit of faith. The behavior that tests Pamela arises from an incapacity to trust her to carry out the roles he has assigned her. He cannot believe that she is an obedient servant, that she has not encouraged Mr. Williams, that she loves him for himself and not for his position. He is not sure that she can manage his household or social interchange with his peers. He cannot allow her to nurse her child, for he is jealous of her time, fearful of being superseded in her physical affections, and unwilling to live temporarily celibate.[22] In the affair with the countess, he is not seeking a casual sexual adventure but an alternative wife, for he cannot believe that in Pamela he has chosen well and completely. So why, when this particular trial comes to a head, is he converted? Like Walter's, his heart is reached by grace. Pamela knows that this is what is needed, more than any amount of demonstration or argument: "I have said enough to such a heart as yours, if divine grace touches it. And if not, all I can say, will be of no avail!" (*Pamela II*, 4:195). Mr. B responds as Walter did: "His generous heart was touch'd, and seem'd to labour within him for expression" (196). In response he performs two acts of faith, agreeing not merely to give up the countess but also to give Miss Goodwin into Pamela's keeping. Pamela reads this second act as evidence of trust in her capacity to educate his children. We can see in it his confidence that the child's presence will not be the excuse to throw his sexual sins up to him, that he has been truly and completely forgiven.

The marital reconciliation has specifically religious as well as generally moral overtones. B's religious conversion has all along been the goal, as became evident in the renovation-of-the-chapel sequence in *Pamela I*.[23] In the trial scene Pamela alludes to that purpose ("Motives of religion *will* have their due force upon your mind one day, I hope" [*Pamela II*, 4:195), and she writes to her parents about the affair of the countess only after that final conversion has taken place. Pamela presents the infatuation with the countess as an interruption in B's steady spiritual progress (she has always been solicitous of his good name before her parents). She describes how her private devotions, her churchgoing, and her brief Sunday colloquies with the servants had won her husband's approbation for their "good effects" and for the discretion with which they are carried out (for B, like Richardson's worldly readers, fears the appearance of over-righteousness). "But still I wanted, and I waited for, with humble impatience, and I made it part of my constant prayers, that the divine grace would at last touch his heart, and make him *more* than a countenancer, *more* than an applauder, of my duties: That he might, for his own dear sake, become a partaker, a partner in them" (*Pamela II*, 4:375). Providentially, the ultimate good results from what might have been the ultimate evil: "But who should pretend to scrutinize the councils of the Almighty?—For out of all this *evil appearance* was to proceed the *real good*, I had been so long, and so often, supplicating for!" (376). Mr. B declares his newfound conviction that "religious considerations" must underpin moral conduct. His wife's rapturous response mimics her reaction to the marital conversion of the trial scene, and the novel is complete.

ELEVEN

Plotting, Sympathizing, and Moralizing

As the eighteenth century proceeded, its philosophical concerns were increasingly epistemological and psychological, and its literary interests increasingly involved the representation of the self-creating and self-revealing personal voice. Richardson's technical innovations in *Pamela* introduced a number of as yet unrefined narrative tools that opened a way into the lived consciousness of the woman at the moment of the test. But in *Pamela* Richardson had not dealt innovatively with the retrospective examinations of the trial phase, nor broached the structural and tonal problems of a tragic version of the tested woman plot, nor dramatized the patriarchal voices that give the plot its social point. While in Mr. B he had created a recognizable personality type, B's exceptional situation obscured the plot's broad fictive applications. Richardson had produced a tour de force but not a fully transportable model. Issues of genre, which involved social attitudes as much as literary technique, were at midcentury still the dominant problem of the plot. Writers were still seeking ways to couple the interaction of drama with the intimacy of first-person narration, and to combine the moral and forensic rigor of the plot's originating structure with the public's desire for sympathetic identification with human joy and sorrow.

Tested Women and Prodigal Sons: Fielding's *Amelia*

Henry Fielding's work as a novelist was carried out from its beginnings in reaction to Richardson. *Joseph Andrews* (1742) was conceived as a parody of *Pamela*. *Shamela*, the brief, anonymously published satire (1741) that presents its heroine as a sexual tease bent on manipulating her master into marriage, was Fielding's as well.[1] His masterpiece *Tom Jones* was written neck-and-neck with Richardson's masterpiece *Clarissa*. At the end of their careers, while Richardson

161

was at work on *Sir Charles Grandison*, Fielding turned his hand to a tested woman story, making *Amelia* (1751) a straight rather than a parodic homage to Richardson's influence. *Amelia's* story line returned to stock characters by blending tested woman and prodigal son plots. Renaissance plays had repeatedly married these two plots, and two anonymous comic versions, *How a Man May Choose a Good Wife from A Bad* (1602) and *The London Prodigal* (1604), show the stereotypical coupling. In them a good woman marries a weak husband who gambles away his substance or otherwise makes himself and his family a prey to unscrupulous creditors and finally the law. The wife continues wise, loving, and supportive throughout her torments, which include having her dowry sold off, her chastity called into question, and her children impoverished. She may have to tolerate her husband's infidelity or be pressured to exchange sexual favors in return for his relief. Sometimes she is aided by a good man sprung to her defense in the interest of reforming the prodigal.

That *Amelia* shows signs of Fielding the dramatist is unsurprising. As a playwright and theater manager he was the most vigorous figure on the London theatrical scene for nearly a decade, staged or encouraged a number of innovative plays, and developed a style of political burlesque so successful as to bring down the wrath of the Walpole government and lead to the repressive licensing act of 1737.[2] Thus Fielding had an intimate acquaintance with a generation's worth of dramatic properties, like Colley Cibber's *Love's Last Shift*, the tested woman/prodigal man play about the reformation of one Loveless that inspired John Vanbrugh's even more successful sequel, *The Relapse*.[3] Fielding probably knew Joseph Mitchell's one-act play *The Fatal Extravagance* (1721), a rewriting of *A Yorkshire Tragedy*, which in 1726 was revised with the help of Aaron Hill into a full-length play that added another prodigal son/tested woman plot to fill it out.[4] Fielding wrote the epilogue to Charles Johnson's *Caelia* (1732), in which a young woman is seduced, impregnated, then locked up in a brothel by an indifferent wastrel.

In *Amelia* Fielding's hero, Billy Booth, is prodigal in all the received ways. He begins the novel with adultery with Miss Matthews and extends his career by unwise expenditures, gambling debts, and unfortunate speculations. In the course of his decline he uses up not only his own substance but his wife's, and when his financial troubles make Amelia the sexual target of his "rescuers," he adds jealousy to his misdeeds. Like any good triple-plotted play, *Amelia* has three tested women, who represent the categories of maid, wife, and widow. Miss Matthews's history is told in her long jail account to Booth. Her story is a seduction device which prepares us to fear for Amelia, for Miss Matthews the genteel whore, seemingly possessed of more independence and peace of mind than her virtuous rival, initially looks like an exemplar of the all-too-happy fall. Later in the novel we hear the history of Mrs. Bennet—her persecution by her stepmother and father; her escape into a love match with a young clergyman; her seduction through poverty, Mrs. Ellison, and a lord's drugged cup; her husband's fury and physical abuse; his illness and death, and the death of her child; her attempts to prevent the same from happening to Amelia. This is fall and recovery—Mrs. Ellison's punishment and expiation prepare her to become Mrs. Atkinson and live happily. Finally there is Amelia, who successfully runs both the test failed by Miss Matthews—a passionate love affair that might have led to "keeping"; and that failed then risen above by Mrs. Bennet—seduction by the lord followed by her husband's ruinous fury.

Readers of *Amelia* have always traced in it Fielding's life and marriage to his beloved Charlotte Cradock. Richardson was sure his rival had nothing to say that did not come from sordid experience: "His brawls, his jars, his gaols, his spunging-houses, are all drawn from what he has seen and known. As I said . . . he has little or no invention."[5] Lore in the family of Fielding's cousin Lady Mary Wortley Montagu tells a more sympathetic story, as her granddaughter Lady Louisa Stuart recounts:

> He loved her passionately, and she returned his affection; yet led no happy life, for they were almost always miserably poor, and seldom in a state of quiet and safety. All the world knows what was his imprudence; if ever he possessed a score of pounds, nothing could keep him from lavishing it idly, or make him think of to-morrow. Sometimes they were living in decent lodgings with tolerable comfort; sometimes in a wretched garret without necessaries; not to speak of the spunging-houses and hiding-places where he was occasionally to be found.[6]

Despite these similarities, however, Fielding's influences in *Amelia* are essentially literary, some of the particulars indebted to Richardson.[7] Fielding has no qualms about borrowing plot structures, event sequences, and motifs. Not only was plotting not his strong suit, but theatrical practice took such borrowing for granted.

In the combined tested woman/prodigal son plot, the husband's education (rather than the wife's sensibility) can be made the center of the novel. This focus on the husband's psychology is the structural reason *Amelia* begins with Booth in jail. Beyond the virtues of an *in medias res* opening, satire on Judge Thrasher, and a look at London underlife, this opening allows Booth's week-long adultery with Miss Matthews, which he finds it impossible to reveal to his wife. As the family's circumstances become more desperate, Booth learns to confess other extravagances and errors to her; only this does he keep hidden. When for the third time he finds himself in the hands of the bailiffs, and Amelia comes in her one remaining undershift to comfort him, he confesses at last. That dam burst, the denouement proceeds in a rush. But the downward trend cannot be stopped, the novel cannot come to rest, until Booth purges himself of the evil that set it going. To do that he must come to have faith that his wife will forgive him, which she already has, having been in receipt of an accusatory letter from Miss Matthews some time before. The novel ends when Booth's conviction of his wife's virtues becomes total and absolute—when he makes his leap of faith.

Yet unlike Richardson's novels, *Amelia* is not driven by psychological concerns. Without question the theme of authority is important. By the time of its composition, Fielding was a London magistrate, and the prodigal son plot is particularly open to overt attention to magistracy and the law. Throughout the novel Fielding satirizes the denizens of the legal world, but his target is really the system itself: the inequities and downright absurdities of the law, the ingrained custom of bribery, the web of patronage in which it operates. He is not primarily concerned to probe the individualized human psyches of his wide range of characters. Quite the contrary: in his authorial intrusions, including the classical allusions, he delights in referring them to their traditional character types. Though he inveighs against legal abuses, he does not personalize the abusers as rounded human beings. Caricature and burlesque are his weapons instead. But authority is also exercised in the family, and here Fielding individualizes somewhat more. None of Amelia's family—a dead father and brother, the spiteful, greedy older sister, and the well-heeled mother, Mrs. Harris, who tightens and releases the purse strings as her children work on her sympathies—is a characterized presence in the novel. But Amelia has an honorary father in the person of Dr. Harrison (the name echoes the mother's), who treats her as his daughter. Dr. Harrison is a clergyman, an older man, a learned man, and a propertied man, so many authority functions can be vested in him. He counsels and preaches, he lends money and withholds it, he punishes Booth with a legal action when things have gone too far, he is the energetic instrument of the young family's eventual salvation, he lives with them until his death. He is a tool father, free to be Amelia's defender without having to undertake the more difficult authority functions with which the real father would be burdened.

Recognizing how conveniently the tool father appears to solve plot problems and convey moral messages tells us a lot about *Amelia*. There is much talk of Providential concerns. The hand of God is seen in the presence of Dr. Barrows's sermons in the bailiff's room or in Robinson's sighting of Amelia pawning her last object of value. But what chiefly operates is the providence of genre. When the tested woman plot is comic, the usual treatment is for the woman to stand in virtuous bemusement while the men go into a moral tailspin around her. Her agonies are largely external; she does not suffer a great deal (though she undergoes mistreatment) because she is not guilty of anything. Her business is to wait it out in the expectation that the men will come to their senses. In comedy, they do. *Amelia's* opening sentence announces "The various accidents which befell a very worthy couple, after their uniting in the state of matrimony, will be the subject of the following history." Since their marriage began with the seeming disinheritance of Amelia, it ends with her reinstatement as rightful heir—once the education of her husband is complete. Fielding's tested woman novel uses a plot combination that allows him to put his attention where his talent is—on the charming scapegrace whose euphorias and misadventures continue until he is taken out of circulation by a good woman. The formula is comic not primarily because so open to satire and caricature, or so welcoming to exuberant mixtures of social classes, but because real-world causation need not operate. Rescue is always at hand; Providence in this context means rescue. Some version of it can appear at a moment's notice, for the story is not designed to carry his principals' lives to their probable conclusion.

Yet despite being presented as the same sort of "comic epic in prose" as the fabulously successful *Joseph Andrews* and *Tom Jones*, *Amelia* did not sell well.[8] Some readers complained about Fielding's sordid characters and episodes, yet *Clarissa* (1749), in some ways no less sordid and a lot more depressing, had been a sensation. Fielding clearly thought he was making concessions to the readership that had created that sensation. Yet despite his use of the tested woman plot, with its examination of sexual relationships, familial dynamics, and moral decision-making, his novel did not sell. Perhaps by 1751 the public had come to expect the tested woman plot to explore characters' internal states, in which Fielding has little interest. Not only does he not use the epistolary form, the only narrative voicing then available for such exploration; he also uses little morally or emotionally probing conversation. During the 1740s so much had changed so radically that Fielding's manipulations and coincidences, exactly what make swift-moving comic drama, may not have seemed emotionally rich enough for narrative fiction based on this plot. Moreover, the moral and social endangerment of women was coming to be seen as a serious social evil, and for all that Fielding displays social problems like the havoc created by arbitrary parental control of marriage portions, these issues are treated as they would have been on stage. Occasions for vivid but stock characterization and witty but throwaway satire, they lack emotional engagement.

SENTIMENTALITY AND THE TESTED WOMAN PLOT: THE PATTERN OF *CAELIA*

Writing the serious drama of contemporary life was nearly impossible in England for much of the eighteenth century. The stage revived tested woman tragedies from the old repertory, and opera made use of time-honored sources of tragicomedy in works like Handel's *Ariodante* (1734) and the *Griselda* of Giovanni Bononcini (1722), which Steele's Biddy Tipkin discusses with her suitor in *The Tender Husband*.[9] But serious plays with a contemporary setting, which Renaissance London theaters had produced by the dozens, hardly existed, the fame of George Lillo's *London Merchant* and *Fatal Curiosity* speaking to their rarity. The example of French theater offered only the warmed-over Roman imperium or other ancient and exotic settings. The theoretical radicalism of Denis Diderot's *Le Fils naturel* (1757) and *Le Père de famille* (1758) with their discussions of bourgeois family morals and their pleas for "fourth-wall" naturalistic acting, was not matched by their dramatic strength, nor was pre-Revolutionary Parisian theater a breeding ground for citizen drama. In English drama sources of resistance included the leftovers of dramatic decorum, which hindered serious treatment of "low" people and the affairs of daily life, the hold of fashionable London audiences on what theatrical troupes dared present, and the absence of a literary style both suitable to the discussion of social issues and free from the preachment of the conduct book. In poetry and fiction the social programs of Wordsworth and George Eliot were decades away—but the theater was even further behind. Whereas the relative freedom of pre-1737 theatrical practice and the proliferation of troupes with a variety of constituencies might eventually have broadened London theatrical practices, the licensing act, which once more restricted theaters to two, each mirroring the other, stamped out experimentation.

Yet some experiments were tried, of which Charles Johnson's *Caelia; or The Perjur'd Lover* (1732) is known by reputation to readers of *Clarissa*. Johnson's tragic treatment of a contemporary tested woman is up against customary practice, as the cautiously anonymous author admits in his prologue: "He knows the wags will laugh, and call him, dull, / Unfashionable, windmill-fighting fool!" Fielding's epilogue responds with the sneer that represents the voice of "the town":

> Lud! What a fuss is here! what blood and slaughter!
> Because poor miss has prov'd her mother's daughter.
>
> . . . .
>
> Here does the wretch his stupid muse invoke,
> And turn to solemn tragedy—a joke![10]

The "joke," which is the seduction, impregnation, and sale of Caelia, is to the town a matter of jest because it takes seriously the sexual victimization of a woman. In the epilogue we see the break from the play's moralizing tone which so incenses Pamela in regard to *The Distressed Mother* and so neatly exemplifies Johnson's moral point. The rake's code, which insists that a gentleman must keep his word (but never to women or other inferiors) and honor his obligations (but not about sex or paying his tradesmen's bills), is Johnson's direct target. But the epilogue further points the "joke," which is that to the town, the double standard exhorting young women to maintain their chastity in the face of male predation is really a triple standard. Chastity is a matter of reputation only, not of fact, and a woman who fails to exploit that discrepancy is merely stupid:

> The girl was in the fault, who strove to smother
> That case she shou'd have open'd to her mother;
> All had been hush'd by the *old* lady's skill,
> And *Caelia* prov'd a good town-virgin still.

Caelia is informative about the tested woman plot in the eighteenth century for several reasons. Taken together, its prologue, epilogue, advertisement to the reader, and stage fortune suggest how little place there is for a play however lively and well constructed—and Johnson's is both—that does not cater to expectations about character decorum. In his advertisement to the reader in the printed edition, Johnson comments on the outrage over the brothel owner Mother Lupine and her women:

> When I communicated this play to Mr. *Booth*, he advis'd me, very justly, to alter my plan with relation to the comic characters, and to wait until another season; but the natural impatience and vanity of an author prevail'd, and I persuaded him to bring it on the stage as it is—I think everyone will allow I have acted with judgment, in concealing my name; yet I beg leave to say, a moral of this kind, and which has not, to my memory, been set in so full a light by the dramatic writers, might have been of use and instruction. How many families have suffer'd irreparable Injuries of this sort? yet it is look'd on by many as a *fashionable amusement*, rather than the *highest injustice: Quae olim vitia fuerunt, mores sunt*, says *Seneca*.[11]

The characterization of the prostitutes that was too much for Johnson's audience is the freshest work in the play. Mother Lupine is a delicious role. Old, lively, managerial, lascivious but not gross, by her lights a benefactor of people in awkward situations, she welcomes the six-months-pregnant Caelia who, despite her condition, is to be put right to work. Lupine reads like a precursor to Richardson's Mrs. Sinclair, whether or not Richardson knew *Caelia*.[12]

But Johnson's focus is different from Richardson's. Though several scenes highlight Caelia's pathetic situation, the action is male-focused: on Wronglove, the friend of her dead brother who seduces Caelia; on Bellamy, Wronglove's friend, who kills him in a duel; on Meanwell, the family steward, who comes to London in search of Caelia; and on Lovemore, Caelia's father, who arrives in time for her to die in his arms. Accusation is deflected from the woman to her victimizer. By the time she comes on stage, her choice is so far past as to be nearly forgotten, her pathetic situation heightened by her grief-killed mother's exhortation to her father to forgive her. The play's indignation is turned against Wronglove. After seducing Caelia he has pretended to send her to the country for a safe lying-in, while actually delivering her to a brothel to get her off his hands, a lie that prevents her family from finding her until she has collapsed. Johnson's master stroke is presenting Wronglove as heedless rather than gross. His evil is monstrous because it is so banal. When Bellamy confronts him about "honor, the characteristic of a gentleman," Wronglove persists in presenting his treatment of Caelia as a sexual game and Bellamy's concern as evidence of sexual rivalry, exposing the male code as the self-justification of a powerful caste against an entire category of inferiors. Though Wronglove claims to hold himself accountable to no one, when Bellamy demands satisfaction Wronglove feels obliged to draw. This is the male equivalent of "town-virginity": the gentleman need not behave honorably even to his friend's family; he need only make public displays of "honor" on demand.

Yet Johnson's moral rigor gets smudged when Bellamy repeats the standard sentiment: "Now, now we will try whose cause is best." The convention originally meant that in trial by combat God directs the arm of the just man. But that is neither what Bellamy says nor what the play argues. This is no longer a society of trial by combat, and in any case the play has already tried Wronglove's cause. Further loss of rigor comes with the news that Wronglove has died declaring himself Caelia's husband and begging his father to care for her and their child. Wronglove's contrition shows the plot's powerful urge to reintegrate the male network. The bond with Wronglove's friend and slayer, Bellamy, is reestablished, while Caelia's father's acceptance restores his ties with his dead son's friend. Caelia is grateful: "My *Wronglove*'s sudden death, as he died mine, repenting, sorrowful, and just at last; whatever I have suffered by his unthinking conduct, Oh! let me drop one tear upon his grave." Her father approves his daughter: "Thy piety is just; so was his end: what reparation he could make, he made.—Unhappy youth!" Though Caelia's description of her seducer's conduct as unthinking is an accurate reflection of his callowness, the sequence is bathetic. The fifth act is really focused on father and daughter, and Johnson's point is their capacity for forgiveness. Caelia is thankful for her father's presence, and her father thankful for his daughter's pure heart.

Caelia was prescient, for its version of the tested woman plot became enshrined in the sentimental novels of the second half of the century. That this is the plot of Emily's story in Henry Mackenzie's *The Man of Feeling* (1771), the type specimen of the sentimental novel, suggests that it is constructed to elicit the strongest emotions at the greatest number of points and that the reunion between daughter and father has become the plot's necessary climax.[13] The story line is set: naive young woman is seduced (usually by an acquaintance of the family and usually by means of promises of marriage or a fake ceremony), taken away (usually to London), abandoned by her seducer (usually pregnant and usually by being turned over to a bawd), imprisoned (usually for debt), succored by a man of feeling, and reunited with her forgiving family. While Caelia dies, Emily does not, but since Mackenzie's fiction is constructed as fragments, each abandoned once its emotional work is completed, his necessary events are already accomplished in the destruction of the daughter's hopes and the grief and forgiveness of the father. Olivia's story in *The Vicar of Wakefield* (1766) varies this pattern only in ways that facilitate Oliver Goldsmith's legitimate-marriage ending. Olivia eludes prostitution and is not definitively pregnant (though she is ill), and her imprisonment for debt is softened into being holed up at an inn unable to pay her bill. That the father is the narrator increases the detail, intensity, and pathos of disappearance, search, rescue, and forgiveness.

The stereotyping of the events suggests their potential for re-metaphorizing the plot. Norman Holland argues that the great change from Jacobean to

Restoration comedy a hundred years before had been the literalizing, or de-analogizing, of its worldview.[14] The reformative events of the Caelia/Emily story, however, come once more to carry metaphorical weight. Making the tempter a friend of the family figures the breaking of family harmony and polity. When the tempter is a friend of the son, the aggression moreover is cross-generational, directed at the father. The elopement to London figures the woman's alienation from her family, since a rural or small-town setting is conventionally the scene of close relationships, while London is the locale of individual action, depersonalization, and disappearance. The sale of the deflowered woman to a bawd makes explicit the sex/money exchange behind both marriage and prostitution, and her prospective downward trajectory—kept companion to brothel worker to streetwalker—shows her progressive economic and moral cheapening. The transfer to prison or sponging house figures the bondage of vice and the inequitable nature of the exchange.

Compared with Renaissance versions of the tested woman plot, neverthe-less, this depersonalization of authority constitutes an immense change. When the woman is succored by a man of feeling rather than defended in a forensic setting, the chief consideration is the emotion her misery evokes, not the judg-ment her behavior deserves. Parental authority is largely replaced by parental emotion. There is scant attention to the seduction itself and next to no sense of a moral test. In fact, responsibility is largely removed from the woman. There is little systematic scrutiny of either the woman's or her tempter's past. The function of accuser (in the classical configuration accusation is directed against the woman) has largely disappeared. In the sentimental version, the defender succors or sympathizes with the woman; he does not examine and defend her actions. What brings Johnson and Mackenzie to these changes is their common search for strong emotion, whether outrage or pathos and sympathy.

Whose outrage and sympathy? One of *The Man of Feeling*'s structural features is the narrator/observer, whose responses guide the reader's. Actually there are several layers of guidance. There is the MacKenzie-like editor of the fragmented bundle of letters rescued from the curate's shooting bag, about which he slyly admits that "had the name of a Marmontel, or a Richardson, been on the title-page—'tis odds that I should have wept: But one is ashamed to be pleased with the works of one knows not whom."[15] Then there is the mysterious stranger from whose cache the papers have come and who may be construed as the narrator of the third-person segments. Finally there is the voice of one or another of the characters, including Harley, the Man of Feeling himself, telling his own story of response to the woes of others. By the date of Mackenzie's novel, the narrator observing simultaneously the pathetic events in others' lives and his own sympathetic response has become, together with the conventionality of the stock situation, sentimental fiction's chief means of guiding the reader's sentimental journey. Eighteenth-century drama cannot achieve this effect, as it has neither narrating observer nor narrating participant. The spectator or reader must work out her own reaction,

in the case of the theater one heavily influenced by group response. In *Caelia*
Johnson seeks to control audience response through Bellamy, who teaches the
audience to condemn Wronglove. But Bellamy cannot be present in all the
scenes. The final act escapes from condemnation into pathos, while the brothel
scenes have no normative voice but only comic predators and pathetic victims,
a combination that made Johnson's audience uneasy.

Refusing the Sentimental Plot: *Clarissa*

Radical as *Caelia* is, it is most interesting for how it shows off Richardson's
deeper radicalism. Nothing quite prepares us for *Clarissa*, though we know
what moral and psychological features of the tested woman plot most stimulated his imagination. Though there is no direct evidence that Richardson
knew Johnson's play, some of *Caelia*'s story components occur in the novel. For
example, Wronglove's acquaintance with Caelia's brother and his presence in
her home on accepted business is a variation on Lovelace's presence among the
Harlowes; Bellamy's relationship with Wronglove seems a precursor to Belford
and Lovelace; Wronglove's patronage of Lupine and her women follows the
same pattern as Lovelace's use of Sinclair; the removal of Caelia from brothel
to prison is echoed in Clarissa's removal from brothel to bailiff's; Caelia's
request to be buried beside her mother is reminiscent of Clarissa's request
to rest in the family tomb. There are differences on approximately the same
scale. Clarissa's brother is still alive, her father unforgiving, and her mother
weak; Lovelace, though vicious, is neither shallow nor boring; Belford begins
as Lovelace's close friend, only gradually becomes his accuser, but is not his
slayer; though emotionally seduced, Clarissa is physically raped; there is no
character who acts as a go-between (Meanwell's function) except Lovelace's
creation, "Capt. Tomlinson." But these differences in plot details pale beside
genre characteristics which separate play from novel.

The first difference involves the distinctiveness of Richardson's epistolary
technique. Richardson's experiments in *Pamela* tapped a self-perpetuating
histrionic creativity. But not even *Pamela II*, where Pamela's voice is joined
by those of her correspondents, could have readied Richardson for what must
have happened in his psyche when, having written the first letters between
Clarissa and her sharp-tongued confidante, Anna Howe, he found himself
inventing the voice of Robert Lovelace. Mr. B never comes fully alive because
he never speaks for himself. At the end of *Pamela* one wonders whether
Richardson can "do" a man, an intellectual, a libertine. Richardson must
have wondered, too. Then comes Lovelace—and Belford and the other rakes,
brother James and uncles John and Antony, Dr. Lewin and the Rev. Mr.
Brand and Cousin Morden. There is equal variation among the women: ill-
tempered sister Arabella, Mrs. Howe, Aunt Hervey and Mrs. Norton and
Mrs. Sinclair and Sally and Polly—all the extraordinary voices that make the

novel. Given this virtuosity, Richardson's catty remarks about Fielding's lack of invention become almost forgivable. By mining his own imagination he had revolutionized literary characterization, a fact he almost recognized and of which he was not a little proud.[16]

There had been epistolary novels before *Pamela* and *Clarissa*, of course. By positing an individualized addressee, any epistolary fiction makes possible an unmediated, individualized voice. But epistolary fiction before Richardson had not made the same breakthrough in terms of currency of events; the fiction in letters had typically been a life story reflected in post-catastrophic tranquility. It was "writing to the moment" that distinguished Richardson's work from what had gone before, which was why he called it "dramatic narrative." *Clarissa* includes plot manipulations that keep characters separated and give them time to write. It exploits narrative tools, including the emotion-mimicking appearance of the words on the page—the unfinished sentences, the various forms of emphatic punctuation, the short paragraphs alluding to events that have just broken into the character's train of thought. These transcription effects are dependent on the more fundamental tool of interruption itself— the convention that the writer may rise from an uncompleted letter and, making that fact part of the action, return to recount the intervening events. All these techniques give the narrative the forward-moving breathlessness of breaking action. Slowing the action through rumination, in which the character transcribes the backing and filling of emotional exploration and moral decision-making, also contributes to the sense of immediacy. Epistolary response aids the intimacy of soliloquizing. The addressee answers with another letter responding to the writer's ruminations and adding facts from the characters' shared world. Correspondence may be multilayered, as when one letter encloses or copies another. The most fundamental tool for suspense is the fraught situation itself, its outcome influenced by the response the letter writer is eliciting. In *Clarissa* any correspondent can use any of these tools (many characters use the enclosure technique), but interruptions are common only with the principals, who are most closely caught up in immediate action. Interruptions both characterize the writer and advance the plot, since they arise from the writer's lack of control over life and surroundings. Where Lovelace's manipulation of events and agents is responsible for Clarissa's house-arrest, there are interruptions in her correspondence, but not his. As her illness progresses, and Belford informs Lovelace of her condition by periodic bulletins, interruptions in Lovelace's letters mark his inability to control either Clarissa or his own frenzy.

Combining the tested woman plot with a to-the-moment epistolary technique also makes possible the focus on psychological and social maturation. It is hard to overstate the importance of this innovation. Pre-Richardsonian fiction, notably Defoe's, had female characters who described the course of their lives and moral decisions. Roxana, for example, looks back on her behavior and her choices with frankness and some attention to her own motivation. But

Richardson presents the growth of consciousness from the inside—while it is happening. For this there is no literary tradition, which is why Fielding's parody was both possible and inevitable. *Shamela* argues from the perspective of the sexually predatory adult male who invents a voice and a correspondence for the woman his lust has created. By contrast, with *Pamela* Richardson seriously imagines the perspective of the fifteen-year-old child-woman. To credit and enunciate such a perspective, a culture must have begun listening to women's voices. It must have become interested in the nature and growth of consciousness itself, must have started to invent childhood and adolescence, which means modern psychology.

In *Clarissa* Richardson retains the expressive excitement of this innovation. Clarissa is no Pamela. Higher-class, better-educated, less socially isolated, living in a more complex family setting, she is also a crucial two years older. Considered marriageable, she has begun the process of winnowing suitors, with the growth in personal and social awareness forced by that process. She has a confidante with whom she has had the luxury of discussing her life from childhood. She knows she is at the natural testing moment for young women of her class, and she is eager for the test of her prudence, which she expects to pass with exemplary grace. Then, to her confusion and humiliation, what she is is not enough. The tested woman plot usually demands that the woman find the will to stay as she is, which is why the test can be over quickly. With Clarissa, Richardson gives us a woman whose testing, while it demonstrates the solid core of her integrity, changes her profoundly. The kind and depth of her growth is partly a function of her youth. Richardson is writing a pioneering *bildungsroman*, and Clarissa is a young person in the process of making her self. As she enters the adult world, she learns only slowly and painfully what she is living toward, and it comes in a form more complex and savage than she could project. Her encounter with Lovelace tantalizes her with the hope of having met her intellectual, social, physical, and moral equal—and endangers her with that imagined equal's simulacrum. With the release of her adult powers, the precarious equilibrium the Harlowes have established around the myth of the beloved child is shattered into its lethal components of paternal control, maternal capitulation, and sibling envy, and Clarissa learns that pleasing is not her life's work. Writing the psychological processes of such a character, as of her tempter, became for Richardson an obsession different in its recursiveness from the relative linearity with which he wrote his first novel. When he was driven to write more about Pamela, he continued her life. When the responses of first his manuscript-reading friends and then his novel-reading public drove him to reconsider *Clarissa*, he went back into the novel, adding explanatory episodes and revealing more of his characters' inner workings.

What drove both his readers' critiques and Richardson's revisions was the problem of the ending. If Clarissa was indeed virtuous, then she should live to be happy. Though I have been distinguishing the tools and effects of Richardson's epistolary fiction from drama, in their theoretical writing

Richardson and his contemporaries assigned his work to the category of drama for the same reason that Fielding assigned his to epic: there was no genre theory for fiction. Richardson chose to situate his work within drama because the time of action is the present and the dialogue-in-letters is carried out without the intervention of an authorial voice.[17] It was in the context of contemporary dramatic theory that Richardson fought his battle over *Clarissa*'s ending.

Richardson had let his readers into the debate by sending portions of the manuscript to his friends and by using the installment release that became novel-publishing practice for the next 150 years. *Clarissa* appeared in three installments of two, two, and three volumes respectively, and the volumes up through the rape were being devoured by his public as he was revising the conclusion. Both friends and the general public took the novel participatorily, and they were not shy about telling him how it ought to come out. What they wanted was a happy ending; wedding bells had rung for Pamela and Mr. B, and they should ring for Clarissa and Lovelace. There were two arguments to be made for this ending: it would "have the appearance of good nature and humanity," as Richardson acknowledged,[18] and it would satisfy the requirements for "poetical justice." Clarissa, being good, should live and be happy, and because only marriage to the perpetrator of her rape could recover her life prospects, Lovelace should be shaped into a suitable husband. In short, the public wanted some combination of tested woman and prodigal son plots, as in *Amelia*. Richardson's conclusion, in which both Clarissa and Lovelace die, was sufficiently wrenching to prompt him to defend his contrary practice in a postscript. There he brought to bear the biggest critical guns he could muster, Aristotle (as interpreted by Joseph Addison) and René Rapin,[19] with footnotes giving a boost from Horace via Alexander Pope and making the suggestion that the young actor/manager David Garrick might be the brave new man to bring back the original *King Lear* (he wasn't). All these authorities were for the purpose of denying that "poetical justice" was the preferred practice of either the ancients or the greatest of the moderns.

But classical precedent was not where Richardson's deepest rationale lay; he was compelled by his understanding of the relationship between the testing pattern of his plot and the testing pattern of Christian life:

> Nor can it be deemed impertinent to touch upon this subject at the conclusion of a work which I designed to inculcate upon the human mind, under the guise of an amusement, the great lessons of Christianity, in an age *like the present;* which seems to expect from the poets and dramatic writers (that is to say, from the authors of works of invention) that they should make it one of their principal rules, to propagate another sort of dispensation, under the name of *poetical justice,* than that with which God by Revelation teaches us he has thought fit to exercise mankind; whom, placing here only in a state of probation, he hath so intermingled good and evil so as to necessitate them to look forward for a more equal distribution of both.

> The history, or rather the dramatic narrative of *Clarissa*, is formed on this
> religious plan; and is therefore well justified in deferring to extricate suffering
> virtue till it meets with the completion of its reward. (1495)

In making this argument, Richardson has extended his heroine's working
life into the hereafter, joining the tested woman plot firmly with the Christian pilgrimage that underlies so much Western literature.[20] After citing his
authorities against the necessity of poetic justice, Richardson goes to the
heart of his argument. If considered on a Christian plan, the novel does
observe poetical justice, for is not Lovelace, "this great, this wilful transgressor,
condignly *punished*"? And Belton and Tomlinson and Mrs. Sinclair, with her
minions, and the whole Harlowe family—"*are they not all likewise exemplarily
punished*"? And are not the noble characters, along with "the repentant and not
ungenerous Belford . . . *made signally happy*"? But Richardson knows that these
characters' fortunes were not what troubled his readers. The heart-wrencher
is the heroine, with whom he clinches his point: "And who that are earnest in
their profession of Christianity but will rather envy than regret the triumphant
death of *Clarissa*, whose piety from her early childhood; whose diffusive charity;
whose steady virtue; whose Christian humility; whose forgiving spirit; whose
meekness, whose resignation, HEAVEN *only* could reward?" (1498). With this
passage, which stresses the range of Christian virtues and the concept of life as
the preparation for afterlife, Richardson puts Clarissa squarely in the tradition
of the Christian heroine whose entire existence is a triumphant affirmation of
her courage, integrity, and faith against the worst temptation has to offer.

And what is that worst? It is not the appeal of concubinage with the most
gifted and charismatic man Clarissa has ever met, though such is Lovelace's
purpose. Whenever she is able to penetrate the obscuring cloud of his artful
practices, she is able to refuse his intentions. Her most difficult test is mimicked by the one Richardson is undergoing with his readers: having refused
the extortionary threat of rape, Clarissa must refuse the blackmail of rape's
aftermath. Her world tells her that there is only one way, marriage to the
rapist, to put right the evil of rape. When she refuses to hide the fact that
she has been raped, but equally refuses to marry a man capable of committing
the act, many of Richardson's readers accused him of having forgotten how
his plot was supposed to go.

What they were demanding was a sentimental denouement, which Richardson was unwilling to supply. The "sentimental" in literature has many strains
and manifestations. That of Addison or the Abbé du Bos was primarily aesthetic
and psychological: the raising of emotion through literature or other representational arts as a means to the pleasure arising from the release from tedium.
Such heightened sensibility is pleasurable in itself, and the sentimentality
that results from seeking it as an artistic end is founded on emotion "cut
adrift from more rational meaning" and "out of proportion in relation to
it," as Henry Hitch Adams and Baxter Hathaway describe it. Cutting adrift

from meaning was far from Richardson's intention. He fought against it, often heavy-handedly, in all his novels. By contrast, the sentimentality of *The Man of Feeling* is a moral matter, more closely allied to "an abstract ethical system that involved doing good by a 'moral sense' and that found weeping and the expression of pity signs of a properly adjusted moral sense, exhibits of an emotionality to be treasured for its moral value."[21] This "moral sense" was construed by some philosophers as an innate (hence "common") psychological capability or "sense" analogous to the physical senses and on a par with imagination, judgment, taste, and the passions. But Richardson was not primarily attempting to cultivate an abstract moral sense in his readers either, though he was willing to profit from its presence. Not only had he no theoretical interest in abstract philosophy, he was hostile to the "common-sense" philosophers for their perceived undermining of the revealed morality of Christianity. He was more open to the associationist psychology of David Hartley's *Observations on Man*, which he printed for its publisher, James Leake of Bath, his wife's brother, in 1749.[22] What Richardson found most appealing about Hartley seems to have been his embedding of a psychological system in a frame of Christian apologetics. The more Richardson worked at novel writing, the more he became interested in how the dramatization of a character's entire life, a coherent moral view attempting with its all-too-human vicissitudes to behave wisely throughout its course, could be made to convey a system of Christian ethics. Hartley's associationist theory integrated all aspects of a person's physical, mental, and spiritual makeup and applied them to daily behavior.

Clarissa seems deliberately to include features conventional to a sentimental use of the plot in order to subvert them. Richardson includes all the events of the *Caelia* model only to twist them all. Though Clarissa leaves home with a tempter who is an acquaintance of the family, she is not naive in the usual sense, her motive in the immediate event is to protect her family from physical violence, and she is not open to seduction. Taken to London, she is housed with a bawd, not so that her fall can be disguised or exploited, but so that her resistance can be forced. She is arrested for debt, but the charge is phony, brought against her because she has found the means to escape from the brothel. Belford, who comes to her aid, is no man of feeling but a professional rake who learns to admire and help her only through a slow moral education. Above all there is her family. The sentiment of the *Caelia* model depends on the fact that Caelia's father (or Emily's or Olivia's) has been searching from the moment of his daughter's disappearance to find her and return her to the bosom of the family. Not Mr. Harlowe. Far from being the emotionally generous standard by which the action is judged and our responses guided, he combines irascibility, intellectual rigidity, and administrative weakness, losing stature on every page as he abdicates to his pathologically envious son. These changes do not result from the "unhappy ending": a novelist could induce more tears by having the villain hide the woman from the yearning family until after her death or continuing the family's misinformation about their daughter beyond the point of her death to allow them an orgy of posthumous reconciliation and uplifting grief. *Clarissa* is not in that business. The Harlowe family are barely recuperated; the parents die oppressed by guilt, and the siblings live on as the victims of their own bad tempers. And the novel ends with Lovelace, whose increasingly hollow claims to sensibility, wit, and passion are silenced by Colonel Morden. Though "the pity of it" may be our response, that is not a sentimental ending.

TWELVE

Theorizing the Obligation
to Self

F ROM THE MID-EIGHTEENTH CENTURY ONWARD, GIVEN THE WANING
of a morally demanding social and religious authority, how can there
continue to be stories built on the tested woman plot? What is the moral
authority that creates moral choice? One way the plot stays viable is by
being pushed down the social scale. As fiction increasingly takes seriously the
portrayal of characters of low degree, it can for a while retain a socially atavistic
plot. The restricted lives of lower-class, especially rural, people allow the
exercise of entrenched social, familial, and religious authority in ways no longer
practiced overtly among the upper classes, mobile urban dwellers, or educated
professionals. So the tested woman plot continues to be operable among
characters on the lower fringes of middle-class respectability. Among such
characters some version of patriarchal authority, personally exercised, can still
operate, because social and psychological sanctions on human behavior always
far outlive either their practical rationale or their unquestioned enforcement.
A woman can suffer agonies of guilt over behavior forced on her by evolving
social norms. In a world in social flux, in fact, the moral nature of remnant or
archaic social demands is underlined by the very absence of supportive social
structures. When female chastity has no extrinsic purposes, its maintenance
becomes purely a moral requirement, its loss the deepest form of personal
weakness or culpability.

The changes in worldview that vitiate patriarchy also create a new source
of moral authority. Literary sentimentality is a manifestation of the shift in
consciousness that accompanied and enabled the Western European journey
into the modern era. Nowhere is that shift more revolutionary than in its
construction of the modern sense of the self. Part of that construction is owing
to Christian emphasis on the individual soul and Protestant emphasis on the
sanctity of ordinary life. Part results from social leveling and the increasing
individual opportunities enabled by vernacular literacy, global mercantilism,

and technological change. The shift is one aspect of the eighteenth-century philosophical concern with epistemology—the nature of the mind, the relationship between mind and the external world, the distinction between intellect and emotion. The eventual result is an often tacit philosophical consensus about what Charles Taylor terms "the dignity of self-responsible reason." Accompanied by belief in the significance of ordinary nature and in the imperative of benevolence toward others, this notion comes to constitute not just an intellectual assumption of the late eighteenth and nineteenth centuries but one of its moral sources.[1]

Access to "self-responsible reason" requires access to the self. Since "self-responsible" must first mean "self-responsive," the eighteenth century had to learn to describe and cultivate the responses of the self. This "painful breaking of the seed of the self from the hard soil of an irrational and tradition-bound society," as John Fowles characterizes the process,[2] occurred more or less simultaneously in all ranks of British society. In 1739, for example, the young Anglican priest John Wesley addressed a new message of inner light to the miners of Bristol; the even younger philosopher David Hume's *Treatise of Human Nature* provided analytical language to explain the reciprocity between pride in oneself and love of others that created the new concept of sympathy;[3] and the aging printer Samuel Richardson had nearly finished the first draft of *Pamela*. What in literary or aesthetic terms is called the Age of Sensibility is a fundamental and definitive cultural reordering. The threads of this reordering, expressed in the language of sensibility, worked changes in the tested woman plot.

THE DOUBLE BIND

Because the waning of a controlling familial patriarchy does not eliminate the moral imperative of female obedience or filial piety, a new version of moral conflict develops in the serious literature of the plot from *Clarissa* onward. That this new version lies at the center of Jane Austen's *Mansfield Park* (1814) shows how quickly it becomes naturalized into the plot. Fanny Price is the good little girl in a family that has inherited a tradition of male authority and female obedience without being able to make it function. Her own father lacks any effectiveness other than progenitive. Her Uncle Bertram has only the husk of moral authority in the form of a rigidity that expresses itself in emotional and physical absence and cannot see beyond its own habits to the needs of the family of which he is head. Thence Fanny's predicament. Having transferred her filial obligation to this surrogate father, she nevertheless knows him misinformed about her feelings for Edmund, the happenings in his household, and the character of Henry Crawford, whose suit he requires that she entertain. Renaissance drama would have played out this family romance in terms of its male relationships. Though using the women as the plot center, it would have focused its psychological attention on the bondings and ruptures among the men—Sir Thomas and his sons, Crawford the interloping friend, Rushworth the cuckolded son-in-law. A Neoclassical play would have compressed the same focus into a thirty-six-hour flurry of betrayal, seduction, and revenge, taking advantage of the women's roles to saturate the play with female arias of hope and longing. Though when applied to the Bertrams such scenarios seem comical, they help us see what Austen does instead. Rather than centering attention on the male polity or balancing the female roles among the Bertram women's jealousies, the novel's second half takes us deep into Fanny's moral development, where her sense of what she owes to those who rescued her and allowed her to love comes to be countered by her sense of obligation to her own increasingly sophisticated emotional convictions. Even her faith in Edmund's godlike sagacity is revised by her deepening sense of his besottedness about the Crawfords and his inattentiveness to her devotion. In addition to owing willing fealty to the authority of her adopted family, Fanny comes to feel the moral force of her own independent, contradictory insights.

What has been assimilated by the time of *Mansfield Park* is the moral valuing of strong emotion. Finding this phenomenon in Austen, who was so antipathetic to the excesses of high Romanticism, makes its matter-of-factness the more striking. Fanny has a moral obligation to honor her own carefully founded and continually examined distrust of the Crawfords and dislike of the behavior they have stimulated in her family. She also has a moral obligation to honor her love for Edmund. Both obligations fly in the face of the behavior expected by her surrogate father, whom she also intends to honor and oblige. This double bind differs from earlier forms of the test, in which a woman is faced with an externally imposed choice expressed in terms of absolute right versus wrong or truth versus error. The new development involves both a growing conviction of the psychological primacy of the self in the human cultural enterprise and the rise of philosophically motivated arguments justifying consciousness of and service to the self as a moral good. New theories of the nature of emotion provide the language for expressing the inalienable rights of the self. The result is women who face obligations to both external and internal authority.

A certain concept of the self has been a concern throughout the history of Christianity. But in the eighteenth century the development of a psychology of emotion created a vocabulary and a theoretical base for a philosophy of selfhood. Sentimentality is one manifestation of this development because it is concerned with the psychology of emotion.[4] In its literary forms sentimentality is designed to arouse pity for the sufferings of others. This is pity expressed in words and tears by characters, author, and audience reacting in concert. Hume proposes that the emotions directed at others—love and hate or their adjuncts compassion and malice—are based on our sense of self and on others' resemblance to us. Pity, for instance, results from no abstract act of intellection—of "I know not what subtle reflections on the instability of fortune, and our being liable to the same miseries we behold" (418)—but from imaginative response to the resemblance to ourselves. Sympathetic responses gain strength and richness from the "reverberating" effect whereby, reacting to our common humanity in others, we strengthen our sense of our own humanness and thus our sensitivity to them.[5] The philosophical underpinnings of sentimental literature give rise to a criticism based on the psychology of reader response. Making this point, Janet Todd cites Edmund Burke on the affective nature of literature: "'We yield to sympathy, what we refuse to description.' The aim of literature is 'to affect rather by sympathy than imitation; to display rather the effect of things on the mind of the speaker, or of others, than to present a clear idea of the things themselves.' Here works of art do not necessarily contain an intellectual meaning; instead they primarily provoke the reader's participation in a mood. We respond to the description of response as much as to the portrayal of action. It is a lesson taken to heart by writers of sentimental fiction."[6]

Sympathy, or fellow feeling, like the newly invented faculty of taste, becomes a mark of gentility in mind and manner. Like a classical education it conveys distinction, but one open to cultivation by all, including women. Its development has conspicuous social effects, such as concern for the reform of madhouses, prisons, and chattel slavery. But it also takes a less activist, more aesthetic form—what Northrop Frye terms "pity without an object"—a generalized sense of fellow-feeling, of "all nature bursting into human life."[7] Within the reach of all, sympathy is subject to endless refinement, so that the "trifling" nature of Mackenzie's affecting passages serves as the guarantor of the editor's nobility of soul. As with princesses, the smaller the pea and the thicker the mattress, the more delicate and thus admirable the capacity for feeling.[8]

The psychology of emotion also leads to literary investment in sophisticated description and analysis of the workings of the mind. For this development the term is "sensibility," which to modern ears has a more cognitive ring than "sentimentality." The term "sensibility" carries a variety of related meanings in the eighteenth century. Narrowly it is physiological, referring to the relationship between external stimuli and the response of sensate organisms, including human beings.[9] More broadly, sensibility involves sensitivity to the state of one's own emotions in relation to their external causes. In its most thoughtful manifestations, the cult of sensibility attempts to do science, to build human philosophy on the minutely felt and analyzed movements of the individual mind. The more attentive the feeling and the analysis, the more firmly they ground philosophical categories and moral distinctions. Both reasoning powers and affective powers become bases for individual worth and individualized moral codes. Reason and sensibility, one traditionally the province of the male and the other of the female, go hand-in-hand as the two tools of the new philosophy of human nature, and both must be cultivated by fully educated people. By uniting them, for example, the three young lovers of Rousseau's *Julie* become intellectual and moral equals and partners: "In teaching us to think," says Julie's cousin to St. Preux, "you have learnt of us sensibility."[10]

POPE'S ELOISA AND ROUSSEAU'S JULIE

Feminist literary critics have brought our attention back to *Julie, ou La Nouvelle Héloïse* (1761) as one of a cluster of radically women-focused fictions of the mid-eighteenth century.[11] This work, which among his contemporaries was Rousseau's most popular, is really as much philosophy as novel. Like *Emile*, published the following year, *Julie* is an educational utopia. But whereas *Emile* is about the education of (male) children, *Julie* is about the emotional and moral education of adults, and that more mature education requires the enlivening and focusing effects of sexual longing, fulfillment, and frustration, for sexual love is one of the major educative experiences. That the philosophies of Rousseau's two works on moral education are disjunctive—that the mind boggles at creating a Julie or a Claire from the Sophie whose enfeebling upbringing is presented in *Emile*—seemed not to occur to him. Rousseau had very little imagination, if by that is meant the ability to be interested in, or even to conceive of, what he had not himself undergone. What he did have was a passion for reliving, revising, and generalizing from his own experience, and the philosophical determination to take his own emotional life seriously as representative of key facts about human nature.[12]

In *Julie*, or *Eloisa*, in William Kenrick's translation, Rousseau lays out the double bind of the morally sensitive woman, the conflict between the obligation of filial piety and the obligation to the emotional life of the self. In the plight of the historical Héloïse, as represented in eighteenth-century redactions like Alexander Pope's heroic epistle "Eloisa to Abelard," Rousseau evidently saw something like the type expression of an increasingly urgent modern quandary. Not that he uses precisely the original story: among other changes, he eliminates the religious milieu, lowers the age and professional status of his philosopher/lover, and redistributes authority functions from the hyperconcentration on Abélard to the more dramatically serviceable male configuration of father, lover, husband, and friend. But his heroine is, he argues, "la nouvelle Héloïse," the woman caught between obligation to the patriarchy and obligation to self.

Pope's "Eloisa to Abelard" is perhaps the first full literary expression of the double bind I am discussing. Certainly it is a powerful and, for 1717, historically precocious herald of literary sensibility. Pope's poem invites sympathy not just through its portrayal of Eloisa's pitiable devotion and frustration but through its meticulously elaborated Gothic apparatus of geographically inaccurate cliffs and grots and anachronistically baroque Catholicism. Eloisa's sensibility is also displayed by means of these descriptions, but even more through her

dramatistically presented internal debate, what the poem's Argument calls
"the struggles of grace and nature, virtue and passion."[13] Much about the
poem's technique is not new. Its genre, the complaint of the woman abandoned
by her lover, has its origin in Ovid's *Heroides*. As for appeals to the laws of
nature against the laws of God or man, since classical times they have been the
argument of the rebel. But Pope's Eloisa uses the appeal to nature differently.
She is a woman, not the usual man, and she offers fidelity rather than seeking
variety. Constraint, obedience, and lifelong devotion have only charms for
her. The nature against which she struggles is not the rake's "Nature," that
font of arguments in favor of sexual freedom after the analogy of heifers and
horses. It is her nature as an impassioned lover, spouse, and friend that is
denied Abelard's tutelage and bodily presence. She argues that sexual desire
is a natural passion from which he is free thanks only to a grossly unnatural
act that has liberated him into "a long, dead calm of fix'd repose" (l. 251)
more than halfway to death. Tellingly, the charge both Pope's Eloisa and the
historical Héloïse bring most bitterly against Abelard is his failure of sympathy,
his refusal to imagine her condition. Or is it his inability? If sympathy is a
natural human emotion, the unnatural act of castration has deprived Abelard
not merely of the means or the interest in sex but of a crucially human
imaginative capacity. Never does she complain of his inability to complete
the sexual act; she complains that his looks, his words, his love have not been
available to relieve her woe. "Give all thou canst—and let me dream the rest"
(l. 124) is her memorable plea. Her bitterness, at her darkest moments, is that
he has lacked even the wish to give. The interconnected human capacities of
sensibility and sympathy work symbiotically. Eloisa's sensibility—her detailed
comprehension and analysis of her condition—invites our sympathy as well as
Abelard's. And we understand, though less poignantly than she, how unnatural
acts destroy that link.

Eloisa also uses her situation as abandoned woman differently from traditional treatments. The usual male justification—Aeneas's justification—is that
the lover has more virtuous duties than answering the claims of passion in the
arms of Dido. By contrast, Eloisa invites Abelard to take up his duties, not
just to her but to her "sisters," his "daughters." One of the most attractive
passages of the poem is her description of the convent of the Paraclete, its
"plain roofs" raised by piety and "vocal with the Maker's praise" (ll. 139–40),
which Abelard built, gave to her and her nuns, and now has the obligation to
nurture. Abelard's career has given him all the patriarchal roles by which that
nurturing can be carried out. Owner of the land, spiritual as well as physical
begetter of the buildings on it, her lover, her husband, he is also a fellow
Benedictine, a priest, and her teacher. The conversation for which she pleads
may be carried out in many forms, all of which she reminds him of: "Come
thou, my father, brother, husband, friend!" (l. 152).[14] These words raise the
most fundamental issue underlying Eloisa's distress—its origin in what, given
the Christian terms of her profession, she can only admit to be idolatry of

Abelard. The poem opens with her admission that in her heart, "mix'd with God's, his lov'd Idea lies" (l. 12), but by the poem's midpoint the full confession has been made. Not God but Abelard: "Ah wretch! believ'd the spouse of God in vain, / Confess'd within the slave of love and man" (ll. 177–8). The historical Héloïse is even more frank and insistent regarding her total commitment to the man: "At every stage of my life up to now, as God knows, I have feared to offend you rather than God and tried to please you more than him. It was your command, not love of God which made me take the veil" (letter 2, 134). She knows that her only hope for peace of mind lies in using one nail to drive another out (letter 3, 159). Thus Pope's Eloisa pleads:

> Oh come! oh teach me nature to subdue,
> Renounce my love, my life, my self—and you.
> Fill my fond heart with God alone, for he
> Alone, can rival, can succeed to thee.
>
> (ll. 203–6)

The emotional logic of the patriarchal analogy has taken literal form: for this woman, the God in Abelard is God indeed. Both her dependence and her obedience are absolute. Therefore, ironically, what he has commanded, that she transfer her devotion to his God, she finds herself unable to perform. "*Make* my soul quit Abelard for God," she begs him (l. 128; my emphasis). Yet both the entire poem and what we know of the historical Héloïse's life tell us that her heart cannot be forced, only seduced.

This historical event takes on a literary life partly because it conforms to a preexisting plot. Abélard the seducer challenges the patriarchal interest and honor of Fulbert the uncle, who first attempts to defend his niece, then, when the marriage has confirmed his dispossession without restoring the family's honor, turns accuser, taking a horrible revenge against them both. This looks like the test stage of the tested woman plot, and it ends in catastrophe, pain, dishonor, and loss, seemingly salvaged by Héloïse's return to the patriarchal fold through her religious profession. After a hiatus of some years, there follows an extended examination of the facts of the past and the situation of the present conducted by the principals themselves. But because with her seduction and marriage Héloïse gave her allegiance to Abélard, and because with the religious vows taken at his command she then committed herself to a higher authority to which she cannot be obedient, the trial stage involves new tests. The odd twist is that Abélard—the husband, brother, father, and spiritual guide—is now attempting to reason or, it may be, command Héloïse out of her allegiance to him. And this time, though she can be silenced, she cannot be moved.[15] This odd twist accounts for the psychological restlessness of the trial stage. Here it is the woman who, seizing the occasion of Abélard's *Historia calamitatum*, reopens the account books. No calm physician to the tormented husband who abused and lost her, it is she who is raw with the anguish of loss and longing, he the cold and vestal one. The emotional situations of Leontes and Hermione, of Pericles and Thaisa, have been reversed.

Had we lacked the historical account of Abélard and Héloïse, it would have been a bold creator of fictions who would have dared a tested woman story in which the test is so doubled and the male character functions so concentrated. The peculiar intensity of this trial stage arises partly because, in the present time of the exchange of letters, Abélard, who carries out all patriarchal plot functions, takes on contradictory roles. It also arises because Héloïse feels her obligations both to God and to Abélard as matters of personal moral intention.[16] Despite never having read the authentic correspondence, Pope captures Eloisa's psychological dilemma, especially the tension between the demands and promises of a religious vocation and the demands of physical passion. Part of the brilliance of his rendition lies in his choice of form. The heroic epistle concentrates the story as the single epistolary voice presents Eloisa's closed world without the distractions of a full exchange.

The success of Pope's poem is a reminder that in its historical form, or even in the unauthentic Bussy-Rabutin/Hughes/Pope version, the story of Héloïse, like that of Griselda, concentrates patriarchal character functions too much to make good drama. When Rousseau created his fully epistolary version of the story, though determined not to lose the double bind of competing forms of obligation, he gave us four men rather than one to fill the roles of father, lover, husband, and friend. First Julie's father, the baron d'Etange, then her husband, Wolmar, represent patriarchal possession, which leaves sexual passion the province of St. Preux, the seducer. This distribution of characters is utterly conventional for the tested woman plot, but then, there is no evidence that Rousseau had an interest in innovative story-making. His innovations lie elsewhere.[17]

Julie is fully epistolary in the sense that the novel is related in letters from various correspondents. In calling the work as much philosophy as novel, I am alluding to its style and narrative pacing. Stylistically the characters' voices are individualized only sporadically. The secondary characters such as Julie's father and mother or even Lord B are distinguishable primarily by the topics of their letters. The main characters and correspondents—Julie, St. Preux, Claire—sound alike, write alike, think alike. I do not mean that they necessarily agree on matters moral or tactical; but their debates, remonstrances, and ecstasies sound like the conflicted positions of a single sensibility. Unlike *Clarissa*, when one opens *Julie* at random, it is often necessary to go back to the salutation, or even back several letters, to tell who is writing to whom. This is not totally an imaginative shortcoming, since the three central characters are construed as having taught each other to think and feel alike. Part of the novel's point is that they have shared a sentimental education; they take delight and comfort in thinking of themselves as one. The triangle is not devoid of multidirectional erotic undertones, but their effect is to stress similarity rather than difference. Eventually the widowed Claire openly admits her long-standing sexual interest in St. Preux, while he responds to her beauty and charm and confides in her almost as to another lover. The relationship between the cousins is intimate in that pre-twentieth-century way we err to characterize as lesbian but no longer quite understand under the name of friendship. Like Clarissa and her Anna Howe, Julie and Claire think of themselves as "lovers," or "the inseparables" as St. Preux calls them (4:60). They openly declare their passionate affection, craft lifelong links, live together whenever possible, and even share children, providing a proving ground for Rousseau's doctrines of friendship and communal life.

In its narrative pacing also, *Julie* also seems as much treatise as novel. Not just St. Preux's trips to France and England, but many of the novel's more intimate events introduce philosophical topics. Much of the work reads like set pieces: on naturalistic landscaping, on the manners and morals of Parisians, on French versus Italian music. Even segments emotionally bound into the story often have an air of philosophical presentation, whether they concern the scenery of Lake Geneva, social relations with a villager, household economy and dining habits, the lover's confession of an episode at a brothel, or the causal relationship between sensibility and religious faith. As a fiction about the moral education of adults, *Julie* is programmatically concerned to consider different aspects of conduct. The work is driven as much by the need to present its philosophical case fully as it is by narrative concerns. The catastrophe of Julie's accident and death occurs where it does because the characters have completed their discussions of every other possible topic. St. Preux and Julie having resumed their correspondence to say all that can be said about religious devotion, a possible marriage between lover and cousin, and their own capacities for a Platonic lifetime together, how Julie will conduct her dying and how those she loves will respond is all that remains.

Reading Rousseau's story against that of the historical Héloïse and Abélard turns up several major differences. Unlike the stalking to which Abélard admits, in Rousseau tutor and pupil, equal in youth and ardor, fall freely in love with each other. As St. Preux writes to the furious father, "Between two persons of the same age there can be no *seducer* but love" (2:208–9). Unlike Héloïse, Julie never suffers the withdrawal of her lover's ardor; rendered impotent by her inaccessibility, he remains obsessed with her. And Rousseau eliminates the functional concentration on Abélard. After distributing those functions among a quartet of male figures and carrying them forward to the climax of the test stage where the father bestows the woman on his choice of husband, Rousseau confirms the salient trajectory of the plot by spending the third and fourth volumes reconciling male conflicts around the focal woman.

In the novel's first half, the testing action is played out under the shadow of the father. The baron d'Etange is mostly absent, making it possible for Julie's mother to welcome St. Preux as the cousins' tutor and give emotional support for her daughter's love. The baron's position, however, is understood by both wife and daughter. He would not tolerate the plebeian St. Preux as

Julie's suitor, and in any case she is promised to the Russian nobleman Wolmar, to whom the baron owes his life. When the baron gets wind of his daughter's infatuation, he writes to St. Preux, castigating him as a seducer and demanding an answer to the enclosed message from "an unhappy girl, whose heart you have corrupted, and who should no longer exist, if I could suppose her to have carried the forgetfulness of herself any farther" (2:208). St. Preux's response releases her from her vow, and the test stage ends with the bond between the baron and Wolmar confirmed by marriage. The seducer is driven off to travel abroad in the service of the English Lord B.

The novel's second half consists of Julie's life with her husband under the shadow of her lover. Her father's actions had aimed at excluding the lover, but Wolmar brings him back into the family as his own companion, friend of the reconciled father, Platonic admirer of the wife, and tutor to their sons. Unlike the baron, Wolmar knows that Julie's affair with St. Preux was consummated. As the rational man, however, he grounds his faith in her faultless marital conduct on her marriage vows and the active pleasures of a richly domestic life. He understands that if a longing absence would be the best encouragement to continued passion, its best cure may be an honorable friendship. Gradually he reintroduces his wary wife to her lover's presence, creating an extended community of family and friends in which St. Preux can occupy a comfortable place. These domestic reorderings are eased and abetted by Lord B. Though his initial presence in the principals' lives is clumsily motivated, he comes to provide not just the epistolary advantage of a distant correspondent but the moral usefulness of an intellectual companion to the husband and a patron to the poverty-stricken lover. Along with Claire's suitor and eventual husband, M. Orbe, Lord B plays the role of adviser to both women, giving them and us a comforting sense of Wolmar's delicately benevolent rationality and the virtuous behavior whereby Mme. Wolmar recommends herself to all. Nevertheless, on her deathbed Julie admits that, despite the felicity of her married life, St. Preux has had her heart.

THE MORAL USES OF SENSIBILITY

Julie lives, where it lives for us at all, through Rousseau's capacity to make deeply attractive both modes of life: the obsessively passionate, intensely private love affair and the exquisitely balanced communal life. Rousseau is conscious of this diptych-like structure: his philosophical business, he says in *The Confessions*, is morality and marital fidelity on the one hand, harmony and public peace on the other.[18] This accounts for the fact that the two sections of the work are so different; as the interlocutor points out in Rousseau's introductory "Dialogue on the Subject of Romance," "one would imagine them to be two different books" which, he continues with comic censoriousness, "ought not to be read by the same people."[19] The attractions of both modes, however, depend on a patriarchal model of family life. The intensity of the love affair requires subversion. Had Julie not had to develop her sensibility in opposition to the opinions of her father, had St. Preux not brought with him a philosophy of selfhood contrasting with what tradition had taught her, the bond would never have been made. But the delight of the communal life of Clarens also depends on its relation to the patriarchal model, in this case the patriarchal family revised. Between the isolation of the individual (or the pair of lovers) and the pointless tumult of the great world, preaches Rousseau, lies the golden middle ground of family life. His family is reconstituted around the bonds of friendship rather than blood; the sustainable productivity of rural life rather than feudal, commercial, or military exploitation; the stimulating intercourse of generations, sexes, nationalities, and even ranks rather than the gloomy tyranny of the patriarch. Clarens is a domesticated revision of the equally utopian dream of the convent of the Paraclete, for the story of Héloïse presents a medieval version of the conflict between the same two compelling modes of life.

In this utopian diptych Rousseau's most influential contribution is to make an intellectual case for the moral power of sensibility. Several structural innovations do this work, but the most important is the profession of the tempter. St. Preux is neither hereditary enemy nor disloyal family friend but tutor and philosopher, so that philosophical conversation becomes natural with his presence. With this gesture toward Abélard, Rousseau acknowledges a precedent, though he bases St. Preux on his own voluptuously intellectual nature. Since the man who explores and theorizes at the heart of the plot is too delicious to lose, Rousseau carries St. Preux into the trial stage, where the amateur philosophizing of Wolmar and Lord B joins his own. Once the type of the tutor/philosopher is established, subsequent practitioners of the plot hardly know how to do without it. Mackenzie's Savillon guides Julia's hand as she draws, Edmund tutors Fanny, Dimmesdale the spiritual adviser seduces Hester, Angel Clare philosophizes to Tess, Benson educates Ruth, and the scholars Casaubon and Chillingworth owe their power, real or illusory, to their esoteric knowledge. Not all these figures are tempters. Their positions serve a variety of story purposes, including rationalizing access to young women. In all cases, however, they are the excuse for the psychological and social analysis that is one of the principal features of their stories; discussion is made natural by their presence. St. Preux, the philosopher of the self, sets the pattern.

Wolmar is also a philosopher in the tradition of serious-minded Enlightenment gentlemen. The marital and emotional opposite of St. Preux, his presence allows a contrastive dissection of the moral power of sensibility. Throughout Wolmar presents himself, and is presented by others, as the man who, because of his deracinating personal history and his innate propensities, is cold, passionless, without the common measure of human sentiment. One expression of this nature is his regrettable inability to shed tears, which in an age of sensibility are the mark of fellow-feeling, and in an age of medical theories still based on purging the humors provide a health-restoring vent for anguish or joy.[20] As the man of reason, refusing all excesses—including those of sexual passion and jealousy—Wolmar attempts to create for his family and friends a rational paradise on earth.

Characters, author, and readers must acknowledge the inadequacy of Wolmar's rationality alone. Claire delicately alludes to the sexual deprivation his character and age must cause her friend.[21] St. Preux discusses the greater deprivation created by Wolmar's religious skepticism. Julie's religious devoutness is made possible by her unceasingly sensitive and joyful reading of the created world, a reading of which her husband is incapable. The result is an unresolvable emotional and intellectual tension: "Imagine to yourself the situation of a married couple, having a sincere regard for each other, who, for fear of giving offence, dare not indulge themselves in such sentiments or reflections as the objects around them inspire; but who are bound in duty, even from their reciprocal affections, to lay themselves under continual restraint" (4:10–1).[22] The discussion raises the question of the relationship between sensibility and the capacity for religious faith. Justifying her own intensifying faith to St. Preux and scorning his caution against excessive devotion, Julie points out that in her youth reliance on reason did not serve her well: "I thought I knew my own strength, I relied on it, and was deceived. All the resistance which was in my own power I think I made; and yet I fell" (4:192).[23] Julie needs more than rationalist moral sustenance and protection. She craves the strengthening force of a morality based on her powers of identification and emotional response. By turning first to the objects of emotion available through her extended family and community, then to those of the natural world and its creator, she attempts to expand the bases of her emotional life away from a fixation on the single Other. This expansion is why the second half of the work has far less sexual interest and far more cultural interest. The deprivations of Julie's married life do not arise from restricted objects of sensibility, for her attention is broadened and her perceptions deepened by her situation and her husband's tutelage. The deprivations arise rather from the "continual restraint" enforced by the absence of the soul mate, the one whose quickness of passionate response would call forth her own.

La Nouvelle Héloïse is an early exemplar of "the argument of sensibility," which, says Stephen Cox, "might be very loosely defined as persuasive discourse that tends to equate intellectual authority with the power to display or elicit emotional susceptibility." Cox cautions that such argument does not lack factual bases: "It would be incorrect to say that the argument of sensibility distinguishes itself from other types of argument by eliminating inference from facts," but, he points out, "the facts involved in this type of argument are the facts of subjective states."[24] Such argument is so easily subject either to flaccid universalizing or to the valorizing of selfishness that it quickly becomes subject to satire and disrepute.[25] What modern thought never loses, however, is the conviction that sensitivity to emotional states is a moral resource that can enrich individual lives and promote social good. Such a deep version of sensibility even seems, for many moderns, a necessary basis for any genuine theory of morality.

The best practitioners of the literature of sensibility know how easily it can be abused. Responding to Lord Kames's challenge to write a tragedy in which all the characters are "naturally virtuous,"[26] Henry Mackenzie spends much of *Julia de Roubigné* (1777) exploring the difference between misguided passions and the moral fruits of genuine sensibility. Julia's error lies in agreeing to marry her father's benefactor, Montauban, when her heart is devoted to her childhood soul mate and tutor, Savillon (though there was never a sexual affair and she believes he is married). When Montauban withdraws his suit in the face of her reluctance, yet still pays off her father's debts, Julia's heart "swell[s] to a sort of enthusiastic madness," and she "offers that hand to his generosity, that she refused to his solicitation" (524). But she knows that she is the victim of her filial piety, as does her father, who finds her reading Racine: "'Iphigenia!' said my father, taking up the book, 'Iphigenia!' He looked on me piteously as he repeated the word. I cannot make you understand how much that single name expressed, or how much that look" (517). The problem of the marriage is the admission of both Montauban and Julia that they are temperamentally ill-suited. The wife must steel herself to be just to her husband, while the husband fears that such constraint must presage infidelity. Because Mackenzie respects the integrity of the double bind, his story ends in tragedy, tapping the convention of hot-blooded Latin excess (the husband is a Spaniard) for a violent denouement: when Savillon returns unexpectedly from Martinique and the childhood friends meet for a last parting, Montauban assumes his wife's infidelity, poisons her, and on learning his error kills himself. This ending is *Othello* without Iago, as the beginning was *La Nouvelle Héloïse* without sexual consummation.

Choosing the tested woman plot for his tragedy of the naturally virtuous, Mackenzie understands that the choice of one good against another is the plot's essence; by taking seriously the argument that honoring the integrity of the heart is as much a duty as filial love, he pinpoints what is emotionally at stake in the transfer of the woman's obligation from father to husband. The argument for sympathy as a human good is at last available to give moral valuing to a human need traditionally dismissed as mere carnality. The schematics of Mackenzie's moral argument are well served. But his epistolary drama has the faults of its virtues: too much the drama, it offers too little sustained exploration of emotional states. Because the three principals, who have their own confidants, write little to one another, they are not open to mutual influence through their expressions of interiority. Their emotional natures are static. The situation controls, the characters are what they are, and the catastrophe is forecast from the opening.

By contrast, Richardson, also practicing a version of the argument of sensibility, uses the tested woman plot to explore how the heart changes. For

instance, the prenuptial scenes reconciling Pamela and Mr. B with Pamela's
father and Mr. Williams, though they are given moral grounding by preceding
events, make an intellectual argument by means of the participants' joyful tears.
That argument, however, is not made chiefly among the principals, but to
the onlookers. Mr. B insists on having witnesses to father's and daughter's
acceptance of his terms and happiness in his beneficence. The onlookers'
rejoicing in the emotions of the two makes the case for the correctness of
his behavior, countering the revulsion arising from his marriage to a social
inferior. A deeper form of the argument of sensibility lies in the protagonists'
motivations for reconciliation. When Pamela breaks off her journey home
and returns to Mr. B in his illness, she has read his letter pleading for her
generosity: "You cannot imagine the obligation your return will lay me under to
your goodness" (216).[27] She is moved by his warm impetuousness of heart, his
sympathetic reaction to her journal, his "obliging" language in blaming himself
for his behavior and in attempting amends: "Now this is a dear generous
manner of treating me. O how I love to be generously used!" (217). Modern
readers are inclined to sneer at Mr. B's "condescension." To some it seems a
paltry thing in light of his offenses; to others it recalls a social inegalitarianism
of which we feel we must disapprove. But through reading Pamela's writing,
B has come to participate in her emotional life, and his emotions have become
responsive to hers. His pride in self has been fractured by a movement toward
the other, and as Hume tells us, love is the name of that movement. Pamela
made her admissions earlier, to her parents: "I must own to you, that I shall
never be able to think of any body in the world but him!—Presumption, you
will say; and so it is; But love is not a volunteer thing:—Love, did I say!—But,
come, I hope not!—At least it is not, I hope, gone so far, as to make me *very*
uneasy; for I know not *how* it came, nor when it begun; but creep, creep it
has, like a thief upon me; and before I knew what was the matter, it look'd like
love" (214). Now, knowing what his admissions have cost her master, she is
obliged to reciprocate his generosity.

Is this the obligation that Cervantes' lovesick swain seeks to force upon
Marcela? By no means. That notion of obligation is founded on the principle
of male sexual right that motivates Mr. B's initial pursuit. Because Richardson
has made Pamela's tempter a gentleman, he is able to develop a contrastive
view of the obligations created by sensibility. Mr. B retains the privileges of
his class. What he partially relinquishes is the caste-privileges of the male,
putting in their place the obligations created by the emotional reciprocities of
sympathetic perception. When Mr. B refers to the obligations Pamela has put
him under (as she refers to his), he means more than the social requirement
that civility be met with civility. He means that, in giving him access to her
emotional life, she has created in him a corresponding emotional life to which
he must be responsive. Privy to Mr. B's self-description, readers can watch
his texts develop a facility in that responsiveness and self-awareness in which
Pamela has preceded him. His pride in his newly trained sensibility becomes

the engine for his moral progress, as his pleasure in Pamela's pleasure responds to and is mirrored by his pleasure in his own emotional responsiveness. The reciprocities of Humean sympathy are being presented before our eyes.

Though she enjoys such reciprocating mutuality of response with Miss Howe, whom she describes as her other self, Clarissa cannot establish it with either her father or Lovelace because such mutuality would require them to engage her individuality with their own, undermining their self-images as powerful and controlling people. Mr. Harlowe refuses to engage the argument of sensibility. Lovelace, superb mimic that he is, periodically practices that language; if occasionally his mimicries engage him fundamentally, causing a momentary shudder in his psyche, they never transform him. Thus, though Clarissa continues obligated to her family by her sense of filial duty, she never becomes more generously obligated by reciprocities of perception and feeling. Nor does she, finally, fall into the trap of feeling obligated by Lovelace's declarations of suffering and remorse.

But Clarissa's sensibility does create obligations to her own self. Resulting from a painfully constructed self-knowledge whose authority is not just *what* she feels but *that* she feels, these are the reasoned operations of what Richardson calls prudence and modern readers would call wisdom.[28] Clarissa has discovered both how she must live and how she cannot live. Deepened by her struggle with her feelings for Lovelace, she refuses to marry Solmes, to submit to her family's bullying, to submit to Lovelace's extortionary rape, and to marry him on demand. This is self-responsible reason, and it is self-responsibility that Austen's Fanny Price both feels and reasons her way to. Her obligations include refusal—she cannot marry Henry—but they also embrace the responsibilities of the adult. She learns to manage as well as be managed; she learns where she cannot please, and ceases to torment herself about the fact; she learns to be a mentor and teacher as well as a willing pupil; she learns to suffer herself to be admired. Many women learn such things, but Austen's novel is built to show us the journey.

PART IV

Narrating the Self

THIRTEEN

Innocence as Ignorance: Teaching Interpretation

THE FIRST TESTED WOMAN STORY, EVE IN THE GARDEN, MAKES TWO incompatible moral arguments. The state of innocence in which mankind knows neither good nor evil is the perfect state, it proclaims, from which all else is decline. And, proclaims the tale, human beings are responsible for their actions. Although the incompatibility of these two positions is not detectable before the entrance of the tempting interloper, once the serpent has made the offer to Eve—once choice has become necessary—the quandary becomes pressing. If one does not know, how can one choose, how be responsible? Yet knowing already represents a fall, because the injunction is, "Thou shalt not know." Until the modern era, tested woman stories typically bypass this fundamental paradox because they operate in cultures that put intermediary requirements between the woman and the possibility of knowledge, especially forbidden sexual knowledge. Whatever the specifics of her duty, the obligation of obedience to the patriarchal representative is foregrounded over the behavior to which such obedience has reference. The problem of the innocence that is ignorance is thus avoided, since the woman knows enough to behave virtuously when she knows to whom she belongs. Virtue consists in not looking beyond the sphere of the father or the husband. If, as in the case of a widow, a woman has no familial superior, custom, religion, and the law provide constraints.

DEVELOPING THE TECHNICAL TOOLS

By *Paradise Lost* the modern era is upon us. When Milton returns to the generative myth, he insistently engages the paradox of ignorant innocence, faceting and refaceting his scenes of warning, tutelage, and interpretation into a massive script exploring moral development and the meaning of free will. In this psychological equivalent of the Ptolemaic universe, with mankind at its

195

center, the epic narrator is the literary device that makes a multifaceted tale possible. The characters' minds are available to us only in framed conversation or soliloquy. Though the poem's capaciousness allows reiteration, its bursts of inward focus are both formally paced and limited in length. By contrast, the eighteenth-century invention of the inward-focused epistolary novel, coupled with its validation of individuals' emotional perceptions, creates the opportunity to explore the paradox of the Garden developmentally. New third-person narrative techniques allow expressions of interiority without potentially clumsy resort to soliloquy, diary, epistolary exchange, or artificially revelatory conversation. Early nineteenth-century novels are in a technical position to deal directly with the problem of ignorance implicit in the tested woman plot.

The development of *style indirect libre*, the narrative technique whereby characters' thoughts are re-presented by the authorial voice without speaker tags and without necessarily referencing actual speech, was, argues Margaret Anne Doody, the creation of Fanny Burney and other English women novelists of the late eighteenth century, and Jane Austen was their beneficiary.[1] When in 1777, under the guise of editor, Henry Mackenzie comments on his decision to present in epistolary form the supposedly authentic letters making up *Julia de Roubigné*, he expresses the assumptions of authors and readers for whom the indirect free style is not yet quite available: "I found it a difficult task to reduce [the letters] to narrative, because they are made up of sentiment, which narrative would destroy" (introduction, 503). That subtlest of the artists of sensibility, Mackenzie is playing an elaborate game with his pretense of authenticity. Even if it had been available to him, he might have feared that the double voicing of indirect free speech and thought would "destroy sentiment" because it conveys the inevitably discrepant judgments of both character and narrator. On the other hand, Doody notes, "What might appear at first glance to be simply an ironic technique is also and at the same time fundamentally sympathetic" (288). To appreciate the worldview of a novel narrated in indirect free style, readers must enter it through the character's thoughts and emotions, often emotions and thoughts too intimate or too tentatively formed to be spoken or written by the character herself. This accessibility to an interiority too embryonic or disturbing even to be capable of expression by the character, in addition to its ironic possibilities, has the potential for taking sensibility to a level of delicacy and suggestiveness impossible for the essentially rhetorical epistolary mode.

The new technical means are timely, for the founding of morality in patriarchal authority is becoming an intellectual and social problem. In a world that increasingly grounds morality in the worth of the individual, what basis can there be for a moral obligation to the mere fact of time-honored social structures? The force of economic and legal power aside, what obligates a woman to accept situations or behavior she finds morally distasteful? On the other hand, if her moral compass is expected to be internal, how in the absence of genuine education and a certain amount of tutelage in the ways of the world can she be expected to develop her bearings? How, especially by the early age at which she is attractive to men more experienced and powerful than she, is she to shape an effective personal morality to replace the absent familial authority that once decided for her? Shamefastness is insufficient protection even for a girl child thrown on her own resources; for an adult woman attempting to lead an active and honorable life, it is laughably inadequate. Caught in the double bind of changing standards, how does a good girl learn what to do?

The problem of the ignorance of innocence lies at the heart of George Eliot's *Middlemarch*. Dorothea's story is consciously built on the tested woman plot, as Eliot's schematically structured character functions and chapter head-notes, with their allusions to Renaissance tested woman drama, make explicit. It is no mystery why Eliot chose this plot as the heart of her most complex examination of the relationship between intellectual and moral life, a topic distinctively her own. Structured around the problem of a woman's moral choice, the tested woman plot cries out to be taken up by a writer who sees this choice as an intellectual opening as well. And opening it still is, for in 1870 the story of the intellectually ambitious, ardent, and innocent young woman had yet to be written. It may seem strange to group Dorothea Brooke with exemplars of the ignorance of innocence, for she is continually in intellectual motion. But she is estranged from her social setting and from social knowledge. For a precariously long time, she is blind to the minds and motives of others. The novel's Prelude and Finale, with their reference to the heroic ardor of St. Theresa of Avila, draw readers' attention to the centrality of the theme of Dorothea's frustrated passion to *do*, both greatly and beneficently. The tested woman plot is preeminently the story of the great female martyrs, as Eliot knows in giving us the winsomely reduced version of the future saint toddling out hand in hand with her little brother to seek martyrdom among the Moors. But Theresa's accomplishment is not primarily a matter of supernaturally supported suffering. Further, Dorothea's passion to give her life greatly is just one aspect of her encompassing intellectual hunger. Ignorance is the failing for which she most often scores herself, deep book learning the only worldly advantage she craves. That her most crippling ignorance stems not from an absence of the learned languages but from a myopia about the human self is part of the revelation of the complicated test and trial she undergoes. And indirect free discourse is Eliot's chief technical tool for portraying her gradual emergence into knowledge.

But the problem of the ignorance of innocence had become salient in the nineteenth-century novel's use of the plot well before *Middlemarch*. Like Eliot's, the novels by Elizabeth Gaskell and Jane Austen that we consider in this chapter share a common starting point. They often posit young, secluded, unworldly women for whom patriarchal lines of authority are blurred or absent. Though none has personal vanity, all these women live in emotional worlds of their own. All of them have developed a capacity for emotional responsiveness that far surpasses their social knowledge, and all feel detached, even estranged, from those around them. Drama or the epistolary novel can do little more with such characters than present their confusions or dawning comprehensions and invite us to rejoice or weep over their fortunes. In a first-person format, they have little to offer because they know little about themselves and the world. This is why the first-person novels of the eighteenth century thrive on witting heroines—the Molls, Roxanas, Pamelas, Clarissas, and Evelinas who, whatever these characters' youthful naïveté and regardless of how many things they get wrong, have a scrappy, gossipy, practical view of life from the opening page.

With the novel of indirect free narration comes the capacity to present the dream-state ignorance of innocence from the inside while analyzing it from the outside. The development of this technique is one reason the exploration of the psychology of ignorant or naive characters comes into its own in the nineteenth century. The other reason is that among radical social critics, the infantilization of women as a caste comes to be understood as a social problem contributing to private misery and the public scourges of prostitution, illegitimacy, and child neglect. The testing of the innocence that is ignorance thus has the makings of a subtle social problem novel that is also deeply psychological, one in which the woman's own education in self and in the world underlies the novel's broader social critique.

Ruth's Case: Social Causes and Social Consequences

Elizabeth Gaskell's *Ruth* is a social problem novel in the classic nineteenth-century sense, with an interest not just in the presenting phenomena of seduction and illegitimacy, but in typhus epidemics, election fraud, the ethnography of dissenting congregations, and the moral education of children. The sexual problem has all the sensational indicators prominently flagged: selfish gentleman, lower-class girl, bastard child, public rejection, redemption through self-abnegating service, and death.[2] But the tested woman plot is the structure on which sensation and sentiment are built. Because Ruth is an unprotected young woman, Gaskell must create family surrogates, spelling out the male character functions and explicitly linking social with sexual politics in the process. The defender, Benson, and the accuser, Bradshaw, are portrayed as long-term allies and twin pillars of a single congregation because, in social terms, they represent reciprocal patriarchal functions. One would integrate the woman into the group in the name of sympathy, while the other would shun her in the name of purity. Because Bradshaw must learn from the inside about temptation and sin, Gaskell introduces the tempter, Bellingham/Donne, into the same circle. Bradshaw becomes contaminated by the man who has contaminated Ruth and, indirectly, Benson as well.

Within these social and structural conventions, the novel offers a striking presentation of estranged innocence. Raised on a secluded farm, her parents now dead, Ruth knows only the dressmaker to whom she is apprenticed and the old country people she visits on her long walk with Bellingham. At barely sixteen, she is beautiful and physically mature but intellectually and emotionally unformed, and she lacks even theoretical instruction in social or sexual behavior. When Bellingham seeks her company she has no idea of his sexual interest, but is simply grateful for a friendly presence and a respite from drudgery.[3] Nor, when she goes off with him, does she understand what is happening; she is trying to escape Mrs. Mason's wrath at having found them together, though she does not understand its basis. At one poignant moment, as she waits for Bellingham to fetch a coach, she thinks it might be better to go to the old couple, but she is reluctant to pass the innkeeper standing in the door because she has no money to pay for her meal, and Bellingham returns to hustle her off to London. With this touch, Gaskell reminds how, for a child, minor social embarrassment carries infinitely more emotional weight than the unimaginable reality of future degradation. Because no one has a stake in what she does with herself, even seduction fails to give Ruth notions of sexual morality in any familial or social sense. When we next meet the pair in a small town in Wales, she is surprised by her first exposure to public contempt, for London was too impersonal for her to be noticed. Though she is later taught that she has offended against God's will, the only offense in human terms is against social opinion. Thus the Bensons can allow themselves to hide the truth, passing her off as the widowed Mrs. Denbigh and raising her son as part of their household.

Joining the Benson household does not totally change Ruth's apartness. Having a child gives her the need to live in the world, and she is grateful to Mr. Benson and his sister and takes full part in family life, but she is never one of them. Some things she keeps secret: not even Mr. Benson knows the identity of Leonard's father until after Ruth's death. Some things are not in her nature: though her behavior is impeccable, and she joins Benson's congregation, Gaskell does not present her as doctrinally Christian. Yet she is not the kind of outcast typical of Charlotte Brontë's novels, for she is neither rebellious nor without family. It is her child who focuses her attention beyond herself: "Oh, my God, I thank Thee! Oh, I will be so good!" (118), she promises when she learns she is pregnant, and her life's goal becomes the raising of her son. Still, she remains emotionally aloof from the community; when she volunteers as matron of the fever hospital, the quarantined world she enters is a literal expression of her social state. Though the community learns to admire her, she values their regard primarily on her son's behalf. Her labor, like the studies she undertakes with Mr. Benson, has been performed to make her a fit mentor for Leonard.

Much of this sense of Ruth's emotional separateness arises from Gaskell's strong use of the tested woman plot's two-stage structure. Rosemarie

Bodenheimer's discussion of the pastoral quality of the novel's opening corroborates my view. Bodenheimer sees the novel's structure as grounded in the
tension between Gaskell's personal commitment to a Wordsworthian view of
the naturalness of sexuality and maternity and her fears about the novel's public
reception. "But the split between Ruth as a private conception and as a public
issue had already been inscribed in the text itself. It takes the form of a division
between a pastoral argument about private feeling, which occupies the first
nine chapters, and a social argument about the treatment of the fallen woman,
which dominates the rest of the novel." Exactly so. Whereas Bodenheimer sees
the motivation for this division in the gap between Gaskell's "personal and maternal commitment to the story"[4] and its public life as a social document, I see
it more fundamentally as a variation on the salient feature of the plot structure
itself, which Gaskell's personal commitment sought to use. When developed to
its fullest, the test is indeed a representation of the woman's personal identity,
and this is what Gaskell's pastoral/social division accomplishes. If the pastoral is
a pre- or nonmoral world—a world that blessedly demands no moral choices—
the entrance into a social world is an entrance into moral choice. Hence the
reappearance of Bellingham. Because Ruth's seduction occurred when she was
too naive to understand it, vitiating the moral (though not the social) point,
Gaskell replays the test: resurfacing as Donne the parliamentary candidate,
Bellingham finds Ruth acting as governess to the Bradshaws and stages a
carefully graduated series of moves to get her back. First attempting to re-
seduce her sexually and emotionally, then to bribe her with education for
Leonard, as a last resort he offers marriage and adoption of the boy. In social
terms this would give her everything—she would become the respected wife
of a prominent man, and her child would never suffer the humiliation attached
to his birth; even the fiction of her widowhood would be maintained. Despite
her yearning for the love she felt for Bellingham, however, Ruth energetically
refuses each of these offers out of contempt for the shallow, self-centered man
Donne so demonstrably is—now that he lacks even his youth to excuse him.
She wants no contact between him and her son; better that Leonard should
work on the roads all his life, she says. At last she can understand and reject
what Bellingham is, and the trial stage begins only when she does.

In some nineteenth-century novels, the woman's real growth occurs during
the trial, as she takes the function of judgment on herself. In *Ruth* Gaskell's
primary interest is rather the moral psychology of defense and accusation
and the social mechanism of public judgment. Ruth's test once replayed in
terms that require conscious choice, the town finds out that Ruth is unmarried
and Leonard a bastard. All along, however, a struggle has been under way
in Benson over his use of evil means to attain good ends. Though Ruth's
agony at encountering her seducer again is cruel, it is almost exclusively
emotional. Benson's struggle, however, is truly moral. By hiding Ruth's antecedents Benson has given her the opportunity to heal her psyche, raise her
child, and find employment as governess to the Bradshaw girls. But he has

also imposed a lie on the entire community, including his parishioner and patron Bradshaw. This dilemma haunts him until it affects his personality. His sister is untroubled, for her commitment first to Ruth and then to Leonard is emotional, not moral. Though Sally, the Bensons' servant, initially accosts Ruth, cuts off her hair and makes her wear a widow's cap, Ruth's reaction is so meek that eventually Sally, like Miss Benson, defends in her deepest heart the necessity for the pretense of widowhood. Benson can never do this; he begins to recover his sense of integrity only when, to his relief, Bradshaw finds out the truth about Ruth.

With Bradshaw's discovery the triad of tempter (Bellingham), defender (Benson), and accuser (Bradshaw) is complete, and the novel is free to focus on the psychological state of the men among whom Ruth lives. During this trial stage Bradshaw throws her out of his house and employment, ceases to attend chapel, and cuts himself off from Benson's company; Leonard hides from the town and goes into a mental and physical decline; Bradshaw's partner, Farquhar, whose vexed attachment to Jemima Bradshaw and hers to him has formed the novel's subplot, feels fortunate not to have proposed to Ruth. Here the novel's attention turns to communal truth-finding, judgment, and reconciliation. Behind the social question of whether Ruth was ever married is the moral question of how the person she is, past and all, is to be viewed. As she takes up private nursing and then, during the typhus epidemic, volunteers as matron of the hospital, the community comes to accept her courage, suffering, and service. The poor of the town, whom she has served for years, speak first, and Leonard, standing among them under the windows of the infirmary, hears their praise and is able, after years of shame, to claim his parentage publicly: "I am her son"; "she is my mother" (430).

The novel ends with Ruth's death from typhus, contracted when she insists upon nursing Bellingham/Donne. Critics have been tempted to ascribe this conclusion to the demand for the erring woman's punishment. Though Gaskell's situation openly demands judgment, and her narrator's viewpoint is openly Christian, it is simplistic to assume that she could have brought her novel to no other conclusion. Ruth has already expiated her sins and has already been judged. More convincing is a reading in terms of the dramatic and even mythic shape of the novel, which gains some of its vitality from what Terence Wright, comparing Ruth's death to Clarissa's, calls the "clash . . . between virtue as a product of trial and failure and virtue as an inviolable wholeness" (92). A victim at the beginning, Ruth ends her life a martyr, willingly sacrificing herself to nurse Bellingham as she was prevented from doing in his first illness. "No one can bar the door against Ruth," says Wright, "and it could be said that now, for the last and only time, she really has him. Her victory over him is not merely in possession, but in making a sacrifice which he does not deserve and which he cannot repay" (94). Literary convention enjoys the final spasm of sympathy, and Jenny Uglow speaks to both that convention and the underlying mythic shape:

Ruth had to die, if only to wring a final tear of sympathy from readers and hard-ened critics. The sacrificial altar is that of literary as well as moral convention: madness or death is the fate of all fallen women. The manner of Ruth's death, however, subtly suggests that she does not perish because of her sin but because of her forbidden love, which could have no place in the Victorian world. She is the Psyche of Greek myth as well as Psyche the purified soul: a woman who embraces death because she returns, against all reason, against all entreaties, to hold up the lamp and look openly—as her author was forced to do in writing her story—on the forbidden face of her own desire.[5]

To the degree that the manner of Ruth's death allows her to rewrite her victim-hood, it is a move familiar from the stories of Iphigenia and Lucretia. Another purpose is also at work in Ruth's death: by educating the patriarchal figures who must decide about her, it examines the nature of moral education itself. Like the death of many a protagonist, Ruth's death allows for what Peter Brooks calls the transmissibility[6] of her whole life, which may serve as an example in both its weaknesses and its strengths. Of all Gaskell's novels, *Ruth* is the one most concerned with education, especially the effects of systems, precepts, and role models in shaping the character of the young. Bradshaw preaches a rigid system of morality to his family and associates. In his condescension to Benson, his endless discussions of business ethics with his partner Farquhar, Jemima's angrier debates with Farquhar and her suppressed rebellions against her father, the turpitude of Richard the hypocritical "pattern" son, and the little girls' matter-of-fact analysis of their father's pressure and their mother's domestic tale-bearing, we see the Bradshaw household as the locus of a pathological relationship between preachment and ethical practice.[7] Gaskell's admiring portrayal of the Benson household is equally sharp-eyed. Miss Benson, exulting in her ability to fill out Ruth's notional background with vivid detail, mortifies her brother, who is already agonizing under the burden of the necessary lie; Sally, forcefully preventing Mr. Benson's reluctant punishment of Leonard for childish fantasizing, alludes to the deeper fiction of Ruth's widowhood that underlies their familial life. The concern about Ruth's employment as governess is what kind of model she provides for the young Bradshaw girls. Her death allows both characters and readers to draw conclusions from the whole shape of her life without the distraction or crutch of her presence. That death forces the fundamental question of her adulthood: how well her life, for which she was so totally unprepared, has educated her orphaned son for his.

READING TEXTS AT *MANSFIELD PARK*

Critics have increasingly come to appreciate that Jane Austen, too, wrote social problem novels, and that her portrayals of the precariously dependent lot of the English gentlewoman constitute an integrated social critique.[8] Her novels are even sprinkled with cautionary evidence of seduction, betrayal, and illegitimacy, beginning with the offstage Elizas of *Sense and Sensibility*. The presenting conditions that separate her fictive world and its moral problems from Gaskell's are in good part a matter of class-based economics and manners. In the working- and lower middle-class world that Ruth inhabits, a capacity for honest (though distasteful) labor is of the moral essence; in Austen's world moral strength, to be effective, must be coupled with social grace and the power it confers. In *Mansfield Park*, the Austen novel that most deeply explores the double bind of incompatible obligations, Fanny's lack of social skill and poise is just one of the traits that exaggerates the incompatibility. Both Fanny's shyness and her adoption into Sir Thomas Bertram's family give her a sense of awe and obligation toward her uncle. Though he tells her she does not owe him the duty she would owe a father, she knows she owes her own father little but the power of negative example. Yet Edmund's friendship has made Fanny morally and emotionally sensitive and scrupulous. She observes, she thinks, she judges, and—of course—she loves. If the men whom her world casts as her defenders and judges see erroneously and choose badly, that makes more urgent her obligation to exercise her own moral powers.

Fanny's bind is an intellectual one, a matter of education and experience in interpretation. Though Fanny is the center of a tested woman plot, the male functions, other than the tempter's, are downplayed. Once Fanny refuses Henry Crawford, Sir Thomas briefly accuses and Edmund briefly defends, but neither is capable of the truth-seeking required by the circumstances, and Fanny cannot bring herself to explain her reasons. She must hold out until Henry's infirmity of purpose yields to Maria's marital misery, Mary's exquisitely modulated concern with appearances finally destroys Edmund's hope in her, and the novel turns toward its quietly domestic conclusion. Two different tested woman plots that share a single tempter provide the novel's skeleton without dominating its external form.

Austen is not submerging some formal features of the tested woman plot from lack of intimate acquaintance, as the Lydia and Wickham action of *Pride and Prejudice* shows. But the Lydia action is atypical because Lydia learns nothing. In the absence of either sensibility or interpretive skill, experience is not enough. In *Mansfield Park*, however, sensibility and interpretation are very nearly everything. The tested woman plot is not ostentatiously schematized in the novel's structure; its presence and significance must be detected and interpreted, in part by means of the subterranean presence of other texts that themselves demand interpretation. With the departure of Sir Thomas and the arrival of the Crawfords, who pull Edmund irresistibly away from her side, pious, dependent Fanny is thrown on her own interpretive resources. Much occurs in the family that Sir Thomas would disapprove, but the indolence of Lady Bertram and the folly of Mrs. Norris allow or encourage. Further, Edmund's increasing infatuation with Mary makes Fanny jealous. Such emotions in herself and such contradiction among her moral arbiters are new to her. One way she learns to interpret them is by learning to read the texts that underlie the novel. August von Kotzebue's *Das Kind der Liebe* (The child of love), which appears in the novel as *Lovers' Vows*, is the most prominent of these. The richness of text and situation provided by setting Kotzebuan theatricals within the dramatistics of the novel gives the first third of *Mansfield Park* a literary allusiveness that, for Austen, is unusually overt.[9]

Austen expects her readers to supply the allusion in detail, for *Das Kind der Liebe* was a famous play at the time. Between 1790 and 1810, August von Kotzebue was the most popular playwright in the Western world. A sometime civil servant to Catherine II of Russia, von Kotzebue was assassinated in 1819 by a student infuriated by his mockery of Sturm und Drang pretension and rising German *volk* fervor. He wrote some 230 plays, ranging from tearjerkers to satires, was translated and performed everywhere in Europe and the European New World, formed the staple of Goethe's theater in their common hometown of Weimar, and wrote tested woman dramas not only because they allow social criticism but because they make for titillating sexual situations, heartwarming reconciliations, and a great deal of rant.[10] Mr. Yates, practicing Baron Wildenhaim before Sir Thomas Bertram's astonished eyes, especially appreciates the rant.

Kotzebue's first play, *Menschenhass und Reue* (Misanthropy and remorse [1788]), had made his name notorious all across Europe. It tells the story of a nobleman's wife who is seduced into a short affair with her husband's closest friend, leaves husband and children to lead a life of pseudonymous remorse, self-abnegating charity, and hard work as housekeeper at a neighboring castle, and is eventually reconciled to the husband, who has been living as a misanthropic recluse in the nearby hunting lodge. Kotzebue's audiences were delighted to shed tears over the virtues of the penitent wife and the agonies of the abused husband; what they found shocking was the husband's willingness to take his wife back. When the play was translated for the English stage by Benjamin Thompson and published as *The Stranger* in 1798, the publisher, Elizabeth Inchbald, explained in her preface how the problem had been solved for morally sensitive English audiences: Kotzebue's final scene, in which the children are brought on to be embraced in a family tableau as the curtain comes down, has been bowdlerized by having the husband's forgiveness speech cut. As in the original, the parents end in each others' arms with the small boy and girl clinging to their legs, but since the husband does not actually say the offending words, any pandering to female vice is strictly the weakness of the beholder.[11]

Though the play made Kotzebue's name as a dramatist, it caused him difficulties with censors and the public. In his next, *Das Kind der Liebe* (1790), which Inchbald published, also in 1798, in her own English version, he tried an erring-man version of the tested woman plot.[12] *Das Kind der Liebe* has a less morally offensive reconciliation because the fault is partly the man's. The nobleman (the Baron) seduced the farmer's daughter (Agatha) under a promise of marriage then abandoned her and married in a foreign country. Twenty years later, his wife having died, he returns to the family estate with his daughter (Amelia), accompanied by a fatuous suitor (Count Cassel) and a serious-minded young clergyman tutor (Anhalt). There he encounters a starving woman in the care of a pair of poor peasants (Cottagers). Her strapping son (Frederick) is, he comes to learn with help from the butler (Butler), his own son as well. Happy to claim the young man, eager to set Agatha up somewhere in the neighborhood where father and son can go for crypto-familial visits, he is informed by both son and tutor that the only right thing to do is to marry her. He agrees, and this time *she* gets to forgive *him*. Meanwhile Anhalt has been wooed by Amelia while on commission from the father to soften her up for Count Cassel, and when the Baron agrees to the match all ends happily (except for the indifferent Cassel).

This play, which Austen had the opportunity to see at Bath, is the one the young people are rehearsing at Mansfield Park.[13] Though Sir Thomas would be opposed to any theatricals out of a generally dampening personality, and Edmund is opposed in part because he knows his father's inevitable objection to having "his grown up daughters to be acting plays" (127),[14] it is hard for Austen's modern readers to see the harm in it. But Fanny is obliged to be more subtle. Unable from shyness to enter into the precipitous sociability between the Bertrams and the Crawfords, she becomes the observer and choral commentator, required to make an independent judgment. Moreover, Austen expects her readers to know the play, so that Fanny's judgment of it will prompt theirs:

> Her curiosity was all awake, and she ran through it with an eagerness which was suspended only by intervals of astonishment, that it could be chosen in the present instance—that it could be proposed and accepted in a private Theatre! Agatha and Amelia appeared to her in their different ways so totally improper for home representation—the situation of one, and the language of the other, so unfit to be expressed by any woman of modesty, that she could hardly suppose her cousins could be aware of what they were engaging in. (135)

But readers know that her cousins are very well aware. Austen spends time with the casting because, given the relations already pending among the young people, the characters chosen increase the resonances and rivalries among their actors. Count Cassel, whose two-and-forty speeches and pink cloak go to the gratified Rushworth, is a booby—a vicious booby whose final scene with the Baron lays out his chilling attitude regarding the disposability of women, but a booby nonetheless. Too close to Rushworth for comfort, he gives Maria yet more occasions to despise the man she has promised to marry. Mary Crawford, who is coming to feel a serious interest in Edmund and is determined to undermine his choice of a clerical profession, first uses the fact that Anhalt is a clergyman to urge Edmund to take the role opposite her Amelia, then, when circumstances force him into it, hopes to exploit his moral sincerity to deepen his interest in her. The greatest danger, though, arises from the maneuver whereby Maria manages to get the role of Frederick for Henry Crawford, then he to arrange that the role of Agatha shall go to her. This casting confirms Julia in her jealous hatred of them both and troubles Fanny throughout the "needlessly" (165) frequent rehearsals of the opening scene—the highly sentimental encounter of soldier son with swooning mother that allows any amount of loving exclamation and anxious fondling. Happening in on their rehearsal "exactly at one of the times when they were trying *not* to embrace," Mary may slyly assure the increasingly jealous Rushworth that Maria's handling of the role is "completely *maternal*" (169), but Fanny sees and loathes the truth. The heart of the matter becomes both what Maria means by this role-playing and what Henry does not. Maria's assurances of his intentions are raised to a certainty when, interrupted by her father's return, he retains her hand pressed to his heart.

Behind the particulars of these individual moments, the play thematically underlies the novel. The bowdlerized title that disguises Frederick's bastardy and Agatha's condition as fallen woman also speaks to its social and ethical import in both its own world and the world of Mansfield Park. The vows of lovers make and break human lives and happiness, women's vows and men's vows have different consequences, men's choices can be written over but women's choices are indelible. For the actors the play is laden with the psychological subtleties and complexities of theatricality itself, for the question is always to what degree the actors speak for themselves, or persuade themselves, in speaking their roles. Separating the actor from the action turns out to be impossibly fraught, as Edmund intuits when he compares the pleasure of seeing "real acting, good hardened acting" to the discomforts inherent in the "raw efforts" of "a set of gentlemen and ladies, who have all the disadvantages of education and decorum to struggle through" (124). The realities of intimacy underlying amateur play-acting allow Henry to wilfully mislead and Maria to wilfully misread. His precipitous departure shocks her into marriage with Rushworth out of anger and spite, yet the intimacies of the play have also prepared for the later flight with Henry from which she, though not he, can never recover.[15]

Since women's choices, usually sexual choices, are the stuff of the tested woman plot, it is not difficult to see in Austen's text how Kotzebue's play contributes to this plot feature. But the tested woman plot is just as much about male competition within the patriarchal world. Austen uses this aspect of the play more lightly. Yet the trace is there, for in Kotzebue, Frederick is imprisoned for attempting to kill his father, while in *Mansfield Park*, allusion to the prison scene is part of the maneuver that gives the role of Agatha to Maria and excludes Julia. Both the Baron and Frederick have their soliloquies of anger, doubt, and resolve: no wonder Mr. Yates would be content with either part. By giving the defender function to the bastard son, who stands in opposition to the tempter father, Kotzebue has focused more on the struggles among the men than on the fall and redemption of the woman, and as much on the education of the Baron as father as on his conversion from seducer. Here is one more fact that Inchbald's title change disguises. In *Mansfield Park* Austen gives us a study in a father's education through his children's rebellion.[16]

But another literary allusion runs deeply through Austen's treatment of Henry Crawford and his courtship of Fanny. To point the allusion, imagine a young man of wealth, education, intelligence, wit, and easy grace who is introduced into a highly respectable and well-to-do country family consisting of parents, brothers and sisters, aunts and cousins. He is quickly understood to be courting the family's daughter, though which daughter is curiously unclear and raises hopes and jealousies in both. After a strategic retreat when the initial relationship develops too demandingly for his taste, he returns to pursue the youngest woman of the family, the moral paragon. Imagine further that he is on the best of terms with his influential uncle and doting sisters, one of whom fills us in on his general history of conquering and abandoning female hearts (he is frankly averse to marrying). To her he openly confides his motives and intentions:

> "My plan is to make Fanny Price in love with me."
>
> "Fanny Price! Nonsense! No, no. You ought to be satisfied with her two cousins."
>
> "But I cannot be satisfied without Fanny Price, without making a small hole in Fanny Price's heart." (229)

This man's profession, we come to see, is women. The emotionally virginal paragon is a piquant challenge. From this point we watch him work with ever-increasing deliberation to conquer her mind and her affections. In observing Fanny's openhearted, loving response to her brother William, for instance, he learns that her seeming aloofness from the world of the Bertrams is not emotional indifference or lack of sensibility: "He was no longer in doubt of the capabilities of her heart. She had feeling, genuine feeling. It would be something to be loved by such a girl, to excite the first ardours of her young, unsophisticated mind! She interested him more than he had foreseen. A fortnight was not enough. His stay became indefinite" (235–6).

Austen has deliberately presented Henry Crawford in a way that reminds the reader of Richardson's Lovelace. This observation is not new. Jocelyn Harris, discussing the literary influences permeating Austen's work, notes the special importance of Richardson's rakes to Austen's and especially emphasizes the play-acting and self-dramatizing similarities between Lovelace and Crawford.[17] My reading accounts for the likeness in terms of the plot structure that creates the tempter figure in both novels. Not all the circumstances are the same. Henry has no male confidant, and his relationship with the men of Fanny's family is quite different. So is his psychology, for though he is predatory and self-indulgent, he is not fixated or pathologically angry. As for frightened, overlooked, just blooming Fanny, in love from childhood with another man, she is no Clarissa. Nevertheless, Austen's presentation of Crawford helps us understand Fanny, with whom we need help. Like Clarissa, Fanny is subjected to premeditated emotional assault, to which the novel's second half is largely devoted. Austen is wittily aware that more or less benign versions of such assault are what her world calls courtship, and that for young women courtship is the crucial educative experience. Given the skill and attractiveness of the assailant, for both Clarissa and Fanny the prime concern must be to interpret fully and accurately. The texts of courtship presented to them are saturated with paradoxes, ambiguities, moments that provoke profound unease in the midst of what seems innocent pleasure.

Again Fanny must learn to read, this time on her own behalf, but this time she has no revelatory script, only the man himself. She learns to appreciate that everywhere Henry is a master actor. When he wishes, he can please anyone, can draw her into the billiard room even for those needless rehearsals with Maria, can captivate and mesmerize her against her fixed intention with his reading of Shakespeare, for her taste responds vividly to his talent.[18] She knows that he is masterful at conferring favors and creating obligation. His intervention with his uncle to obtain William's promotion gratifies her deeply, but even more astute, because simpler, is his refusal of her father's invitation to dinner, which saves her from humiliation over the Prices' domestic habits. Though at first she is offended by his ingratiating attentions, once her refusal of him to her uncle surprises Crawford into the recognition that she is no easy game, he begins truly to study her. It is not just her homesickness for Mansfield Park during her entrapment at Portsmouth that makes his visit there seem so welcome and his manners so improved. It is that his exquisite adaptability has taught him how to approach her.

This adaptability, reminiscent of Lovelace's, taxes the reader's powers of interpretation as much as Fanny's, for as Joseph Litvak points out, "theatricality wreaks havoc on intentions."[19] Most taxing, perhaps, is the fact that Austen has so subtilized the male competition of the tested woman plot that not one man in the family, except Rushworth the discredited son-in-law, sees Henry as a threat. This absence of male competition concentrates Austen's version of the plot on the women's acts and arts of interpretation. With the exception of a comparatively few direct exchanges with Mary or Mrs. Grant, Austen's text about Henry is almost always filtered through the mind of another character on the watch for what she or he wants to see. What the men of the family see, and what until the catastrophe they never see beyond, is the entertainingly adaptable companion and eligible suitor. The young women see much more. Yet each seems untrustworthy in her judgment. Is not Julia too soon secure in her expectations of Henry, and thus too rapidly jealous? Does not Maria, on the rebound from her error in accepting Rushworth, encourage and use Henry as much as he does her? As for Fanny, is she not tiresomely prim and diffident? Until recently, critics have tended to think that all these young women misconstrue Henry's sociability and high spirits to make their own misery.

Yet the fact is that Henry comes as seducer into the bosom of the family where he lodges himself with everyone. What confuses Fanny most is this all-purpose, chameleon charm.[20] "How could *she* have excited serious attachment in a man . . . who was everything to everybody, and seemed to find no one essential to him?" (305–6). When for a short passage Austen works with Crawford's mind from the inside, what we see best is his assurance of universal conquest: "Must it not follow of course, that when he was understood, he should succeed?—he believed it fully. Love such as his, in a man like himself, must with perseverance secure a return, and at no great distance; and he had so much delight in the idea of obliging her to love him in a very short time, that her not loving him now was scarcely regretted. A little difficulty to be overcome, was no evil to Henry Crawford. He rather derived spirits from it. He had been apt to gain hearts too easily. His situation was new and animating" (327). Like Richardson, Austen has brought her master seducer up against the challenge of time. Faced with refusal, Lovelace becomes obsessed; since time is the chief medium of his artistic deployments, only Clarissa's death can deprive him of his profession. By contrast (for Austen is writing comedy), Fanny's deepest moral intuition about Henry is that he lacks staying power, and she is right. Sir Thomas believes that time, distance, and a little hard living at Portsmouth must soften Fanny, but it is Henry who breaks.

Fanny's interpretive journey from ignorance to wisdom, her education in the reading of character, has thus far involved two major texts, one the Kotzebue play as cast and rehearsed at Mansfield Park, the other the text of Henry's presentation of himself. The climactic move in Fanny's education is, however, her return home to Portsmouth. Fanny needs no practice with interiority; what she needs is practice in social interpretation—the reading of a range of human types and experiences and the toughening effects of making unsupported, independent decisions about them. So she goes home—but of course she has two homes, and returning to the first allows comparison with the second by her nearly adult eye. At Portsmouth she has time to reflect on the Bertram family dynamic and Henry's place in it in light of the chaos and slovenliness of her parents' home, and then to reflect again on the dangers as well as the attractions of genteel life. Portsmouth gives the distancing of both space and time, and in it Fanny learns to see anew. One effect is that she is cured of her nostalgia for her childhood home. She sees that her chronically flurried mother is incapable, for all her fussing, of creating familial ease or comfort. She admits that her father is lazy and feckless. And she realizes with a shock that her parents are indifferent to her needs and her very existence. Their indifference liberates her to make independent choices. Having to cope with her biological parents allows her to return to her adoptive ones with less awe and more genuine appreciation for their virtues. Money is undeniably one of those virtues, but their solicitude for her is the greater one. Above all, Fanny returns having learned to take charge of her own life by actively helping others. She learns to use her money for human ends, settling with it the problem of sibling rivalry over the spoon Mary bequeathed to Susan. She learns to exploit her gentlewoman's skill for the family's advancement, outfitting her brother Sam for his midshipman's posting. She learns to be a mentor as well as an adoring pupil, taking Susan under her wing, modestly deepening her reading, subtly smoothing her manners, and giving her the hope of a future better than the squalor of her home and a marriage like her mother's. These are the actions of an adult, and they can be summed up by the notion of leadership. Rather than merely reacting, Fanny takes responsibility for improving lives, including her own.[21]

The whole Austen corpus presents the conditions of courtship in the genteel family as constituting a pressing social problem. How marriage is prevented or made possible by economic forces that individuals cannot control, the inequality of education and of worldly power and experience between men and women, the early age at which women must make their most important and irrevocable life decision, the premium such a pattern of social behavior puts on less than universally available parental sense and sensibility—all these contribute to poising Austen's marriageable characters on the threshold of a catastrophe many of her married couples have not avoided. If the young people she brings her readers to care for the most seem to avert the fate of their elders, their rescue is owing to the providential hand of comedy, and Austen always invites us to contemplate the narrowness of their escape. The relative darkness of *Mansfield Park* arises from the number of young people enmeshed by a common problem and a common family dynamic, as well as from the openness—here Kotzebue gives her a means and a structural model—with which Austen explores the causes and consequences of their errors. Until recently critics have not thought of Austen as a writer of social problem novels because of the privateness of her novelistic worlds. Yet however private, the social configurations they contain are universal. And their theme is always the willed achievement of social and psychological health in an increasingly dysfunctional patriarchy. In *Mansfield Park*, the underlying presence of the tested woman plot helps us see how savagely that patriarchal structure can malfunction and how high the stakes can be.

FOURTEEN

Dream States and Landscapes

IN TERMS OF THE PORTRAYAL OF RURAL MORES, GEORGE ELIOT'S *ADAM Bede* (1859) and Thomas Hardy's *Tess of the D'Urbervilles* (1891), both using seduction versions of the tested woman plot, lie like sociological bookends to the nineteenth century. *Adam Bede* opens in 1799 at the commencement of the Napoleonic era. In this world the rector wears his powdered hair tied back with a ribbon, laborers form a stable class on the local estates and farms, Methodists are peripatetic evangelists from a recently formed proletariat who still allow their womenfolk to preach, and the skills of the carpenter Adam Bede presage a new class of technically sophisticated farm managers comfortable within the old rural order. In Tess's late Victorian world, by contrast, milk from a Wessex dairy farm reaches London breakfast tables by overnight train, rural villages are being depopulated in a process resembling "the tendency of water to flow uphill when forced by machinery,"[1] and Tess's skills as a dairy- and poultrywoman are eventually marketable only as rough labor. Many of the bare events of the novels are similar: a young, beautiful, ignorant farm girl is seduced by a patronizing young squire, undergoes pregnancy in shame, bears and buries an infant, engages herself to marry a more nobly natured man, endures a wandering journey across the rural English countryside, is brought to trial for murder, and is sentenced to be hanged.

Despite the possibilities for the growth of consciousness inherent in the characters of Hetty and Tess—both their stories begin in the same adolescent dream state in which we first encounter Ruth—neither novel is primarily about their psychological growth. Hetty never attempts to take control of her life, despite the final paroxysm that enables her to tell Dinah her story. At this point her author is finished with her; she is no more than mentioned in the remainder of the novel. Tess is the more developed character. With infinitely more varied experiences, she grows rapidly to full consciousness. Recounting the changes wrought by her pregnancy and the care and burial of her child, the narrator describes them as the beginning of her adulthood: "Almost at a leap Tess thus changed from simple girl to complex woman" (139). But whereas Eliot's narrative technique seeks at its most compelling to achieve an interiorized voicing of a character's mental states, so that Hetty's limited horizons express her intellectual and emotional vacancy, Hardy's narrative voice more closely resembles that of the Immortals, and Tess's mind never truly seems an independent entity. When Angel Clare, Alec d'Urberville, or circumstances are not doing her thinking for her, the narrator is. All Hardy's characters are picked up, examined, and dropped; especially is this true of Tess, toward whom the narrator seems yet another male gazer: "Her eyes grew larger and more eloquent. She became what would have been called a fine creature; her aspect was fair and arresting; her soul that of a woman whom the turbulent experiences of the last year or two had quite failed to demoralize" (139).

Though the psychological growth of the woman is not the focus of either novel, examination of the sources of moral authority impinging on her emphatically is. This examination incorporates questions of social responsibility and providential design in new ways. Placing the woman in a rural setting, for instance, allows an examination of her moral relationship to the natural world. Hetty and Tess come of age in the midst of cultivation and procreation, where their business is to promote fecundity by dairying, feeding poultry, tending flocks of children, and attracting suitors. They are at their most appealing when in greatest synchrony with the creatures they tend. How can such physical creatures be prepared for a test that puts so much of that world off limits? And what moral purpose can such a test have? Moreover, positing a lower-class family reinvigorates the issue of patriarchal authority. Has a father of Hetty's or Tess's class the authority to demand the woman's traditional obedience or the power to protect her from threats from outside her social group? Given that modernity has muddied old clarities, has the young woman the knowledge to carry out her obligations? In fact, to what degree is the social demand for the mechanics of female chastity a fetish with no moral basis in the physical world?

Middlemarch, *Ruth*, and *Mansfield Park* counter such pressures by pushing the woman toward a morally integrated, productive family life. *Adam Bede* and *Tess of the D'Urbervilles*, however, increasingly detach the woman from family. Hetty's and Tess's family relations expose the inadequacy of the patriarchal model to supply either training and protection for the girl or a rational role for the woman. Hetty Sorel's detachment is initially emotional, though physical flight follows; Tess's detachment, though unwilled, is both. Capitalizing on Tess's filial piety, her mother effectively sells her to her seducer, and her husband's revulsion at her past cuts her off even more brutally. Eliot makes the point through the contrastive upbringing of Hetty's cousin Dinah Morris, the only female character who systematically makes conscious choices about her life. Dinah is a professional woman. An orphan like Hetty, she was raised by her maiden aunt in a female household devoted to spiritual training and social service, and from adolescence she has been both a Methodist preacher and a wage-earner. The contrast is made possible by popular stereotyping about the wage-earning folk of the northern manufacturing towns—that they are more intellectually active, socially democratic, and theologically independent (or, it may be, more contentious, politically radical, and doctrinally fanatic) than the stolid peasants of the rural south. Through its setting on the border between Loamshire and Stonyshire, Eliot's novel can contrast the opportunities and mindsets of the two ways of life. Mrs. Poyser may distrust Dinah's Methodism and despise the hardships of her home country, but these influences are what have given her niece her independent character, and it is in part the narrow comforts and received opinions of the Poyser farmstead that have trapped Hetty.

Unlike Hetty, Tess's capacity for deep, other-focused emotion creates a devotion to her family that persists precisely because of their helplessness and need. Most of her disasters—losing the horse during the night drive with the beehive, coming to Alec's attention by claiming kin with the Stoke-d'Urbervilles, going back to Alec in exchange for a house for the family and schooling for the children—come from her efforts on their behalf. But instead of contrasting them with another, more functional, family, Hardy compares their present state with the family's history: from d'Urbervilles to Durbeyfields, Norman landholders to a cottager's lapsed life-lease, family portraits to Tess's face, ancestral vaults sheltering the homeless descendants. Neither Hardy's characters nor his readers can bridge this gap. Though the novel posits a great family of the past and a link between it and Tess, there is no getting from one to the other. Angel Clare is at his moral nadir when he thinks to salve his marriage by presenting his wife as a d'Urberville. The buildings that jut above graveyards and copses house portraits and funeral monuments, but no life is associated with them. Only the Gothic tale of the family curse about the d'Urberville coach and its associated murder sets the past in action, sketching another tested woman who was punished for a deed not of her doing. In *Tess of the D'Urbervilles* there is no alternative to familial decay and collapse.

HETTY SOREL BEFORE THE MIRROR

For Hetty Sorel the compelling focus of life is a vague but passionately felt sense of her physical self. The most striking sequences in *Adam Bede* are the two that present her in a solitude in which that focus can be explored. The second, her anguished journey to and from Windsor (chapters 36 and 37, "The Journey in Hope" and "The Journey in Despair"), is a tour de force. Its power, however, depends on the earlier scene (chapter 15, "The Two Bed-Chambers") where Hetty poses in a candlelit ecstasy of expectation before the mirror of her own self-absorption. Weighted with more significance than the stereotype of the vain woman at her toilette, Hetty's narcissism echoes a classic topos of the tested woman, classic at least since Milton gave Eve her first awakening beside a "clear / Smooth lake" so still it seemed "another sky":

As I bent down to look, just opposite
A shape within the wat'ry gleam appeared,
Bending to look on me. I started back,
It started back; but pleased I soon returned,
Pleased it returned as soon with answering looks
Of sympathy and love.

(Paradise Lost, 4:460–5)

This moment is Eve's first temptation. "There I had fixed / Mine eyes till now, and pined with vain desire / Had not a voice thus warned me" (4:465–7) that the unobtainable image she sees is herself, and that she is destined for an obtainable Other. Yet when she sees Adam, "less fair, / Less winning soft, less amiably mild, / Than that smooth wat'ry image" (4:478–80), she turns back toward her lake-mirror and must be pursued and gently seized before she is reconciled to him. The temptation of Milton's Eve is to gaze upon and adore the self rather than the patriarch from and for whom she has been created.

Hetty's temptation revisits many of the Miltonic motifs. Much of it is self-temptation. Though she understands that Adam Bede quietly courts her and is approved by her family, though her hunger for admiration is fed by the knowledge that she controls his heart, his desire gives her no personal interest in him, only a more vivid sense of her own physical attractiveness.[2] Arthur Donnithorne's attentions heighten her rapturous self-absorption, providing both an imaginary future of silks and satins and an internalized male gaze before which to perform her acts of self-admiration: "Hetty looked at herself to-night with quite a different sensation from what she had ever felt before; there was an invisible spectator whose eyes rested on her like morning on the flowers. His soft voice was saying over and over again those pretty things she had heard in the wood; his arm was round her, and the delicate rose-scent of his hair was with her still" (195).[3] Repeatedly both Hetty and the narrator compare Arthur's gentlemanly smoothness of body, manners, and language to Adam's relative roughness. Arthur's soothing, ingratiating, flattering courtship, compared with the rough-hewn Adam's, represents not just the voice of the serpent or the toad at the ear, but the narcissistic self turning back to feed its desire by gazing on its own perfections. Hetty is physically a Miltonic Eve, with Adam's "hyacinthine locks" (4:301) transferred to her. Her "wanton ringlets waved / As the vine curls her tendrils" (4:306–7). As she lets down her hair, says the narrator, "the dark hyacinthine curves fell on her neck. It was not heavy, massive, merely rippling hair, but soft and silken, running at every opportunity into delicate rings" (195). As for Adam Bede, he is a Miltonic Adam, his sense of her a compound of his response to her beauty and his lordly notions of connubial bliss:

How she will dote on her children! She is almost a child herself, and the little pink round things will hang about her like florets round the central flower;

and the husband will look on, smiling benignly, able, whenever he chooses, to withdraw into the sanctuary of his wisdom, towards which his sweet wife will look reverently, and never lift the curtain. It is a marriage such as they made in the golden age, when the men were all wise and majestic, and the women all lovely and loving.

It was very much in this way that our friend Adam Bede thought about Hetty. (198)

Arthur Donnithorne views her much the same, though without the scenes of marriage and children, and with the additional sense that "the poor thing is so clingingly fond of him. God made these dear women so—and it is a convenient arrangement in case of sickness" (198).

Though Hetty's story is a fully developed exemplar of the tested woman plot, down to the struggle of the defender Adam Bede against the tempter Arthur Donnithorne, a struggle that George Henry Lewes encouraged Eliot to emphasize,[4] the accuser figure is underplayed. Hetty's uncle, whose patriarchal image is reinforced by the shadowy presence of his own aged father, speaks primarily through Hetty's horror of being shamed before the people she knows—for shame "was poor little Hetty's conscience" (382). Martin Poyser's response is uncompromising. To Mr. Irwine's surprise, this "kind-hearted" man is more severe than his sharp-tongued wife: "Hetty had brought disgrace on them all—disgrace that could never be wiped out. That was the all-conquering feeling in the mind of both father and son—the scorching sense of disgrace, which neutralized all other sensibility." Poyser cannot be reconciled. He will pay money toward Hetty's legal defense, " 'but I'll not go nigh her, nor ever see her again, by my own will' " (459).

What is fresh about Hetty's treatment is that the novel dwells on an ignorance and moral obtuseness it does not dispel. The confession scene in the prison breaks through Hetty's instinctual attempt at self-protection to permit her to tell Dinah her story and ask Adam for his forgiveness, but the moment signals no conversion.[5] Hetty's few weeks of agonized independence on the journey to Windsor and back might in another character have been the beginnings of a competent understanding of the world, but for her they become another form of mirror-worship, a solipsistic drowning in the dark pool she sees as the only alternative to her shattered dream life with Arthur. The pool first appears in the chapter entitled "The Hidden Dread," in which even Hetty comes to understand that she is carrying a child and then seeks to conceal it from all, including herself: "After the first coming-on of her great dread, some weeks after her betrothal to Adam, she had waited and waited, in the blind vague hope that something would happen to set her free from her terror; . . . All the force of her nature had been concentrated on the one effort of concealment, and she had shrunk with irresistible dread from every course that could tend towards a betrayal of her miserable secret" (411). The impending marriage, however, means that she can wait no longer, and she seeks out the "dark shrouded pool" in the Scantlands: "She has thought of this pool often in the nights of the month that has just gone by, and now at last she is come to see it. She clasps her hands round her knees and leans forward, and looks earnestly at it, as if trying to guess what sort of bed it would make for her young round limbs" (411). But she cannot do it. She lacks the courage. Besides, they might find her, find out why she drowned herself. The pool recurs in the Warwickshire countryside Hetty returns to after her fruitless search for Arthur: "She would go away from Windsor—travel again as she had done the last week, and get among the flat green fields with the high hedges round them, where nobody could see her or know her; and there, perhaps, when there was nothing else she could do, she should get courage to drown herself in some pond like that in the Scantlands" (426). When she finds the pool, it is "black under the darkening sky: no motion, no sound near" and she sits looking into it in a "fixed, dreamy attitude" (431), only to sleep and wake to "the horror of this cold, and darkness, and solitude," memories of the lost "sweets of her young life" (432), and the sudden exhilaration of finding herself still alive. We last meet the dark water in Hetty's search for a way to rid herself of the child: "I thought I'd find a pool, if I could, like that other, in the corner of the field, in the dark" (498). She walks, and sleeps, and wakes again: "And I saw a wood a little way off . . . I thought there'd perhaps be a ditch or a pond there. . . . But I went on to the wood, and I walked about, but there was no water" (498–9). The pond has become the mantric means for the concealment of shame as the mirror was for the reflection of admiration, and each promotes her self-absorption.

The "kitten-like" Hetty develops little more capacity for self-understanding and self-direction than an animal, and the animal to which she is in some comically grotesque way compared is Bartle Massey's Vixen. There are repeated hints that Massey, the lame, eccentric schoolmaster, had woman troubles back home in the south; at any rate, the only female he can bear to have around is his short-legged little turnspit bitch. He keeps house better than any woman, he insists to Adam. His table, the narrator tells us, is "as clean as if Vixen had been an excellent housewife in a checkered apron" (285). Massey's language about Vixen is bizarre: "He always called Vixen a woman, and seemed to have lost all consciousness that he was using a figure of speech" (284). The episodes of the dog's life repeatedly call up Hetty's story. The "sly, hypocritical" Vixen's pups are "against the law" in Massey's bachelor household (284), the result of an illicit affair: " 'I'm pretty sure the father was that hulking bull-terrier of Will Baker's—wasn't he now, eh, you sly hussey?' " (292). Vixen contrived to be " 'brought to bed on a Sunday at church-time,' " says Massey "in a rasping tone of reproach," causing him to miss his usual singing at the service: " 'I wished again and again I'd been a bloody-minded man, that I could have strangled the mother and the brats with one cord.' " Vixen was herself nearly drowned as a pup: " 'If I'd known Vixen was a woman, I'd never have held the boys from drowning her.' " Part of the comedy stems from the disparity between

Massey's bark and his bite: he should have let the boys drown her, " 'but when I'd got her into my hand, I was forced to take her' " (284). Nevertheless the bark allows plain speaking about his expectations of females: " 'Now, I shall be obliged to take you with me, you good-for-nothing woman. . . . but if you do anything disgraceful I'll disown you—mind that, madam, mind that!' " he lectures Vixen (465) as the two hurry toward Stoniton to watch over Adam during Hetty's trial.

The episodes and language of Vixen's story are too closely analogous to the animal accidents of Hetty's seduction and childbearing to be fortuitous, and their framing in Bartle Massey's fear of the emotional dominance of women enables an openness about sex, reproduction, and male-female power struggles that cannot be incorporated directly into Hetty's story. (Already the Hetty material may have been too frank to be deemed suitable for *Blackwood's Magazine*, which was the original publication venue.)[6] Yet however similarly bound to her own ignorant physical destiny, Hetty has the misfortune not to be a mere animal. She lacks Vixen's slavish affection for her domestic benefactors, and she is no hoveringly instinctual mother to the "babbies." Though without the education or the experience that would give her a way to envision a realistic future beyond her daily round, she is still held to the moral code with which Vixen is merely threatened. "What's the use of talking to a woman with babbies?" Massey asks himself in a twisted prefiguration of a later scene, "she's got no conscience—no conscience—it's all run to milk!" (292). Alas for Hetty, even that is untrue.

TESS AND THE AUTHORITY OF THE NATURAL WORLD

Hetty has been offered the moral instruction of her time and class, yet readers with their ears full of Mrs. Poyser's unending admonitions can understand how she has learned to shut it out. Moreover, "religious doctrines had taken no hold on Hetty's mind: she was one of those numerous people who have had godfathers and godmothers, learned their catechism, been confirmed, and gone to church every Sunday, and yet, for any practical result of strength in life, or truth in death, have never appropriated a single Christian idea or Christian feeling" (430). For the self-absorbed Hetty, admiration and luxury are the sole objects of desire and shame the sole sanction. She can learn from no moral authority but forceful experience, and of that she has none.

Tess Durbeyfield is no Hetty. As the oldest child of drunken, fecund parents, she is wise in household responsibilities and the psychology of fecklessness. Nevertheless, like Ruth and Hetty she is mature-looking beyond her years, and for such a girl-child the sexual test comes so early she has no realistic way to be prepared. It is true that Joan Durbeyfield is criminally at fault. When she blames her daughter for not getting her seducer to marry her, and Tess charges her with never having educated her in what d'Urberville's attentions meant, her mother tells the truth: "I thought if I spoke of his fond feelings and what they might lead to, you would be hontish wi' him and lose your chance" (117). "Hontish"—this dialect word is ironically appropriate to their Norman antecedents; shamefast, it means, and yet the greater irony is that Tess did conduct herself with native integrity and responsibility.

Hardy is bent on examining the matter of education. In "Phase 2, Maiden No More," after the child Sorrow has been christened and buried, he begins the next chapter thus:

> "By experience," says Roger Ascham, "we find out a short way by a long wandering." Not seldom that long wandering unfits us for further travel, and of what use is our experience to us then? Tess Durbeyfield's experience was of this incapacitating kind. At last she had learned what to do; but who would now accept her doing?
>
> If before going to the d'Urbervilles' she had vigorously moved under the guidance of sundry gnomic texts and phrases known to her and to the world in general, no doubt she would never have been imposed on. But it had not been in Tess's power—nor is it in anybody's power—to feel the whole truth of golden opinions while it is possible to profit by them. (138)

By the Ascham quotation and the phrase "vigorously moved," Hardy insists that both time and moral insight are required to become wise or prudent, comprehending of the past and realistic about the future. Neither event nor precept alone is enough. Some version of the long wandering of Tess's sexual and maternal experience is necessary. Living with and applying the gnomic texts is the only way for them to enter us and do their work.

But where is the alternative to the family-scape that has failed Tess so badly by its sins of commission—the mother's dream of the fine marriage, the father's dream of the ancestral vaults—and its sins of omission—the failure to supply either precept or story, to name Alex d'Urberville for what he is, to be provident in any way? Earlier in phase 2 Tess awaits the birth of the child:

> At times her whimsical fancy would intensify natural processes around her till they seemed a part of her own story. . . . But this encompassment of her own characterization, based on shreds of convention, peopled by phantoms and voices antipathetic to her, was a sorry and mistaken creation of Tess's fancy—a cloud of moral hobgoblins by which she was terrified without reason. It was they that were out of harmony with the actual world, not she. Walking among the sleeping birds in the hedges, watching the skipping rabbits on a moonlit warren, or standing under a pheasant-laden bough, she looked upon herself as a figure of Guilt intruding into the haunts of Innocence. But all the while she was making a distinction where there was no difference. Feeling herself in antagonism she was quite in accord. She had been made to break an accepted social law, but no law known to the environment in which she fancied herself such an anomaly. (121)

Tess is reading the countryside as a moral landscape, and Hardy is reading Tess's reading. Both characters and narrator read landscape this way many times and recur to some of the specifics of this description, for example the "pheasant-laden bough" first encountered on the night of Tess's rape, then again during her flight from Angel when the pheasants, killed by the likes of Alec d'Urberville, fall with soft plops. This is not a vague pantheism proposed as an antidote to human ills. Hardy is explicit that although Tess rightly reads herself into this landscape and the natural processes around her, she is unnaturally solitary. This interlude she is living is less than human life. Because temporary, it is not cruel but healthy. But the expansion that follows at Talbothays under the kindly eye of Dairyman Crick and among her fellow milkmaids tells us that Tess is meant for the world of human beings, even if there were no Angel Clare to heighten her responsiveness. Her character must develop in the world of people, not just of buds and birds and gusts of wind.

Hardy is not wallowing in an escape to the "natural" world or even setting it against the "human" world. He is, however, distinguishing between an actual world and a world "based on shreds of convention" and "peopled by phantoms." He works the issue of convention versus actuality in showing how Angel changes at Talbothays, adopting some country ways and striking his brothers, when he returns home, as coarse, they him as stiff and diminished. In parallel we see Tess burgeoning under an absence of social cares, in the enjoyment of her competence as a farm woman, in response to Angel's intellectual tutelage. Talbothays makes both Tess and Angel more actual than they were before they came. This does not eliminate their distinctiveness. Angel continues to take his meals at the separate table that Mrs. Crick sets for him; he is not one of them. As for Tess, she recoils at the tale of Jack Dollop, the philanderer turned in the churn, and later, when Jack marries, hearing the debate over the undisclosed secret of his widow-bride, she writhes again as they laugh. She is not one of them either. But "they" do not lack their moral trials and sorrows, as the story of the heartsick fellow milkmaids makes clear, and Tess is at her morally most wrenched when faced with the quiet heroism of Marian, Retty, and Izzy.

What is the actuality that Tess and Angel take on at Talbothays? Comparing phase 3 of the novel with phase 1 at Marlott and Trantridge demonstrates a difference in how authority is construed. The novel's opening makes the way things are—we might call it the *truth*—perfectly plain. What is ludicrous and evil about John Durbeyfield's pretensions to gentility is his incompetence in his everyday sphere. He has no moral authority as a father because he has none as a man. Nothing he does or thinks corresponds with how the world is, and the tale of his d'Urberville origins is just the latest and most extreme of those disjunctions. The world of Tess's parents is a world of lies, of which Joan's dreams and John's pretensions are twin manifestations. The other sources of human authority in phase 1 are equally bankrupt. The local clergyman perpetrates the d'Urberville hoax, the "young squire" is a caricature of the real thing, the "lady of the manor" is blind. Only the chickens and the bees and the horse are real—and the endless children Tess cares for as best she can. So much for authority at Marlott or at Trantridge.

At Talbothays the sense of authority is all-encompassing. Dairyman Crick is its expression, but he is not its source. The dairy, which has no resident landlord (241), takes its authority from the meads and bartons and rushing water; from the yearly, seasonal, and daily dairying routines; from the demands of hiring and breeding and marketing. When Dairyman Crick takes on labor or lays it off, rouses his hands at three in the morning or sends them off in the rain to the railway station, he is less making decisions than expressing truths. No one carps at losing a job, for no one expects to work when there is no work. No one complains about the hours, for the job sets the hours, and the job is the same as life. Even the marketing, that feature most connected with human institutions, has a natural inexorability about it, as Tess reflects when driving home in the rain from the railhead. The people of London will drink tomorrow what we shipped tonight; if we did not ship, they would not drink. This is not to say that there is no variation in the natural world: one of its manifestations is Hardy's insistence on the individuality of milk cows. This bovine facticity is the authority of cows—and, we could say, the authority of the natural world, which means of landscape in the broad sense. For Hardy, as for nineteenth-century Europeans in general, what is here imbued with moral authority is not a world without people, not "wilderness" in the modern American sense. Landscape is inescapable from, and significant by reason of, man-in-landscape. Hardy never stays long with a scene without turning to man's impress on it.

To some extent Hardy is waxing nostalgic for the bucolic. He is helping create a novelistic tradition: Tolstoy, D. H. Lawrence, and John Fowles also have their harvesting scenes, with the slaughter of the little beasts caught inside the square. Yet life-in-landscape need not bring the pleasures of Talbothays; there is winter and rain, the coarse farmer, and the chopping of swedes. Farmer Groby is instructive. He first appears as the passerby who recognizes Tess from her time at Trantridge and remarks in Angel's hearing that she is no maid. She encounters him again on the road during her wandering and flees his recognizing eye for the safety of the woods. But on his farm Tess is neither frightened nor emotionally wearied by him. She has her place as a laborer, and that place has no sexual aspect. Though in his harshness he takes revenge for having been knocked down by Angel, Groby's life and manner principally reflect the hardscrabble land he farms, and his recognition of Tess is the reporting of fact. In Farmer Groby, as in Dairyman Crick, life and manner follow from the land and its occupations, giving rise to the sense of conviction that accounts for the novel's best moments. When Tess is at work in those occupations, whether pleasurable or exhausting, the action is authentic and tied to the requirements of rural life. Tess is born into these requirements and must respond to them. She must work to live, and this is the work she does. The plot of her seduction, her marriage, her struggle toward death comes from a separate sphere patched into the givens of her life. And in the presentation of the givens of her life, the narrator takes on the function of defender.

Comparing the settings of Renaissance tested woman drama, we see the radical change Hardy has worked. There the primary setting is the patriarchal family and its power relationships. The milieu in which the woman lives her entire dramatized existence is the family structure, and that is all the setting we get. There is no separate physical, economic, or social sphere with independent authority over her life. In such plays setting and plot are coterminous, for they embody the same structure and carry the same moral weight. The life of the literary work is subsumed into one authority structure. In *Tess of the D'Urbervilles*, by contrast, two incompatible realms, two incompatible sources of authority, are in competition.

FINDING AN ENDING

Though both dreamscape and landscape can be used to stage the human psyche, though both are powerfully evocative and explanatory about states of innocence and naïveté, neither can bring the tested woman plot to a close. The only way the plot can evade staging a trial is for the woman herself to face her accusers, set aside her defenders, and take the role of judgment upon herself. In some fashion this is what Dorothea and Fanny, like Clarissa and Hester Prynne, grow to be able to do. The absence of such psychological and moral maturity and independence in the tested woman, however, forces a return to external judgment. *Tess of the D'Urbervilles*, *Adam Bede*, and *Ruth* all incorporate public judgment and end by refocusing the action on the men. And all their endings are troublesome to readers.

Ruth's simplicity keeps her from preempting the trial functions of accusation, defense, and judgment as more intelligent and self-aware women may do. These functions are ethical positions as much as social roles, and Ruth's intellectual absence gives Gaskell room to dissect them. Playing the tempter to the last pages of the novel, Bellingham/Donne learns nothing and grows not at all, which prevents his participation in the reestablishment of patriarchal harmony. His return as the patient who causes Ruth's death, in fact, gives Benson his final task as defender. When Donne offers to support Leonard, Benson learns that he is the father and drives him away as Ruth had done, grateful that Donne has no claim on the child. Benson is thus able to complete the defense of Ruth he began when he saved her from suicide. The hunchbacked little minister has put himself at moral risk to save Ruth from moral risk. He has suffered financially, socially, and emotionally for what it would be cheap to call his charity. It is his story as much as Ruth's that Gaskell is concerned to shape to a satisfactory close.

Bradshaw, the self-righteous pillar of the dissenting community, is the accuser writ large. When his candidate Donne runs for Parliament, he connives at bribery; feeling tainted, he is doubly self-righteous when he hears of Ruth's background. He must undergo the purgatory of his son's embezzlement of Benson's stocks and near-fatal accident before he can admit his responsibility for his son's character and his own need for forgiveness. By the time of Ruth's death Bradshaw has begun to discover the humility that will lead to reconciliation with Benson.

But the accusatory function is also taken up by Leonard. The narrator states that Ruth had wished for a girl (160–1), and Gaskell's work might lead us to expect a daughter,[7] but this particular plot needs a male child to reestablish the patriarchal configuration. About seven years old when public exposure forces his mother to tell him of their background, Leonard suffers hideously, terrified of anyone who may say the shameful words that describe his and his mother's condition. In his relationship with Ruth, which to this point has been open and sunny, he plays out both defender and accuser roles, sometimes smothering her with kisses and attentions, sometimes acting hostile or depressed. Leonard's torment is presented as partly a function of his age, of the necessary break with his mother that must make possible his entrance into the world of men. It is also, however, the classic shaming of the patriarchy created by the woman's sexual disobedience.

Because there is no human father or husband against whom Ruth has offended, the community assumes the function of judge. What people will say has been the bugbear all along; the fear of shunning is what drove Benson and his sister to their benevolent lie. Except for a few people in the Welsh town, the milliner who spreads the news, and Bradshaw, no one overtly abuses Ruth. But the stigma is heavy. First Ruth can get no work, and then, when she turns to nursing, only the poor will employ her. This period of her life, extended as so often during the trial stage, allows the community to scrutinize her choice and arrive at its expiatory judgment. Following the praise of the poor with whom Leonard stands outside the infirmary come the commendations from the rector, representing the hospital board, and from Dr. Davis, representing the town's doctors. Davis, who offers to apprentice Leonard to his practice, becomes an important figure late in the novel. His professional admiration for Ruth and the motive that he himself is illegitimate matter less than that, like the rector, he speaks for the community. Since Ruth has harmed no one, she can be taken for herself alone. Only time and purgatorial struggle can make that self clear and evident, but when at last it is, the town speaks.

The last pages of the novel explicitly present the restoration of patriarchal harmony. Once judgment about Ruth has been spoken and the tempter definitively rejected, reconciliation becomes the pressing need. Bradshaw, the erstwhile accuser, learns to follow the community's lead. No longer able to pretend to moral leadership, he has returned to his church pew too humiliated to reestablish his friendship with Benson. Yet reconciliation, like the rupture that preceded it, comes about by Ruth's means, and it closes the novel. Seeking by ordering a tombstone "to testify his respect for the woman, who, if all had entertained his opinions, would have been driven into hopeless sin," Bradshaw finds Leonard weeping on her grave and escorts the boy home. "The first time, for years, that he had entered Mr Benson's house, he came leading and comforting her son" (458).

Gaskell's schematic use of the trial stage rationalizes many narrative needs. It provides time for first Ruth, then the community, then Leonard to grow to moral consciousness. It provides time to explore the figures of accuser and defender. To a degree with Bradshaw, but even more with Benson and his moral dilemma, Gaskell has brought fresh attention to a traditional structure, dramatizing the relationship between ethos and deed. Rather than letting Ruth's story dissipate into the life events of the virtuous unwed mother, Gaskell keeps it focused on the struggle toward judgment.

In Eliot's version of the intellectually vacant woman, the elimination of the woman's centrality in favor of patriarchal reconciliation is even more striking. As Hetty's story moves toward its inevitable judgment, she ceases to be the psychological focus, which turns to the male world of Hayslope reconstituting itself in the mutual respect with which the novel opened. The Reverend Mr. Irwine earnestly counsels Adam against succumbing to either passion for or acts of revenge, and he is right not merely from an emotional or theological point of view, but from the needs of the plot. As for Arthur, shocked by the truth of Adam's bitterest charges, he acts energetically to make what restitution he can, acknowledging his responsibility (though we never see the scene) and riding for the pardon that saves Hetty from hanging. More significant for the plot's purposes is Arthur's self-exile to a military life on the Continent, which allows the Poysers to continue their long tenancy at Hall Farm and Adam to remain in his home. Arthur's relinquishment of his fantasy of playing the admired young squire is hardly self-sacrifice pure, nor is it so presented. He has spoiled his own dreamscape forever and could not stay except to be despised. But his plea to Adam to help convince the Poysers to stay at Hall Farm begins the softening process between the two men, and the epilogue shows the three-way reconciliation of tempter, defender, and accuser, for when Arthur returns after eight years, Adam's nostalgic meeting with him carries an invitation from the Poysers. This ending is possible because Hetty has been purged from the configuration. Arthur returns to the news that she has died on the way home from her seven years' transportation, and the reconciliation is made complete with his admission to Adam, "You told me the truth when you said to me once, 'There's a sort of wrong that can never be made up for'" (584). Agreeing on this truth, the men may live in harmony again.

In terms of the traditions of the tested woman plot, this treatment of male functions is unexceptional. It receives its strength from its careful adaptation not just to Hetty's psychology but to the novel's geographical and historical setting. Pastoral Hayslope is the milieu in which this rendering of the plot can operate. If it were shifted to Stonyshire or set two or three decades later, the fit would be impossible. It is not an intact blood-kin patriarchy that allows the plot. When the novel opens, Hetty is orphaned, Adam is in revolt against the incapacity of his father, and the adult generation between nonage and dotage is absent among the Donnithornes. But the community has a stable population, with grandfathers, uncles, and teachers acting as placeholders for the vacated paternal functions until the sons mature to fill them. As the novel progresses, enough time and torment pass for Arthur, Adam, and even Seth to take their adult male places with Martin Poyser, Mr. Irwine, and Bartle Massey.

Hardy, too, ends his novel with attention focused on male character functions. Again the enabling mechanism is murder. One of the difficulties of *Tess* is that, since those male functions never made up an actual social community, only a cluster of assumptions about the relations of men and women, the social interconnectedness we get in *Adam Bede* and *Ruth* is not available to be reconstituted. Hardy handles the judgment function by means of the Immortals who sport with Tess, represented by the court system that, indifferent to her sexual behavior, must condemn and execute her for the murder of Alec d'Urberville. That nothing is shown of this formal trial but the distant raising of the flag demonstrates how, in Tess's private world, there has been no one who naturally occupies—much less is worthy of occupying—the position of judge.

Hardy cares most about the functions of accusation and defense, where he puts all the energy of the novel's end. He cares nothing about Alec, a plot necessity in whose depiction extravagance substitutes for personality. But Hardy is fascinated by the psychology of male response to the fallen woman. From the wedding-night confession, the point of shift from test to trial, Angel Clare has been the accuser, and the exploration of his wretchedness in that role becomes the novel's focus. Part of the wretchedness is created by Hardy's deliberate schematic plot twist. In a sense Tess has misrepresented herself to Angel, yet the patriarchal authority against which she could be said to have been disobedient no longer exists, or exists only newly in Angel, the husband. Hence Angel's attempt to evade his role as accuser by only half-believing Tess's confession. Hence the sleepwalking scene that repeats the motif of "carrying over the water" from the earlier rescue on the way to church.

The trial time of the novel's second half has two purposes. It chronicles Tess's increasing desperation, but it also makes possible Angel's conversion to defender, which is what he believes he comes back from the purgatory of Brazil to be. The reconciliation of male character functions should thus take place within Angel himself. But Hardy faces two technical problems in making that move. One is the shift in tone and focus as the narrator ceases to perform the defense function that has been his from the novel's opening. Defending Tess has made the narrator intimate with her, and the moment that function is relinquished to Angel, narrative intimacy ceases. The other technical problem lies in the defender's psychology. For Angel legitimately to defend Tess's essential purity, he must be forced to confront and defend an act of disobedience directed against him, and this is what Angel cannot do. Once he knows of Tess's return to Alec, his impulse toward pity and protection vanishes. Yet the return has been meticulously motivated. Tess's first fall was a rape, and this second fall was also an enforcement. By it she saved her family at the expense of herself. So Angel's second round of revulsion looks like another failure of sympathetic imagination. Neither Hardy nor his character, it seems, can bear to give not just the name but the actuality of wife to a tainted woman.

Alec's murder relieves Angel of the burden of his second rejection. There will be closure, and it will be swift, justified, and distant. Only once this certainty is available is Angel freed to be defender. The murder finesses the necessity of Angel's having to deal with the implications of Tess's second sexual fall. His recoil and revulsion are overwhelmed by her strangely bold confession, creating the moral holiday in which he can love her. Clearly Angel's defense function depends on Hardy's ability to resolve the need for judgment. Judgment—the judgment of the patriarchal community, not alone of the reader or the narrating voice—still seems a requirement of the plot's ending in a novel that has declared the woman pure from its title page on. From the opening pages of *Tess* the function of judge has been left vacant within the story. The purpose of the murder is to fill that function definitively and unequivocally, so that the story can be brought to an end within the configurations of the plot. Because there is no way to construct a familial, communal, or societal judge around the issue of Tess's sexuality, Hardy has Tess perform a nonsexual act that calls up the needed authority. Society as a whole cares nothing about Tess's sexual behavior. She is caught at the modern moment, in which individual and communal shaming responses have far outlived the social structures in which they could find purpose and closure. Society still, however, has mechanisms for judging murderers.

The problems many readers perceive with the endings of *Ruth*, *Adam Bede*, and *Tess of the D'Urbervilles* lie in the relationship between the tested woman's fate and the novel's conclusion. It is difficult to bring formal judgment to bear on a woman who has been so carefully presented as ignorant and victimized. It is not merely that readers and authors are no longer prepared to tolerate draconian punishments for sexual failings, so that murder must be introduced to make up the difference. The structural problem runs deeper. The disjunction seems to arise from the absence of a personalized authority figure against whom the woman has offended sexually. In the absence of a perceived reciprocity between patriarchal authority and its violation, judgment is troubling. Yet the plot has no other finishing point available to it.

FIFTEEN

Telling and Witnessing

A FUNDAMENTAL MOVE OF THE TESTED WOMAN PLOT IS THE ACTION of revelation. Because the nineteenth-century tested woman novel is bent broadly upon an examination of women's separateness, and more narrowly on the social ramifications of seduction and illegitimacy, revelation, especially under the aspects of telling and being told on, is one of its central themes. And speaking is its customary mode. Tess Durbeyfield tells her mother and eventually Angel about her life with Alec; Hester Prynne refuses even before the highest authority to tell the name of her child's father; Ruth Hilton never reveals the name of hers; Hetty Sorel's whole attention is fixed on not revealing anything; at the climax of *Middlemarch*, Rosamond tells of her relationship with Will to Dorothea, who has agonized over her contacts with Will that she kept from her husband; in Walter Scott's *Heart of Midlothian* the whole issue at Effie Dean's trial is whether Effie told her sister about her pregnancy.

This plot emphasis on the woman's speech is hardly surprising. For individuals and groups occupying subordinate positions, speaking in general, and certainly speaking out in public, tends to be a political act. Feminist scholars have described the strong reciprocity in patrifocal cultures between the demand for women's obedience and the demand for their silence. "All domination begins by prohibiting language," remarks Roland Barthes.[1] In any hierarchical and authoritarian culture, speech by the subordinate comes close to being the fundamental act of disobedience. Revelation, or "telling," takes the matter further. The character who tells or can be told on has a guilty secret.

Though in real time it may pass swiftly, revelation is a complexly structured action weighted with multiple ideas and interactions, as is clear from its kinship to the Aristotelian dramatic devices of reversal (peripety) and recognition (anagnorisis).[2] Unlike these devices, however, revelation has intentionality built into it. It carries with it the idea of decision, whether forced or free, for both revelation and concealment represent choices. Further, the vernacular expression "telling" carries with it the sense of a fact or deed that might better remain hidden. In the form of telling, revelation prominently draws attention to its operation in threefold time: it takes place in the present about a deed or a fact from the past that will affect the future.

Telling also involves agency, the matter of who tells, a fact that emphasizes how past and future conspire together. "She told me everything" speaks of the revelation of secrets. "I'll tell on you" threatens the revelation of secrets. This combination of agency and intentionality appears vividly in the first tested woman stories. Despite Tarquin's confidence that shame will silence her, Lucretia tells, repeating the rape with her own knife as her only form of corroborating evidence. Susanna tells, crying rape against the Elders and provoking their nearly lethal counter-accusation. Though in both these cases telling is coupled with calumniation and extortion, calumniation can happen even where there is nothing to tell. Telling is not Hermione's action, nor is it Imogene's or Desdemona's; though calumniated, they have no secrets. In the traditional context of the plot, how impossible it is that a woman whose virtue is absolute would have any scope for telling is demonstrated by Griselda. Her silence means that there is no separate will, no separate content, in her. But the nineteenth-century novel can no longer present the impeccably obedient woman; in its novels there is much to tell. Moreover, the social and moral issue has developed a technical side: the omniscient narrator becomes an additional character with both knowledge and the means of telling. The structures of telling are fundamental not just in *Adam Bede, Ruth*, and *Tess of the D'Urbervilles*, but in Walter Scott's *The Heart of Midlothian* and Nathaniel Hawthorne's *The Scarlet Letter.*

STYLES OF TELLING

On the evening of Tess's wedding day, the hopefulness that has been building since her arrival at Talbothays, though contaminated by foreboding over her unmentioned past, is shattered by revelation. Disclosure has been repeatedly approached by both Tess and Angel in the weeks before. Now Angel confesses to his wife his single sexual indulgence, forty-eight hours of dissipation with a London woman. Relieved of the barrier that has burdened her speech, Tess joyfully produces her matching revelation, and the section that follows is aptly titled "The Woman Pays."

Hardy's interest in secrecy and revelation goes beyond their social consequences to the use of hiding and revelation as a chief material of plot architectonics. His earlier novel, *A Pair of Blue Eyes* (1873), in some ways a structural study for *Tess*, already is built not so much around the disobedient act itself, or even the need to keep it secret, as around the ways it is made known. The major difference in *Tess* lies in the boldness with which Hardy retains the tested woman plot's traditional moves. In the earlier novel all boundaries are smudged—between obedience and disobedience, sexual innocence and sexual knowledge, not knowing Elfride's secret and knowing it. Even temptation, accusation, defense, and judgment are not clearly separated. The father is present and significant but slightly out of focus throughout. Much of the novel's attention is on the adoring relationship of the defender figure, young Stephen, with the accuser figure, his mentor Harry Knight. In *Tess* the lines are as sharp as possible, as though Hardy is pushing to their limits the emotional conflicts and moral positions the plot gives him. Tess's sexual initiation is total: the child confirms it, her neighbors know it. The tempter, Alec, and the defender, Angel (though drifters both), are psychological antitheses. They never meet, and neither has an intrusive emotional life to deflect his or the reader's attention from his relationship with Tess. Tess is aware of how her experience with Alec is regarded; she believes it impossible for her to marry honorably, and only her passion for the seemingly heterodox Angel tempts her to accept his courtship.

For all the clarity of its character functions, however, *Tess* works a reorientation of the plot's emotional center. Whereas traditionally the moment of the woman's moral choice is the moment of sexual temptation, Hardy makes the choice to tell the major moral decision of the novel. Unlike that telling, Tess's rape overtakes her against her will, and there is no decision in it. In her return to d'Urberville, the necessity is narrated, but not the choice, as circumstances again overtake her. As for the murder, it is a reflexive action; Hardy needs it for his denouement but wisely spends little time with it. Nor is falling in love so much a matter of conscious choice as an effect of life at Talbothays, a world in which companionship founded in sexual desire but completed by intellectual and emotional compatibility is so natural as to grow without deliberation. It is a *habitus*, to use Pierre Bourdieu's term, whose daily operations and behaviors infiltrate and reshape even the most strongly held conscious positions. Because they have shifted worlds, Angel and Tess come to think of each other as life mates in the teeth of their every intention and long before they have brought the difficulties carried over from their previous worlds to consciousness.[3] But when Angel's marriage proposal brings Tess to an anguished deliberation such as she has never undergone before, it is the issue of telling that occupies her. Her letters to her mother asking for advice, her repeated assertions to Angel that the other three milkmaids are "better," her painfully written letter of revelation accidentally thrust under the carpet, her recoil from the debate over Jack Dollop's deceptive widow, the encounter with the man who recognizes her, all are emotionally traumatic occasions tending toward the telling Tess cannot manage. After the revelation, her traveling is motivated to evade knowledge about her, and all of Hardy's convergences are collected under the rubric of revelation—the encounter with Farmer Groby, with Alec d'Urberville as preacher, between the Reverend Mr. Clare and Alec, even, it seems to Tess, with the man with the paint pot inscribing accusatory texts before her eyes. Her return to Alec owes much to his persistence and more to her family's need, but most to the fact that he is the only resource (unlike the Cricks or the Clares) who already knows about her past. With him she is spared the trauma of telling.

Yet Tess's very mobility makes speech traumatic. At home, where everyone knows, no one need be told. The field folk with whom she harvests turn away discreetly to give her privacy to nurse her child, and their conversation is no longer of her. But away from home she can be forced to speak. In the central revelation scene of the wedding night, instead of exploring each other's bodies, husband and wife explore the separate bodily experiences of their pasts. The talk is veiled: Angel veils his in a preliminary declaration of his scrupulousness, while Tess veils hers physically.[4] The shame of the telling is part of Hardy's point about its moral quality, which he contrasts with Tess's revelation of the murder: "Angel, do you know what I have been running after you for? To tell you that I have killed him!" (405). Here the eagerness to tell is what strikes Angel most: "his horror at her impulse was mixed with amazement at the strength of her affection for himself and at the strangeness of its quality, which had apparently extinguished her moral sense altogether" (406).

In novels less frank than *Tess*, revelation tends to be accomplished not by speech but by emblematic scenes and objects. Often the evidence linking the woman to her tempter is their presence together in a tableau: Stephen and Elfride on the railroad platform; Bellingham and Ruth on the road; Will in Dorothea's drawing room or library, or on Rosamond's rug or sofa; Arthur kissing Hetty under the beech tree at the curve of the path. These moments throw the observers—Mrs. Jethway, Mrs. Mason, Casaubon or Chettam, Dorothea, Adam—into agonies of suspicion and accusation. None of these moments, not even (argues Arthur) the scene under the beech tree, need have seductive import. Yet they do—the novels build toward them, prepare their discovery by other characters, and revisit them to confirm their significance. In a novelistic convention that cannot enter the bedroom, proximity in solitude is emblematic; Eliot can illustrate Dorothea's social naïveté by her slowness to recognize her husband's objection to her receiving his cousin in his absence.

If emblematic tableaux can tell, so can emblematic objects, though more ambiguously. Hetty's locket, which seems to reveal her secret to the dumb-founded Adam, does not initially do so. He makes the connection only by means of the beech tree scene. By contrast, in *The Scarlet Letter* Hester's "A" seems to be the supremely intelligible emblem. Unlike Hetty's locket, unlike the tableaux of proximity, it stands for what is already known and condemned. Yet Hawthorne makes a point of how quickly its original meaning is blurred and another meaning ascribed by citizens who admire Hester's expiatory behavior: "Such helpfulness was found in her,—so much power to do, and power to sympathize,—that many people refused to interpret the scarlet A by its original signification. They said that it meant Able; so strong was Hester Prynne, with a woman's strength" (131). The narrator tells us that the scarlet letter has the effect "of the cross on a nun's bosom. It imparted to the wearer a kind of sacredness, which enabled her to walk securely amid all peril" (132). What the "A" means first, however, is Pearl, for in these novels the most intimate and unequivocal telling comes from pregnancy and childbirth. Hester dresses

Pearl in the shape and colors of the letter so that the child is a living emblem, a conceit that merely adds to Pearl's already revelatory existence.[5] The narrator acknowledges Hester's acknowledgment of this fact from the opening scene in which, emerging from prison, she overcomes her initial impulse to hide the letter with the child's body, "wisely judging that one token of her shame would but poorly serve to hide another" (57).

In all versions of the tested woman plot, the woman's illicit pregnancy literally embodies her disobedience, giving it an objective existence that bespeaks the presence of the tempter within her. In pregnancy the erstwhile maiden's body changes. Both womb and breasts respond to the child's presence until the woman becomes a living text. Pregnancy also gives the novelist an explicit time line to exploit and manipulate. Because the doctor detects Ruth's pregnancy in the aftermath of her suicide attempt, Gaskell may broaden the secrecy motif to include the Bensons' concealment of her unwed state. Because Tess arrives back home at Marlott in the early stages of her pregnancy, Hardy may suspend her in the soul-deepening solitude required for her emotional maturation. In *Adam Bede* the scrupulously dated sequence of Arthur's departure to his regiment, Hetty's betrothal to Adam, and the onset of her secret knowledge shows us how long it has taken Hetty to detect her pregnancy, how completely the betrothal to Adam has trapped her, how total is her incapacity to face inevitabilities before she is forced to the brink. This sequence also engages us in foretelling consequences; it is the reader's mind, not Hetty's, that casts back and forth over the nine-month term and projects possible life trajectories.

Pregnancy also gives the novelist an efficient way to enter the seasonal rhythms of the natural world. Seasons are a matter of indifference to Bellingham, who has the resources to take Ruth off to London. But the seductions of Tess, of Hetty, of Effie all occur when the long evenings and warm temperatures of a northern summer make privacy possible. A social phenomenon of winter is also exploitable: pregnancy can be more easily hidden under winter clothes than summer clothes. Still, how could Hetty's condition have escaped the censorious eyes of Mrs. Poyser? By the same device Scott uses in *The Heart of Midlothian:* Mrs. Poyser is confined to her upstairs room with pneumonia for much of the fateful winter, as Effie's employer, Mrs. Saddletree, is confined to hers, while the young women do the downstairs work. In Scott others notice: "Neighbours, . . . and fellow-servants, remarked, with malicious curiosity or degrading pity, the disfigured shape, loose dress, and pale cheeks, of the once beautiful and still interesting girl. But to no one would she grant her confidence, answering all taunts with bitter sarcasm, and all serious expostulation with sullen denial, or with floods of tears" (104). Scott nearly tells straight out. The reader of Hetty's misery, by now at home in the Poyser household, needs no telling.

But no revelation is so total and so public as the babe in arms. Hence the opening chapters of *The Scarlet Letter.* Yet out of this fact the novelist may multiply the sin/secrecy motif: that Effie or Hetty has no child in her arms is evidence of an even greater guilt. The move from the sin of fornication to the crime of murder brings official intervention, of course, but it also brings irreversibility. Irreversibility is a key moral motif in *Adam Bede;* there are some things that cannot be remedied. A marriage might pretend to patch up the damage of seduction, Arthur might not take seriously the destruction of a young girl's dreams or even those of the man who is his friend, but murder and a sentence of hanging he must notice. In Scott's novel George Staunton's childlessness commences when old Meg buries Madge Wildfire's infant, and the reprise of the motif in his relationship to Effie merely makes events from what is already fact. The irreversibility of Tess's lot, against which she struggles with vigilance and love, is completed by her murder of Alec. She did not kill their child. She nurtured it body and soul and grieved over its death. It is the irreversibility of Alec's murder, a last spasmodic attempt to wipe out that past, as Hetty's burial of her infant is an attempt to erase hers, that closes Tess's life.

Part of Tess's tragedy paradoxically lies in the death of the child Sorrow, then, for it makes the pretense to secrecy possible. The child in arms eliminates the tormenting necessity to tell. So Hester uses the child's presence to tell what matters most to her, and her seeming boldness as she holds Pearl bespeaks both "the woman pays" and "the woman possesses." The child is hers. Until she speaks, it has no father, and she is nowhere moved to reveal the father except when she fears Pearl will be taken from her. By not speaking she declares herself outside domestic patriarchy, an independence she protects with tenacity. Though the sight of Chillingworth shakes her self-possession, it does not shake her possessiveness toward the child, and his failure to publicly acknowledge her frees her from domestic control. The death of Tess's child, by contrast, returns her to a male-centered world.

THE NARRATOR TELLS

Revelation is fundamentally an action of the trial stage of the tested woman plot. It is designed to create or respond to accusation, to bolster or undermine defense, to influence judgment. In traditional versions of the plot, revelation is elicited by and directed toward accuser, defender, and judge, and such character connections occur in the nineteenth-century novel as well. But compared with the revelation sequences of Renaissance drama, say, the novels we are considering also include an additional layer of revelatory voicing, for the motif of telling has been transformed by indirect free discourse. The story's creator has always known the content and outcome of the story. In Genesis, though scene, actors, and dialogue are God's, the author is privy to them all. God's plot (the *mythos* or action) and the story are intended and presented as one.[6] The latent terror, impiety, and power of the making of drama lies largely in the fact of taking on God's role, performing a creative act analogous to the divine fiat. The third-person narrative of the classic nineteenth-century novel adds the narrative voice as a new kind of character, both complicit with and judgmental of the characters it has access to. By means of indirect free style, the narrator not only plays the creator God but imitates God's omniscience, his divine eavesdropping within the human psyche. The fact that "(only) God knows" our innermost thoughts becomes the fact that "the narrator knows."

Moreover, the narrator tells. But narrative telling is an ambiguous matter. Though knowledgeable about the inner states of a character, it is far from being the equivalent of the character's own presentation of self. In these novels narration is socially, morally, and sometimes psychologically *more* knowing. Unlike the narrative texts of Genesis or of Hellenistic romance, the narrator is not only knowledgeable about the shape of the story, but opinionated, urgent, sorrowing, continually ethically intrusive. Though the presence of such a narrator affects the test stage of the plot relatively little, it changes the import, conduct, and authority of the trial stage. *Because* the narrator knows and tells for the community as well as for the tested woman, to various degrees the narrator takes over the functions of accuser, defender, and judge. These functions cease to be the exclusive prerogative and obligation of the family or the community in the story and become vested in the private congress between narrator and reader. Not only is that private congress preoccupied with the individual psyche under stress, it cannot present the views of family or community exactly as the principals would view them. The result is narration in which the judgment of the community within the story is both complexified and undercut.

Abetted by the woman's comparative muteness, *Adam Bede* presents a nuanced example of this kind of narrative involvement. Eliot's narrator knows Hetty Sorel unsettlingly well, subtly individualizing the adolescent type of the self-absorbed, self-protective, ignorant, and narrowly cunning personality housed in a precociously attractive body. To the fortunate adult, every one of these qualities exists to be lived beyond; Hetty, however, is fixed in a state intended to be transitory. The narrator's interpreting voice is deeply empathetic: the explicit vagueness of Hetty's construction of self, the coolly ironic depiction and dissection of varieties of male desire, the inexorability of the countdown to exposure that tells an age-old woman's story, all are moving feats of imaginative art. There is likewise no question about the moral accusation in the narrating voice. That Hetty's self-absorption is pre-moral and thus comprehensible points up a truth fundamental to Eliot's worldview, that mankind's life task is nevertheless to ethicize nature.

The presence of narrative attitude means that the narrator tends to take up one or more of the trial functions of the tested woman plot, a permutation impossible to either drama or the epistolary novel. In *Tess* the narrator's function is declared to be defense. In *Adam Bede* it feels to many readers like accusation. My concern here is not which side the narrator lines up on, but how such lining up affects the depiction of character functions. For instance, Martin Poyser's accuser function is only sketched. But though the accuser character is undeveloped, there is a deep-seated critique in every moment of Hetty's depiction. This is more than the author carrying out a plot that prevents Hetty from evading the results of her ignorant choice. (Such authorial presence is common to all stories, in whatever genre.) Nor is it overt sermonizing. Rather it is the ceaseless probing of the eventually culpable limits of Hetty's worldview, inviting our judgment that, young and limited as she is, abused as she has been, she is nevertheless responsible for what she has done and failed to do. Yet the accuracy of the presentation precludes narrative rancor. It is rather that, given the facts, the narrator's deep imaginative comprehension is bound to become accusation as well as defense.[7] The contrast with Adam, whose character function of defender is strongly developed, is instructive. Despite the attractiveness of his struggle to protect Hetty, he knows little of her life or mind. Adam can intuit Arthur's culpability, but about Hetty he knows only his own desire. It is the narrator who sees her pitiable nature and life as they are.

If the narrator sees and judges, so does the reader. The tested woman plot is designed to bring its audience, which both participates in the test and takes sides in the trial, into the ethical action. The original purpose was to bring the audience's judgments into agreement with the community's. The presence of a narrator with inside knowledge, however, puts the reader in a position to understand differently from the community or from the characters. *Adam Bede* shows this double perspective in the way it handles the question of what constitutes the test. Traditionally the plot views the sexual sin as the moment of choice, but Eliot complicates the matter by preventing any public view of Hetty's year until its end. Her community learns of the sexual act only when it knows of the birth of the child, which it discovers by discovering the child's body. Until that point Adam is the only person who notices Arthur's interest in Hetty, and he is too naive to project a sexual consummation. The community has no emotional way to separate fornication from the death of the child, and for its members the greater sin may swamp the lesser or seem its unsurprising consequence. Either way hindsight gives the illusion of an inevitable downward trajectory, which suggests an innate viciousness first manifested by the sexual sin.

Yet the reader knows that sexually Hetty is more sinned against than sinning. Moreover, the novel seems uninterested in a fetishized virginity; the characters' emotional and social illusions are the narrative focus of the love affair. Nevertheless, Hetty must undergo pregnancy and motherhood. Here she is clearly culpable, and here she tells at last. Hetty has been given little dialogue, being presented almost exclusively through the narrator's voice and the community's observations. Her confession to Dinah is the only time she tells a portion of her story, yet it is hardly a confession in any moral sense, as Hetty has no sense of sin and no moral view of herself. Her mental sound track of the baby's wailing is its substitute: "Will he take away the cry?" she asks, making God the next patriarchal figure onto whom she can attempt to shift her burden. That the episode about which Hetty speaks is the abandonment of the child is crucial. Her intention here is of the essence to the reader's judgment, if not to the law, and only she can demonstrate the moral vacancy of her actions. If we are to judge, this is the passage we must hear for ourselves. Though the narrator has prepared us well, its primitive lack of sentiment is still shocking.

Because the narrator of *Adam Bede* is absorbed in the delineation of character in action, her entrance into the dynamic of accusation, defense, and judgment is indirect and subtle. In *Tess of the D'Urbervilles*, where the author is interested first in a social thesis, the narrator's functional participation is blatant. The novel's subtitle—"A Pure Woman Faithfully Presented by Thomas Hardy"— is as bold an announcement in defense of a fornicating murderer as one could ask for, and it was too much for Hardy's readership. That the tested woman plot should effectively finish its career with so explicit a highlighting of the narrator's encroachment on the internal structure of the plot is appropriate, for by this historical point the woman's intention has become a central issue, and sympathy for her socially constructed plight an expectation. The moment the tested woman's life was presented from the inside—in *Pamela* and *Clarissa*—the plot became open to dispute about its morals. Once authors had the technical means to provide an argumentatively framed presentation with running commentary on that inside story, taking sides became natural. The dramatic versions of the plot have always invited observer participation in accusation, defense, and judgment. Given the narrative tools, authors are unable to turn down the same invitation.

This involvement is a different matter from a generalized expression of the narrator's judgment such as we find in the Clerk's approving summation of Griselda's patience: "This storie is seyd. . . . / . . . for that every wight, in his degree, / Sholde be constant in adversitee / As was Griselde" (1142; 1145–7). Judgment is always required by both characters and readers; naturally it is open to narrators as well. In the case of *Tess*, however, the defending narrator takes over the function from the character. The defender's task is primarily interpretive, not to save the woman but to tell her truth as he understands it. In *Clarissa* Belford is a classic defender. Though Clarissa tells her own story at length and in depth, Belford develops an explanatory function as compiler and interpreter of the complete record for the defense. Not so Angel Clare. His function as defender is never complete because he gives so little impression of understanding Tess's story. The absence of a defender as a character is striking—or would if the narrator were not so insistently present on her behalf.

This presence and the related underdevelopment of Angel's defender function seem responsible for the major structural flaw of the novel, the use of the murder of Alec as the plot's catastrophe. Hardy's narrator makes a three-stage biological and sociological argument on Tess's behalf. The first involves Tess's family and establishes that there is no genuine patriarchal authority to be offended by her behavior. (That she has developed a quasi-middle-class sensibility about manners, including sexual manners, is a different matter.) The second stage, constructed around her pregnancy and child, is that Tess's sexual and maternal experience have made her more womanly physically and emotionally and therefore more in tune with the natural world. The third stage, made by the contrast between her confession and Angel's, is that the moral reading of men's and women's sexual experience should be the same but is not. The fact that it is not is a failing, but the failing is not Tess's.

Yet as defender the narrator can do little for Tess within the story because he cannot bring either her psyche or her community to adopt his ethical position about her sexual behavior. The author's adjective of choice to his readers— that Tess is a "pure" woman—is blatantly coded for sexual behavior, the only arena in which he really wages his narrative defense. In plot terms, however, he undercuts that defense. At the moment when Angel must come to a serious acceptance of her sexual past, Tess kills Alec, changing the whole moral and legal shape of the novel. Angel's sexual reconciliation becomes an encapsulated coda sealed off from the prospects of an extended life, another version of the "dissipated forty-eight hours" with the London woman. The murder has relieved him from making good on his marital contract in other than sexual terms or from understanding and forgiving Tess's return to d'Urberville under the pressure of familial poverty and spiritual hopelessness. Tess cannot escape legal retribution for the murder, but Hardy does not argue that she should. After her return to d'Urberville, Hardy never engages her psyche; Angel has all his attention.

The Scarlet Letter provides a third variant on the theme of the narrator's intrusion into the trial. Hawthorne's narrator is even more deeply embedded in the text than are Hardy's and Eliot's, paradoxically as a result of his lack of authority. To a degree this is owing to Hawthorne's concept of romance, with its deliberate pose of partial and uncertain knowledge. But we must note what the narrator is uncertain about. Generally speaking, it is not Hester's or Pearl's natures or the events of their lives. Great chunks of Hester's seven years' purgatory are missing from the narrative, and the final chapter professes no more than conjecture about the events after Chillingworth's death, yet the narrator knows in detail the crises of her freethinking struggle to come to terms with her lot. He even seems to know her reasons for returning to Boston. The narrative consistently expresses certainty about its interpretation of her life, even in moments where her opinions and actions are most fraught with indecision.

Hawthorne's narrator professes much more uncertainty about Chillingworth and Dimmesdale, the putative accuser and defender. This uncertainty is most obvious regarding the relation between Dimmesdale's physical and his psychological state. There is expressed uncertainty about the cause of his decline—"whether it was his failing health, or whatever the cause might be, his large dark eyes had a world of pain in their melancholy depth" (98). There is ambiguity in the exposure of his breast, first during his deep sleep when Chillingworth unveils him, then on the scaffold when the community debates the physical facts. In part we may ascribe the uncertainty about Dimmesdale and the certainty about Hester to Surveyor Pue's document: what "The Cus-tomhouse" tells us of the document mentions only the woman, her sentence, and her scarlet "A." Dimmesdale, Chillingworth, or even Pearl herself may be present in Pue's document, or they may be among "the figures with which" (says the narrator) "I did my best to people" the tale (45). This narrative uncertainty both motivates and sometimes becomes indistinguishable from the dynamic of investigation and concealment between the men. When the patient asks his doctor to speak frankly about his health, Chillingworth's answer is disguised and paradoxical: "I know not what to say—the disease is what I seem to know, yet know it not" (113). Yet when Chillingworth takes his next accusatory step, reminding Dimmesdale that physical conditions may have spiritual causes, Dimmesdale starts away in frantic self-protectiveness. Chill-ingworth's accusatory energies have shifted from the woman to her seducer. Dimmesdale's defensive function, which prior versions of the plot as well as his own guilt insist should be his, remains focused on himself. Yet since no telling has been forced on Dimmesdale, the two men can remain veiled in uncertainty and disguise.

The result is that, as in *Tess*, the woman lacks a defender except where that function is taken up by the narrator. And it is; that is why the text is so certain about Hester's long purgatory and her shifting emotional and intellectual states. The reader is meant to see all her facets: her strength, her conquest of despair, her nostalgia for love, her grief and anger and maternal foreboding. They make the impression they do because this woman outlives all the male functions brought to bear on her. No male hegemony or reconciliation is established, except in negative form. Dimmesdale's death robs Chillingworth of both purpose and life, and the magistrates dwindle into ordinary men. Hester's escape from the patriarchy is total, if at heroic cost. The contrast with *Tess of the D'Urbervilles* could not be more stark.

WITNESSING AND AVOWAL

Despite its powers of investigation and judgment, a knowing narrative voice cannot substitute for conscious understanding and commitment in the char-acters. Such self-consciousness is ultimately created by an obligation-shaping milieu; characters understand themselves as moral agents because of the social structures in which they are bred. In more historically remote versions of the tested woman plot, the theme of revelation does not require a social or institu-tional setting beyond the patriarchal family. But the nineteenth-century tested woman novels I am examining uniformly share the presence of an extrafamilial moralizing institution, that of dissenting or evangelical Protestantism. The hectoring magistrates of *The Scarlet Letter* who loom so threateningly in the isolation of the New England frontier, the covenanting Lowland Scots of *The Heart of Midlothian*, the Methodist preachers of *Adam Bede*, the dissenting congregation in *Ruth*, the low church evangelizing of the Clare circle in *Tess of the D'Urbervilles*, Bulstrode's evangelical background in *Middlemarch*—all respond to the fracturing of traditional hierarchies and patterns of authority. By institutionalizing a confessional form of public witnessing, evangelicalism gives the theme of revelation a social location beyond the family, which explains its presence in these novels. Within the evangelical congregation the sign that the message of salvation has touched the listener is confessional response—the admission of sins and the expression of remorse—which brings forgiveness and (re)admission into the social group. Public confession replaces the personal and familial power of fathers or priests with a theocratically based communal power.

In these novels confession is first of all the obligation of the tested woman. Public pressure to confess is found in Dinah Morris's cajoling confrontation with Bessy Cranage, the blacksmith's daughter, and it prepares us for her pleading encounter with Hetty in prison. It appears when Tess passes the door of the barn where the converted Alec is preaching, as it already has in her encounter with the gnomically accusatory texts of the man with the paint pot. The pressure is found in the social mechanism behind Scott's entire plot, for Calvinist congregations in Scotland, attempting to stem a rash of illegitimate births by public shaming ceremonies, drove up the incidence of infanticide. As for *The Scarlet Letter*, public confession is the overarching frame, motivating the scaffold setting where the novel commences, climaxes, and concludes.

Legal trials have always been a salient feature of the tested woman plot. Given the political configuration of Boston society, Hester Prynne's trial is both ecclesiastical and secular. Even strictly secular trials are designed to urge the accused toward confession. Though *The Heart of Midlothian* is filled with judicial proceedings of every stripe, confession is what is demanded of Effie— the law that has no interest in accusing her of fornication has every reason to think her guilty of child murder, and every iota of legal persuasion is put into getting her to confess to it. The court that tries Hetty also wants her confession and is baffled by its inability to persuade her of the pointlessness of silence.

Forensic trials are, however, much less fundamental to these novels than are patterns of Christian self-scrutiny and witness. Over and over appear elements of religious structure and ritual: Dinah's composition of the person of the longing and welcoming Christ; Dorothea's dark night of the soul on the floor of her bedroom; Benson's pastoral care of the suicidal Ruth; the ritualized doctrinal fencing between Douce Davie and Reuben Butler; Jeanie's encounter with the Reverend Staunton, not to mention Staunton's pastoral pressure on his prodigal son. Hester's and Tess's (third-person) spiritual journals, the return of the prodigal Angel to his parents, Leonard's public claiming of kinship with his mother—all are recognizable by their religious types.

The phenomenon is most consciously examined in George Eliot's treatment of Arthur's non-confession to the Reverend Mr. Irwine, where she emphasizes by negative example how the ritual structure of public disclosure makes possible the trauma and release of revelation. Arthur chooses to go to Mr. Irwine at breakfast time, as he used to in his pupilhood, because that event, unlike the old rituals, has no sacramental character and every opportunity of evasion: "there was this advantage in the old rigid forms, that they committed you to the fulfilment of a resolution by some outward deed: when you have put your mouth to one end of a hole in a stone wall, and are aware that there is an expectant ear at the other end, you are more likely to say what you came out with the intention of saying, than if you were seated with your legs in an easy attitude under the mahogany, with a companion who will have no reason to be surprised if you have nothing particular to say" (207). So it comes as no surprise, even to him, that Arthur cannot tell. For all his good intentions, he is too callow to understand the enabling function of sacramental moments, while Mr. Irwine, for all his acuteness at social interpretation, is too doctrinally relaxed to recognize its need.

In Hetty's case the absence of confession is seen in its relation not to Anglo-Catholic ritual but to Methodism. In the prison scene with Dinah, Hetty tells and experiences relief. Nevertheless she does not confess in any genuine sense. Dinah's desire is to bring Hetty into genuine moral self-consciousness. We know that Hetty has bodily self-consciousness—that is, she sees herself as she imagines others seeing her. Dinah wishes to teach a moral way of seeing the self as well, yet although she gets Hetty to tell, she fails to achieve that breakthrough. The narrator has described Hetty's lack, despite years of routine performance, of any kind of religious impulse and the concomitant absence of confessional urges or practices. When she finds herself in trouble she fears shaming (we cannot even say that she is ashamed), so she conceals. What she lacks is any practice in avowing her engagements in the world, or any practice with the introspection that makes such avowals possible. Such self-consciousness need not be overtly religious, as Adam's demonstrates. Unlike his brother Seth, Adam is not caught up in the fervor of vivid religious practice, but he is unceasingly introspective, and in his need he finds confession and avowal necessary and possible. At its deepest his avowal is framed in the sacramental quality of the meal he shares with Bartle Massey. This spiritual quality, trained through introspection, brings him and Dinah together, as it brings Dorothea through her spiritual struggle. It is this quality that is absent in Hetty.

What Hetty cannot do is bring her story about herself into agreement with her actions. By contrast what Dorothea and Dinah and even Adam learn to do, and what Eliot's novelistic technique is able to show them doing, is what the moral philosopher Herbert Fingarette calls "spelling out." In probing the relationship between motivation and act, Eliot examines the discrepancies between what her characters suspect about themselves, unspokenly and often uneasily, and what they choose to avow actively as a way of defining their identities. Eliot is a master at representing various forms of self-deception, of which Hetty's is particularly deep. How is it even possible, Fingarette asks, for there to be such a thing as self-deception, as distinct from mere hypocrisy? Is that not a logical paradox, an impossibility? His answer lies in the distinction between passive consciousness and explicit commitment. Exploring the phenomenon as it occurs in autobiography, where the writer's motives may seem undeniably sincere yet produce an account strongly discrepant with the facts, Roy W. Perrett paraphrases Fingarette's concept of self-deception as "a motivated failure to become explicitly conscious of some part of one's engagement in the world. Becoming explicitly conscious . . . is not something that just happens to us, it is something we *do*. . . . In other words, self-deception involves—as a matter of policy—the persistent avoidance of spelling out some feature of one's engagement in the world" (32). Perrett goes on to argue that such spelling out "is roughly telling a story about oneself, or episodes in one's life, that acknowledges that engagement as part of one's self-identity." Self-identity, in the subjective sense of a person's self-image, is "a narrative construction" (33).[8]

Fingarette's concept of spelling out links the notion of a narrative construction of self to the practices of evangelicalism. The confession of the sinner is a subcategory of the broader Christian idea of witnessing—giving testimony about one's spiritual state and life intentions. *The Heart of Midlothian* makes the link unusually explicit. Much of the strength of Scott's characterization of Jeanie Deans lies in his understanding of the relation between her religious faith and her capacity for self-identifying avowal. The forebearing acuteness with which she allows for or circumvents the more fanatical of her father's shortcomings is no failure of filial piety. Rather, her paternally inculcated belief in a personal God as observer, participant, and interlocutor overrides other authority. Explaining her journey to London in a letter to her father, she acknowledges that leaving him without his knowledge and consent was perhaps a guilty act, "for Scripture says, that 'the vow of the daughter should not be binding without the consent of the father,'" but a greater command has taken precedence over both Scriptural and paternal authority: "it was borne in upon my mind that I should be an instrument to help my poor sister" (272). "It was borne in upon my mind" is the Calvinist formula by which Jeanie expresses her belief that God has spoken directly to her and that it is her unimpeachable duty to obey. David Deans recognizes the import of the phrase; he must acknowledge for his daughter the same right of independent interpretation that he reserves unyieldingly to himself.

The Heart of Midlothian is not about the pathological effects of concealment per se, then; quite the contrary. Jeanie's reason for not testifying falsely in court has to do with the formal nature of oaths: "It is not man I fear . . . the God, whose name I must call on to witness the truth of what I say, he will know the falsehood," she tells George (156). But she repeatedly conceals information that she does not consider hers to reveal: she will not tell George's father about her sister's catastrophe or his son's role in it; will not tell Reuben about Effie's correspondence with her; will not for a long time reveal Staunton's identity, much less his past, to her husband. What she does not do, on the other hand, is hide her commitments from herself. Her case helps us see how essential to genuine revelation is the revealing of the self to itself. A different milieu may exclude any implication of a divine voice (as when Emma suddenly realizes that Mr. Knightly should marry no one but herself), but self-conscious speaking to the self is required. In Jeanie's case, her religious beliefs train the conscious self in a continuing scrutiny of its own motives and a continuing process of avowal of its engagements.

Because of the openness of Jeanie's self-avowals, motifs of disguise and hiding the past are used in *The Heart of Midlothian* to forward plot events more than to stage a moral debate. By contrast, though Hester's survival and hard-won sanity are grounded in the revelation that childbirth forces on her, concealment is the sin explored throughout *The Scarlet Letter.* The narrator purports to tell us outright the chief moral of the tale: "Be true! Be true! Be true! Show freely to the world, if not your worst, yet some trait whereby the worst may be inferred!" (198). However we regard this strangely undercut injunction, it is evident that Dimmesdale dies the way he does because he has not had revelation forced upon him and has been too weak to embrace it himself. Hester's case is much less clear, for concealment has been her mode, too. Like Jeanie's, her concealment is on others' behalf, but unlike Jeanie, she comes to regard it as pathological. Her first concealment is to refuse to name Dimmesdale as the father, and though it looks like mercy, or heroism, or pride in her own strength, or the angry desire that he have the courage to take up his rightful burden, she comes to recognize it as fatal to him. That concealment makes possible the subsequent one, hiding Chillingworth's identity from Dimmesdale, which she undertakes both to protect her lover's reputation and as a form of equity to her husband. Hester must finally recognize that this further concealment has been instrumental in turning Chillingworth into the fiend he has become: "Here was another ruin, the responsibility of which came partly home to her" (137). When during her climactic encounter with the minister in the forest she begs his forgiveness— an extraordinary reversal of the plot move one might expect—it is because her lie on his behalf proves heavier than the motive for that lie.

What of Dimmesdale? His illness comes to a head because Hester has re- tracted her vow of silence to Chillingworth and told Dimmesdale her husband's identity. That truth-telling accomplished, Dimmesdale can take the scaffold to stand with Hester and Pearl, expose his bosom, escape Chillingworth's clutches, and die with his child's kiss on his lips. So has Hester's truth-telling enabled Dimmesdale's? In fact, no. Dimmesdale never confesses openly. He merely suffers openly. He never states his relationship to his child any more than Chillingworth acknowledges his relationship to her mother. Chilling- worth's willing of his estate, like Dimmesdale's baring of his bosom, could be so interpreted; that is all. As the narrator tells us, "when time sufficed for the people to arrange their thoughts in reference to the foregoing scene, there was more than one account of what had been witnessed on the scaffold" (197). One fact only is unequivocally presented to the town—that Hester has borne a child. Only the woman must tell.

Dimmesdale's failure is the absence of avowal in Herbert Fingarette's sense, the spelling out in unequivocal terms of his physical and emotional engagement with Hester and the child. Nowhere—not on the scaffold, in conversation with Hester, or in the indirect free rendering of his mental states—does he state his deed and its consequences in a way that would commit him to his past role of lover and his present role of parent. Neither does Hester, but she has no need to. Bearing and caring for her child is her avowal. Dimmesdale has no choice but to work in words. But why should he need to avow? There is his Christian sense of guilt, of which he wishes to purge himself. In plot terms this is insufficient explanation, however, for the tempter is allowed to flee the story undetected; he has no purpose in the trial stage. Paradoxically it is Dimmesdale's desire for a continued role in Hester's and Pearl's lives that gives him the opportunity to fail again. The plot's deep structure informs us that the true function of the defender is to witness to the truth about the woman's deed and her moral condition. If Dimmesdale wishes to perform this function, he must wish to implicate himself, he must desire a commitment to explicit involvement with her deed and its consequences. As it stands, his solipsistic efforts at self-protection and self-purgation never even recognize this need: self-deception underlies to the end his deception of the community.

SIXTEEN

Epilogue

IN *THE SCARLET LETTER* HAWTHORNE EXPLICITLY CONNECTED THE tested woman plot's dramatic need for concealment and revelation to the religious and social themes inhering in his story material, bridging the gap from the historically bound milieu of a theocratic culture to romance's fundamental function as secular scripture. "Secular scripture" is Northrop Frye's term, and by it he means something broader than Hawthorne's starting point in Puritan Boston might suggest. Despite its historical and transcendental trappings, Hawthorne's tale is a secular statement of Frye's fundamental trajectory of romance, its descent into and ascent out of the demonic realm into a regained individual identity.[1] The tested woman plot is well-suited to Frye's romance pattern: Shakespeare's *Winter's Tale* and *Pericles*, with their tales of male madness and female sequestration, marry full-blown renderings of the plot to the romance schema. Yet the plot's flexibility of development and denouement is one of its attractions. Open to a wide variety of tones and textures, it is also at home in both heroic tragedy and social comedy.

Various genres or authorial intentions are able to play to different aspects of the plot. Livy's exemplary stories of the history of Rome extend the complications of patriarchal conflict and reconciliation and spend little time with the moment of the woman's moral choice. Early Renaissance homiletic drama lingers over the woman's moral witnessing and makes her sacrifices the focus of the work. In drama and the novel, the plot adapts itself to the opportunities of genre. The relatively stark, agonistic characterizations and rapid rhetorical actions typical of drama bring to the fore the schematic relationships of the plot's character functions. Though the form is open to stock figures and stereotyped moves (amply revisited by nineteenth-century melodrama), at its most gripping the result can be, as in *Othello*, a compelling presentation of the pathology of male competition. The epistolary novel and the novel of *style indirect libre*, with their access to characters' interior processes, take advantage of the plot's concern with moral choice. This interiority, combined with novelistic extension, gives modern renditions of the plot the enormous advantage of attention to character maturation. Both extension and interiority

243

have their dangers, naturally. The danger of extension is that the plot will be tediously replayed. The danger of interiority is that the plot's shape—its test/trial stages and character functions—will be attenuated into a story of the events, perhaps even the confessions, of a life.

But the greatest dangers to the tested woman plot lie in cultural changes, and they have made the plot hard to sustain in the modern world. Built on a structure of male control and female obedience—most fundamentally on the story of fathers and daughters, the originating patriarchal authority practiced on the natural subordinate—the plot can live at its fullest only in a world in which patriarchal power is clearly delineated, carried out through personal relationships, and supported by individual morality. Such an environment is increasingly unavailable in modern Western culture. Because the plot is a structure about absolute character traits and extreme social measures, it is ill-suited to the world of impersonal sanctions and of mundane duties with their monotonies and moral ambiguities. It depends on verities that increasingly can be made believable only by social or historical distance.

The nineteenth-century novel was already showing the strain. The classic feel to *Ruth*'s treatment of the tested woman plot comes in part from its historical distancing. Though the period of the novel is not specified, though the trip to the seaside is taken by railroad and the election appears to be carried out under the provisions of the 1832 Reform Bill, Gaskell emphasizes a world of carriages and stagecoaches, introducing her tested woman as living in a time "now many years ago" (3). *Tess of the D'Urbervilles* also depends on the historical lag attendant on rural isolation. There are trains at the edge of Tess's world, but her people walk or catch rides on slow-moving carts. Other novels go further back: *Adam Bede* to 1799, Scott's and Hawthorne's novels by generations. All are placed in rural or small-town settings, among ordinary people far from modern sophistications and social innovations.

Though pushed back in setting, these novels nevertheless have distinctly modern concerns, ones that do not appear in earlier renditions of the plot. One concern is social class. With the exception of the somewhat aberrant Griselda story and its analogues (*Pamela*, for instance), in which the man marries down in order to ensure his total control over his wife, the tested woman plot traditionally operates between characters of the same class. In the nineteenth century, however, the seduction of a lower-class girl by a gentleman becomes the usual version, one way of expressing the modern vitiation of paternal authority. Another example is the theme of mothering. Sexual disobedience is traditionally expressed by the child's mere existence; the modern world adds the ability to find moral expiation in the quality of the woman's care. Gaskell's and Hawthorne's tested women perform their trials in a mother's world, and what they do there gradually takes precedence over their past. Both novels allude to nearly a generation's worth of mothering time. Both track the bond between mother and child, the child's realization of the mother's offense, and the blame that follows. Leonard sulks and rebels,

Pearl forces her mother to resume wearing the scarlet letter. Both Hester and Ruth must do the work of outcasts, but their skill at this drudgery makes their children's lives possible.

Expiation through parenting seems not to be available to the tempter, however. The absence of fathering in the novels I have considered owes something, no doubt, to the nineteenth-century fear of sanctioning illicit sexual activity. The mother's obligation to care for the ill-begotten child is undeniably a higher moral duty than abandoning it, but the novel still has difficulty socially regularizing her life. Confronting male involvement and responsibility, which would all too explicitly return our minds to the genital act, seems out of the question. The absence of fathering perhaps owes as much to the fact that, the very American *Scarlet Letter* aside, all these novels are as burdened by class as by sexual politics. In theory there could be a novel in which the tempter, converted to defender and grieving over the death of the woman in childbirth, might raise the child as an act of propitiation for his own behavior. But I do not know of one: such an action is too far from the original center of the plot—the woman's choice and the collective patriarchal interpretation of it.

Up to the mid-eighteenth century, the imitation of literary types and the traditions of character decorum drew both the author's and the audience's attention to the repetition of literary patterns. When Davenport has the friend accuse the husband who wants to test his wife of borrowing a hackneyed plot move, or Shirley has his tested woman turn the tables on a lover he has named Trier, we are still in a literature that calls attention to its types. When Chapman carries the testing of the wife as far as a botched trial we suspect him of using consciousness of the plot's stages to emphasize his satire. When Ford calls his play *The Lady's Trial*, discusses sexual attempts on wives in the first scene, gives his tempter, accuser, and defender similar names, and stages their reconciliation as preparation for a public trial, we know he is flagging the plot's entire shape. When Richardson has Pamela arrange her chairs into a bar and invite her husband to be both accuser and judge, he shows his awareness of the forensic functions her terminology calls up.

In a literature that pretends to originality and attempts to disguise literariness as individual experience, however, the degree of an author's or an audience's plot consciousness is less certain. Some authors still openly reference the plot: several of George Eliot's chapter epigrams for *Middlemarch*—quotations from Renaissance dramatists or her own dramatic pastiches—revisit plot segments appropriate to the action. But in *Mansfield Park* it is left to the reader to see the structural relationship with Kotzebue, namely, that Henry, playacting the son and defender of the fallen woman, is actually the tempter of Maria, and that Fanny, too, will come to find herself tempted. As for *Ruth*, for all its close adherence to the plot structure, Gaskell makes no overt literary allusions at all.

If the social conditions of the nineteenth century were already causing strains and adjustments, how is the tested woman plot possible in the post-modern world? Given that it requires a patriarchal structure and makes its drama from an examination of a woman's place in that structure, is the plot seriously available to contemporary writers? There is no question that its remnants are present in some versions of popular romance. In series where extramarital sex is prohibited, there is enough of the obedience issue, in attenuated form, to spice the heroine's dilemmas. Barbara Cartland was not one of the twentieth-century's bestselling authors for nothing. Nevertheless, modern popular romances are novels of courtship, not novels of the testing of obedience—much less the quest for individual reintegration in Frye's sense. Yet memory of the tested woman plot and consciousness of its power hangs on, exercising both a formal and a psychological fascination.

Some of the fascination comes from familiarity. Because the plot has been so widespread and powerful in our literary culture, because its flourishing has been based on social phenomena out of which the modern world has erupted, it seems in some sense natural. We easily borrow its motifs and resurrect its references. Rakish tempters are still Lotharios, patient women Griseldas. Wallace Stevens's Peter Quince dreams Susanna. Yet motifs and characters are not the entire plot, though they call it up. Dependent as it is on fixed social relations and attitudes about female obedience that are being lost, the plot's overall form does not translate well into postmodern literature. Its psychological fascination, however, is more transportable. The eighteenth-century breakthrough primarily enlarged two themes in the plot, allowing the deep exploration of the pathology of the tempter and the deep exploration of the psychological integrity of the tested woman. These two psychologies are the center of the achievement of *Clarissa*. Capitalizing on the development of notions of the individual self and exploiting the opportunities inherent in the immediacy and extension of the epistolary form, Richardson brought the plot fully into the modern world. These possibilities are still usable by twentieth- and twenty-first-century writers and can carry remnants, or even the entire skeleton, of the tested woman plot with them, as in John Fowles's *The Collector* (1963) and William Trevor's *Felicia's Journey* (1994).

In both Fowles and Trevor the plot is used to engage the violent social anomies of the present. Both novels feature psychologically fixated, socially estranged, predatory men who seek to control young, unwitting women so as to glory in their imaginatively stimulating possession. That plot move has its historical antecedent in Lovelace's pathology. Though Lovelace's announced motives, not to mention his class, are very different from those of Fowles's and Trevor's predators, his behavior is markedly similar. In all three there is the spite against the woman's family, the physical and mental stalking, the absence of any strong impulse to genital sex, the fantasies about life together (in the case of Trevor's predator even resulting in psychological collapse and suicide following the woman's escape). Yet though for both Fowles and Trevor much of the fascination lies in male psychopathology, both, like Richardson, give full voicing to their tested women, so that the struggle between male pathology and female integrity is made the heart of the novels.[2]

Trevor's novel has the more obvious remnants of the tested woman plot structure, made possible by Felicia's Irish origins. When the pregnant Felicia flees her home to escape the judgmental eye of her father and search for the boyfriend who has deserted her, she seeks him in the mazes of an English Midlands city. She finds instead Mr. Hilditch, fat, fifties, and avuncularly helpful. As the novel moves between Felicia's consciousness and Hilditch's, the reader realizes early on what Felicia comes to understand only later: Hilditch is a psychopathic murderer of young women, and she is being positioned as his seventh victim. Initially the functions of tempter and judge are classically deployed. The father is the controlling moral figure, both in the family's interactions and in Felicia's mind, making it impossible for her to imagine returning home. Johnny vanishes early, his role as enemy of the family clear from his treatment of Felicia and his flight to the British army. Hilditch plays what is left: defender first, for that is his entrapment procedure, then eventually accuser, as Felicia prepares to leave. Giving her rides, feeding her in pubs and canteens, pretending to help her look for her boyfriend, pressuring her to have an abortion and paying for it, Hilditch feeds his need to be *seen* with a young woman, to be understood in his fantasies and among his acquaintances to be attractive to women. Warped by a smothered childhood culminating in coerced incest with his mother, he displays no interest in actual genital sex with any of his girls. His deepest fear is that they will leave him. The trigger of that fear is their plan to do so. And the orgasmic moment is the death he administers to each in his little humpbacked car. Buried in his backyard, they become nostalgic characters in his Memory Lane.

John Fowles takes the motif of male pathology a step further. Frederick Clegg, a lower-class misfit contemptuous of his roots and envious of middle-class social and intellectual ease, finds his youthful devotion to collecting butterflies mutating into a fixation on collecting the perfect specimen woman, which he finds in the art student Miranda. Having won the football pools, he is able to quit his job, send the remnants of his family to Australia, and live his fantasy of perfect possession. Miranda's capture, immurement, and death follow. When Miranda is first kidnapped, she assumes that her collector is the classic tempter, seeking sexual conquest. Then, as sex seems not, after all, to be his purpose, she realizes that Clegg is just what he professes, a man obsessed by ownership. When she seeks to break the stasis by trying to seduce him, his response is panic and disgust, which he translates with a pseudo-moral tag: "I no longer respected her" (240). His sexual prissiness is both motive and manifestation. Sex is "some crude animal thing I was born without," he tells us. The self-justification follows: "(And I'm glad I was, if more people were like me, in my opinion, the world would be better)" (11).

The swings between grandiose self-inflation and abject psychological collapse, the torrent of self-justification, the dependence on the approval of the object of obsession, the pleasure of scheming, the enormous organizational effort to pull off the pretenses aimed at disguising the mania for possession—these traits are present in both Clegg's and Hilditch's inventions. Lovelace is their great predecessor. But for modern writers the emphasis has shifted from traditional, socially sanctioned morality to an ethics of the self, and in both Fowles and Trevor the woman triumphs through psychological maturation, expressed by the growth of independent decision-making. This independence is at its bitterest in Miranda's case, for she dies of pneumonia in a cellar. Where is her victory? It lies in her capacity to use the months of captivity to examine her life: her relationships with her family, with her older mentor and would-be lover, with her captor; her attitudes toward her body and toward the use of violence, even in defense of her life. This self-examination, undertaken in her journal, matures and strengthens her. Writing late, though before the full anguish of her dying, she notes, "A strange thought: I would not want this not to have happened. Because if I escape I shall be a completely different and I think better person. Because if I don't escape, if something dreadful happened, I shall still know that the person I was and would have stayed if this hadn't happened was not the person I now want to be" (229). This insight echoes Clarissa's gratitude that Lovelace's villainy has given her her spiritual opportunity.

In keeping with this psychological focus, both Fowles and Trevor adopt dramatistic techniques of voicing. Fowles's novel is first person and double-voiced. Glegg narrates his story; Miranda writes hers in her journal. Trevor's novel is third person, but it switches between Felicia's and Hilditch's views and is narrated primarily in the present tense. These fictional techniques increase the immediacy of our experience, but they also invite introspection in the characters. The result facilitates the woman's breaking free into independent self-judgment. Miranda's self-shaping is the more conscious and cultured, her descent into and partial ascent out of the demonic realm closer to Frye's trajectory. But Felicia also ends strangely liberated, a vagrant confident in her ability to survive and to sustain friendships with those needier than herself. The introspective voicing also facilitates our understanding of the accuser/defender reciprocal—the alternating worship and denigration of the woman. In traditional versions of the plot, aimed at external judgment, the two functions are generally allotted to separate characters because they represent different social attitudes or allegiances. In Trevor and Fowles, because the focus is private and psychological rather than public and social, because the final ethical judgment is now in the hands of the woman herself, the male psychodrama between defender and accuser is easily housed in a single obsessed figure.

Despite its links to modern social and psychological concerns, the tested woman plot is an artifact of patriarchal cultures. As such cultures wane in the modern world, the plot in its fully public, socially reflective form is bound to wane with them. The two novels I have just discussed can hardly supply a definitive demonstration of the plot's lingering uses, but they are suggestive.

The man's obsession to possess and the woman's will to resist, to maintain her spiritual intactness, may be the drives at the heart of the plot that will continue to pull at least its shadow into modern works. Modern readers, even authors, are unlikely to identify those shadows explicitly, and certainly not in terms of the schematic relationships I have labeled and discussed. But the plot still lives at the heart of our cultural memory, and we can continue to expect its echoes.

.

NOTES

CHAPTER ONE

1. *The Golden Ass* includes the tale of Cupid and Psyche; *The Satyricon* has the "Milesian Tale" of the Widow of Ephesus; *Don Quixote* includes the account of "El curioso impertinente"; in bk. 1, cantos 3 to 5 of *Orlando Furioso*, Ariosto tells the story of Ariodante and Ginevra.

2. Handel uses the episode from Ariosto for his *Ariodante*; Mozart's exemplar is *Così fan tutte*; Puccini contributes *Tosca*.

3. Cesare Segre's "From Motif to Function and Back Again" examines the term "motif" as used by both Vladimir Propp and non-Proppian formalists, considers issues of stability, portability, and divisibility (my terms), and argues for the existence of thematic kernels that are nonnarrative or formal components of plot structure.

4. Two collections of essays situate structural thematics in relation to narratology, structuralist linguistics, folktale studies, and archetypal or myth criticism: *Thematics: New Approaches*, ed. Claude Bremond, Joshua Landy and Thomas Pavel, which groups papers presented at several conferences held in France in the mid-1980s, and *The Return of Thematic Criticism*, ed. Werner Sollors.

5. Lubomír Dolozel, "A Semantic for Thematics: The Case of the Double," 91.

6. Thomas G. Pavel, "Thematics and Historical Evidence," 130.

7. Entry "type," in *Standard Dictionary of Folklore, Mythology and Legend*, ed. Maria Leach, 1137.

8. A stimulating and magisterial discussion of prototype categorization is George Lakoff's *Women, Fire, and Dangerous Things: What Categories Reveal about the Mind.*

9. Peter Brooks, *Reading for the Plot: Design and Intention in Narrative*, xi.

10. Brooks, *Reading for the Plot*; Allen Tilley, *Plot Snakes and the Dynamics of Narrative Experience*. Tilley's more recent book, *Plots of Time: An Inquiry into History, Myth, and Meaning*, has a less literary focus. The title of Leopold Damrosch's *God's Plot and Man's Stories*, in which he explores the relationship between the Christian assumption of Providential intentionality and the stories of a particular cultural moment (Milton to Fielding), is an apt expression of the relation between plot and ideology. My work is *Clarissa's Plots*.

11. Richard Levin, *The Multiple Plot in English Renaissance Drama*; Vladimir Propp, *Morphology of the Folktale*; Stith Thompson, *Motif-Index of Folk Literature*; Tzvetan Todorov, *Grammaire du "Décaméron"*; Thomas G. Pavel, *The Poetics of Plot: The Case of English Renaissance Drama*; and Roland Barthes, *S/Z: An Essay*, 204.

CHAPTER TWO

1. Ovid, *Amores*, 1.8.43. During her trial John Webster's Vittoria uses this aphorism with striking ambiguity (*The White Devil*, 3.2.200).

2. In *The Secular Scripture: A Study of the Structure of Romance*, Frye distinguishes between the causally driven, linear, "hence" structures typical of (for instance) so-called realistic fiction, and the additive, vertical, "and then" structures of undisplaced romance such as the Hellenistic tales (chap. 2, "The Context of Romance," esp. 47–51).

3. In Thomas Heywood's *Edward IV, Parts I and II*, Jane Shore yields to the king's importunities and becomes his mistress. Then, confronted by her husband, she vows to expiate her sin and spends the remainder of two plays demonstrating her virtue, finally dying reconciled to Shore. Thomas Dekker's *The Honest Whore, Parts I and II* replays the test/trial actions from the opposite direction, initially converting Bellafront to virtue, then providing repeated opportunities to attack her now unshakable "honesty."

4. In Shakespeare's *Cymbeline* Imogen is mistakenly judged unchaste. When she refuses Iachimo's solicitation, he lies in order to establish proof of unchastity, and on the strength of this lie Posthumus orders her death. Opinion and appearance do not correspond with fact and reality until the play's denouement. In Thomas Middleton's *Hengist King of Kent*, Hengist's daughter Roxena, eager to ingratiate herself with King Vortiger, swears to her virginity in a formal chastity trial and becomes Vortiger's wife while continuing as Horsus's mistress. Unchaste, she is judged chaste.

5. A seeming omission of the test action occurs in Shakespeare's *The Winter's Tale*. When Hermione is brought to trial for unchastity, she has not been solicited by Polixenes or engaged in any unchaste thought or behavior. The first, or test, action occurs only in the mind of Leontes. *Edward III* truncates the trial. All test, it begins when the king solicits the countess of Salisbury and ends when he gives up in the face of her intransigence. Because the ultimate judge of the lady, the sovereign, is also the tempter, converted to right behavior by her virtuous rebuff, no trial stage is needed. Opinion and fact are in harmony about the countess's incorruptibility.

6. In John Ford's *The Lady's Trial*, Auria the husband and judge fervently longs to make publicly indisputable his wife's virtue. In *The Revenger's Tragedy* (probably by Middleton), Vindice longs just as fervently for his sister Castiza to resist his solicitations on Lussurioso's behalf. Nancy Cotton Pearse makes this point and its application to Fletcher's plays in *John Fletcher's Chastity Plays: Mirrors for Modesty*. Though I do not always agree with her conclusions, I am indebted to many of her distinctions.

7. In the biblical vignette of the woman taken in adultery, the tempter flees clutching his clothes, as Wendoll in Heywood's *A Woman Killed with Kindness* flees in his nightgown. In the trial scene of Webster's *The White Devil*, Bracciano the tempter as much as admits to being Vittoria's lover, but in the Susanna story the Elders reappear as accusers. In Thomas Garter's *Virtuous and Godly Susanna* the judge tries to pass his judicial function over to the defender, Daniel; in Webster's *The Devil's Law-Case* the judge, Crispiano, steps down from the bench to become a curious kind of defender; and in the anonymous *A Woman Killed with Kindness* the wronged husband, Frankford, is both accuser and judge.

8. The competing creation accounts of Genesis 1 and 2 open interpretive possibilities as well as problems. The contradictions are well-known: humans first or animals first? male human first or both sexes simultaneously? initial creation of two people or of many? These contradictions mean, however, that the tradition is able to choose

what it regards as the "real story." The Christian synoptic tradition hierarchizes by making human creation the culminating act and preferring the drama of individualized creation to the more impersonal creation of the race. All my biblical citations are from the King James Version.

9. Euripides' earlier *Iphigenia in Tauris* has the divinely rescued daughter, now a priestess of Artemis, save Orestes and Pylades from the Taurids. As for *Iphigenia in Aulis*, in the introduction to his translation Charles R. Walker says that it "was produced, together with the *Bacchae* and the *Alcmaeon*, at the Great Dionysia in March, 405 B.C., a few months after Euripides' death. It seems probable that Euripides' son (some say his nephew) produced the play and perhaps filled in parts of the script which Euripides had left incomplete at the time of his death" (290). The extant play includes what is generally regarded as a spurious ending, the tonally jarring messenger's report to Clytemnestra that describes Artemis's divine translation of the girl and substitution of a hind as the sacrificial victim.

10. Michael Cacoyannis's 1979 film of the play (with Costa Kazakos as Agamemnon, Irene Papas as Clytemnestra, and Tatania Papamoskou as Iphigenia) sketches the conditions of the camp at Aulis with visual force and economy and superbly conveys the barely leashed threat of violence from the increasingly restless and sullen troops.

11. My text of Livy is the translation by Aubrey de Sélincourt, but I am using the spelling Virginia/Virginius rather than his Verginia/Verginius for consistency with other versions of the tale.

12. Another figure in Livy is Lucius Junius, son of the king's sister who to escape his uncle's slaughter of rivals has masqueraded as a dullard, "Brutus." Brutus accompanies Collatinus to witness Lucretia's accusation and suicide. Throwing off his disguise, he rallies the mourning husband and father to vow vengeance, then leads the campaign against the Tarquin kings. When the republic elects its first tribunes, it chooses Brutus and Collatinus. In Livy's story the revulsion against the Tarquins must be seen as a general response to a deep-seated Roman problem, not the affair of one or two families only. The abuse of which the rape is the expression requires a reordering of the whole body politic. As Brutus assumes his rightful character and embraces the public cause, he epitomizes the efforts of the Roman state to find its rightful form. Ian Donaldson's *The Rapes of Lucretia: A Myth and Its Transformations* establishes the importance of the Brutus material and discusses iconic treatments of Lucretia and Brutus during the early modern period.

13. I say "typically," for the best-known of the few that survive, Longus's *Daphnis and Chloë*, brings adventure home to interrupt the pastoral idyll rather than sending its young lovers over road or sea. In *The True History of the Novel*, Margaret Anne Doody argues against the terminology "Hellenistic romance," principally the "romance" part, preferring the more inclusive term "Greek novel" or simply "ancient novel." Since my interests have been shaped first by plot and only second by genre, I have retained the term "romance" for its connotations of gender equality and far-flung adventure. These characteristics make the genre open to celebration in drama (Shakespeare) and verse (Chaucer) as well as prose narrative. I use "Hellenistic" because it implies a distinctively eastern Mediterranean mixture of cultures, races, topographies, empires, and historical periods.

14. Mikhail Bakhtin, "Forms of Time and of the Chronotope in the Novel," in his *Dialogic Imagination: Four Essays*.

15. Doody, *True History*, 2. In *Sexual Symmetry: Love in the Ancient Novel and Related*

Genres, David Konstan also disagrees with Bakhtin's emphasis on stasis, stressing that "fidelity . . . tends to displace original erotic attraction between hero and heroine, and it becomes the basis for their association as a wedded couple, recharacterizing the nature of their bond over and against the passionate infatuation that inaugurated the relationship" (46).

16. Warren E. Blake's introduction to his 1939 translation of Chariton gives a history of the novel's fortunes in English. The only previous translation into English, "of anonymous authorship and dating from 1764, was based upon an Italian translation of the imperfect text of the first Greek edition" printed in Rome in 1752 (vi). That earlier translation has its own historical interest. Its anonymous editor describes himself as the father of two young daughters whom he is having educated in the modern languages and whom he set to translate Chariton from "an elegant Italian translation." After giving an accurate history of the recovery of Chariton and the current state of editions and scholarship as described in the notes and commentary to the Latin translation by d'Orville published in Amsterdam in 1750, this father shows his familiarity with the whole corpus of Hellenistic romance and his appreciation, given his pedagogical purposes, of Chariton's chaste matter and plain style.

17. Achilles Tatius, *Clitophon and Leucippe*, bk. 6, § 22, p. 347. Recent scholarship on the ancient novel is signposted by Tomas Hägg's *The Novel in Antiquity* and by the translations in *Collected Ancient Greek Novels*, ed. B. P. Reardon. Frederick A. Todd's *Some Ancient Novels* (1940), though it lacks the advantage of the upsurge in scholarly and critical interest, provides a useful brief overview of the texts and English publication history of Longus, Achilles Tatius, Apuleius, and Petronius. Unlike Chariton, Achilles Tatius's *Clitophon and Leucippe* was preserved in a number of thirteenth-to-sixteenth-century manuscripts. The Greek text was first printed in Heidelberg in 1601, but the sixteenth century had numerous Latin printed translations (including that of Cruceius, or Benedetto della Croce), French (including that of Belleforest), and Italian. The first English translation was published by "W. B." (William Burton, older brother of Robert Burton, the author of *The Anatomy of Melancholy*) in 1597, dedicated to Henry Wriothesley, third Earl of Southampton and Shakespeare's patron, and died aborning. Todd notes, "From 1597, the year of its publication, to 1897, exactly three centuries, no mention of it has been found anywhere" (12). In 1897 a single copy surfaced, in 1923 another, and it is now available in facsimile as Tatius Achilles, *The History of Clitophon and Leucippe*. Burton's translation was made primarily from the Latin of Cruceius (Todd, 13). An English translation by Anthony Hodges, long thought to be the first, was published anonymously in 1638 at Oxford under the title *The Loves of Clitophon and Leucippe*.

18. Many Latin versions of *Apollonius of Tyre* were available in the Middle Ages, and the story became part of the *Gesta Romanorum*. Shakespeare's sources were book 8 of John Gower's *Confessio Amantis* (1393) and Laurence Twine's *Patterne of Painefull Adventures*, which was first entered in the Stationer's Register in 1576. Geoffrey Bullough's *Narrative and Dramatic Sources of Shakespeare* reprints the Twine text and, with the Arden edition of *Pericles*, is the most easily available source of *Apollonius of Tyre* and its Renaissance provenance and influence. My summary of the plot features is based on Twine. Doody describes the Roman/Christian flavor, transmission history, and influence of *Apollonius*, and notes (*True History*, 224) the existence of at least one published English version before Twine's, Robert Copelande's 1510 translation from a French text.

19. Doody's discussion of Apuleius's *Metamorphoses* (*The Golden Ass*) (*True History*, chaps. 5 and 8) demonstrates what the novelistic teleology so evident in *Apollonius* owes not just to its Christian flavor but also to the Roman novel of spiritual journeying, recovery, and transformation.

20. That "blasphemy [will] bring its certain and immediate consequence" of death, a consummation surely to be wished under the circumstances, is the interpretation preferred by Samuel Terrien in his exegesis of Job in *The Interpreter's Bible* (3:921).

21. "It is amazing to see how easily Yahweh, quite without reason, had let himself be influenced by one of his sons, by a *doubting thought*, and made unsure of Job's faithfulness. With his touchiness and suspiciousness the mere possibility of doubt was enough to infuriate him and induce that peculiar double-faced behaviour of which he had already given proof in the Garden of Eden, when he pointed out the tree to the First Parents and at the same time forbade them to eat of it. In this way he precipitated the Fall, which he apparently never intended. Similarly, his faithful servant Job is now to be exposed to a rigorous moral test, quite gratuitously and to no purpose, although Yahweh is convinced of Job's faithfulness and constancy, and could moreover have assured himself beyond all doubt on this point had he taken counsel with his own omniscience" (Carl Gustav Jung, *Answer to Job*, 375).

CHAPTER THREE

1. For a bibliography of English debate over the "woman question" and of the social, religious, and educational environment of women, see Rosemary Masek's "Women in an Age of Transition, 1485–1714," in *The Women of England from Anglo-Saxon Times to the Present: Interpretive Bibliographical Essays*, 138–82; other essential sources include Carroll Camden, *The Elizabethan Woman*; Coryl Crandall, *"Swetnam the Woman-Hater": The Controversy and the Play*; Suzanne W. Hull, *Chaste, Silent, and Obedient: English Books for Women, 1475–1640*; Ruth Kelso, *Doctrine for the Lady of the Renaissance*; Chilton L. Powell, *English Domestic Relations, 1487–1653*; Eileen Power, *Medieval Women*; Katharine Rogers, *The Troublesome Helpmate: A History of Misogyny in Literature*; Lawrence Stone, *The Family, Sex, and Marriage in England, 1500–1800*; Francis L. Utley, *The Crooked Rib*; Louis B. Wright, *Middle-Class Culture in Elizabethan England*.

2. For a general background to Renaissance rhetoric, see Wilbur Samuel Howell, *Logic and Rhetoric in England, 1500–1700*; for the effect of antilogistic rhetoric on classical and Renaissance drama, Charles O. McDonald, *The Rhetoric of Tragedy: Form in Stuart Drama*, and Joel B. Altman, *The Tudor Play of Mind: Rhetorical Inquiry and the Development of Elizabethan Drama*; and for the effect of rhetorical training on the conduct of the *querelle des femmes*, M. A. Screech, *The Rabelasian Marriage*, 5–13.

3. The social, legal, and political background to dualism in the classical treatment of women is provided by Sarah B. Pomeroy in *Goddesses, Whores, Wives and Slaves: Women in Classical Antiquity*; studies of its medieval manifestations include Marina Warner, *Alone of All Her Sex: The Myth and the Cult of the Virgin Mary* on Mariolatry, and, for information on dualistic portrayals of women in medieval art, Henry Kraus, *The Living Theatre of Medieval Art*, 41–62. See also Marjorie M. Malvern, *Venus in Sackcloth: The Magdalen's Origins and Metamorphoses*, for a treatment of the radical dualism in the figure of Mary Magdalene.

4. An influential Stuart contribution to the genre of exemplary biographies came from Thomas Heywood, whose *Gunaikeion; or, Nine Books of Various History Concerning*

Women appeared in 1624. His *Exemplary Lives and Memorable Acts of Nine of the Most Worthy Women of the World* was published in 1640.

5. Key studies of the hierarchical philosophy of the Renaissance include Arthur O. Lovejoy, *The Great Chain of Being;* Theodore Spencer, *Shakespeare and the Nature of Man;* E. M. W. Tillyard, *The Elizabethan World Picture.* A good synopsis appears in Herschel C. Baker, *The Image of Man,* 223–40.

6. Virtually any entry in the literature of the "woman question" provides examples. For a particularly influential support of female superiority, see Henry Cornelius Agrippa von Nettesheim's *De Nobilitate et Praecellentia Foeminei Sexus* (1529), translated as *A Treatise of the Nobilitie and Excellencie of Womankynde* (London, 1542). Rosemary Masek lists some of the many Tudor and Stuart works based on Agrippa. The anonymous French work of the early fifteenth century entitled *Les quinze joyes de mariage,* which Thomas Dekker translated as *The Batchelors Banquet* (1603), ironically lays out the fifteen joys of marriage (the title parodies the fifteen joys of the Virgin Mary) that entrap the husband prey to his wife's lust, pride, covetousness, and desire for domination.

7. Raleigh, *The History of the World,* bk. 1, chap. 2, § 5, p. 126.

8. "I had listened to the truth of the Spirit's long discourse with bowed head, because I realized my error. Hearing him finish and fall silent, I raised my head and said somewhat tearfully, 'Blessed Spirit, you have showed me clearly the duties of one [of] my age and learning, and, especially, the baseness of that woman whom my mistaken judgment revered as noble, and had chosen for the lady of my mind, and also her habits, her defects, her marvelous virtues, and many other things; and by reproving me with words far sweeter than my sin deserved, you have shown me how much men naturally surpass women in nobility, and who I am in particular. These things, one by one and all together, have so completely reversed my opinion and changed my mind, that without any doubt at all, I now think the opposite of that I thought before'" (Boccaccio, *The Corbaccio,* 70–1).

9. Madeleine Doran, *Endeavors of Art,* 216–32, lays out the doctrine of decorum as it applied to the English theater.

10. The collection of articles entitled *Medieval Women* and edited by Derek Baker gives a sense of the richness, variety, and turmoil in the more extreme relations between the church and women in the Middle Ages. The articles' focus on remarkable women rulers, mystics, ascetics, religious administrators, and family heads shows both the range of possible attitudes toward women and the almost inevitable tendency of conservatives to fear women in positions of power.

11. Rosalie Colie, *Paradoxia Epidemica: The Renaissance Tradition of Paradox,* 53.

12. Thomas Laqueur, *Making Sex: Body and Gender from the Greeks to Freud,* gives detailed information about medical attitudes regarding sex differentiation and sexual behavior from classical, medieval and Renaissance sources. Robert Con Davis, *The Paternal Romance: Reading God-the-Father in Early Western Culture,* provides background in his discussion of Greek medical and philosophical attitudes towards women. Medical theory through the eighteenth century followed the traditional one-sex model of human reproductive anatomy that regarded male and female organs as analogous. In this model the penis was an extruded vagina, the vagina an inverted penis. Both women and men experienced sexual arousal and orgasm, and in fact, the argument from analogy assumed that female orgasm was necessary to conception, or at least to the production of healthy children. But a one-sex theory also had to account for the fact of sex differentiation

and, given the hierarchical bias and ignorance of the role of the ovaries, it produced a deficit model that located the defect in the female. Medical opinion from Aristotle generally held that (as the metaphor suggests) the male seed was the life-giving material of human reproduction. The womb was just a repository for the fetus or, at most, the supplier of material lacking the essential life force. The pathology model carried into humoral physiology and its attendant faculty psychology which categorized women as innately imbalanced rather than as subject to the full range of male possibilities (Baker, *Image of Man*, 275–92, surveys Renaissance physiology; Lawrence Babb, *The Elizabethan Malady: A Study of Melancholia in English Literature from 1580 to 1642*, provides an extended application). Female anatomy created this humoral imbalance, for medical opinion as far back as Hippocrates, influenced by the etymology of the word *hysteria*, held that the woman's uterus was a semiautonomous organ or even an autonomous animal that longed independently for generation, producing the humors that stimulate the passions. Women were the victims of this organ's (or animal's) insatiate lusts, for containment required extraordinary control, overindulgence was morally reprehensible and physically dangerous, yet deprivation could bring on the deathlike fits of the medical condition called hysteria. (Screech, *Rabelasian Marriage*, 87–95, surveys this opinion among classical and humanist medical authorities and its importance to the woman question.) Despite the pathology model, virtually no one questioned that woman's purpose in the human and divine scheme was reproductive. In fulfilling her reproductive function properly, woman might even aspire to a kind of general, if not individual, health and perfection. So Aquinas, forced to answer his own question why God can have created a creature "defective and misbegotten," replies in terms of her reproductive role: "On the other hand, in relation to the universal nature, woman is not misbegotten, but is included in nature's intention as ordered to the work of generation" (*Summa Theologiae*, 1:489).

13. The insistence of a St. Jerome or a St. Clement on the superiority of virginity over the married state was in part an argument from the notion that the maximally pure are those whose bodies retain as much as possible of their original state. Here is St. Jerome in a letter to the virgin Eustochium: "That you may understand that virginity is natural and that marriage came after the Fall, remember that what is born of wedlock is virgin flesh and that by its fruit it renders what in its parent root it has lost" (*Select Letters of St. Jerome*, letter 22, p. 93). How different the Protestant position was is exemplified by Milton's depiction of ideal marriage—and sexual attraction—before the Fall.

14. Among others, see Claire Cross, " 'Great Reasoners in Scripture': The Activities of Women Lollards, 1380–1530"; Keith V. Thomas, "Women and the Civil War Sects"; and Christopher Hill, *The World Turned Upside Down: Radical Ideas during the English Revolution*, 247–60.

15. See Stone's overview of the role of Protestantism in the strengthening of patriarchy (*The Family, Sex, and Marriage in England*, esp. 154–5).

16. John Foxe, *The Acts and Monuments of John Foxe*, 1:83–4.

17. In interpreting St. Paul, John Foxe is clearly thinking primarily of the sexual nature of males: "What order and rule St. Paul hath set for marriage in his epistle to the Corinthians it is manifest; where, as he preferreth single life, in such as have the gift of continence, before the married estate, so again, in such as have not the gift, he preferreth the coupled life before the other; willing every such one to have his wife, 'because of fornication' " (*Acts and Monuments*, 1:83).

18. Citations from *Don Quixote* are from Samuel Putnam's modern translation. The

first English translation was that of Thomas Shelton. Part 1 of Shelton's translation was published in London in 1612 (though probably translated in 1608) and part 2 in 1620.

CHAPTER FOUR

1. David M. Bevington, *From "Mankind" to Marlowe: Growth of Structure in the Popular Drama of Tudor England;* Bernard Spivack, *Shakespeare and the Allegory of Evil: The History of a Metaphor in Relation to His Major Villains;* and Thomas Stroup, *Microcosmos: The Shape of the Elizabethan Play,* all trace the relationship between testing patterns in the miracle and morality plays and the structures and themes of Tudor and Stuart drama.

2. V. A. Kolve argues (*The Play Called Corpus Christi,* esp. 146–51) that the entire Wakefield cycle is shaped around a theme of obedience or "maisterye" illuminated by the frequent comments on women's follies (in the *Second Shepherds' Play,* the *Judgement,* and presumably the lost *Fall of Man*) and worked out in the marital failures of Adam and Eve and of Noah and his wife.

3. Murray Roston's *Biblical Drama in England* describes the ways medieval and Renaissance biblical drama staged sacred subjects and the developments by which, under the influence of Protestant translations into the vernacular, all biblical material came to be regarded as sacred and thus unavailable for staging.

4. Unless otherwise specified, the dates for English Renaissance plays are as given in Samuel Schoenbaum's revision of Alfred Harbage's *Annals of English Drama, 975–1700.*

5. See Bevington, *From "Mankind" to Marlowe,* for an analysis of morality drama and its literal transformations.

6. Patient Griselda has attracted attention from folklorists, literary scholars, and Jungian mythographers. Various tale types have been advanced as the folkloric antecedents of the literary story that first appeared in the *Decameron.* D. D. Griffith, in *The Origin of the Griselda Story,* sees it as a variant of "The Monster Bridegroom" (best known to literature in Apuleius's story of Cupid and Psyche). William E. Bettridge and Francis L. Utley, in "New Light on the Origin of the Griselda Story," point out the flaws in Griffith's work and advance a related eastern Mediterranean tale, "The Patience of a Princess," as a more likely source for Boccaccio. Jan-Ojvind Swahn, in *The Tale of Cupid and Psyche,* gives background for both positions. J. Burke Severs, *The Literary Relationships of Chaucer's Clerkes Tale,* describes how the story made its way into English literature. Erich Neumann, *Amor and Psyche: The Psychic Development of the Feminine,* explores the testing patterns of the Cupid and Psyche tale as embedded in *The Golden Ass.*

7. The comparison to Job comes in the narrator's summation:

> Men speke of Job, and moost for his humblesse,
> As clerkes, whan hem list, konne wel endite,
> Namely of men, but as in soothfastnesse,
> Though clerkes preise wommen but a lite,
> Ther kan no man in humblesse hym acquite
> As womman kan, ne kan been half so trewe
> As wommen been, but it be falle of newe.
>
> (932–8)

I am using F. N. Robinson's *Works of Geoffrey Chaucer*, 2d ed., for all Chaucer citations except where noted.

8. In his prologue to *Ancient Scripts and Modern Experience on the English Stage, 1500–1700*, Bruce R. Smith overviews the competing ideas and cultural tensions accompanying the introduction of classical drama to Renaissance humanist education and thence to the English stage.

9. Scholars have argued for dates ranging from 1534 to 1554 for *Ralph Roister Doister*. I am persuaded by a dating of 1552, which precedes the publication of the third edition of Thomas Wilson's *Rule of Reason*, in which Roister Doister's letter is quoted. For a summary of the evidence on dating, see William L. Edgerton, *Nicholas Udall*, 89–94, the same author's "Date of *Roister Doister*," David Bevington's overview in *Tudor Drama and Politics: A Critical Approach to Topical Meaning*, 121, and Nicholas Udall, *Ralph Roister Doister*, introduction by Charles W. Whitworth, xxxii–xxxiii.

10. This estimate of its significance and antecedents appears with almost every mention of the play. See Frederick C. Boas, *An Introduction to Tudor Drama* (1933); Alan S. Downer, *The British Drama* (1950); Thomas Marc Parrott and Robert Hamilton Hall, *A Short View of Elizabethan Drama* (1958); F. P. Wilson, *The Elizabethan Drama, 1485–1585* (1969); Joel B. Altman, *The Tudor Play of Mind* (1978); Charles W. Whitworth, introduction to *Three Sixteenth-Century Comedies* (1984); Jill Levenson, "Comedy," in *The Cambridge Companion to English Renaissance Drama* (1990). Edgerton's *Nicholas Udall*, 94–101, reviews the play's Roman elements. For an overview of trends in twentieth-century scholarship and criticism, see Philip Dust and William D. Wolf, "Recent Studies in Early Tudor Drama: *Gorboduc, Ralph Roister Doister, Gammer Gurton's Needle* and *Cambises*." Dust and Wolf remark that "there is still much to be done with analysis of *Roister Doister*'s dramatic effectiveness" (112).

11. See Bevington, *From "Mankind" to Marlowe*, 33; Edgerton, "The Date of *Roister Doister*," 559; Edwin S. Miller, "Roister Doister's 'Funeralls' "; A. W. Plumstead, "Satirical Parody in *Roister Doister:* A Reinterpretation"; T. W. Baldwin and M. Channing Lithicum, "The Date of *Ralph Roister Doister*"; William Peery, "The Prayer for the Queen in *Roister Doister*." In *Tudor Drama and Politics*, Bevington emphasizes the dramatic and moral centrality of Custance and describes her confrontation with Roister Doister as "essentially a battle of the sexes, reminiscent of the division between female virtue and male vice in *Respublica*" (122). Edgerton represents the stock attitude: "The plot can be traced to the sub-plot of Terence's *Eunuchus*. In both plays the hero tries to win a woman's favor in her lover's absence; in both, he relies on the counsel of a mischievous parasite; in both, his actions reach the same height of absurdity in an unsuccessful attack on a woman's house; in both, there is a general reconciliation at the end" (*Nicholas Udall*, 95).

12. The struggle in Roman comedy is most often between two people for legal possession of a soulless, helpless third—usually a woman as sexual object, though sometimes a child or a slave. The winner generally employs elaborate trickery and the ability to coax or bully an authority figure, in most cases a father, into acquiescence. Terence's *Eunuchus* pits the braggart soldier Thraso against the young man Phaedria for the favors of Thais the courtesan. Phaedria (or mainly his slave, Parmenio) makes a fool of Thraso (whose parasite, Gnatho, simplifies the operation by encouraging his dupe's posturing) in the course of protecting Thais's interest in the slave Pamphila. Since bamboozling Thraso helps establish that Pamphila is really freeborn and can be married to Phaedria's brother, who in the meantime has raped her, the grateful

father approves Phaedria's liaison with Thais. But since keeping Thais will cost money, Gnatho convinces Phaedria to allow Thraso continued access to the courtesan. The braggart's generosity will support them all, while his loutishness assures that he is no rival for Thais's heart.

13. Since Udall knew Chaucer (Arthur R. Moon, "Two References to Chaucer Made by Nicholas Udall," 426–7), I am assuming his familiarity with the Man of Law's Tale. Indisputably he knew some version of the story of Constance (in Chaucer's spelling Custance), for whom he named his protagonist. He does not tell the traditional Constance story any more than he tells the traditional Susanna story. But in addition to the heroine's name that leads the audience to expect fortitude and Christian victory, the Constance story provides other motifs. When Chaucer's Custance is falsely accused of murder, she, like Udall's Custance, prays for divine aid, citing the example of Susanna (Man of Law's Tale, ll. 639–44). Faced with rape aboard her boat, Chaucer's Custance fights back and in the struggle knocks her attacker overboard to his death. To the question how this woman found the strength to defend herself, the narrator gives the received answer: like David confronting Goliath and Judith Holofernes, Custance received strength from God. Even "wayke" women can attain moral victory by physical means (ll. 932–45).

14. In the sixteenth century the Apocrypha was mined for literary and homiletic examples of upright and valiant heroes supported by divine grace. See Marvin T. Herrick, "Susanna and the Elders in Sixteenth-Century Drama," for a discussion of English and Continental Susanna plays.

15. "Playing with both hands" reaches its apotheosis in the vice Ambidexter in *Cambises.* See Spivack, *Shakespeare and the Allegory of Evil,* 286–91, and A. P. Rossiter, *English Drama from Early Times to the Elizabethans: Its Background, Origins and Development,* 142–3. The vice Ill Report in Thomas Garter's *The Most Virtuous and Godly Susanna* (1569) helps stone the Elders whose lascivious approaches he encouraged.

16. See George Buchanan, *Tragedies,* introduction by P. Sharratt, 3–4, for the probable dating of *Jephthes sive votum* and Buchanan's three other plays (*Baptistes sive calumnia* and Latin translations of Euripides' *Hecuba* and *Alcestis*); *Jephthes* was first published in Paris in 1554. For background about Christopherson's *Jephthah,* see Wilbur O. Sypherd's introduction to the English translation.

17. In his dedicatory epistle to Lord Parr, Christopherson tells how he chose his plot: "since, from the very beginning of my studies, I had been devoted to Greek literature, I thought it worth while to take some plot from Sacred Scripture and to treat it at somewhat greater length and in Greek. . . . Now, when I read diligently the stories of the Old Testament, I found none more suited to this purpose than the story of Jephthah in Judges XI." His dedication to Bishop Tunstall explains his rationale: "This [story], so at least I thought, offered appropriate material for tragedy, for, as I examined the eloquent *Iphigenia* of Euripides, I saw clearly that the heroines were not dissimilar" (Sypherd, introduction to *Jephthah,* 10).

18. Erasmus's Latin version was published in Paris in 1506, by the Venetian printer Aldus Manutius in 1507, and in eighteen European editions by 1540; see Sharratt, introduction to Buchanan, *Tragedies,* 6–7. Sypherd's introduction to Christopherson, *Jephthah* (1–2), discusses the medieval and Renaissance popularity of the Jephthah story and its relation to the reception of Erasmus's *Iphigenia.* Margaret M. Phillips' *Erasmus and the Northern Renaissance* discusses Erasmus's connection with Aldus Manutius (57).

The availability of Erasmus's translation probably accounts for the play's use as a school exercise by Lady Jane Lumley, who appears to have made her still extant English version (c. 1558) from the combined resources of the Greek original and Erasmus's Latin (T. W. Baldwin, *William Shakspere's Small Latine & Lesse Greeke*, 1:261).

19. The edition of Buchanan's *Tragedies* I use gives both the Latin text and an English prose translation by P. G. Walsh. Line numbers refer to the Latin text and page numbers to the English.

20. Sharratt's introduction to Buchanan's tragedies briefly describes Buchanan's influence on the French and Scottish Renaissance and his career as a scholar and teacher in Paris, Bordeaux, and Coimbra before he settled in his native Scotland and became the most important intellectual influence on James VI of Scotland, later James I of England. During his years at the *collège* in Bordeaux (1540–43) one of Buchanan's fellow teachers was the French humanist Marc-Antoine Muret; his most famous pupil was Michel de Montaigne. Though Buchanan is not in the direct line of English vernacular drama, his Latin plays influenced the development of sixteenth-century British drama not just by their own power and the vigor of their Latin, but, in the case of his translations, for their role in familiarizing Europe with Euripides. Samuel Johnson consistently praised Buchanan as a Latinist and "a great poetical genius" (James Boswell, *Life of Johnson*, 2:96; see also 1:460, 4:185, and 5:398).

21. Also not possible in the Renaissance is the linguistically exacting reading of the story of Jephthah's daughter by Phyllis Trible in *Texts of Terror: Literary-Feminist Readings of Biblical Narratives*. Situating it in the context of other Old Testament tales of terror directed at women—Hagar, Tamar, the unnamed concubine of Judges 19—Trible unpacks the particulars of the tale of a courageous daughter whose private sacrifice exalts the public stature of a faithless father (107–8).

22. None of Radcliffe's plays has survived, but his Griselda play was probably written between 1546 and 1556 (Roston, *Biblical Drama*, 67).

23. Stone (*The Family, Sex, and Marriage*) argues that "under pressure from the state and from Protestant moral theology" (216) increasing patriarchal control became one of the salient characteristics of the sixteenth- and seventeenth-century middle- and upper-class English family.

24. Dekker's editor Fredson Bowers says, "For authorship, there is common agreement that the main plot is Dekker's; otherwise, Haughton and Chettle are usually assigned varying portions of the two underplots" (*The Dramatic Works of Thomas Dekker*, 1:211).

25. My text of *A Yorkshire Tragedy*, ed. A. C. Cawley and Barry Gaines, provides information on the Calverley murders, including the text of the pamphlet that was the play's main source, and gives the rationale for a date of 1605. It also discusses the issue of authorship, including the reasons for its sometime ascription to Shakespeare and recent arguments in favor of Middleton.

26. My source for Webster's text of *Appius and Virginia* and its probable date is F. L. Lucas, *The Complete Works of John Webster*, vol. 3. Lucas argues (3:131) that Webster took the bulk of his material from Dionysus of Halicarnassus's *Roman Antiquities* (an edition with Latin translation had been published in 1586), but probably also used Philemon Holland's 1600 translation of Livy. Giovanni Fiorentino's *Il pecorone* (published 1558 but written several decades earlier), a paraphrase combining Livy's and Dionysus's versions of the story, may also have been a source. For evidence of Webster's chief authorship of the play and his probable collaboration with Heywood, see Lucas, *Works of John*

Webster, 3:134–45. For the uses of Livy in the Tudor grammar school curriculum, see Baldwin, *William Shakspere's Small Latine,* esp. 2:564–68, 573–4.

27. In "Chaucer and the Sacrifice of Isaac," Anne Lancashire describes how motifs and patterns from the Abraham and Isaac story are used in Chaucer's and R. B.'s versions of the tale of Appius and Virginia to increase the emphasis on parent/child relationships and on the child as sacrificial victim.

28. For descriptions and evidence of the intensification of patriarchy in the English Renaissance, see Stone, *The Family, Sex, and Marriage;* Carl Bridenbaugh, *Vexed and Troubled Englishmen, 1590–1642;* three works by Christopher Hill, *The Century of Revolution, 1603–1714; Society and Puritanism in Pre-Revolutionary England;* and *The World Turned Upside Down;* Gordon J. Schochet, *Patriarchalism in Political Thought: The Authoritarian Family and Political Speculation and Attitudes Especially in Seventeenth-Century England;* and John W. Gough, *The Social Contract,* 2d ed. Susan Amussen, *An Ordered Society: Gender and Class in Early Modern England,* examines the power structures and the workings of the patriarchal analogy in family and village life in seventeenth-century Norfolk. For the analogy's use in Restoration drama, see Susan Staves, *Players' Scepters: Fictions of Authority in the Restoration,* chap. 3.

29. Hill, *Society and Puritanism,* esp. 443–8.

30. Ibid., 448.

31. In Plato's *Crito,* Socrates accepts his death sentence in part on the grounds of the analogy between the citizen's duty to the state and the child's to the parents. In *The Politics* Aristotle, whose justification of social hierarchy by natural hierarchy lies prominently behind medieval and Renaissance ideas of order, consistently equates children, women, and slaves as natural subjects. Examples of the patriarchal analogy abound in both Old and New Testaments. The following commonly evoked texts show some of the most obvious analogical progressions: "As a man chasteneth his son, so the Lord thy God chasteneth thee." Deut. 8:5; "For the husband is head of the wife, even as Christ is the head of the church: and he is the saviour of the body. Therefore, as the church is subject unto Christ, so let the wives be to their own husbands in everything." Eph. 5:23–4; "But I would have you know, that the head of every man is Christ; and the head of the woman is the man; and the head of Christ is God." 1 Cor. 2:3. David L. Balch's *Let Wives Be Submissive: The Domestic Code in 1 Peter* surveys the Greco-Roman topos Concerning Household Management with its three analogical pairs—father/child, husband/wife, and master/servant—and the relation of this topos to New Testament texts on domestic relations.

32. Elaine H. Pagels, *The Gnostic Gospels,* writes on the relationships among matriarchal theology, cultural feminism, and the Gnostic strain in early Christianity.

33. The pervasiveness and power of the patriarchal analogy is brought home by the diversity of circumstances under which it was used. King Edward's Catechism, interpreting the Fifth Commandment, gave it classic expression: in addition to obliging children to "love, hear, and reverence" their biological parents, the commandment "bindeth us also most humbly and with most natural affection to obey the magistrate: to reverence the ministers of the church, our schoolmasters, with all our elders and betters" (cited by Schochet, *Patriarchalism,* 79–80). For the Anglican Richard Hooker, fathers naturally had supreme power in their families, "for which cause we see throughout the world even from the foundation thereof, all men have ever been taken as lords and lawful kings in their own houses" (*Of the Laws of Ecclesiastical Polity,* 1:191). The Puritan William Perkins also saw patriarchy as based in nature: "A family is a natural

and simple society of certain persons having mutual relation one to another under the private government of one" (*Christian Oeconomie* [1609]; cited in Bridenbaugh, *Vexed and Troubled Englishmen*, 29). Insubordination in one relationship implied insubordination in all. In 1641 Sir Thomas Aston understood that for the threatened patriarch "true liberty" was knowing "by a certain law that our wives, our children, our servants, our goods are our own" (*A Remonstrance against Presbytery* [1641]; cited in Hill, *The World Turned Upside Down*, 281). During his sojourn in New England, Hugh Peters accused Anne Hutchinson of trying through her spiritual leadership to step out of all her places: "You have rather been a husband than a wife, and a preacher than a hearer; and a magistrate than a subject" (Thomas, "Women and the Civil War Sects," 49). The world-turned-upside-down motif of popular broadsheets depicted the inversions of wife over husband, servant over master, son over father, pupil over teacher, as equivalents, with the female-male inversion the most prominent and dangerous (David Kunzle, "World Turned Upside Down: The Iconography of a European Broadsheet Type," esp. 42–3). Legal relationships were understood to be controlled or at least explained by the patriarchal analogy. From the fourteenth to the nineteenth centuries English law categorized as petty treason the killing of a husband by his wife, a master by his servant, or a prelate by his cleric. The term "treason" underlined the analogy to the rebellious act of a subject against a sovereign (Natalie Davis, "Women on Top: Symbolic Sexual Inversion and Political Disorder in Early Modern Europe," 150).

34. *The Political Works of James I*, 272; Robert Sanderson, *XXXV Sermons* (1681; cited in Hill, *Society and Puritanism*, 461, 459); Justus Lipsius, *Six Books of Politics or Civil Doctrine*; the Star Chamber debate (cited in Hill, *Century of Revolution*, 64); Sir Henry Shirley is quoted by Lawrence Stone, *The Crisis of the Aristocracy, 1558–1648*, 265.

35. Sir Robert Filmer, *Patriarcha and Other Political Works*.

36. James Daly, *Sir Robert Filmer and English Political Thought*, argues that Filmer's view is idiosyncratic and unrepresentative of most patriarchalist arguments.

37. See Schochet, *Patriarchialism*, for a survey of patriarchalism from Plato to Locke, with particular attention to Filmer and his heirs and opponents.

38. I have not cited specific passages from *Patriarcha* for these two issues as examples of debate because Filmer's strength of argument lies in their deployment throughout the whole work, which is short. See Peter Laslett's introduction to *Patriarcha*, specifically 11–15, for an overview of Filmer's opinions on the biblically based origins of human society.

39. In his chapter "Thomas Hobbes on the Family and the State of Nature," Schochet examines the "familial aspect" of Hobbes's thought in *Leviathan*, *De Cive*, and other works, and shows the various ways Hobbes uses patriarchal political theories (*Patriarchalism*, 225–43).

40. John Locke, *Two Treatises of Government*, 163, 167, 198, 202–4, 328–9, 336–7. See also the editor's introduction, esp. 34–6.

41. Ernst H. Kantorowicz, *The King's Two Bodies: A Study in Mediaeval Political Theology*, cites Aquinas's gloss on Aristotle, *Politics* 1259a (Thomas Aquinas, *In libros Politicorum Aristotelis expositio*, 1, lect. x, § 152), 217.

42. John Knox, *First Blast of the Trumpet against the Monstrous Regiment of Women*, Geneva, 1588.

43. Schochet, *Patriarchialism*, 229–33.

44. Michael McKeon, "Historicizing Patriarchy: The Emergence of Gender Dif-

ference in England, 1660–1760," explores the contradictions inherent in women's roles and the "differential interaction" of sex-based and class-based hierarchies during the shift to modern systems of gender and class.

CHAPTER FIVE

1. M. Joan Sargeaunt, *John Ford*, 149–52, mentions connections with Griselda character types and notes Ford's innovation in placing the story of a maritally level-headed husband in an Italian setting.

2. Juliet S. McMaster, "Love, Lust, and Sham: Structural Pattern in the Plays of John Ford," argues for the consistency of Ford's structuring of subplots. In *The Lady's Trial* the stories of Levidolche and Amoretta have thematic parallels with Spinella's, including those of sexual appropriateness or homecoming and of the purging of humors.

3. Citations of *The Lady's Trial* are adapted from the edition of Henry de Vocht, *John Ford's Dramatic Works*, which follows the act divisions of the 1639 edition and provides consecutive line numbers. I have supplied scene divisions and identified citations by both act/scene numbers and Vocht's line numbers, which are set off by semicolons.

4. I read "her breach of truth" to mean "the breach of truth against her" and "her trespass" to mean "the trespass against her." The usage is an example of the rhetorical scheme of exchange called *permutatio* or *enallage*. Richard Sherry, *A Treatise of Schemes and Tropes* (1550), calls this specific version *antiptosis* or *casus pro casu*, the exchanging of one grammatical case for another (31–2). See Lee A. Sonnino, *A Handbook to Sixteenth Century Rhetoric*, 140–1, for ways other Renaissance rhetoricians describe the figure. Nothing in this speech or elsewhere in the play suggests that Auria here assumes Spinella guilty. His "justice" would have been directed solely against Adurni.

5. John Florio's Italian-English dictionary *A World of Words* (1598) provides the obvious gloss, "golden" or "shining." Nothing so obvious is available for Adurni, though it is tempting to turn to Florio's definition of the durian: "Durione—a fruit in Malacca, of that excellency that it exceedeth all other fruits whatsoever in sweetnesse of taste . . . some are of the opinion that this was the apple that Eve tempted Adam to disobedience with, it is so delectable in taste" (Florio, *Queen Anna's New World of Words*, 1611 [a revised and augmented version of the 1598 dictionary]).

6. "I'm too blame sure": According to the *Oxford English Dictionary* (hereafter OED), s.v. "blame," 6, the dative infinitive "to blame," a common predicate after "be," was commonly misunderstood in the sixteenth and seventeenth centuries, with "to" misconstrued as "too" and "blame" taken as an adjective meaning blameworthy, culpable. Ford's phrase thus collapses two different modern constructions: "I am to blame," as in "worthy to be blamed" and "I am too blameworthy," as in "excessively guilty." I have left this ambiguity.

7. Mark Stavig, *John Ford and the Traditional Moral Order*, emphasizes the public necessity of the trial: "By going through with a formal trial scene, [Auria] is able to prove for the record both that he has not glossed over a slight to his honor and that Spinella and her family can defend themselves nobly and convincingly" (87).

8. In the 1730s George Frideric Handel composed several operas based on stories from *Orlando Furioso*. Now considered one of Handel's finest both musically and on the basis of its strong libretto by Antonio Salvi, *Ariodante* opened at the Theatre Royal in Covent Garden in January 1734. The Italian text with English translation was published

concurrently for the benefit of the theatergoing audiences as well as for readers. (It is available in facsimile in *The Librettos of Handel's Operas: A Collection of Seventy-One Librettos Documenting Handel's Operatic Career*, vol. 7.) Jonathan Keates, *Handel: The Man and His Music*, comments on Salvi's own comments about the liberties he took with Ariosto, blackening Polinesso and whitening Dalinda by making her "somewhat more decent in manner" (183). The biggest change is the elimination of the frame character Rinaldo, so that Ariodante rescues Dalinda, learns the truth about Ginevra's innocence, and defends her honor by refusing to fight his brother and by revealing the villain's machinations. Lurcanio, who has killed Polinesso, receives Dalinda's hand, and the opera ends with exquisite duets.

9. With the exception of the one Harington quotation noted, I am using Guido Waldman's prose translation for the virtues he describes as most characteristic of Ariosto: its narrative vigor and its stylistic nuance and flair (xv–xvi).

10. John Harington, *Orlando Furioso in English Heroical Verse* (1591). Harington was proud of this beautifully printed book, supplying organizational and interpretive aids and commenting on the quality, clarity and rarity of the brass plates used for the illustrations. Each canto has its plate in which, as he notes, one who has read the canto can return to read it again in visual form.

11. Bk. 2, canto 4. I have retained the original spelling, deliberate archaism being part of Spenser's literary style.

12. Peter Ure, "Cult and Initiates in Ford's *Love's Sacrifice*," charts Bianca's and Fernando's relationship in terms of Platonic conventions. Other work on Platonism in Ford's characters includes Juliet Sutton's "Platonic Love in Ford's *The Fancies, Chaste and Noble*" and George F. Sensabaugh's *The Tragic Muse of John Ford*. I agree essentially with Mark Stavig, *John Ford*, who regards the passion of Bianca and Fernando as a perversion of genuine Platonism (see his chapter on *Love's Sacrifice*, esp. 131–2).

13. R. J. Kaufmann, "Ford's Tragic Perspective," discusses an aspect of the schism when, comparing the play to *Othello*, he faults Ford for failing to place Caraffa at its center, thereby denying him an "interior function" (364), and for centering the play "to one side of the issues that characterize a normal adultery-revenge play" (365). For a fuller reading of the structural difficulties of *Love's Sacrifice*, see my article entitled "Role-Splitting and Reintegration: The Tested Woman Plot in Ford," from which portions of this chapter are adapted.

14. A kneeling, clandestine ceremony carries the same emotional weight in *The Duchess of Malfi* and (as reinforcement of a previous vow) in *The Broken Heart*. In Chapman's *The Gentleman Usher*, more elaborate clandestine vows are designed to forestall a forced marriage.

15. Incest cannot have been vastly more common in the English Renaissance than at other times and places. The frequency of the motif doubtless has less to do with contemporary morals than with its power and economy as a dramaturgical tool. See my article entitled "The Structural Uses of Incest in English Renaissance Drama."

16. These lines are ambiguous as well as allusive, as is much of Penthea's mad speech. Not only are they loaded with ill-referenced pronouns, but Penthea could conceivably be addressing any of the men present—Bassanes, Ithocles, Armostes her uncle. But the center of the sentence is clear: "our hands" are Penthea's and Orgilus's; "my father, he" is the dead Thrasus, who promised the two to each other. I take it that after her previous lines, which are evidently addressed to Bassanes, Penthea turns to address Ithocles, who took the place of the father to make the illicit but binding ceremony

with Bassanes, and who, if he had carried out her father's promises, would have been her father indeed. The next lines couple the two addressees together as the sources of her disease: "Oh, my wracked honour, ruined by those tyrants, / A cruel brother and a desperate dotage!" (144–5).

CHAPTER SIX

1. The authorship of *The Revenger's Tragedy* has been in question for decades, the seventeenth-century attribution to Cyril Tourneur probably stemming from the similarity of the title to his *Atheist's Tragedy*. Most recent critics seem persuaded that the work is by Thomas Middleton. My text citations are from Brian Gibbons's edition, which retains the traditional authorial attribution to Tourneur.

2. Citations are from *The Second Maiden's Tragedy*, ed. Anne Lancashire. This anonymous play is generally ascribed to Middleton partly on the basis of its similarity to *The Revenger's Tragedy*, raising the problem of circular argument. Lancashire deals evenhandedly with the evidence about authorship in her introduction (15–23).

3. In my edition of Robert Davenport's *The City Night-Cap*, edited by Willis J. Monie, lines are numbered consecutively throughout the play. I have indicated this practice with a semicolon.

4. Cyrus Hoy, *The Hyacinth Room: An Investigation into the Nature of Comedy, Tragedy, and Tragicomedy*, begins with a consideration of the generic possibilities of the "Widow of Ephesus" story.

5. My judgment of the brilliance of Chapman's final scene goes against the critical grain. In her introduction to *The Widow's Tears*, Ethel M. Smeak summarizes: "The very last action of the play—the scene of the imbecile Governor and the resolution—has been condemned by all hands" (xxii), and she goes on to quote critics from Swinburne to T. M. Parrott. Smeak to my mind rightly argues that, by not giving judicial, intellectual, or moral authority to the Governor, Chapman's ending maintains the play's satiric edge and throws the burden of judgment on characters and audience. Another critic to find value in the ending and understand how much the play is based on the rivalry between the brothers is Henry Weidner ("Homer and the Fallen World: Focus of Satire in George Chapman's *The Widow's Tears*"), who sees Tharsalio as a Machiavellian malcontent and lord of misrule and the expression of everything Chapman denounces. I find Chapman less invested in approval or disapproval of his characters than in a demonstration of the moral distinctions his sophisticated plot combination allows. "Knowing," in all its meanings and permutations, is the controlling theme of the play.

CHAPTER SEVEN

1. *The Works of Sir William Davenant*, London, 1673; I have added scene divisions and line numbers to the folio's acts.

2. Kantorowicz, *The King's Two Bodies*, 497. He is discussing Francis Bacon's "precepts of remembrance" concerning kings.

3. Maynard Mack, Jr., *Killing the King: Three Studies in Shakespeare's Tragic Structure*, explores how this incompatibility is dramatically exploited in *Richard II*, *Hamlet*, and *Macbeth*.

4. In addition to Mack, *Killing the King*, see Jonathan Goldberg, *James I and the Politics of Literature*.

5. Having reminded his son Prince Henry of the sovereign's double obligation to God—"first, for that he made you a man; and next, for that he made you a little GOD to sit on his throne, and rule over other men," James extends the metaphor of the two bodies to discuss that obligation: "But as you are clothed with two callings, so must ye be alike careful for the discharge of them both" (*The Political Works of James I*, 12, 18).

6. Kantorowicz's chapter "Shakespeare: King Richard II" in *The King's Two Bodies* discusses the dramatization of the metaphor in the person of Richard, whose prison meditation—"Thus play I in one person many people" (5.5.31)—summarizes his plight.

7. Peter Saccio, *The Court Comedies of John Lyly: A Study in Allegorical Dramaturgy*. Saccio argues both what Lyly's play is and what it is not. He demonstrates that it is a drama of situation rather than story, that it is lucidly intellectual, and that its nodes are connected in an elaborate network of ideas. I go a step further, arguing that *Campaspe* is able to spend its time on situation and not story because the tested woman plot provides a recognizable, potent structure.

8. The anonymous author or authors, probably Shakespeare in at least the king/countess action, followed the accounts of Edward's life in Froissart and Painter; hence the progression of events. The thematic emphasis on contracts in their various forms is, however, the author's invention. My edition is *The Raigne of King Edward the Third*, ed. Fred Lapides. Act/scene indications are editorial, and line numbers are consecutive; hence my use of semicolons. Eric Sams's *Shakespeare's Edward III* presses the argument for Shakespeare's single authorship, surveys the evidence (largely based on language patterns), and includes the play's text with modern spelling and punctuation.

9. The supposed titillations of supposed incest have narrowed criticism of *A King and No King* to an unproductive degree. Robert K. Turner, Jr., surveys the classic twentieth-century criticism of the play, which tended to focus on moral themes and purposes (*A King and No King*, xv–xviii). Eugene M. Waith, *The Pattern of Tragicomedy in Beaumont and Fletcher*, countered this emphasis with attention to Beaumont and Fletcher's dramatic stylization and use of rhetorical forms. Arthur Mizener, "The High Design of *A King and No King*," emphasized the play's theatrical virtuosity. More recently, Lee Bliss's *Francis Beaumont*, which surveys the play's Hellenistic and Renaissance sources, reads *A King and No King* (the last of the Beaumont and Fletcher collaborations) as moving away from the tragic potential of *Philaster* and *A Maid's Tragedy* by means of a "frustration of affective engagement" (111) that largely detaches us from the dramatic action. In *The Plays of Beaumont and Fletcher: Sexual Themes and Dramatic Representation*, Sandra Clark, whose opening chapter recaps the history of Beaumont and Fletcher's reception and reputation as related to both political and sexual themes, briefly discusses *A King and No King* as "a contribution to the debate on the politics of absolutism." Clark sees the play as making a "serious examination of the king's relation to law through his relation to desire" (120). My article entitled "Structural Uses of Incest" makes a more detailed case for incest as a genre-linked dramaturgical device.

10. Jonas A. Barish's stimulating article "*Perkin Warbeck* as Anti-History" argues that the play is indeed about who ought to be king.

11. The commendatory poems suggest that Ford's contemporaries were struck by this kingly manner, as Ralph Eure argues in "justify[ing] . . . the glorious Perkin, and thy poet's art, / Equal with his in playing the king's part" (*Perkin Warbeck*, 5).

12. Jonas Barish, "Anti-History," 157–63, comments on some of those changes.

13. In "John Ford," T. S. Eliot, who admired *Perkin Warbeck* as the best chronicle play outside Shakespeare as well as the best of Ford's work, comments on how difficult

it is for the playwright to make Katherine such an exemplar of constancy. On the contrary: given the presentation of the preternaturally faithful and constant woman over two thousand years of literary history, it is the easiest move the playwright could have made. What is remarkable is the persistence and overtness with which Ford lays out the political analogies.

14. As Warbeck seeks the apotheosis of martyrdom, his language becomes increasingly Christological. Announcing "How constantly my resolution suffer'd / A martyrdom of majesty" (5.3.74–5), he pretends to a victory over death not merely through historical fame, but by analogy to the martyrdom and eternal life of Christ. As he exhorts his followers, his language sounds the note of the Protestant martyr: "I read / A triumph over tyranny upon / Their several foreheads.—Faint not in the moment / Of victory!" (5.3.187–90). Their deaths fulfill the divine will—"Heaven be obey'd" (195)—and promise to bring them a kind of eternal life: "Be men of spirit! / Spurn coward passion! So illustrious mention / Shall blaze our names, and style us kings o'er death" (5.3.205–7). The whole final scene has a flavor of the abused man/god as Warbeck turns the taunts of his tormenters, says good-bye to his wife and her family, and exhorts his followers to steadfastness. Ford even capitalizes on a morality motif in which a virtuous figure preaches from the stocks, as in the early sixteenth-century morality play *Hickscorner* (mentioned in Spivack, *Shakespeare and the Allegory of Evil*, 157) and in *King Lear*. Warbeck's death is thus enriched by the Christological analogy that any king may use, but a martyr may use most poignantly.

CHAPTER EIGHT

1. Paul Ricoeur, *The Rule of Metaphor*, 11.

2. Critics agree that most of *The Changeling*'s main plot is by Middleton and that the entire subplot is William Rowley's. Together *The Changeling*, *A Game at Chess*, and *Women Beware Women* show Middleton's skill with the tested woman plot, a skill honed through its earlier uses in city comedy, chronicle play, and tragedy (assuming his authorship of *The Second Maiden's Tragedy* and *The Revenger's Tragedy*).

3. J. W. Harper, introduction to *A Game at Chess*, xii–xv.

4. The Ciceronian description of deliberative persuasion identifies prudence as one of the four divisions of honesty, the virtue of which the White Queen's Pawn should be the exemplar. In his Ciceronian *Art of Rhetoric* (1553), Thomas Wilson's definition explicitly interconnects the places of prudence to show how its operations educate and protect innocence: "the memory calleth to account those things, that were done heretofore, and by a former remembrance, getteth an after wit, and learneth to avoid deceit" (46).

5. N. W. Bawcutt's introduction to *The Changeling* provides a thorough overview of the question of authorial attribution.

6. The extended word-linking is akin to a typically Rowleyan form of punning that D. M. Robb calls "cue-catching" ("The Canon of William Rowley's Plays," 129). For instance,

ALIBIUS   I am old, Lollio.
LOLLIO   No, sir, 'tis I am old Lollio.
                       (1.2.19–20)

Middleton's patterns differ from Rowley's puns by developing a systematic psychological point; they make part of a rhetorical matrix in the play that is largely but by no means exclusively stylistic and is based on the theme of change. My article entitled "The Rhetoric of Change in *The Changeling*" deals with these patterns.

7. My source for the text and provenance of the *Soliloquies* is Gerard Watson's edition. Augustine's description of his work is from the *Retractationes* 1.4.

8. Samuel Richardson, *Pamela or, Virtue Rewarded*, ed. T. C. Duncan Eaves and Ben D. Kimpel, 217; based on Richardson's first edition of 1740.

CHAPTER NINE

1. Michel Beaujour, "Rhetoric and Literature," gives a theoretical and historical overview of this European shift away from rhetoric and toward expressive literature.

2. Robert D. Hume, *Henry Fielding and the London Theatre, 1728–1737*, details Fielding's immense entrepreneurial and dramaturgical talent. His career was sufficiently threatening to the Walpole government to provoke the licensing act of 1737 that closed his theater and drove him into novel writing.

3. Fanny Burney, *The Diary of Fanny Burney*, 24–8. I have borrowed the term "playbook scene" for this format shift from Mark Kinkead-Weekes, *Samuel Richardson: Dramatic Novelist*.

4. Mary Edmond, *Rare Sir William Davenant: Poet Laureate, Playwright, Civil War General, Restoration Theatre Manager*, says of Davenant: "His importance as a champion of continuity can hardly be over-estimated" (140). One form this influence took was his professional friendship and collaboration with John Dryden, with whom he adapted *The Tempest* (1667) and whom "he first taught," according to Dryden, "to admire" Shakespeare (Edmond, *Davenant*, 199–200). James A. Winn, *John Dryden and His World*, discusses Davenant's stylistic influence on Dryden (72–8).

5. See Malcolm Goldstein's introduction to *The Fair Penitent*, xiv–xvi, on Rowe's relation to his source.

6. "The Rapin Preface," in *The Critical Works of Thomas Rymer*, 2.

7. Rosalie Colie, *The Resources of Kind: Genre Theory in the Renaissance*, surveys the importance of genre and the stimulating place of mixed genres.

8. John Vanbrugh's *Relapse*, ed. Curt Zimansky, prints as blank verse some scenes in which the language is really a looping prose, but it is hard to determine whether this is a printer's decision, an indication of the vitiated state of the English dramatic blank verse line, an additional weapon in Vanbrugh's satire on the convention of moral reform, or a reflection of his poor ear for meter. In his introduction to *The Complete Works of Sir John Vanbrugh*, Bonamy Dobree takes the no-ear-for-meter position (xxv). Zimansky's introduction to *The Relapse* (xvii–xviii) discusses Vanbrugh's style briefly but inconclusively.

9. Though the concept of just deserts is an old one, Rymer's "poetical justice" is his own coinage. Used first in his essay "The Tragedies of the Last Age" (1677), it rapidly became the accepted term. In the postscript to *Clarissa*, Richardson uses this terminology in his argument about the novel's ending: "Nor can it be deemed impertinent to touch upon this subject at the conclusion of a work which is designed to inculcate upon the human mind, under the guise of an amusement, the great lessons of Christianity, in an age *like the present;* which seems to expect from the poets and dramatic writers (that is to say, from the authors of works of invention) that they should make it one of their principal rules, to propagate another sort of dispensation, under the name

of *poetical justice*, than that with which God by Revelation teaches us he has thought fit to exercise mankind" (*Clarissa*, ed. Angus Ross,1495).

10. Dryden's Crites, the interlocutor who represents the neoclassical position derived by French critics from Aristotle's *Poetics* and Horace's *Art of Poetry*, gives a judicious presentation of the doctrine of the unities that is conspicuous for its reasoned justification of principles and its fudging of specifics ("An Essay of Dramatic Poesy," in *The Works of John Dryden*, 17:17–20).

11. Thomas Sprat, *Observations on M. de Sorbière's Voyage into England* (1665). Earl Miner calls Sprat's work the first piece of Restoration literary criticism (commentary on "An Essay of Dramatic Poesy," *The Works of John Dryden*, 17:345). The trope of *theatrum mundi*, which lies at the root of serious defenses of the stage in a Christian culture, had been elaborated by Thomas Heywood in the preface to *An Apology for Actors* (1612). "The world's a theater, the earth a stage, / Which god and nature doth with actors fill," Heywood begins, and after describing the cast of characters from king to clown, from chaste lady to courtesan, from gentlemen to shepherds and seamen, and the "continual actions" of good and ill in which they spend their days, he draws his conclusion against those who condemn it: "He that denies then theaters should be, / He may as well deny a world to me" (introductory material to *Edward IV, Parts I and II*, in *The Dramatic Works of Thomas Heywood*, vol. 1).

12. *The Works of John Dryden*, 11:205–6.

13. With André Dacier's recognition that the desirable reinstitution of the chorus as a requirement in tragedy would make all locations public, since a chorus cannot accompany a king into his private chambers, we have the admission that a king is not to be portrayed as a private man. Dacier's translation and commentary on Aristotle's *Poetics* was published in 1692. Rymer leans heavily on it in *A Short View of Tragedy* (1692). Rymer's editor, Curt Zimansky, summarizes Dacier's point: "Since tragedy represents a public action it is not possible for it to pass without many people observing it, whose fortunes are also concerned, and therefore the chorus is necessary for verisimilitude. It has been wanting in French tragedy, where much happens in the private apartments of kings which the chorus cannot enter. But since the spectators can no more come into such a place than the chorus can, the place should be changed and the chorus reintroduced. In that way tragedy will again be restored to its first luster" (*Critical Works of Thomas Rymer*, 235).

14. Lamb notes, "The whole is a passing pageant, where we should sit as unconcerned at the issues, for life or death as at a battle of the frogs and mice" (Charles Lamb, "On the Artificial Comedy of the Last Century," *Elia* (1823), in *The Works of Charles and Mary Lamb*, 2:144).

15. Dryden's *examen* of *The Silent Woman* in "An Essay of Dramatic Poesy" is the first example of extended critical analysis in English, a technique adopted from Pierre Corneille. See Miner commentary, *Works of John Dryden*, 17:339.

16. John Fletcher and Francis Beaumont wrote *Philaster, The Coxcomb, The Captain, The Maid's Tragedy*, and *A King and No King* between 1609 and 1611. After Beaumont dropped out of the partnership, Fletcher continued to write, both alone and in collaboration, until his death in 1625. *Rollo Duke of Normandy, or The Bloody Brother*, probably written between 1617 and 1620, was revised in the late 1620s by Philip Massinger and perhaps others (*The Dramatic Works in the Beaumont and Fletcher Canon*, 10:155–9).

17. Dryden's response appears in his "Heads of an Answer to Rymer": "The faults of the character of the *King and No King* are not, as he makes them, such as render

him detestable; but only imperfections which accompany human nature, and for the most part excused by the violence of his love; so that they destroy not our pity or concernment for him. This answer may be applied to most of his objections of that kind" (*The Works of John Dryden*, 17:188).

18. In discussing the extreme Aristotelianism of the Averroists that overturned the medieval commitment to the Augustinian view of time as created, finite, temporary, and purgative for mankind in favor of time as permanent by the law of nature, a perpetual continuum of successive moments, Kantorowicz notes that time thereby became "the symbol of the eternal continuity and immortality of the great collective called the human race, of the species of man, of the seminal powers, of the forces of germination. It gained, through its connection with ideas of religious and scientific progress, an ethical value when one recognized that 'the daughter of Time was Truth.'" (*The King's Two Bodies*, 277, 277 n.). In "*Veritas Filia Temporis* and Shakespeare," Soji Iwasaki describes the motto's emblematic currency, its links to the calumniated wife theme, and its use in *King Lear* and *The Winter's Tale*. The figure is used twice in Ford's *The Broken Heart*, at 3.5.62 (Penthea: "my fame . . . I bequeath / To Memory, and Time's old daughter, Truth") and at 4.3.39 (Crotolon to the king, interpreting the oracle: "Truth is child of Time").

19. *A Short View of Tragedy*, chap. 7, in *The Critical Works of Thomas Rymer.*

20. Johnson feels that Rowe has succumbed to the double hazard inherent in the use of "mythological stories": "We have been too early acquainted with the poetical heroes, to expect any pleasure from their revival; to shew them as they have already been shewn, is to disgust by repetition; to give them new qualities or new adventures, is to offend by violating received notions" (*The Works of Nicholas Rowe*, 3).

21. But the play held the stage for the next century for other reasons. The appeal of Rowe's quasi-historical story lies in its sentiment. The story, as Johnson says, "lays hold upon the heart. The wife is forgiven because she repents; and the husband is honoured because he forgives" ("Life of Rowe," *The Works of Samuel Johnson*, 10:64).

22. Harry W. Pedicord, xvi–xviii, in the introduction to his edition of Rowe's *Jane Shore.*

23. Several sensitive lines bearing on issues of succession were canceled by the lord chancellor in licensing the production (ibid., xiii–xiv).

24. After suggesting that Jane's meekness ought to find favor with modern husbands, whose own intrigue-pursuing wives might cuckold them in revenge for being restrained, the actress who has played the role of Jane continues:

> Well, peace be with her; she did wrong most surely,
> But so do many more who look demurely.
> Nor should our mourning madam weep alone,
> There are more ways of wickedness than one.
> If the reforming stage should fall to shaming
> Ill-nature, pride, hypocrisy, and gaming,
> The poets frequently might move compassion,
> And with she-tragedies o'errun the nation.
>
> (22–9)

25. A comparison of the number of performances listed in *The London Stage* from first run through the season of 1746–47, when both were revived to great acclaim by John Rich's Theatre Royal at Covent Garden, shows *Jane Shore* and *The Fair Penitent*

performed with more or less the same frequency until the late 1730s. Thereafter *The Fair Penitent* seems clearly to have been the more popular. See also *The London Stage*, 3:cliii, for a description of the excitement generated by Rich's acting troupe. Over the longer haul, argues Pedicord, *Jane Shore* proved most popular of Rowe's "she-tragedies," holding its place in the repertory well into the nineteenth century (*Jane Shore*, xix).

26. T. A. Dunn, introduction to *The Fatal Dowry*, 4. Dunn remarks that such a structure "looks like a defect in the plotting" (5) which Rowe usefully avoided by beginning his version after the marriage. Dunn's comment demonstrates how neoclassical practice obscures the very different structure and intentions of Renaissance plays.

27. As the Devil in G. B. Shaw's *Man and Superman* puts it, "To this day every Briton believes that the whole of [Milton's] silly story is in the Bible."

28. Bakhtin, "Epic and Novel," in *The Dialogic Imagination*, 13.

29. In "When Eve Reads Milton: Undoing the Canonical Economy," 331–3, Christine Froula discusses the effect of Eve's perceived completedness on Adam, though her argument takes a different direction from mine.

CHAPTER TEN

1. Regarding this tradition see Thomas O. Sloane, *Donne, Milton, and the End of Humanist Rhetoric*.

2. "Consecrates the writer": The expression is Paul Bénichou's and is used by Beaujour in "Rhetoric and Literature" (155), where he explores the vexed modern confusions between rhetoric and literature and discusses the peculiarly impoverished understanding of the history of rhetoric by most francophone philosophers and literary critics.

3. For *Pamela II* I am using the third and fourth volumes of the "Shakespeare Head" *Pamela*, ed. William King and Adrian Bott. For the discussion of Phillips's epilogue see 4:76–8.

4. Much of the contemporary commentary on *Pamela* involved whether and how the voice of the lowborn should be represented. Seeing his readers' reactions helps us understand just how radical Richardson was in this respect. In later editions he elevated his character's diction and smoothed her grammar, showing his insecurity about this feature of his work.

5. Our chief source on Richardson's youth is his letter to his Dutch translator, Johannes Stinstra, written 2 June 1753, in which he describes his ventures from the age of eleven in writing to and for women and in telling stories of his own invention to his schoolmates (William C. Slattery, ed., *The Richardson-Stinstra Correspondence and Stinstra's Prefaces to "Clarissa,"* 26–7).

6. *Grammaire du "Décaméron,"* "au nom de l'audacieuse initiative personnel" (81). The translations from Todorov are mine.

7. "Il est à noter que, dans ces cas, l'échange ne s'établit pas avec l'objet de l'action, mais avec une personne tierce, le législateur, qui peut même être totalement absent de la nouvelle: si on couche avec une femme mariée, c'est avec son mari que l'on échange" (ibid.).

8. T. C. Duncan Eaves and Ben D. Kimpel, eds., introduction to Samuel Richardson, *Pamela*, xv.

9. I use the Eaves and Kimpel text for the 1740 version of *Pamela I*. Two other modern editions allow comparison of Richardson's revisions. The 1761 version, the last printed in his lifetime, has been edited by William Sale (New York: Norton, 1958), and the 1801 version has been edited by Peter Sabor (London: Penguin, 1980). The text of the 1801 edition was printed from a complete revision in Richardson's own hand and represents his final intentions.

10. See Roy Roussel, *The Conversation of the Sexes: Seduction and Equality in Selected Seventeenth- and Eighteenth-Century Texts*, esp. 81–6.

11. B's response to his sister's provocation—What would you have said if I had married my father's groom?—plays over the interrelated issues of class and gender hierarchy from a slightly different perspective to arrive at the same conclusion: "The Difference is, a Man ennobles the Woman he takes, be she *who* she will; and adopts her into his own Rank, be it *what* it will: But a Woman, tho' ever so nobly born, debases herself by a mean Marriage, and descends from her own Rank, to his she stoops to" (*Pamela I*, 349).

12. Richardson's letter to Aaron Hill (1741), in *Selected Letters of Samuel Richardson*, ed. John Carroll, 39–41.

13. Carol Houlihan Flynn devotes a chapter in *Samuel Richardson: Man of Letters* to the "romance" elements in Richardson's work ("Horrid Romancing: Richardson's Use of the Fairy Tale"), mentioning many of the recurring motifs of the popular culture of the day.

14. A. D. McKillop, *Samuel Richardson: Printer and Novelist* (45–6), gives an example for this contemporary linking of the two stories: "In 1744 William Whitehead, with a light touch but hardly with satiric intent, associated *Pamela* with other stories of lowly damsels who made great matches, with the Patient Griselda, Marivaux' *Marianne*, and Mouhy's *Paysanne parvenue* (translated as *The Fortunate Country Maid*):

> Did never Nobles mix with vulgar Earth,
> And City Maids to envyed Heights translate,
> Subdued by Passion, and decay'd Estate?
> Or sigh, still humbler, to the passing Gales
> By turf-built Cots in daisy-painted Vales?
> Who does not, *Pamela*, thy suff'rings feel?
> Who has not wept at beauteous *Grissel*'s Wheel?
> And each fair Marchioness, that *Gallia* pours
> (Exotic Sorrows) to *Britannia*'s Shores?

15. In the Clerk's Tale Chaucer uses the Job comparison to argue that the "humblesse" of the tested woman eclipses that possible to any man (932–8). See also ll. 1149–62, which refer to the Epistle of St. James about how men are proved by God.

16. Inscribed "Intended Letter to Dr. Cheyne on Pamela's Plan" (Richardson, *Selected Letters*, 46).

17. By November 1739, when Richardson started his first novel, the Griselda story was available in several forms, having been a staple of popular literature from Elizabethan plays to the ballad and chapbook versions printed into the eighteenth century. Allusions occurred in popular art, as we see from Charles Cotton's reference to the broadside woodcuts with which people decorated their homes—"We in the country do not scorn, / Our walls with ballads to adorn / Of Patient Grizell, and the Lord of Lorne" (from the Prologue to *Burlesque upon Burlesque: Or, The Scoffer Scoft*, in *The Genuine*

Works of Charles Cotton, Esq., London, 1715; cited by Albert B. Friedman, *The Ballad Revival: Studies in the Influence of Popular on Sophisticated Poetry*, 47). When, years later, Sarah Fielding wrote to Richardson that the ability of two women of her acquaintance to read *Sir Charles Grandison* together without peeping ahead made credible the fable of Patient Grizzle, she was assuming that he knew its outline (letter of 6 July 1754; cited by Eaves and Kimpel, *Biography*, 203). But some features of *Pamela* suggest that Richardson knew an original version of the story, perhaps even Chaucer's. Those with antiquarian and literary interests could obtain Renaissance editions of Chaucer, a reissue of an Elizabethan edition had been printed in 1687, and in 1721 there had appeared a new edition by John Urry (for other post-Restoration editions of Chaucer, see Caroline Spurgeon, *Five Hundred Years of Chaucer Criticism and Allusion, 1357–1900*, 168–70, 259–60, 353–6, 377–8, 381–2). There was a flurry of interest in publication of Chaucer in the several years preceding *Pamela*'s composition. In 1737 John Morrell published the first volume in a proposed new edition of *The Canterbury Tales*, his work having been introduced the previous year by a spate of name-calling letters in the London papers with a would-be rival editor. Though the edition was never completed and did not include the Clerk's Tale, the dispute must have come to Richardson's attention: Morrell's side of the argument was published in the *Daily Gazeteer*, which Richardson printed, Morrell was a friend of various members of Richardson's circle, and Morrell's foundering single volume was reissued in 1740 by John Osborn, the bookseller behind both the *Familiar Letters* and *Pamela*. For the history of the Morrell-Entick controversy, the publication of Morrell's volume, and Morrell's friendship with Stephen Duck, to whom Richardson wrote regarding *Pamela II*, see William L. Alderson and Arnold C. Henderson, *Chaucer and Augustan Scholarship*, 141–61.

Or Richardson might have read a modernized version of the Clerk's Tale. At the time he was writing *Clarissa* he was familiar with Dryden's *Fables Ancient and Modern* (1700); his characters refer to Dryden's work several times. In his preface Dryden mentions Chaucer's indebtedness for the Griselda story to Boccaccio and Petrarch, though he does not include it in his *Fables* (*The Poems of John Dryden*, 4:1450). Having read Dryden as well as having been on the fringes of the Morell publishing venture might have interested Richardson in George Ogle's *Gualtherus and Griselda: Or The Clerk of Oxford's Tale*, a version "modernis'd by several hands," including those of Dryden and Pope, and issued for the bookseller Robert Dodsley in 1739 (Spurgeon, *Chaucer Criticism*, 1:384–6, 389–90; Derek Brewer, *Chaucer: The Critical Heritage*, 202–4).

18. I am using David Wright's prose version of the *Canterbury Tales* in modern English for comparison with Richardson's own text. The following references give Wright's page numbers first, Chaucer's line numbers second: "not in the least put out," 236, ll. 1011–2; "My lord, you know," 233–4, ll. 862–68, 871–5, 881–8.

19. The frequent discussion of clothing also educates us about Pamela's working life. Critics who condescend to Pamela's commentary need to remember that her chief art and occupation as lady's maid and hard-working gentlewoman is making clothes, as carpentry is Adam Bede's or whaling Ishmael's.

20. Richardson's preface to part 2 emphasizes that the novel is about the *"general conduct of life,"* and he hopes that the continuation will not be "disproportioned to the more exalted condition in which Pamela was destined to shine as an affectionate *wife*, a faithful *friend*, a polite and kind *neighbour*, an indulgent *mother*, and a beneficent *mistress;* after having in the former Part supported the character of a dutiful *child*, a spotless *virgin*, and a modest and amiable *bride*" (*Pamela* [London: J. M. Dent, 1914]).

21. Wright's translation, 236–7. Chaucer's text reads:

> And whan this Walter saugh hire pacience . . .
> This sturdy markys gan his herte dresse
> To rewene upon hire wyfly stedfastnesse.
>
> (1044; 1049–50)

22. Medical opinion in the eighteenth century held that sexual intercourse during breast-feeding harmed the quality of the woman's milk and thus the health of the child. See Stone, *The Family, Sex, and Marriage*, 398, 426–7, 496–7.

23. James Fortuna, *"The Unsearchable Wisdom of God": A Study of Providence in Richardson's "Pamela,"* stresses the explicitly Christian nature of Richardson's moral concerns in all his work. That Richardson regarded the issue of Providential intervention in the reformation of B's character as central is indicated in his postscript to the third edition of *Clarissa* (1751). Writing in the third person of his refusal to capitulate to his readers' demands for Lovelace's last-minute conversion and a happily-ever-after ending, he continues "Nor is reformation, as he has shown in another piece, to be secured by a fine face, by a passion that has sense for its object, nor by the goodness of a wife's heart, or even example, if the heart of the husband be not graciously touched by the divine finger" (8:278).

CHAPTER ELEVEN

1. *An Apology for the Life of Mrs. Shamela Andrews.* See Sheridan W. Baker, Jr.'s, introduction for a discussion of publication and attribution.

2. See Hume, *Henry Fielding and the London Theater.*

3. Both *Love's Last Shift* and *The Relapse* were first performed in 1696 (*London Stage*, part 1).

4. The prologue and epilogue of Joseph Mitchell's one-act *Fatal Extravagance* were written by Aaron Hill, who in the play's preface was thanked by its young Scots author for putting him on to "Shakespeare's Yorkshire Tragedy" (*The Dramatic Works of Aaron Hill, Esq., in Two Volumes*, [London: T. Lownds, 1760], vol. 2). In the 1721–22 season at Lincoln's Inn Fields, the one-act play appears on the bill with other plays or with musical or dance performances (*London Stage*, part 2). A version with the same title, published under Joseph Mitchell's name in 1726, is described on its title page as "improved into five acts" (my citation copy is in the Huntington Library). When in 1730 the play appears again in the theatrical record, it is still at Lincoln's Inn Fields but this time in its five-act version and under Aaron Hill's name (*London Stage*, part 3).

5. Letter of 22 Feb 1752 to Mrs. Donnellan. Richardson, *Selected Letters*, 197.

6. Lady Louisa Stuart, "Introductory Anecdotes," *The Letters and Works of Lady Mary Wortley Montagu*, ed. Lord Wharncliffe, rev. ed. W. Moy Thomas (1861), 1:105–6; cited in Martin C. Battestin, introduction to Henry Fielding, *Amelia*, xvii–xviii.

7. The genteel bawd Mrs. Ellison, proprietress of the boarding house where the Booths stay and cousin of the delicately importunate lord who brought about Mrs. Bennet's downfall and seeks Amelia's, is physically so noticeably a dragon lady of the Jewkes/Sinclair type that a reader of Richardson will suspect her even when there is no other cause for uneasiness. The lord's seduction techniques include a visit to the oratorio, another to the Ranelagh masquerade, the dinner afterward, and a poisoned drink, all imitations of Lovelace. Some details of Amelia's family are

reminiscent of Clarissa's—the nasty older sister, the escape with the lover over the wall, the parent who through the sibling's machinations appears to have cut her off completely, the foster brother. On the other hand, the foster brother is no sickly, inconvenient disembodiment, but a vigorous secondary character.

8. Fielding's publisher, Andrew Millar, who had vastly underrated the appeal of *Tom Jones* and had had to scramble to meet demand, took nearly a decade to sell off *Amelia*'s first edition of five thousand copies. See Battestin, introduction to *Amelia*, xlv–l.

9. Giovanni Bononcini's *Griselda* had a run of fifteen performances during spring 1722 (*London Stage*, part 2). Its popularity is also attested by the existence in the British Library of two printed collections of its arias by different publishers, both designed for amateur performance. In the early eighteenth century the Griselda story, based on a libretto by Apostolo Zeno, was popular among Italian operatic composers, including Antonio Pollarolo (1701), Tomaso Albinoni (1703), Giovanni's younger brother Antonio Maria Bononcini (1718), Alessandro Scarlatti (1721), and (with a book adapted by Carlo Goldoni) Antonio Vivaldi (1735). See Howard Meyer Brown, introduction to Vivaldi, *La Griselda*.

10. Fielding's epilogue, showing exactly what Johnson was up against, is worth quoting in full (the text lacks line numbers):

> Lud! what a Fuss is here! what Blood and Slaughter!
> Because poor Miss has prov'd her Mother's Daughter.
> This unknown Bard is some insipid Beast,
> From *Cornwall*, or *Northumberland* at least;
> Where if a Virgin chance to step aside,
> And take forbidden Sweetmeats of a Bride,
> The virtuous Ladies, like Infection, fly her,
> And not one marrying Booby will come nigh her;
> But here, 'mongst us so famous for Good-nature,
> Who thinks a Cuckold quite a Fellow-Creature:
> Where Miss may take great Liberties upon her,
> And have her Man, and yet may keep her Honour:
> Here does the Wretch his stupid Muse invoke,
> And turn to solemn Tragedy—A Joke!
> Had some Town-Bard this Subject undertaken,
> He wou'd have match'd, not kill'd, the Nymph forsaken.
> *Wronglove*, as now, had the first Favour carried,
> And *Bellamy* been, what he is fit for, married.
> What else are all your Comic Heroes fam'd for?
> Than such Exploits as *Wrong love* has been blam'd for?
> The Girl was in the Fault, who strove to smother
> That Case she shou'd have open'd to her Mother;
> All had been hush'd by the *old* Lady's Skill,
> And *Caelia* prov'd a good Town-Virgin still;
> For as each Man is brave, till put to rout,
> So is each Woman virtuous, till found out:
> Which, Ladies, here I make my hearty Prayer,
> May never be the Case of any Fair,
> Who takes unhappy Caelia to her Care.

11. Seneca: "What once were vices, are now customs."

12. I have not seen direct evidence that Richardson knew *Caelia*, though Ira Konigsberg finds it "difficult to believe that Richardson was not familiar with Johnson's works" (*Samuel Richardson and the Dramatic Novel*, 40).

13. In *Sensibility: An Introduction*, Janet Todd reminds us of the demographic and economic facts of eighteenth-century life for unmarried middle-class women—increasing numbers of spinsters thanks to improved living standards, the absence of any economic or social role for them beyond the family, their total dependence on the father or the father's male heir. "In sentimental literature the father-daughter tie would be shorn of its social and economic problems and be marvellously extolled" (18).

14. Norman Holland, *The First Modern Comedies*, chap. 17.

15. Henry Mackenzie, *The Man of Feeling*, ed. Brian Vickers, 5. This text is based on the second (corrected) edition of August 1771, which followed the sold-out first edition of April 1771. In the first edition Marmontel's and Richardson's names had been joined by that of Rousseau.

16. Richardson's consciousness of his originality is discussed in Eaves and Kimpel, *Biography*, esp. 115–8, 241–2, 432–5 (on Richardson's role in Edward Young's "Conjectures on Original Composition"), 566–7, and 600–3.

17. Richardson's contemporaries found the attribution to drama natural. In his "Essay on the Genre of Serious Drama" (1767) Beaumarchais argues that Richardson's novels are "true dramas." Moses Mendelssohn, corresponding in 1757 with G. E. Lessing, refers to "Grandison" in his list of dramatic characters who evoke admiration rather than pity (H. H. Adams and Baxter Hathaway, eds., *Dramatic Essays of the Neoclassic Age*, 370, 338).

18. *Clarissa*, ed. Ross, 1495.

19. Joseph Addison, *Spectator* #40 (16 April 1711); René Rapin, *Reflections on the "Poetics" of Aristotle* (1674).

20. This is my argument in *Clarissa's Plots*, chap. 6, "Prudence: The Plot of the Purposeful Life."

21. Both passages are from Adams and Hathaway, *Dramatic Essays*, 251.

22. In 1749 Richardson's friend Edward Young twice recommended Hartley's *Observations on Man* to him. See letters #260 (6 May) and 262 (24 May), in *The Correspondence of Edward Young, 1683–1765*, ed. Henry Pettit, 319–22. In his correspondence with Lady Bradshaigh, Richardson refers to that recommendation (14 February 1754; *Selected Letters*, 294) and a few months later mentions having read the passage from Hartley that she pointed out to him: "He is a good man. One day I hope to read him thro', though without hopes of understanding the abstruser parts" (30 May 1754; *Selected Letters*, 308).

CHAPTER TWELVE

1. Charles Taylor, *Sources of the Self: The Making of the Modern Identity*, 351.

2. John Fowles, *A Maggot*, 463. The novel is set in 1736, the year of the Porteus affair (around which Scott centered his own tested woman novel, *The Heart of Midlothian*) and the birth of the Shakers' Mother Ann Lee.

3. David Hume, *A Treatise of Human Nature*, bk. 2, pts. 1 and 2.

4. According to the OED, the first recorded use of the term "sentimental" in English occurs in late 1749 in a letter from Lady Bradshaigh, writing under the

pseudonym "Belfour," to Samuel Richardson. She comments on the word's sudden faddishness and wonders what he thinks it really means. *The Letters of Samuel Richardson*, ed. Anna Letitia Barbauld, 4:282–3.

5. Hume, *Human Nature*, 414. Carol Kay, *Political Constructions: Defoe, Richardson, and Sterne in Relation to Hobbes, Hume, and Burke*, chap. 3, discusses the way the language of approval and disapproval is related to Hume's concept of sympathy. See Kay's "Sex, Sympathy, and Authority in Richardson and Hume" for Hume's theory of sympathy in relation to *Clarissa*.

6. Todd, *Sensibility*, 30. Todd cites from Burke's *A Philosophical Enquiry into the Origin of Our Ideas of the Sublime and Beautiful* (1757; revised and enlarged 1759).

7. Northrop Frye, "Toward Defining an Age of Sensibility," in *Eighteenth Century English Literature: Essays in Modern Criticism*, 316.

8. Mackenzie is aware of the moral danger inherent in the cultivation of emotional responsiveness. Writing for his own periodical *The Lounger* (essay #20, 1785), he scores the "separation of conscience from feeling" as "a depravity of the most pernicious sort": "In the enthusiasm of sentiment there is much the same danger as in the enthusiasm of religion, of substituting certain impulses and feelings of what may be called the visionary kind, in the place of real practical duties, which in morals, as in theology, we might not improperly denominate *good works*. In morals, as in religion, there are not wanting instances of refined sentimentalists, who are contented with talking of virtues which they never practice, who pay in words what they owe in actions; or perhaps, what is fully as dangerous, who open their minds to *impressions* which never have any effect upon their *conduct*, but are considered as something foreign to and distinct from it" (cited by Louis I. Bredvold, *The Natural History of Sensibility*, 84–5).

9. See Ann Jessie Van Sant, *Eighteenth-Century Sensibility and the Novel: The Senses in Social Context*, for this technical use of the term "sensibility" and its connection with the phenomenon of "gazing upon suffering." John Mullan, "Sentimental Novels," distinguishes the use of the term "sensibility," applied to a person or character, from the term "sentimentality," applied to the features of a text or representation: " 'Sensibility' had originally referred to bodily sensitivities, began to stand for emotional responsiveness in the early eighteenth century, and came to designate a laudable delicacy in the second half of the century. It was a natural human resource or faculty often displayed by characters in sentimental fiction. 'Sentimental,' by becoming a word for a type of text, promised an *occasion* for fine feeling. This fine feeling could be experienced by both the characters in a narrative and the reader of that narrative. A sentimental text depicted 'sensibility,' and appealed to it" (238). In "Nerves, Spirits and Fibres," G. S. Rousseau argues for the fundamental debt of sentimental literature to the scientific investigation of human emotion and sensibility under development from the 1660s forward.

10. Jean-Jacques Rousseau, *Eloisa, or a Series of Original Letters*, trans. William Kenrick, 1:198 (this is the second of the original four volumes). Rousseau's text reads: "En nous apprenant à penser, vous avez appris de nous à être sensible." I am using Kenrick's translation for its historic interest and its linguistic and literary excellence; in the words of Jonathan Wordsworth, introducing the 1989 Woodstock reprint of the 1803 edition, Kenrick "has provided a strong, clear, thoroughly English version, that is true to the spirit of Rousseau and remains extremely readable." In his preface Kenrick explains that he has used the name "Eloisa" for Rousseau's "Julie" "because the public seemed unanimous in distinguishing the work by the former rather than the latter"

(v). I have chosen to refer to Rousseau's heroine as Julie to distinguish her both from Pope's Eloisa and from the historical Heloise.

11. In addition to Richardson's first two novels, these include Denis Diderot's *La Religieuse*. Rita Goldberg's *Sex and Enlightenment: Women in Richardson and Diderot* discusses Richardson's influence on French philosophy and letters; Tony Tanner's "Julie and 'La Maison paternelle': Another Look at Rousseau's *La Nouvelle Héloïse*" develops a Lacanian reading of the paternal presence in Rousseau's novel that indirectly deepens understanding of the familial dynamics in Richardson; and Mary Seidman Trouille's *Sexual Politics in the Enlightenment: Women Writers Read Rousseau* traces the complex influence of Rousseau on such nearly contemporary women as Mary Wollstonecraft, Madame de Staël, and Olympe de Gouges.

12. In *The Confessions*, Rousseau situates the inspiration for *Julie* in his own erotic longing. In June 1756, sighing over the absence of the love objects of earlier years, he turns to wish fulfillment: "The impossibility of attaining the real persons precipitated me into the land of chimeras; and seeing nothing that existed worthy of my exalted feelings, I fostered them in an ideal world which my creative imagination soon peopled with human beings after my own heart. . . . In my continual ecstasies I intoxicated myself with draughts of the most exquisite sentiments that have ever entered the heart of a man. Altogether ignoring the human race, I created for myself societies of perfect creatures celestial in their virtue and in their beauty, and of reliable, tender, and faithful friends such as I had never found here below" (398). When his chimeras turned into characters, he gave them a setting in his personal Arcadia on the shores of Lake Geneva (400–1); by the beginning of the next year he was "altogether seduced" by his fictional episodes, "and my only occupation was to try and impose some order and sequence upon them, to turn them into a sort of novel" (404). The composition of the rest of the novel, he says, followed a more orderly design (404–6). Rousseau's further references to his fiction are infused by his infatuation with Mme. d'Houdetot: "She came; I saw her; I was intoxicated with love that lacked an object. My intoxication enchanted my eyes, my object became identified with her, I saw my Julie in Mme d'Houdetot, and soon I saw only Mme d'Houdetot, but endowed with all the perfections with which I had just embellished the idol of my heart" (410). This representation of the origins and composition of *Julie* is consistent with Rousseau's discussions of his writing largely in emotional terms; unlike his descriptions of his musical composition, say, where he discusses influences, borrowings, and technique, the work of literary and philosophical composition is nearly always presented in emotionally intimate, sometimes nearly mystical, terms. Literary influences must be inferred from the text of *Julie* and from contemporary contexts; Rousseau is silent about them, as though they would contaminate the intimacy of his relationship with his text.

13. My text for "Eloisa to Abelard" is the Twickenham edition of *The Poems of Alexander Pope*, vol. 2. In the introduction to his edition of the poem, *Eloisa to Abelard with the letters of Heloise to Abelard in the version by John Hughes (1713)*, James E. Wellington explains the complicated background to Pope's poem: "What may be called the first modern edition of the Latin correspondence, the curious Duchesne-d'Amboise (Quercetanus-Amboesius) edition, was published in Paris by Nicholas Buon in 1616. This became the basis for a wildly romanticized French version of three of the letters, written in 1687 and privately circulated (until its posthumous publication ten years later) by Roger de Rabutin, comte de Bussy (1618–1693). . . . Six years later, an expanded French version, based on that of Bussy-Rabutin, was published at the Hague

by an author whose identity cannot now be established. After several intermediate publications of individual letters, the whole was reprinted in 1711; and two years later . . . John Hughes produced a somewhat bowdlerized English translation. Hughes' version . . . became in turn the source which Pope utilized in the composition of *Eloïsa to Abelard*" (20–1). The Hughes version included three letters from Héloïse to Abélard. Two were adapted by the Hague author from Bussy-Rabutin, and the third is "an imaginary production of the Hague author for which no Latin prototype exists" (22). These three are printed in Wellington's edition. Pope used all three letters, but especially the first, Héloïse's first response (à la Hughes) to the *Historia calamitatum*. In *The Poetics of Sexual Myth: Gender and Ideology in the Verse of Swift and Pope*, Ellen Pollak discusses charges that Pope's Eloisa escapes his poetic control and details the several points at which Pope appropriates the passions and frustrations of Hughes's Abelard (not a feature of the Latin original) for his Eloisa (183–6).

14. Héloïse's salutation in her first letter to Abélard elaborates this cluster of roles: "To her master, or rather her father, husband, or rather brother; his handmaid, or rather his daughter, wife, or rather sister; to Abelard, Heloise" (Pierre Abelard, *The Letters of Abelard and Heloise*, 109).

15. No reader of the original correspondence can imagine that, when the correspondence ends, the historical Héloïse had ceased to center her life on Abélard or had transferred her emotional devotion, fervor, and longing to the divine lover/father. The opening of letter 3, her last, shows rather that she has elected to cease her recital of the miseries she suffers (as Abélard characterized her letters) or to hope for words of sympathy on other than his terms. Better, she seems to have decided, to have his professional correspondence and help than nothing of him at all. This is obedience without conversion. For a discussion of this point in the context of the authenticity and the personal and intellectual milieu of the correspondence, see Etienne Gilson, *Heloise and Abelard*, 98–104.

16. On Abelard's doctrine of justification from intention, which Heloise seems to follow, see Gilson, *Heloise and Abelard*, 59–65.

17. The degree to which Rousseau had the history of Héloïse and Abélard in mind from the beginning is unclear. Though an entry in Pierre Bayle's dictionary and the Bussy-Rabutin *Lettres* (both 1697) had made the medieval story known in eighteenth-century France, it was with the translation in 1758 of Pope's poem (two years after Rousseau began *Julie*) that it became fashionable. St. Preux comments that he has always pitied Héloïse and despised Abélard, "who knew equally little of either love or virtue" (1:24). By the time of publication Rousseau's intention was to capitalize on the current interest; one of the late revision requests he made of his publisher was to change the subtitle from "moderne Héloïse" to "nouvelle Héloïse" (*La Nouvelle Héloïse*, editors' notes, 1335–9). How much Rousseau was consciously influenced by *Clarissa* is also unclear, though plot echoes are frequent. In his 1758 *Lettre à M. d'Alembert sur les spectacles* he expresses his admiration for the novel. However, the Abbé Prévost's adaptation/translation of Richardson's novel as *Lettres angloises* (1751), which enjoyed great popularity on the Continent, did not give French-speaking readers Richardson's novel, for Prévost cut episodes and greatly reduced the revisiting of events from different characters' points of view which is the heart of Richardson's literary technique and didactic purpose. On the absence of such "perspectivism," and other changes, see Thomas O. Beebee, *"Clarissa" on the Continent: Translation and Seduction*, a study

of Richardson's original, Prévost's translation, and the German translation of Johann David Michaelis.

18. Rousseau, *The Confessions*, 405. Kenrick's four-volume translation makes the diptych structure particularly clear. The original French has six parts, here collated with Kenrick's numbering:

French	Kenrick
Part 1, letters 1–65	Volume 1, letters 1–70
Part 2, letters 66–93	
Part 3, letters 94–119	Volume 2, letters 71–119
Part 4, letters 120–36	Volume 3, letters 120–39
Part 5, letters 137–50	
Part 6, letters 151–63	Volume 4, letters 140–63

19. *Eloisa*, trans. Kenrick, 1:xxi. Rousseau's text reads: "on diroit que ce sont deux livres différens que les mêmes personnes ne doivent pas lire." *La Nouvelle Héloïse*, "Seconde Préface," 17.

20. Kenrick, 4:210; *La Nouvelle Héloïse*, pt. 6, letter 11, 704.

21. Kenrick, 4:101; *La Nouvelle Héloïse*, pt. 6, letter 2, 642.

22. *La Nouvelle Héloïse*, pt. 5, letter 5, 591–2.

23. *La Nouvelle Héloïse*, pt. 6, letter 8, 693.

24. Stephen Cox, "Sensibility as Argument," 64. The argument is supported by the work of philosophers of perception like Hume, who points out that morality itself, like many of the so-called properties of physical objects like heat or color, is not a matter of objective fact but a state of mind.

25. Todd, *Sensibility*, provides a list that, while selective, indicates the fortunes of the term "sensibility": "Its adjectives tell the tale of its rise and fall. It is 'exquisite' in Addison, 'delicate' in Hume, 'sweet' in Cowper, and 'dear' in Sterne. But as it declines from fashion, it becomes 'acute' in Austen, 'trembling' in Hazlitt, 'mawkish' in Coleridge, and 'sickly' in Byron'" (7).

26. Walter Scott, "Prefatory Memoir to Mackenzie," in *Ballantyne's Novelist's Library*, vol. 5 (*The Novels of Sterne, Goldsmith, Dr Johnson, Mackenzie, Horace Walpole and Clara Reeve*), lvi. Citations from *Julia de Roubigné* are from this edition.

27. Richardson's publication practices declared the importance of this sympathetic turn. In the first edition the volume break occurs following B's frank admission to Pamela of his passion for her, his pleasure in her company, and his frustration that they cannot marry (*Pamela*, ed. Eaves and Kimpel, 189). The 1801 edition, based on Richardson's final revisions, places the volume break a little later, at the moment when she has taken leave of him to return home (this occurs in the Eaves and Kimpel edition on p. 210). This emendation allows the second volume to open with Pamela's momentous act of faith in her own inclinations, her decision to break off her journey home and return to B in his illness.

28. On the relationship between wisdom and prudence and their place in Richardson's novel, see my treatment in *Clarissa's Plots*, 43–52 and 130–1.

CHAPTER THIRTEEN

1. Margaret Anne Doody, "George Eliot and the Eighteenth-Century Novel." That novelists like Burney wrote about ordinary people is crucial to the development

of their technique. Says Doody, "In order to deal fairly with the truths of our continuing history and to convey a just understanding of the real plight of those who are struggling, or outcast, or 'low,' the new novelist needed to create a form that did not take short cuts along easy paths marked heroism and villainy. For such a form, the novelist needed first of all a language, a style which at once allowed investigation and judgment both of the individual character and of the society surrounding and influencing the character" (279). The new technique of using indirect speech as well as direct quotation, followed by an extension that allowed "characters' thoughts [to] be echoed without 'he said' and without reference to any particular speech," resulted in *style indirect libre*, "use of indirect quotation freed from specific reference to any actual speech." The development of indirect free style, points out Doody, "is of the highest importance in the history of the novel" because it results in the double voicing characteristic of an Austen or an Eliot, in which "Our judgment develops slowly, under the quiet guidance of the author, and can be completely formed only when we understand a character's point of view. What might appear at first glance to be simply an ironic technique is also and at the same time fundamentally sympathetic. We must understand and sympathize with another way of viewing the world. The sympathy is not soft—the technique does not lead to sweetness. But readers cannot rush to irony and judgment; these have to be earned. The author makes us see the world as the character sees it, and we must comprehend his view before rejecting or modifying it" (286–8).

2. *Ruth* was greeted with outrage in many quarters; several men of William Gaskell's generally liberal Unitarian congregation burned the novel, and others forbade their wives to read it. Gaskell may have been given courage while composing *Ruth* by the literary success of *The Scarlet Letter*, in which the illegitimate child is the instrument of its mother's redemption. She kept up with Hawthorne's career, writing to her publisher in January 1851 for the copy of *The Scarlet Letter* she had ordered bound for her. See J. A. V. Chapple, *Elizabeth Gaskell: A Portrait in Letters*, 133, and Anne Henry Ehrenpreis, "Elizabeth Gaskell and Nathaniel Hawthorne." Ehrenpreis cites parallel passages from the two novels about the rehabilitating effect of the child.

3. W. R. Greg's review article, "Prostitution," written for the *Westminster Review* in 1850, speaks directly to what Amanda Anderson calls the "blank virtue" contributory to the initial seductions of young women: "Many—far more than would generally be believed—fall from pure unknowingness. Their affections are engaged, their confidence secured; thinking no evil themselves, they permit caresses which in themselves, and to them, indicate no wrong, and are led on ignorantly and thoughtlessly from one familiarity to another, not conscious where those familiarities must inevitably end, till ultimate resistance becomes almost impossible" (cited in *Tainted Souls and Painted Faces*, 128–9). Anderson cites this passage in her discussion of Ruth's "attenuated consciousness," noting Aina Rubenius's hypothesis (in *The Woman Question in Mrs. Gaskell's Life and Works* [Cambridge: Harvard University Press, 1950], 207–10) "that Gaskell based *Ruth* specifically on Greg's article, so strikingly similar are the strategies of vindication."

4. Rosemarie Bodenheimer, *The Politics of Story in Victorian Social Fiction*, 153, 152.

5. Terence Wright, *Elizabeth Gaskell "We Are Not Angels": Realism, Gender, Values*, 92, 94; Jenny Uglow, *Elizabeth Gaskell: A Habit of Stories*, 337. Writing about the transformative power of the fall throughout Victorian literature, Nina Auerbach notes, "Conventionally, the fallen woman must die at the end of her story, perhaps because death rather than marriage is the one implacable human change, the only honorable

symbol of her fall's transforming power. Death does not simply punish or obliterate the fallen woman: its ritual appearance alone does her justice" ("The Rise of the Fallen Woman," 35).

6. Brooks discusses this plot function of the focal character's death by evoking Walter Benjamin: "If in Benjamin's thesis . . . 'Death is the sanction of everything that the storyteller can tell,' it is because it is at the moment of death that life becomes *transmissible*" (*Reading for the Plot*, 28). The Benjamin citation is from "The Storyteller" [*Der Erzähler*], in *Illuminations*, trans. Harry Zohn (New York: Schocken, 1969).

7. Gaskell's Unitarian upbringing, convictions, and milieu provided her with a generous and wide-ranging education; her and her husband's involvement in educational concerns extended from their thoughtful tailoring of their daughters' schooling to their own teaching in Sunday schools, workingmen's institutions, and Manchester New College. See Uglow, *Elizabeth Gaskell: A Habit of Stories*, and Coral Lansbury, *Elizabeth Gaskell*. Lansbury points out that Charles Dickens, who "showed far greater appreciation and understanding of *Ruth* than many subsequent readers," borrowed Bradshaw for *Hard Times*, "where he becomes Mr. Gradgrind, whose bleak statistical fictions reduce his wife to a querulous imbecile, his daughter to a repressed neurotic, and his son to a thief" (32).

8. Feminist criticism has resulted in the reassessment of Austen's relation to predecessor novelists and the feminist radicalism of the 1790s. Marilyn Butler's *Jane Austen and the War of Ideas* surveys the politically motivated novels of the latter part of the eighteenth century and situates Austen firmly in the anti-Jacobin novelistic tradition. By way of partial counterargument, Margaret Kirkham's *Jane Austen: Feminism and Fiction* situates Austen in the context of feminist writing of the previous century, from Mary Astell's *A Serious Proposal to the Ladies for the Advancement of Their True and Greatest Interest* (1694) through Mary Wollstonecraft's *A Vindication of the Rights of Woman* (1792). Kirkham maintains that the scandal resulting from William Godwin's publication in 1798 of the personal details of his late wife's life, joined with the increasingly hysterical reaction to the aftermath of the French Revolution that created a monumental antifeminist backlash, helps account for the delayed publication of Austen's early novels and the tonal differences in the later work. Alison G. Sulloway, *Jane Austen and the Province of Womanhood*, argues (though less coherently) that Austen's work fits into the subgenre "satire of the oppressed." In Sulloway's view Austen is an admiring successor to Fanny Burney and Maria Edgeworth, and shares many of the concerns, though not the tone, of the radical feminist works of the 1790s by Wollstonecraft, Mary Hays, and Catharine Macaulay.

9. In *Jane Austen's Art of Memory*, Jocelyn Harris shows the extent and subtlety of Austen's literary influences from Locke, Shakespeare, Chaucer, Milton, and especially Richardson. But she dismisses Kotzebue as unworthy of consideration, without attending to how *Lovers' Vows* works, why it both attracted and scandalized audiences, and what Austen actually does with it.

10. The only recent study of Kotzebue in English is Oscar Mandel's *August von Kotzebue: The Comedy, The Man* (1990). Intent on recovering a specific Kotzebue play, the satiric comedy *Die deutschen Kleinstädter*, which he publishes as *The Good Citizens of Piffelheim*, Mandel has hardly a good word to say for the rest of the corpus. But he does give an overview of Kotzebue's career, provides a bibliography of the modest amount of critical and scholarly work available (most of it Continental), and demonstrates the ubiquity of Kotzebue's influence. There are apparently no modern, which probably

means no unbowdlerized, English translations of either *Menschenhass und Reue* or *Das Kind der Liebe*. That Kotzebue understood both the modest stature and the broad appeal of his work is clear: "I am sure that though none of my plays will be staged in fifty years yet the poets of posterity will use my plots and more often my situations. . . . Turn the play into a story and if it still grips it will live" (epigraph to chap. 16 of Kirkham, *Jane Austen: Feminism and Fiction*; from the introduction to Kotzebue's *Neue Schauspiele*; also quoted by L. F. Thompson, *Kotzebue: A Survey of His Progress in England and France*, 47). Kotzebue's self-appraisal disguises the fact that his plots grip precisely because they are not new, but time-tested.

11. After assuring readers that Kemble, playing the Baron, and Mrs. Siddons, playing Mrs. Haller, have vividly portrayed the agonies attendant on vicious behavior, Mrs. Inchbald continues with lightly veiled satire, "Notwithstanding all these distressful and repentant testimonies, preparatory to the reunion of this husband and wife, a delicate spectator feels a certain shudder when the catastrophe takes place,—but there is another spectator more delicate still, who never conceives, that from an agonizing, though an affectionate embrace, (the only proof of reconciliation given, for the play ends here), any farther endearments will ensue, than those of participated sadness, mutual care of their joint offspring, and to smooth [*sic*] each other's passage to the grave.

"But should the worst suspicion of the scrupulous critic be true, and this man should actually have taken his wife 'for better or for worse,' as on the bridal day—can this be holding out temptation, as alleged, for women to be false to their husbands? Sure it would rather act as a preservative. What woman of common understanding and common cowardice, would dare to dishonour and forsake her husband, if she foresaw she was ever likely to live with him again?" (introduction to August Kotzebue, *The Stranger*, 5).

12. Thompson, *Kotzebue*, includes a comparison (63–5) of some of the differences between Kotzebue's original and Inchbald's rendering of *Das Kind der Liebe*, including omission of characters, elimination of characterizing elements like mannerisms and dialect, addition of songs for the Butler, and softening of episodes and characterizations.

13. In *Jane Austen: Feminism and Fiction*, Kirkham devotes considerable attention to Kotzebue's "catalytic" influence (92) on both *Mansfield Park* and *Emma* (portions of whose plot she traces to Kotzebue's play *The Birthday*), and, more weakly, on *Persuasion*. She also mentions the various performances of Kotzebue and other dramatists that Austen is known to have attended or had access to, primarily at Bath. In early 1803 three plays alluded to in *Mansfield Park* played in Bath at the Orchard Street Theatre Royal: *Lovers' Vows* and Nahum Tate's version of *King Lear* in January, and *King Henry VIII* in March. "As far as we know, [Austen] was in Bath at these times and [is] likely to have seen them" (112). Kirkham argues that Austen saw in Kotzebue an antipathetic exemplar of Rousseauist sentimentality to which she was moved to respond: "Kotzebue becomes the grit which irritates Austen into the production of pearls" (93). In *Jane Austen and the War of Ideas*, Butler describes the political milieu in which Austen wrote and to which she contributed, and characterizes in some detail the anti-Jacobin movement and its attacks on Kotzebue. Regarding Austen's familiarity with *Lovers' Vows*, a possibility is raised by Austen's letter to Cassandra of 2–3 March 1814 (#97 in *Jane Austen's Letters*, ed. Deirdre Le Faye, 256), in which she refers to their friend Major-General Christopher (Tilson) Chowne, as she does in the two subsequent letters, as "Frederick": "I shall be ready to laugh at the sight of Frederick again." Le Faye's note conjectures: "Could it be that [Cassandra and Jane] had once seen an amateur performance of *Lovers' Vows*,

with a much younger Mr (Tilson) Chowne taking the part of 'Frederick'?" (429). The suggestion is plausible: at the time of writing, Chowne and his brother were about to join the Austen party at a play, and Austen's brother Henry was in the middle of reading proof sheets of *Mansfield Park*, so that her letter is full of references to the novel.

14. Jane Austen, *The Novels of Jane Austen*, 3d ed., ed. R. W. Chapman, vol. 3. Chapman's edition also prints the version of *Lovers' Vows* Austen used.

15. Critics can misread as well. Henry's willful misleading is made possible by the fact that he plays "son" to Maria's "mother," so that Maria does *not* have the excuse that "he loves her in the way that the character he plays loves hers" (Harris, *Jane Austen's Art of Memory*, 153). Thence Mary's slyness to Rushworth about Maria's "completely *maternal*" performance. Frederick, the character Henry is playing, legitimately and honorably occupies the function of defender in his plot, whereas Henry's pretense to defense, both here with Maria and later with Fanny, is specious.

16. Though we now know that Austen never remarked in a letter to her sister that *Mansfield Park* was to be about "ordination," as some critics once believed, it is barely possible to see Edmund's struggle against Mary's objection to his chosen profession in those terms. If we conceive the idea more broadly, in terms of pastoral vocation or pastoral duties (where the pastor stands in for the father), *Mansfield Park* is indeed such a study, both in the character of Edmund and in that of his father, for the novel is a study of fatherhood. In addition to Kotzebue's Baron, its contrastive exemplars are Mr. Price, Sir Thomas, and, in a sense, Edmund himself, who from his youth guides Fanny and, like Austen's Mr. Knightly or Gaskell's Mr. Farquhar, raises up a wife for himself. See Austen, *Letters*, 202, for the 29 January 1813 letter in which the word "ordination" occurs, and 411 for Le Faye's note on the misreading.

17. Samuel Richardson's *Sir Charles Grandison* was among the Austen family's favorite reading. The publication as *Jane Austen's "Sir Charles Grandison"* of a playlet in five acts, written perhaps as a collaboration among various members of the family including her youthful niece Anne, perhaps primarily by Austen herself, shows their easy familiarity with the novel. The high point of the playlet comes in act 2, where Richardson's tested woman comedy on the theme of enforced marriage is heightened to swift and riotous farce. As the abductor, Sir Hargrave Pollexfen, stands flummoxed, and the slatternly witness urges force, the spirited Harriet Byron with the cry "No Dearly Beloveds!" snatches the prayer book from the clergyman and hurls it into the grate. But *Clarissa* is not high comedy, nor is it a book about which the world Austen presents in her novels would have found it easy to talk openly, much less in mixed company. There was a copy of the novel in the pair of rooms Jane shared with her sister at Steventon, however (see Christopher Gillie, *A Preface to Jane Austen*, rev. ed., 12, and Harris, *Jane Austen's Art of Memory*, 56).

18. See Kirkham, *Jane Austen: Feminism and Fiction*, 114–7, for a reading of the significance of Fanny's choice of *Henry VIII* and the parallels that may be drawn between Queen Katherine's situation as a tested, accused, and cajoled woman and Fanny's own.

19. Joseph Litvak, *Caught in the Act: Theatricality in the Nineteenth-Century English Novel*, 13. While I am far from persuaded by the conduct of Litvak's argument about *Mansfield Park*, I find useful his insistence on the pervasive theatricality of Sir Thomas Bertram's familial ideal, a theatricality Fanny must learn to become comfortable with performing, and which her exile to the chaos of Portsmouth teaches her to value (23).

20. Harris, *Jane Austen's Art of Memory*, goes so far as to suggest that Henry, who

"takes on other people's colouring," "has no character at all. . . . He may convince himself, nearly persuade Fanny, and puzzle many critics, but nothing holds" (153–4).

21. Butler, *Jane Austen and the War of Ideas*, addresses Fanny's Portsmouth education in terms of the contrast not just with Mansfield Park but with Henry Crawford's Everingham. She points out that Fanny's choice of Mansfield Park represents a conservatively Evangelical preference for "a social life of affectionate service, together with an inner life of meditation" (245).

CHAPTER FOURTEEN

1. *Tess of the D'Urbervilles* was first published in book form in December 1891, though it had appeared in expurgated serial form both in Britain and abroad over the previous two years. My text is Thomas Hardy, *Tess of the D'Urbervilles*, ed. Juliet Grindle and Simon Gatrell. The quotation is from p. 478.

2. The difference between Ruth's ignorance and Hetty's self-absorption is pointed by Gaskell's different use of the same motif. As Anderson, *Tainted Souls*, notes, Bellingham "dresses Ruth's hair with water lilies and instructs her to look at her own reflection in the pond. Although Ruth 'could not help seeing her own loveliness,' she nonetheless 'never thought of associating it with herself'" (136).

3. I am using Stephen Gill's edition of *Adam Bede*, which includes two useful appendixes: George Eliot's account of the novel's composition, "History of Adam Bede," from her journal for 30 November 1858, and a contemporary account of "The Experience and Happy Death of Mary Voce," the historical original whose story formed the germ of her novel.

4. Regarding the relations of Adam and Arthur, Eliot wrote, "While we were at Munich, George [George Henry Lewes, her partner] expressed his fear that Adam's part was too passive throughout the drama and that it was important for him to be brought into more direct collision with Arthur. This doubt haunted me, and out of it grew the scene in the Wood between Arthur and Adam: the fight came to me as a *necessity* one night at the Munich opera when I was listening to *William Tell*" (*The George Eliot Letters*, ed. Gordon Haight, 2:504).

5. Hetty's emotional frozenness is a deliberate act of characterization. When we compare the contemporary account of the arrest and execution of the historical Mary Voce, the "very ignorant girl" whose story sparked Hetty's, we find a young woman caught up in the exhilaration of spiritual birth, on her lips the texts of triumphant redemption, going joyfully to her execution full of love for those who have converted her. Says Eliot, "The germ of 'Adam Bede' was an anecdote told me by my Methodist Aunt Samuel (the wife of my Father's younger brother) . . . how she had visited a condemned criminal, a very ignorant girl who had murdered her child and refused to confess—how she had stayed with her praying, through the night and how the poor creature at last broke out into tears, and confessed her crime. My Aunt afterwards went with her in the cart to the place of execution, and she described to me the great respect with which this ministry of hers was regarded by the official people about the gaol" (Eliot, *Letters*, 2:502).

6. Ibid., 503–4.

7. The relation between Ruth and Leonard never develops the felt specificity of Gaskell's father/daughter pairs; it is a structural phenomenon more than a psychological one. Susan Morgan discusses the importance of the daughter/father relationship in

Gaskell (*Sisters in Time: Imagining Gender in Nineteenth-Century British Fiction*, esp. 99–107). We see a version of this relationship in the pitched battle between Mr. Bradshaw and Jemima, and its reversal in Jemima's attraction to and for Farquhar.

CHAPTER FIFTEEN

1. Barthes, *S/Z*, 68. For global historical instantiation see the collection edited by Lena B. Ross, *To Speak or Be Silent: The Paradox of Disobedience in the Lives of Women*. A helpful treatment of a seminal Christian text and its background in Judaic tradition is Balch's *Let Wives Be Submissive*, an examination of St. Paul's text in 1 Peter. For a treatment of the way the demand for female silence is exposed and complicated in *Clarissa*, see Beebee, *"Clarissa" on the Continent*, 125–42.

2. In *The Pleasure of the Play*, Bert O. States argues for peripety or reversal as not merely a localized structural device but also a "principle of plot development," an overarching dramatic strategy that "occurs in many modes and manifests itself in different forms" (86). Peripety is the master term in a semantic network of contiguous and related ideas. "Crudely, a semantic network is a mental map in which the 'towns' and 'cities'—the terms composing the network—are all connected by neuronal 'roads' and have names that are at least partially synonymical (as one might expect to find North Clearfield next to East or West Clearfield, and so on). Thus on a map encompassing the province of Peripety, the capital city would be Peripety itself, next to which we might find Coincidence, Reversal, Metabasis, Contrast, and so on" (87). On a map depicting Peripety in the nineteenth-century novel, I argue that one of the outlying towns and boroughs is Revelation.

3. In *The Logic of Practice*, Pierre Bourdieu argues for the omnipresence, even the quasi-omnipotence, in all our lives of unconscious and unexamined but coherent daily practices—routines, "scripts," received ways of behaving, cultural patterns and expectations—that create a worldview and the behaviors operating within it. These form the *habitus*. By bringing the very different outsiders Angel and Tess to the world of Talbothays, Hardy is able to explore the impress of a culturally coherent set of practices on their psyches and life stories.

4. As Tess responds to her husband's confession with her own, "She bent forward, at which each diamond on her neck gave a sinister wink like a toad's; and pressing her forehead against his temple, she entered on her story of her acquaintance with Alec d'Urberville and its results, murmuring the words without flinching and with her eyelids drooping down" (243). Tess's posture echoes the confessional moment of her return from Trantridge when her mother asks her whether she has not come home to be married to her cousin: " 'He is not my cousin, and he's not going to marry me.' Her mother eyed her narrowly. 'Come, you have not told me all,' she said. Then Tess went up to her mother, put her face upon Joan's neck, and told" (97). Both scenes capitalize on Tess's shamed veiling of her eyes to emphasize the voice that tells but that the reader does not hear directly and must supply.

5. "It was a remarkable attribute of this garb, and, indeed, of the child's whole appearance, that it irresistibly and inevitably reminded the beholder of the token which Hester Prynne was doomed to wear upon her bosom. It was the scarlet letter in another form; the scarlet letter endowed with life!" And the narrator goes on, "The mother herself . . . had carefully wrought out the similitude; lavishing many hours of morbid ingenuity, to create an analogy between the object of her affection, and the

emblem of her guilt and torture. But, in truth, Pearl was the one, as well as the other; and only in consequence of that identity had Hester contrived so perfectly to represent the scarlet letter in her appearance" (Nathaniel Hawthorne, *The Scarlet Letter*, 90).

6. See States, *The Pleasure of the Play*, 157–79, for a discussion of dramatists' authorial ventriloquism.

7. U. C. Knoepflmacher, *George Eliot's Early Novels: The Limits of Realism*, emphasizes Hetty's lack of comprehension of self, world, act, and consequence, and sees Eliot as punishing her for her moral unresponsiveness (119–24). I see Eliot as more interested in psychology than in sin.

8. Roy W. Perrett, "Autobiography and Self-Deception: Conjoining Philosophy, Literature, and Cognitive Psychology"; Herbert Fingarette, *Self-Deception*.

CHAPTER SIXTEEN

1. Frye, *Secular Scripture*, esp. 183.

2. Victor J. Lams, *Anger, Guilt, and the Psychology of the Self in "Clarissa,"* gives a searching reading of the struggle between male pathology and female integrity. In particular, Lams explores Lovelace's narcissism, the psychological disease that fuels his response to Clarissa and resonates in these twentieth-century treatments.

WORKS CITED

Abelard, Pierre. *The Letters of Abelard and Heloise.* Translated with an introduction by Betty Radice. Harmondsworth, Middlesex: Penguin, 1974.

Achilles Tatius. *Clitophon and Leucippe.* Translated by S. Gaselee. Revised by E. H. Warmington. Cambridge: Harvard University Press, 1969.

Adams, Henry Hitch, and Baxter Hathaway, eds. *Dramatic Essays of the Neoclassic Age.* 1947. Reprint, New York: Benjamin Blom, 1965.

Alderson, William L., and Arnold C. Henderson. *Chaucer and Augustan Scholarship.* University of California Publications in English Studies 35. Berkeley: University of California Press, 1970.

Altman, Joel B. *The Tudor Play of Mind: Rhetorical Inquiry and the Development of Elizabethan Drama.* Berkeley: University of California Press, 1978.

Amussen, Susan Dwyer. *An Ordered Society: Gender and Class in Early Modern England.* Oxford: Basil Blackwell, 1988.

Anderson, Amanda. *Tainted Souls and Painted Faces: The Rhetoric of Fallenness in Victorian Culture.* Ithaca: Cornell University Press, 1993.

Aquinas, Thomas, Saint. *Summa Theologiae.* Edited by Thomas Gilby, O. P. 60 vols. New York: McGraw-Hill, 1969–.

Ariosto, Lodovico. *Orlando Furioso.* Translated by Guido Waldman. London: Oxford University Press, 1974.

Auerbach, Nina. "The Rise of the Fallen Woman," *Nineteenth-Century Fiction* 35 (1980): 29–52.

Augustine of Hippo, Saint. *Soliloquies and Immortality of the Soul.* Translated with a commentary by Gerard Watson. Warminster, England: Aris and Phillips, 1990.

Austen, Jane. *Jane Austen's Letters.* 3d ed. Edited by Deirdre Le Faye. Oxford: Oxford University Press, 1995.

———. *Mansfield Park.* Vol. 3. of *The Novels of Jane Austen.* 3d ed. Edited by R. W. Chapman. Oxford: Oxford University Press, 1934.

[Austen, Jane]. *Jane Austen's "Sir Charles Grandison."* Edited by Brian Southam. Oxford: Clarendon Press, 1980.

Babb, Lawrence. *The Elizabethan Malady, A Study in Melancholia in English Literature from 1580 to 1642.* East Lansing: Michigan State University Press, 1951.

Baker, Derek, ed. *Medieval Women.* Oxford: Basil Blackwell, 1978.

Baker, Herschel C. *The Image of Man.* New York: Harper, 1961. Originally published as *The Dignity of Man* (Cambridge: Harvard University Press, 1947).

Bakhtin, Mikhail. *The Dialogic Imagination: Four Essays.* Translated by Caryl Emerson and Michael Holquist. Austin: University of Texas Press, 1981.

Balch, David L. *Let Wives Be Submissive: The Domestic Code in 1 Peter.* Society of Biblical Literature Monograph Series 26. Chico, Calif: Scholars Press, 1981.

Baldwin, T. W. *William Shakspere's Small Latine & Lesse Greeke.* 2 vols. Urbana: University of Illinois Press, 1944.

Baldwin, T. W., and M. Channing Lithicum. "The Date of *Ralph Roister Doister,*" *Philological Quarterly* 6 (1927): 379–95.

Barish, Jonas A. "Perkin Warbeck as Anti-History," *Essays in Criticism* 20 (1970): 151–71.

Barthes, Roland. *S/Z: An Essay.* Translated by Richard Miller. New York: Hill and Wang, 1974.

Bawcutt, N. W. Introduction to Thomas Middleton and William Rowley, *The Changeling.* London: Methuen, 1958.

Beaujour, Michel. "Rhetoric and Literature." In *From Metaphysics to Literature,* edited by Michel Meyer, 151–68. Dordrecht: Kulwer Academic Publishers, 1989.

Beaumont, Francis, and John Fletcher. *The Dramatic Works in the Beaumont and Fletcher Canon.* Edited by Fredson Bowers. Cambridge: Cambridge University Press, 1966–.

———. *A King and No King.* Edited by Robert K. Turner, Jr. Lincoln: University of Nebraska Press, 1963.

Beebee, Thomas O. *"Clarissa" on the Continent: Translation and Seduction.* University Park: Pennsylvania State University Press,1990.

Bettridge, William E., and Francis L. Utley. "New Light on the Origin of the Griselda Story," *Texas Studies in Language and Literature* 13 (1971): 153–208.

Bevington, David M. *From "Mankind" to Marlowe: Growth of Structure in the Popular Drama of Tudor England.* Cambridge: Harvard University Press, 1962.

———. *Tudor Drama and Politics: A Critical Approach to Topical Meaning.* Cambridge: Harvard University Press, 1968.

Bliss, Lee. *Francis Beaumont.* Boston: Twayne, 1987.

Boas, Frederick S. *An Introduction to Tudor Drama.* Oxford: Clarendon Press, 1933.

Boccaccio, Giovanni. *The Corbaccio.* Translated by Anthony K. Cassell. Urbana: University of Illinois Press, 1975.

Bodenheimer, Rosemarie. *The Politics of Story in Victorian Social Fiction.* Ithaca: Cornell University Press, 1988.

Boswell, James. *Boswell's Life of Johnson, together with Boswell's Journal of a Tour of the Hebrides and Johnson's Diary of a Journey into North Wales.* Edited by G. B. Hill. Revised and enlarged by L. F. Powell. 6 vols. Oxford: Clarendon Press, 1934.

Bourdieu, Pierre. *The Logic of Practice.* Translated by Richard Nice. Stanford: Stanford University Press, 1990.

Bredvold, Louis I. *The Natural History of Sensibility.* Detroit: Wayne State University Press, 1962.

Bremond, Claude, Joshua Landy, and Thomas Pavel, eds. *Thematics: New Approaches.* Albany: State University of New York Press, 1995.

Brewer, Derek, ed. *Chaucer: The Critical Heritage.* Vol. 1, 1385–1837. London: Routledge and Kegan Paul, 1978.

Bridenbaugh, Carl. *Vexed and Troubled Englishmen, 1590–1642.* New York: Oxford University Press, 1976.

Brooks, Peter. *Reading for the Plot: Design and Intention in Narrative.* New York: Knopf, 1984.

Brown, Howard Meyer, ed. Introduction to *La Griselda* by Antonio Vivaldi. In *Italian Opera, 1640–1770*, vol. 35. New York: Garland, 1978.

Buchanan, George. *Tragedies*. Edited by P. Sharratt and P. G. Walsh. Edinburgh: Scottish Academic Press, 1983.

Bueler, Lois E. *Clarissa's Plots*. Newark: University of Delaware Press, 1994.

———. "The Rhetoric of Change in *The Changeling*," *English Literary Renaissance* 14 (Spring 1984): 95–113.

———. "Role-Splitting and Reintegration: The Tested Woman Plot in Ford," *Studies in English Literature, 1500–1900* 20 (1980): 325–44.

———. "The Structural Uses of Incest in English Renaissance Drama," *Renaissance Drama*, n.s., 15 (1984): 115–45.

Bullough, Geoffrey, ed. *Narrative and Dramatic Sources of Shakespeare*. Vol. 8, Romances. New York: Columbia University Press, 1975.

Burney, Fanny. *The Diary of Fanny Burney*. London: J. M. Dent, 1940.

Butler, Marilyn. *Jane Austen and the War of Ideas*. 1975. Reissue with new introduction, Oxford: Oxford University Press, 1987.

B[owers], R[ichard]. *Appius and Virginia*. Edited by Ronald B. McKerrow and W. W. Greg. London: Malone Society Reprints, 1911.

Camden, Carroll. *The Elizabethan Woman*. Houston: Elsevier Press, 1952.

Cervantes Saavedra, Miguel de. *The Ingenious Gentleman Don Quixote de la Mancha*. Translated by Samuel Putnam. New York: Viking, 1958.

Chapman, George. *The Plays of George Chapman: The Comedies*. Edited by Allan Holaday. Urbana: University of Illinois Press, 1970.

Chapple, J. A. V. *Elizabeth Gaskell: A Portrait in Letters*. Manchester: Manchester University Press, 1980.

Chariton's Chaereus and Callirhoë. Translated by Warren E. Blake. Ann Arbor: University of Michigan Press, 1939.

Chaucer, Geoffrey. *The Canterbury Tales: A Prose Version in Modern English*. Translated by David Wright. New York: Random House, 1964.

———. *The Works of Geoffrey Chaucer*. 2d ed. Edited by F. N. Robinson. Boston: Houghton Mifflin, 1957.

Christopherson, John. *Jephthah*. Edited and translated by Francis H. Fobes. Introduction by Wilbur O. Sypherd. Newark: University of Delaware Press, 1928.

Clark, Sandra. *The Plays of Beaumont and Fletcher: Sexual Themes and Dramatic Representation*. New York: Harvester/Wheatsheaf, 1994.

Colie, Rosalie L. *Paradoxia Epidemica: The Renaissance Tradition of Paradox*. Princeton: Princeton University Press, 1966.

———. *Resources of Kind: Genre Theory in the Renaissance*. Edited by Barbara K. Lewalski. Berkeley: University of California Press, 1973.

Collected Ancient Greek Novels. Edited by B. P. Reardon. Berkeley: University of California Press, 1989.

Cox, Stephen D. "Sensibility as Argument." In *Sensibility in Transformation: Creative Resistance to Sentiment from the Augustans to the Romantics*, edited by Syndy McMillan Conger, 63–82. Cranbury, N.J.: Associated University Presses, 1990.

Crandall, Coryl. *"Swetnam the Woman-Hater": The Controversy and the Play*. Lafayette: Purdue University Studies, 1969.

Cross, Claire. " 'Great Reasoners in Scripture': The Activities of Women Lollards,

1380–1530." In *Medieval Women*, edited by Derek Baker, 359–80. Oxford: Basil Blackwell, 1978.

Daly, James. *Sir Robert Filmer and English Political Thought*. Toronto: University of Toronto, 1979.

Damrosch, Leopold, Jr. *God's Plot & Man's Stories: Studies in the Fictional Imagination from Milton to Fielding*. Chicago: University of Chicago Press, 1985.

Davenant, William. *The Works of Sir William Davenant*. 1673. Facsimile edition, New York: Benjamin Blom, 1968.

Davenport, Robert. *The City Night-Cap*. Edited by Willis J. Monie. New York: Garland, 1979.

Davis, Natalie Zemon. "Women on Top: Symbolic Sexual Inversion and Political Disorder in Early Modern Europe." In *The Reversible World*, edited by Barbara A. Babcock, 147–90. Ithaca: Cornell University Press, 1978.

Davis, Robert Con. *The Paternal Romance: Reading God-the-Father in Early Western Culture*. Urbana: University of Illinois Press, 1993.

Dekker, Thomas. *The Dramatic Works of Thomas Dekker*. Edited by Fredson Bowers. 1952. Reprint, Cambridge: Cambridge University Press, 1962.

Deutsch, Otto Erich. *Handel: A Documentary Biography*. London: Adam and Charles Black, 1955.

Dobree, Bonamy. Introduction to *The Complete Works of Sir John Vanbrugh*. 1927. Reprint, New York: AMS Press, 1967.

Dolozel, Lubomír. "A Semantics for Thematics: The Case of the Double." In *Thematics: New Approaches*, edited by Claude Bremond, Joshua Landy, and Thomas Pavel, 89–102. Albany: State University of New York Press, 1995.

Donaldson, Ian. *The Rapes of Lucretia: A Myth and Its Transformations*. Oxford: Clarendon Press, 1982.

Doody, Margaret Anne. "George Eliot and the Eighteenth-Century Novel," *Nineteenth-Century Fiction* 35 (1980): 260–91.

———. *The True History of the Novel*. New Brunswick: Rutgers University Press, 1996.

Doran, Madeleine. *Endeavors of Art*. Madison: University of Wisconsin Press, 1954.

Downer, Alan S. *The British Drama*. New York: Appleton-Century-Crofts, 1950.

Dryden, John. *The Poems of John Dryden*. Vol. 4, *Fables Ancient and Modern*. Edited by James Kinsley. Oxford: Clarendon Press, 1958.

———. *The Works of John Dryden*. Vol. 11, *Plays*. Edited by John Loftis and David Stuart Rodes. Vol. 17, *Prose 1668–1691*. Edited by Samuel Holt Monk. Berkeley: University of California Press, 1978, 1971.

Dunn, T. A. Introduction to Philip Massinger and Nathan Field, *The Fatal Dowry*. Berkeley: University of California Press, 1969.

Dust, Philip, and William D. Wolf. "Recent Studies in Early Tudor Drama: *Gorboduc, Ralph Roister Doister, Gammer Gurton's Needle* and *Cambises*," *English Literary Renaissance* 8 (1978): 110–12.

Eaves, T. C. Duncan, and Ben D. Kimpel. *Samuel Richardson: A Biography*. Oxford: Clarendon Press, 1971.

Edgerton, William L. "The Date of *Roister Doister*," *Philological Quarterly* 44 (1965): 555–60.

———. *Nicholas Udall*. New York: Twayne, 1965.

Edmond, Mary. *Rare Sir William Davenant: Poet Laureate, Playwright, Civil War General, Restoration Theatre Manager*. New York: St. Martin's Press, 1987.

Ehrenpreis, Anne Henry. "Elizabeth Gaskell and Nathaniel Hawthorne." In *The Nathaniel Hawthorne Journal, 1973,* edited by C. E. Frazier Clark, 89–119. Englewood, Colo.: Microcard Editions Books, 1973.

Eliot, George. *Adam Bede.* Edited by Stephen Gill. Harmondsworth, Middlesex: Penguin, 1980.

———. *The George Eliot Letters.* Vol. 2. Edited by Gordon S. Haight. New Haven: Yale University Press, 1954.

Eliot, T. S. "John Ford." In *Selected Essays 1917–1932,* 193–204. London: Faber and Faber, 1932.

Euripides. *Iphigenia in Aulis.* Translated with an introduction by Charles R. Walker. In *The Complete Greek Tragedies,* edited by David Grene and Richmond Lattimore. Vol. 4, *Euripides.* Chicago: University of Chicago Press, 1992.

Fielding, Henry. *Amelia.* Edited by Martin C. Battestin. Oxford: Clarendon Press, 1983.

[Fielding, Henry.] *An Apology for the Life of Mrs. Shamela Andrews.* Edited by Sheridan W. Baker, Jr. Berkeley: University of California Press, 1953.

Filmer, Sir Robert. *Patriarcha and Other Political Works.* Edited by Peter Laslett. Oxford: Basil Blackwell, 1949.

Fingarette, Herbert. *Self-Deception.* New York: Humanities Press, 1969.

Florio, John. *Queen Anna's New World of Words.* 1611.

———. *A World of Words.* 1598.

Flynn, Carol Houlihan. *Samuel Richardson: A Man of Letters.* Princeton: Princeton University Press, 1982.

Ford, John. *The Broken Heart.* Edited by Brian Morris. New York: Hill and Wang, 1966.

———. *The Lady's Trial.* In *John Ford's Dramatic Works.* Edited by Henry de Vocht. 1927. Reprint, Vaduz: Kraus, 1963.

———. *Love's Sacrifice.* In *John Fordes Dramatische Werke.* Edited by Henry de Vocht. 1908. Reprint, Vaduz: Kraus, 1963.

———. *Perkin Warbeck.* Edited by Donald K. Anderson, Jr. Lincoln: University of Nebraska Press, 1965.

———. *'Tis Pity She's a Whore.* Edited by N. W. Bawcutt. Lincoln: University of Nebraska Press, 1965.

Fortuna, James Louis. *"The Unsearchable Wisdom of God": A Study of Providence in Richardson's "Pamela."* University of Florida Monographs in the Humanities 49. Gainesville: University Presses of Florida, 1980.

Fowles, John. *The Collector.* New York: Dell, 1963.

———. *A Maggot.* Boston: Little, Brown, 1985.

Foxe, John. *The Acts and Monuments of John Foxe.* Edited by George Townsend. 1837. Reprint, New York: AMS Press, 1965.

Friedman, Albert B. *The Ballad Revival: Studies in the Influence of Popular on Sophisticated Poetry.* Chicago: University of Chicago Press, 1961.

Froula, Christine. "When Eve Reads Milton: Undoing the Canonical Economy," *Critical Inquiry* 10 (1983): 321–47.

Frye, Northrop. *The Secular Scripture: A Study of the Structure of Romance.* Cambridge: Harvard University Press, 1977.

———. "Toward Defining an Age of Sensibility," *English Literary History* 23 (1956): 144–52. Reprinted in *Eighteenth Century English Literature: Essays in Modern*

Criticism, 3d ed., edited by James L. Clifford, 311–18. New York: Oxford University Press, 1959.

Gaskell, Elizabeth. *Ruth*. Edited by Alan Shelston. Oxford: Oxford University Press, 1985.

Gillie, Christopher. *A Preface to Jane Austen*. Rev. ed. New York: Longman, 1985.

Gilson, Etienne. *Heloise and Abelard*. Translated by L. K. Shook. London: Hollis and Carter, 1953. Originally published as *Héloïse et Abélard* (Paris: Librairie Philosophique J. Vrin, 1948).

Goldberg, Jonathan. *James I and the Politics of Literature*. Berkeley: University of California Press, 1983.

Goldberg, Rita. *Sex and Enlightenment: Women in Richardson and Diderot*. Cambridge: Cambridge University Press, 1984.

Gough, John W. *The Social Contract*. 2d ed. Oxford: Clarendon Press, 1957.

Griffith, D. D. *The Origin of the Griselda Story*. University of Washington Publications in Language and Literature 8:1. Seattle: University of Washington Press, 1931.

Hägg, Tomas. *The Novel in Antiquity*. Berkeley: University of California Press, 1983.

Handel, George Frideric. *The Librettos of Handel's Operas: A Collection of Seventy-One Librettos Documenting Handel's Operatic Career*. Edited by Ellen T. Harris. New York: Garland, 1989. Vol. 7 (1732–36) includes *Ariodante*.

Harbage, Alfred. *Annals of English Drama, 975–1700*. Revised by Samuel Schoenbaum. Philadelphia: University of Pennsylvania Press, 1964.

Hardy, Thomas. *Tess of the D'Urbervilles*. Edited by Juliet Grindle and Simon Gatrell. Oxford: Clarendon Press, 1983.

Harington, John. *Orlando Furioso in English Heroical Verse*. London: Richard Field, 1591.

Harris, Jocelyn. *Jane Austen's Art of Memory*. Cambridge: Cambridge University Press, 1989.

Hawthorne, Nathaniel. *The Scarlet Letter*. Edited by Ross C. Murfin. Boston: Bedford Books, 1991.

Herrick, Marvin T. "Susanna and the Elders in Sixteenth-Century Drama." In *Studies in Honor of T. W. Baldwin*, edited by Don Cameron Allen, 125–35. Urbana: University of Illinois Press, 1958.

Heywood, Thomas. *The Dramatic Works of Thomas Heywood*. Vol. 1, *Edward IV, Parts 1 and 2*. 1874. Reprint, New York: Russell and Russell, 1964.

Hill, Christopher. *The Century of Revolution, 1603–1714*. Edinburgh: T. Nelson, 1962.

———. *Society and Puritanism in Pre-Revolutionary England*. London: Secker and Warburg, 1964.

———. *The World Turned Upside Down: Radical Ideals during the English Revolution*. New York: Viking, 1972.

Holland, Norman. *The First Modern Comedies*. Cambridge: Harvard University Press, 1959.

Hooker, Richard. *Of the Laws of Ecclesiastical Polity*. 2 vols. Introduction by Christopher Morris. London: J. M. Dent, 1954.

Howell, Wilbur Samuel. *Logic and Rhetoric in England, 1500–1700*. 1956. Reprint, New York: Russell and Russell, 1961.

Hoy, Cyrus. *The Hyacinth Room: An Investigation into the Nature of Comedy, Tragedy, and Tragicomedy*. New York: Knopf, 1964.

Hull, Suzanne W. *Chaste, Silent, and Obedient: English Books for Women, 1475–1640*. San Marino, Calif.: Huntington Library, 1982.

Hume, David. *A Treatise of Human Nature*. London: Penguin, 1969.

Hume, Robert D. *Henry Fielding and the London Theatre, 1728–1737*. Oxford: Clarendon Press, 1988.

Iwasaki, Soji. "*Veritas Filia Temporis* and Shakespeare," *English Literary Renaissance* 3 (1973): 249–63.

James I. *The Political Works of James I*. Edited by Charles H. McIlwain. Cambridge: Harvard University Press, 1918.

Jerome, Saint. *Select Letters of St. Jerome*. Translated by F. A. Wright. 1933. Reprint, Cambridge: Harvard University Press, 1975.

Johnson, Charles. *Caelia; or, The Perjur'd Lover*. London: J. Watts, 1733.

Johnson, Samuel. "The Life of Nicholas Rowe, Esq." Preface to *The Works of Nicholas Rowe*, 1–11. London: W. Lowndes, 1792.

Jung, Carl Gustav. *Answer to Job*. In vol. 11 of *Collected Works of C. G. Jung*. 2d ed. Translated by R. F. C. Hull. Princeton: Princeton University Press, 1969.

Kantorowicz, Ernst H. *The King's Two Bodies: A Study in Mediaeval Political Theology*. Princeton: Princeton University Press, 1957.

Kaufmann, R. J. "Ford's Tragic Perspective." *Texas Studies in Language and Literature* 1 (1960): 522–37. Reprinted in *Elizabethan Drama: Modern Essays in Criticism*, edited by R. J. Kaufmann, 356–72. New York: Oxford University Press, 1961.

Kay, Carol. *Political Constructions: Defoe, Richardson, and Sterne in Relation to Hobbes, Hume, and Burke*. Ithaca: Cornell University Press, 1988.

———. "Sex, Sympathy, and Authority in Richardson and Hume." In *Studies in Eighteenth-Century Culture*, edited by Harry C. Payne, 77–92. Madison: University of Wisconsin Press, 1982.

Keates, Jonathan. *Handel: The Man and His Music*. London: Victor Gollancz, 1985.

[Kelly, John]. *Pamela's Conduct in High Life, to The Time of Her Death. Publish'd from her original papers interspers'd with several true, moral, and entertaining incidents and characters*. London: Ward and Chandler, 1741.

Kelso, Ruth. *Doctrine for the Lady of the Renaissance*. Urbana: University of Illinois Press, 1956.

Kenny, Shirley Strum. "Perennial Favorites: Congreve, Vanbrugh, Cibber, Farquhar, and Steele," *Modern Philology* 73/4, part 2 [Friedman festschrift] (1976), S4–S11.

Kinkead-Weekes, Mark. *Samuel Richardson: Dramatic Novelist*. Ithaca: Cornell University Press, 1973.

Kirkham, Margaret. *Jane Austen: Feminism and Fiction*. Brighton, Sussex: Harvester Press, 1983.

Knoepflmacher, U. C. *George Eliot's Early Novels: The Limits of Realism*. Berkeley: University of California Press, 1968.

Kolve, V. A. *The Play Called Corpus Christi*. Stanford: Stanford University Press, 1966.

Konigsberg, Ira. *Samuel Richardson and the Dramatic Novel*. Lexington: University of Kentucky Press, 1968.

Konstan, David. *Sexual Symmetry: Love in the Ancient Novel and Related Genres*. Princeton: Princeton University Press, 1994.

Kotzebue, August von. *Lovers' Vows*. Translated by Elizabeth Inchbald. In *The Novels of Jane Austen*, edited by R. W. Chapman, vol. 3. Oxford: Oxford University Press, 1934.

———. *The Stranger*. Translated by Benjamin Thompson. In *The British Theatre*, edited by Elizabeth Inchbald, vol. 24. London: Hurst, Rees and Orme, 1808.

Kraus, Henry. *The Living Theatre of Medieval Art.* Bloomington: Indiana University Press, 1967.

Kunzle, David. "World Turned Upside Down: The Iconography of a European Broadsheet Type." In *The Reversible World,* edited by Barbara A. Babcock, 39–94. Ithaca: Cornell University Press, 1978.

Lakoff, George. *Women, Fire, and Dangerous Things: What Categories Reveal about the Mind.* Chicago: University of Chicago Press, 1987.

Lamb, Charles. "On the Artificial Comedy of the Last Century." [1823]. In *The Complete Works of Charles and Mary Lamb,* edited by E. V. Lucas, 2:141–7. 1903. Reprint, New York: AMS Press, 1968.

Lams, Victor J. *Anger, Guilt, and the Psychology of the Self in "Clarissa".* New York: Peter Lang, 1999.

Lancashire, Anne. "Chaucer and the Sacrifice of Isaac," *Chaucer Review* 9 (1974–75): 320–26.

Lansbury, Coral. *Elizabeth Gaskell.* Boston: Twayne, 1984.

Laqueur, Thomas. *Making Sex: Body and Gender from the Greeks to Freud.* Cambridge: Harvard University Press, 1990.

Levenson, Jill. "Comedy." In *The Cambridge Companion to English Renaissance Drama,* edited by A. R. Braunmuller and Michael Hattaway, 263–300. Cambridge: Cambridge University Press, 1990.

Levin, Richard. *The Multiple Plot in English Renaissance Drama.* Chicago: University of Chicago Press, 1971.

Lipsius, Justus. *Six Books of Politics or Civil Doctrine.* Translated by William Jones. 1594. Reprint, New York: Da Capo Press, 1970.

Litvak, Joseph. *Caught in the Act: Theatricality in the Nineteenth-Century English Novel.* Berkeley: University of California Press, 1992.

Livy (Titus Livius). *The Early History of Rome.* Books 1–5 of *The History of Rome from Its Foundation.* Translated by Aubrey de Sélincourt. Introduction by R. M. Ogilvie. London: Penguin, 1971.

Locke, John. *Two Treatises of Government.* 2d ed. Edited by Peter Laslett. Cambridge: Cambridge University Press, 1967.

The London Stage, 1660–1800. 3 parts. *Part 1: 1660–1700,* edited by William Van Lennep. *Part 2: 1700–1729,* edited by Emmett L. Avery. *Part 3: 1729–1747,* edited by Arthur H. Scouten. Carbondale: Southern Illinois University Press, 1960–65.

Lovejoy, Arthur O. *The Great Chain of Being.* [1936]. Cambridge: Harvard University Press, 1961.

Lyles, Albert. "Pamela's Trials." *College Language Association Journal* 8 (1965): 290–2. Reprinted in *Twentieth Century Interpretations of Pamela,* edited by Rosemary Cowler, 103–5. Englewood Cliffs, N.J.: Prentice-Hall, 1969.

Lyly, John. *Campaspe.* In *Campaspe; Sappho and Phao,* edited by G. K. Hunter. New York: Manchester University Press, 1991.

Mack, Maynard, Jr. *Killing the King: Three Studies in Shakespeare's Tragic Structure.* New Haven: Yale University Press, 1973.

Mackenzie, Henry. *Julia de Roubigné.* 1777. In *Ballantyne's Novelist's Library,* vol. 5 (*The Novels of Sterne, Goldsmith, Dr Johnson, Mackenzie, Horace Walpole and Clara Reeve*), Prefatory memoirs by Walter Scott. London: Hurst, Robinson, 1823.

———. *The Man of Feeling.* Edited by Brian Vickers. London: Oxford University Press, 1967.

Malvern, Marjorie M. *Venus in Sackcloth: The Magdalen's Origins and Metamorphoses.* Carbondale: Southern Illinois University Press, 1975.

Mandel, Oscar. *August von Kotzebue: The Comedy, The Man.* University Park: Pennsylvania State University Press, 1990.

Masek, Rosemary. "Women in an Age of Transition, 1485–1714." In *The Women of England from Anglo-Saxon Times to the Present: Interpretive Bibliographical Essays,* edited by Barbara Kanner, 138–82. Hamden, Conn.: Archon Books, 1979.

McDonald, Charles O. *The Rhetoric of Tragedy: Form in Stuart Drama.* Amherst: University of Massachusetts Press, 1966.

McKeon, Michael. "Historicizing Patriarchy: The Emergence of Gender Difference in England, 1660–1760," *Eighteenth-Century Studies* 28 (1995): 295–322.

McIntosh, Carey. "Pamela's Clothes," *English Literary History* 35 (March 1968): 75–83. Reprinted in *Twentieth Century Interpretations of Pamela,* edited by Rosemary Cowler, 89–96. Englewood Cliffs, N.J.: Prentice-Hall, 1969.

McKillop, Alan Dugald. *Samuel Richardson: Printer and Novelist.* 1936. Reprint, [Hamden, Conn.]: Shoestring Press, 1960.

McMaster, Juliet S. "Love, Lust, and Sham: Structural Pattern in the Plays of John Ford," *Renaissance Drama* 2 (1969): 157–66.

Middleton, Thomas. *A Game at Chess.* Edited by J. W. Harper. London: Ernest Benn, 1966.

———. *Women Beware Women.* Edited by Roma Gill. London: Ernest Benn, 1968.

[Middleton, Thomas.] *The Revenger's Tragedy.* See Tourneur, Cyril.

[Middleton, Thomas.] *The Second Maiden's Tragedy.* Edited by Anne Lancashire. Manchester: Manchester University Press, 1978.

Middleton, Thomas, and Thomas Dekker. *The Roaring Girl.* Edited by Andor Gomme. London: Ernest Benn, 1976.

Middleton, Thomas, and William Rowley. *The Changeling.* Edited by George W. Williams. Lincoln: University of Nebraska Press, 1966.

Miller, Edwin S. "Roister Doister's 'Funeralls,'" *Studies in Philology* 43 (1946): 42–58.

Milton, John. *Complete Poems and Major Prose.* Edited by Merritt Y. Hughes. New York: Odyssey Press, 1957.

Miner, Earl. Commentary on "An Essay of Dramatic Poesy." In *The Works of John Dryden,* vol. 11, edited by Samuel Holt Monk. Berkeley: University of California Press, 1971.

Mizener, Arthur. "The High Design of *A King and No King,*" *Modern Philology* 38 (1940–41): 133–54.

Moon, Arthur R. "Two References to Chaucer Made by Nicholas Udall," *Modern Language Review* 21 (1926): 426–7.

Morgan, Susan. *Sisters in Time: Imagining Gender in Nineteenth-Century British Fiction.* New York: Oxford University Press, 1989.

Mullan, John. "Sentimental Novels." In *The Cambridge Companion to the English Novel,* edited by John Richetti, 236–54. Cambridge: Cambridge University Press, 1996.

Neumann, Erich. *Amor and Psyche: The Psychic Development of the Feminine.* Translated by Ralph Manheim. New York: Bollingen Foundation, 1956.

Ovid (Publius Ovidius Naso). *Heroides and Amores.* Translated by Grant Showerman. Cambridge: Harvard University Press, 1914.

———. *Ovid's "Metamorphoses": The Arthur Golding Translation.* 1567. Edited by John Frederick Nims. New York: Macmillan, 1965.

Pagels, Elaine. *The Gnostic Gospels.* New York: Random House, 1979.

Parrott, Thomas Marc, and Robert Hamilton Hall. *A Short View of Elizabethan Drama.* 2d ed. New York: Scribner's, 1958.

Pavel, Thomas G. *The Poetics of Plot: The Case of English Renaissance Drama.* Minneapolis: University of Minnesota Press, 1985.

———. "Thematics and Historical Evidence." In *The Return of Thematic Criticism,* edited by Werner Sollors, 121–45. Cambridge: Harvard University Press, 1993.

Pearse, Nancy Cotton. *John Fletcher's Chastity Plays: Mirrors for Modesty.* Lewisburg, Penn.: Bucknell University Press, 1973.

Peery, William. "The Prayer for the Queen in *Roister Doister,*" *Studies in English* (University of Texas) 17 (1948): 222–33.

Perrett, Roy W. "Autobiography and Self-Deception: Conjoining Philosophy, Literature, and Cognitive Psychology," *Mosaic* 29 (December 1996): 25–40.

Phillip, John. *The Play of Patient Grissell.* Edited by Ronald B. McKerrow and W. W. Greg. London: Malone Society Reprints, 1909.

Phillips, Margaret M. *Erasmus and the Northern Renaissance.* London: English Universities Press, 1949.

Plumstead, A. W. "Satirical Parody in *Roister Doister*: A Reinterpretation," *Studies in Philology* 60 (1963): 141–54.

Pollak, Ellen. *The Poetics of Sexual Myth: Gender and Ideology in the Verse of Swift and Pope.* Chicago: University of Chicago Press, 1985.

Pomeroy, Sarah B. *Goddesses, Whores, Wives and Slaves: Women in Classical Antiquity.* New York: Schocken, 1975.

Pope, Alexander. *The Poems of Alexander Pope.* 3d ed. Vol. 2, *The Rape of The Lock and Other Poems.* Edited by Geoffrey Tillotson. New Haven: Yale University Press, 1962.

Powell, Chilton L. *English Domestic Relations, 1487–1653.* New York: Columbia University Press, 1917.

Power, Eileen. *Medieval Women.* Cambridge: Cambridge University Press, 1975.

Propp, Vladimir. *Morphology of the Folktale.* 1928. Translated by Laurence Scott. 2d ed. revised and edited by Louis A. Wagner. Austin: University of Texas Press, 1968.

Les XV Joies de mariage. (*Les Quinze Joyes de mariage.*) Edited by Jean Rychner. Geneva: Librairie Droz, 1967.

The Raigne of King Edward the Third. Edited by Fred Lapides. New York: Garland, 1980.

Raleigh, Sir Walter. *The History of the World . . .* Edited by C. A. Patrides. Philadelphia: Temple University Press, 1971.

Richardson, Samuel. *Clarissa.* Edited by Angus Ross. New York: Viking, 1985. (Based on the first edition of 1747–48)

———. *Clarissa.* 3d ed. [1751]. New York: AMS Press, 1990.

———. *The Letters of Samuel Richardson.* 6 vols. Edited by Anna Letitia Barbauld. London: Richard Phillips, 1804.

———. *Pamela, or Virtue Rewarded.* Edited by T. C. Duncan Eaves and Ben D. Kimpel. Boston: Houghton Mifflin, 1971. (Based on the first edition [1740], with a title page saying 1741)

———. *Pamela.* Vols. 3 and 4. Edited by William King and Adrian Bott. Oxford: Basil Blackwell, 1929. (Richardson's sequel; based on the so-called third edition [1742])

———. *Selected Letters of Samuel Richardson.* Edited by John Carroll. Oxford: Clarendon Press, 1964.

Ricoeur, Paul. *The Rule of Metaphor.* Translated by Robert Czerney. Toronto: University of Toronto Press, 1975.

Robb, D. M. "The Canon of William Rowley's Plays," *Modern Language Review* 45 (April 1950): 129–41.

Rogers, Katharine. *The Troublesome Helpmate: A History of Misogyny in Literature.* Seattle: University of Washington Press, 1966.

Ross, Lena B., ed. *To Speak or Be Silent: The Paradox of Disobedience in the Lives of Women.* Wilmette, Ill.: Chiron Publications, 1993.

Rossiter, A. P. *English Drama from Early Times to the Elizabethans: Its Background, Origins and Development.* London: Hutchinson, 1950.

Roston, Murray. *Biblical Drama in England.* Evanston: Northwestern University Press, 1968.

Rousseau, G. S. "Nerves, Spirits and Fibres: Towards Defining the Organ of Sensibility." In *Studies in the Eighteenth Century 3*, edited by R. F. Brissenden and J. C. Eade, 137–57. Canberra: Australian National University Press, 1973.

Rousseau, Jean-Jacques. *The Confessions.* Translated by J. M. Cohen. Harmondsworth, Middlesex: Penguin, 1954.

———. *Eloisa, or a Series of Original Letters.* Translated by William Kenrick. 4 vols. 1803. Facsimile reprint, 4 vols. in 2, Oxford: Woodstock, 1989.

———. *La Nouvelle Héloïse.* Vol. 2 of *Oeuvres complètes.* Edited by Bernard Gagnebin and Marcel Raymond. Paris: Gallimard, 1964.

Roussel, Roy. *The Conversation of the Sexes: Seduction and Equality in Selected Seventeenth- and Eighteenth-Century Texts.* New York: Oxford University Press, 1986.

Rousset, Jean. *Le Mythe de Don Juan.* Paris: Armand Colin, 1978.

Rowe, Nicholas. *The Fair Penitent.* Edited by Malcolm Goldstein. Lincoln: University of Nebraska Press, 1969.

———. *Jane Shore.* Edited by Harry W. Pedicord. Lincoln: University of Nebraska Press, 1974.

———. *The Works of Nicholas Rowe.* "A new edition to which is prefixed a Life of the Author [by Samuel Johnson]." London: 1792.

Rymer, Thomas. *The Critical Works of Thomas Rymer.* Edited by Curt A. Zimansky. 1956. Reprint, Westport, Conn.: Greenwood Press, 1971.

Saccio, Peter. *The Court Comedies of John Lyly: A Study in Allegorical Dramaturgy.* Princeton: Princeton University Press, 1969.

Sams, Eric. *Shakespeare's Edward III.* New Haven: Yale University Press, 1996.

Sargeaunt, M. Joan. *John Ford.* Oxford: Basil Blackwell, 1935.

Schochet, Gordon J. *Patriarchalism in Political Thought: The Authoritarian Family and Political Speculation and Attitudes Especially in Seventeenth-Century England.* New York: Basic Books, 1975.

Scott, Walter. *The Heart of Midlothian.* Introduction by John Henry Raleigh. Boston: Houghton Mifflin, 1966.

———. "Prefatory Memoir to Mackenzie." In *Ballantyne's Novelist's Library,* vol. 5 London: Hurst, Robinson, 1823.

Screech, M. A. *The Rabelasian Marriage.* London: Edward Arnold, 1958.

Segre, Cesare. "From Motif to Function and Back Again." In *Thematics: New Approaches,* edited by Claude Bremond, Joshua Landy, and Thomas Pavel, 21–32. Albany: State University of New York Press, 1995.

Sensabaugh, George F. *The Tragic Muse of John Ford*. Stanford: Stanford University Press, 1944.

Severs, J. Burke. *The Literary Relationships of Chaucer's Clerkes Tale*. New Haven: Yale University Press, 1942.

Shakespeare, William. *The Complete Works of William Shakespeare*. 3d ed. Edited by David Bevington. Dallas: Scott, Foresman, 1980.

Sherry, Richard. *A Treatise of Schemes and Tropes (1550) and His Translation of The Education of Children by Desiderius Erasmus*. Introduction by Herbert W. Hildebrandt. Gainesville: Scholars' Facsimiles and Reprints, 1961.

Shirley, James. *The Dramatic Works and Poems of James Shirley*. Vol. 2, *Hyde Park*. 1833. Reprint, New York: Russell and Russell, 1966.

Slattery, William C., ed. *The Richardson-Stinstra Correspondence and Stinstra's Prefaces to "Clarissa."* Carbondale: Southern Illinois University Press, 1969.

Sloane, Thomas O. *Donne, Milton, and the End of Humanist Rhetoric*. Berkeley: University of California Press, 1985.

Smeak, Edith M. Introduction to George Chapman, *The Widow's Tears*. Lincoln: University of Nebraska Press, 1966.

Smith, Bruce R. *Ancient Scripts and Modern Experience on the English Stage, 1500–1700*. Princeton: Princeton University Press, 1988.

Sollors, Werner, ed. *The Return of Thematic Criticism*. Cambridge: Harvard University Press, 1993.

Sonnino, Lee A. *A Handbook to Sixteenth-Century Rhetoric*. New York: Barnes and Noble, 1968.

Spencer, Theodore. *Shakespeare and the Nature of Man*. 2d ed. 1949. Reprint, New York: Collier Books, 1966.

Spenser, Edmund. *The Faerie Queene*. In *The Complete Poetical Works of Spenser*, edited by R. E. Neil Dodge. Boston: Houghton Mifflin, 1908.

Spivack, Bernard. *Shakespeare and the Allegory of Evil: The History of a Metaphor in Relation to His Major Villains*. New York: Columbia University Press, 1958.

Spurgeon, Caroline F. E. *Five Hundred Years of Chaucer Criticism and Allusion: 1357–1900*. 3 vols. 1925. Reprint, New York: Russell and Russell, 1960.

Standard Dictionary of Folklore, Mythology and Legend. Edited by Maria Leach. New York: Funk and Wagnalls, 1972.

States, Bert O. *The Pleasure of the Play*. Ithaca: Cornell University Press, 1994.

Staves, Susan. *Players' Scepters: Fictions of Authority in the Restoration*. Lincoln: University of Nebraska Press, 1979.

Stavig, Mark. *John Ford and the Traditional Moral Order*. Madison: University of Wisconsin Press, 1968.

Stone, Lawrence. *The Crisis of the Aristocracy, 1558–1648*. Oxford: Clarendon Press, 1965.

———. *The Family, Sex, and Marriage in England, 1500–1800*. New York: Harper and Row, 1977.

Stroup, Thomas. *Microcosmos: The Shape of the Elizabethan Play*. Lexington: University of Kentucky Press, 1965.

Sulloway, Alison G. *Jane Austen and the Province of Womanhood*. Philadelphia: University of Pennsylvania Press, 1989.

Sutton, Juliet. "Platonic Love in Ford's *The Fancies, Chaste and Noble*," *Studies in English Literature* 7 (1967): 299–309.

Swahn, Jan-Ojvind. *The Tale of Cupid and Psyche*. Lund: CWK Gleerup, 1955.

Tanner, Tony. "Julie and 'La Maison paternelle': Another Look at Rousseau's *La Nouvelle Héloïse*," *Daedelus* 105 (Winter 1976). Reprinted in *Jean-Jacques Rousseau: Modern Critical Views*, edited by Harold Bloom, 119–47. New York: Chelsea House, 1988.

Taylor, Charles. *Sources of the Self: The Making of the Modern Identity*. Cambridge: Harvard University Press, 1989.

Terrien, Samuel. Exegesis of the Book of Job. In *The Interpreter's Bible*, vol. 3. Nashville: Abingdon Press, 1954.

Thomas, Keith V. "Women and the Civil War Sects," *Past and Present* 13 (April 1958): 42–62.

Thompson, L. F. *Kotzebue: A Survey of His Progress in France and England*. Paris: Librairie Ancienne Honoré Champion, 1928.

Thompson, Stith. *Motif-Index of Folk Literature*. 6 vols. Bloomington: Indiana University Press, 1955–58.

Tilley, Allen. *Plot Snakes and the Dynamics of Narrative Experience*. Gainesville: University Press of Florida, 1992.

———. *Plots of Time: An Inquiry into History, Myth, and Meaning*. Gainesville: University Press of Florida, 1995.

Tillyard, E. M. W. *The Elizabethan World Picture*. London: Chatto and Windus, 1960.

Todd, Frederick A. *Some Ancient Novels*. London: Oxford University Press, 1940.

Todd, Janet. *Sensibility: An Introduction*. London: Methuen, 1986.

Todorov, Tzvetan. *Grammaire du "Décaméron."* The Hague: Mouton, 1969.

Tourneur, Cyril. *The Atheist's Tragedy*. Edited by Brian Morris and Roma Gill. London: Ernest Benn, 1976.

[Tourneur, Cyril?]. *The Revenger's Tragedy*. Edited by Brian Gibbons. London: Ernest Benn, 1967.

Trevor, William. *Felicia's Journey*. New York: Penguin, 1994.

Trible, Phyllis. *Texts of Terror: Literary-Feminist Readings of Biblical Narratives*. Philadelphia: Fortress Press, 1984.

Trouille, Mary Seidman. *Sexual Politics in the Enlightenment: Women Writers Read Rousseau*. Albany: State University of New York Press, 1997.

Udall, Nicholas. *Ralph Roister Doister*. 1552? In *Three Sixteenth-Century Comedies*, edited by Charles W. Whitworth. London: Ernest Benn, 1984.

Uglow, Jenny. *Elizabeth Gaskell: A Habit of Stories*. London: Faber and Faber, 1993.

Ure, Peter. "Cult and Initiates in Ford's *Love's Sacrifice*," *Modern Language Quarterly* 11 (1950): 298–306.

Utley, Francis L. *The Crooked Rib*. Columbus: Ohio State University Press, 1944.

Van Sant, Ann Jessie. *Eighteenth-Century Sensibility and the Novel: The Senses in Social Context*. Cambridge: Cambridge University Press, 1993.

Waith, Eugene M. *The Pattern of Tragicomedy in Beaumont and Fletcher*. New Haven: Yale University Press, 1952.

Warner, Marina. *Alone of All Her Sex: The Myth and the Cult of the Virgin Mary*. New York: Knopf, 1976.

Webster, John. *Appius and Virginia*. Vol. 3 of *The Complete Works of John Webster*, edited by F. L. Lucas. [1927]. New York: Gordian Press, 1966.

———. *The White Devil*. Edited by J. R. Mulryne. Lincoln: University of Nebraska Press, 1969.

Weidner, Henry M. "Homer and the Fallen World: Focus of Satire in George Chapman's *The Widow's Tears*," *Journal of English and German Philology* 62 (1963): 518–32.

Weinstein, Leo. *The Metamorphoses of Don Juan*. Stanford: Stanford University Press, 1959.

Wellington, James E., ed. Introduction to Alexander Pope's *Eloïsa to Abelard with the letters of Heloise to Abelard in the version by John Hughes (1713)*. Coral Gables: University of Miami Press, 1965.

Whitworth, Charles W. Introduction to *Three Sixteenth-Century Comedies*. London: Ernest Benn, 1984.

Wilkins, George. *The Miseries of Enforced Marriage*. Edited by Glen H. Blayney. Oxford: Malone Society Reprints, 1963.

Wilson, F. P. *The English Drama, 1485–1585*. Oxford: Oxford University Press, 1969.

Wilson, Thomas. *The Art of Rhetoric*. 1553. Edited by Robert Hood Bowers. Gainesville: Scholars' Facsimiles and Reprints, 1962.

Winn, James A. *John Dryden and His World*. New Haven: Yale University Press, 1987.

Wright, Louis B. *Middle-Class Culture in Elizabethan England*. Chapel Hill: University of North Carolina Press, 1935.

Wright, Terence. *Elizabeth Gaskell "We Are Not Angels": Realism, Gender, Values*. London: Macmillan, 1995.

Wright, Thomas. *The Passions of the Mind in General*. 1604. Edited with an introduction by Thomas O. Sloan. Urbana: University of Illinois Press, 1971.

A Yorkshire Tragedy. Edited by A. C. Cowley and Barry Gaines. Manchester: Manchester University Press, 1986.

Young, Edward. *The Correspondence of Edward Young, 1683–1765*. Edited by Henry Pettit. Oxford: Clarendon Press, 1971.

Zimansky, Curt A. Introduction to John Vanbrugh, *The Relapse*. London: Edward Arnold, 1970.

INDEX